Story thus far

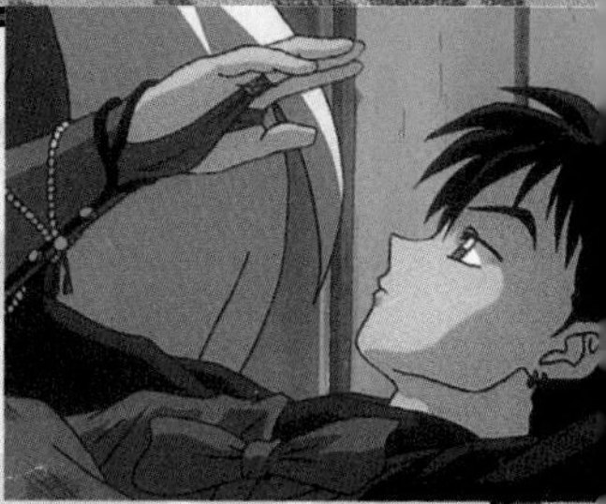

Kagome, a typical high school girl, has been transported into a mythical version of Japan's medieval past, a place filled with incredible magic and terrifying demons. Who would have guessed that the stories and legends Kagome's superstitious grandfather told her could really be true!?

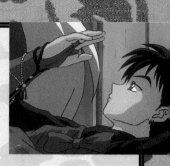

It turns out that Kagome is the reincarnation of Lady Kikyo, a great warrior and the defender of the Shikon Jewel, or the Jewel of the Four Souls. In fact, the sacred jewel mysteriously emerges from Kagome's body during a battle with a horrible centipede-like monster. In her desperation to defeat the monster, Kagome frees Inuyasha, a dog-like half-demon who lusts for the power imparted by the jewel, and unwittingly releases him from the binding spell that was placed 50 years earlier by Lady Kikyo. To prevent Inuyasha from stealing the jewel, Kikyo's sister, Lady Kaede, puts a magical necklace around Inuyasha's neck that allows Kagome to make him "sit" on command.

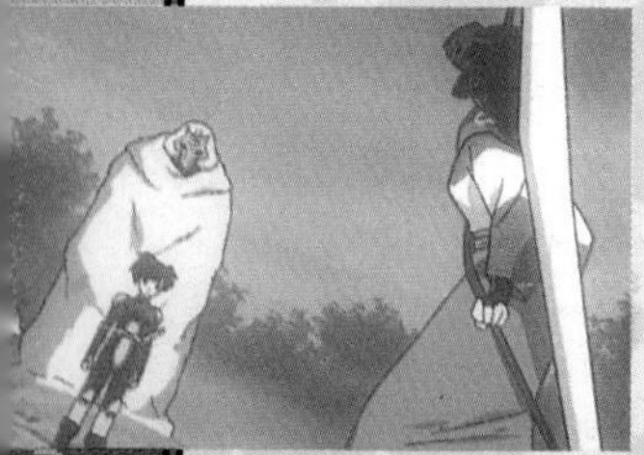

In another skirmish for possession of the jewel, it accidentally shatters and is strewn across the land. Only Kagome has the power to find the jewel shards, and only Inuyasha has the strength to defeat the demons who now hold them, so the two unlikely partners are bound together in the quest to reclaim all the pieces of the Shikon Jewel.

The wind tunnel weapon in flirty monk Miroku's hand is spreading and threatening to consume him, so he seeks out his old mentor, Mushin, for help. Mushin does his best to repair Miroku's hand, but the only way to truly save Miroku is to destroy the evil Naraku, who originally placed the curse of the wind tunnel on Miroku's family. Naraku is up to more dirty tricks when he revives the demon slayer Sango's brother, Kohaku, using a shard of the sacred jewel. He threatens to let Kohaku die again unless Sango brings him Inuyasha's sword, the Tetsusaiga. Though Sango is tempted to accept Naraku's bargain, she realizes that no good will come of it, and she refuses. A standoff ensues, and Kagome comes to Sango's rescue, injuring Naraku with a well-aimed arrow.

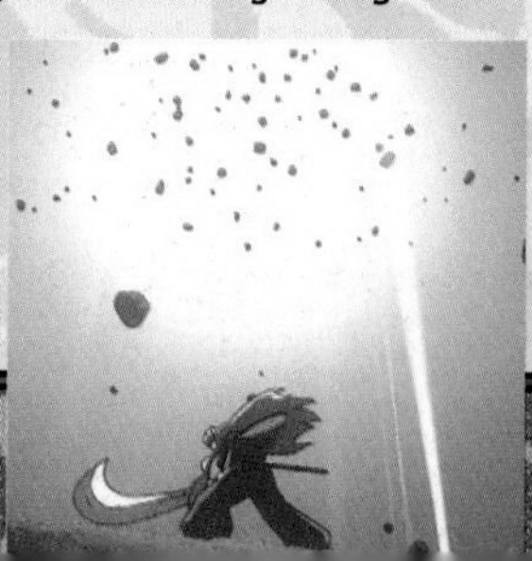

INUYASHA

ANI-MANGA Vol. 11

Contents

31
Jinenji, Kind Yet Sad

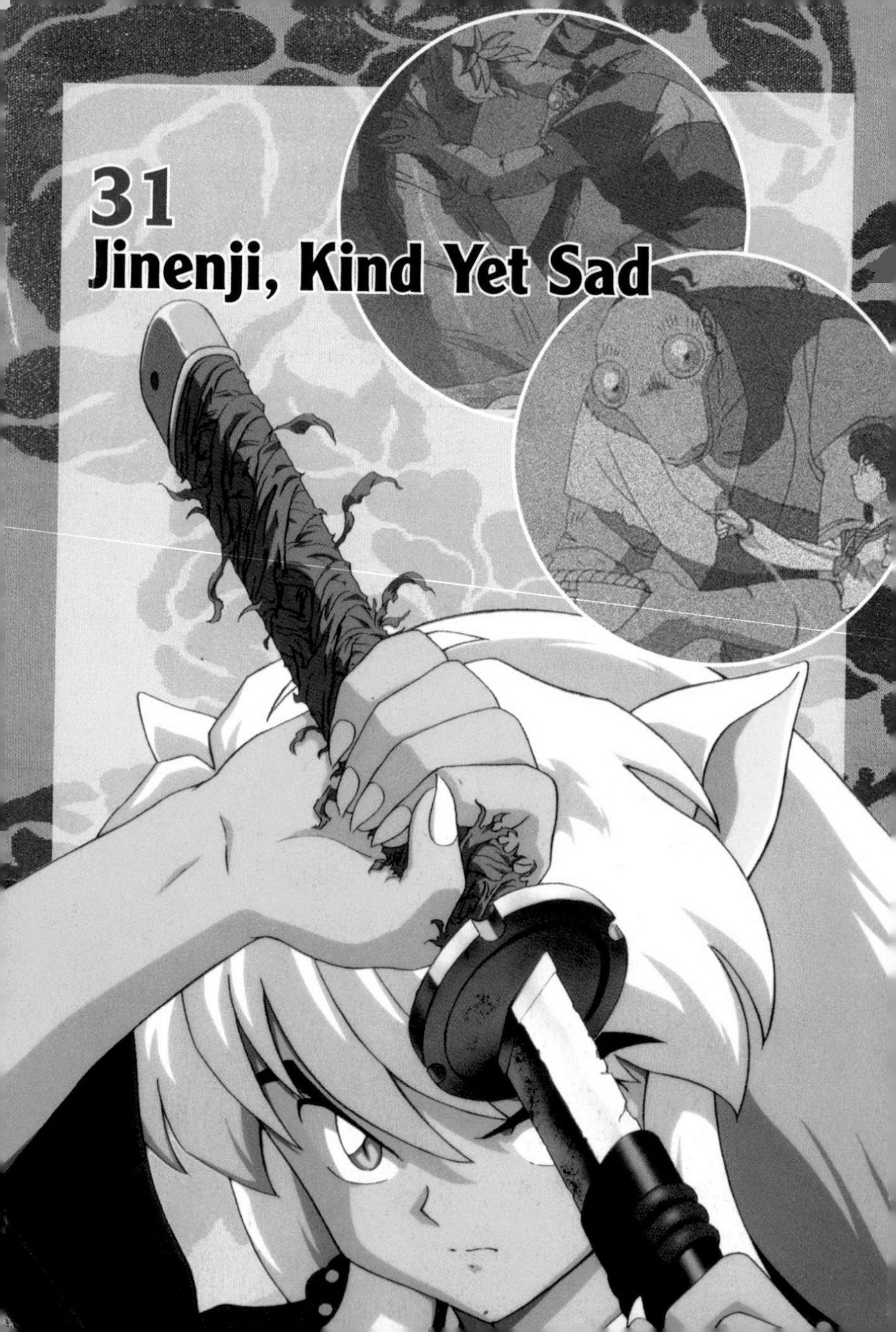

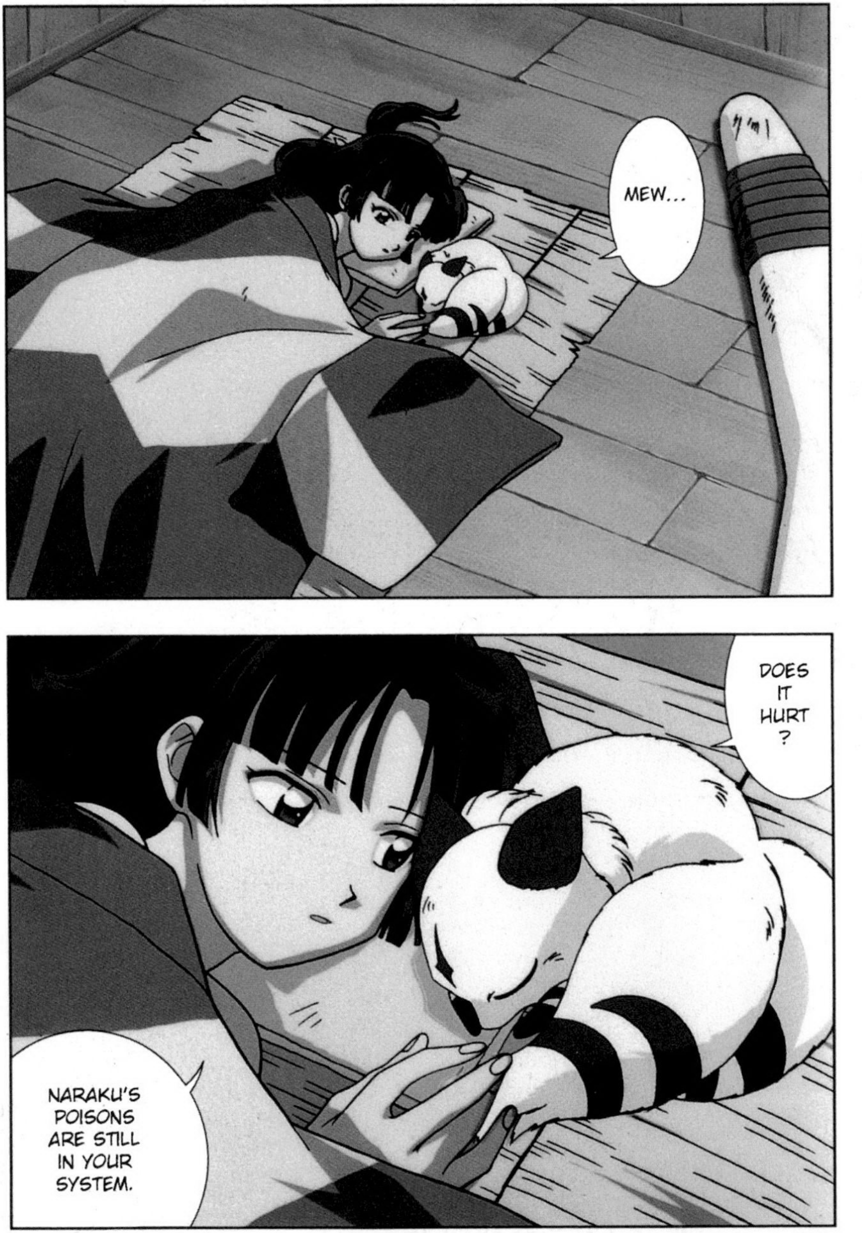
MEW...
DOES IT HURT?
NARAKU'S POISONS ARE STILL IN YOUR SYSTEM.

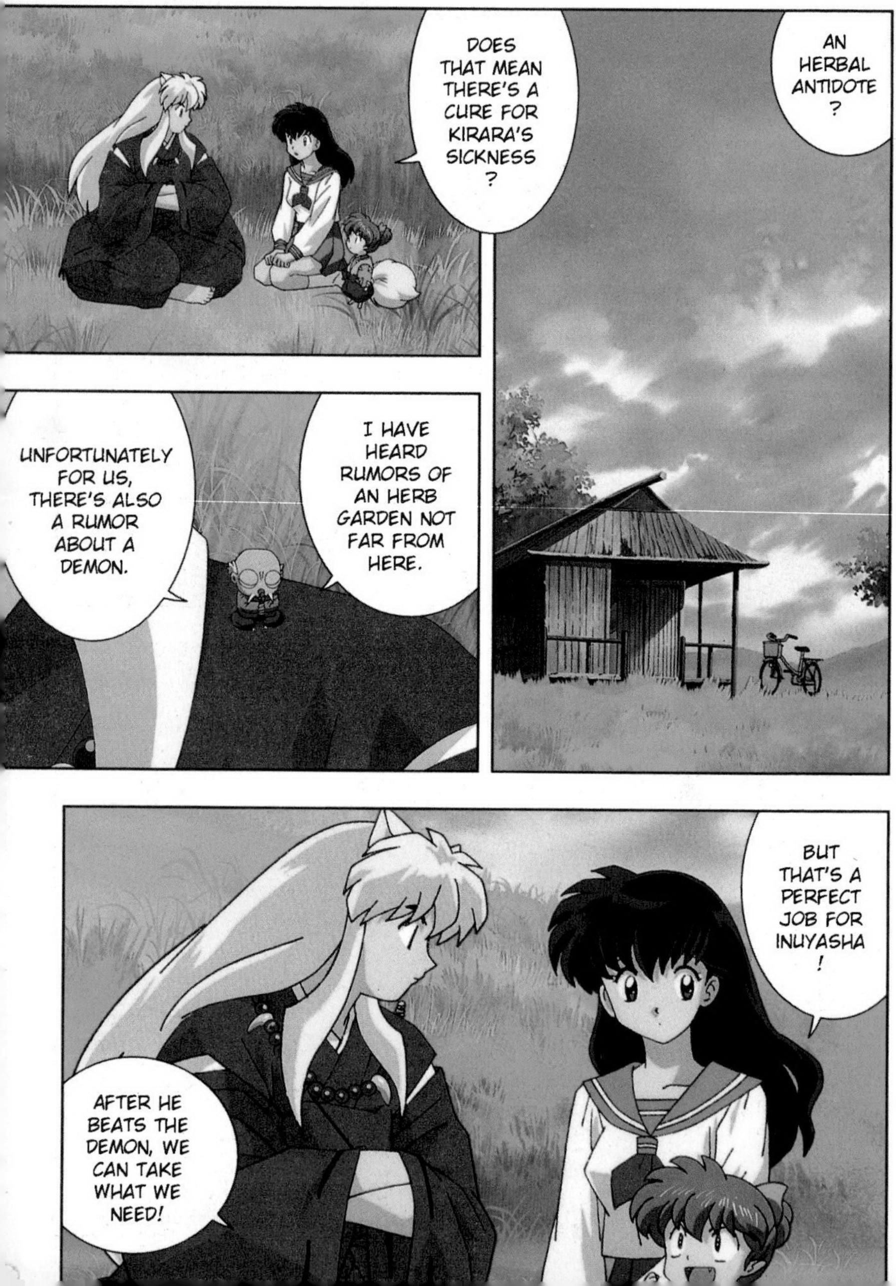
AN HERBAL ANTIDOTE?
DOES THAT MEAN THERE'S A CURE FOR KIRARA'S SICKNESS?
I HAVE HEARD RUMORS OF AN HERB GARDEN NOT FAR FROM HERE.
UNFORTUNATELY FOR US, THERE'S ALSO A RUMOR ABOUT A DEMON.
BUT THAT'S A PERFECT JOB FOR INUYASHA!
AFTER HE BEATS THE DEMON, WE CAN TAKE WHAT WE NEED!

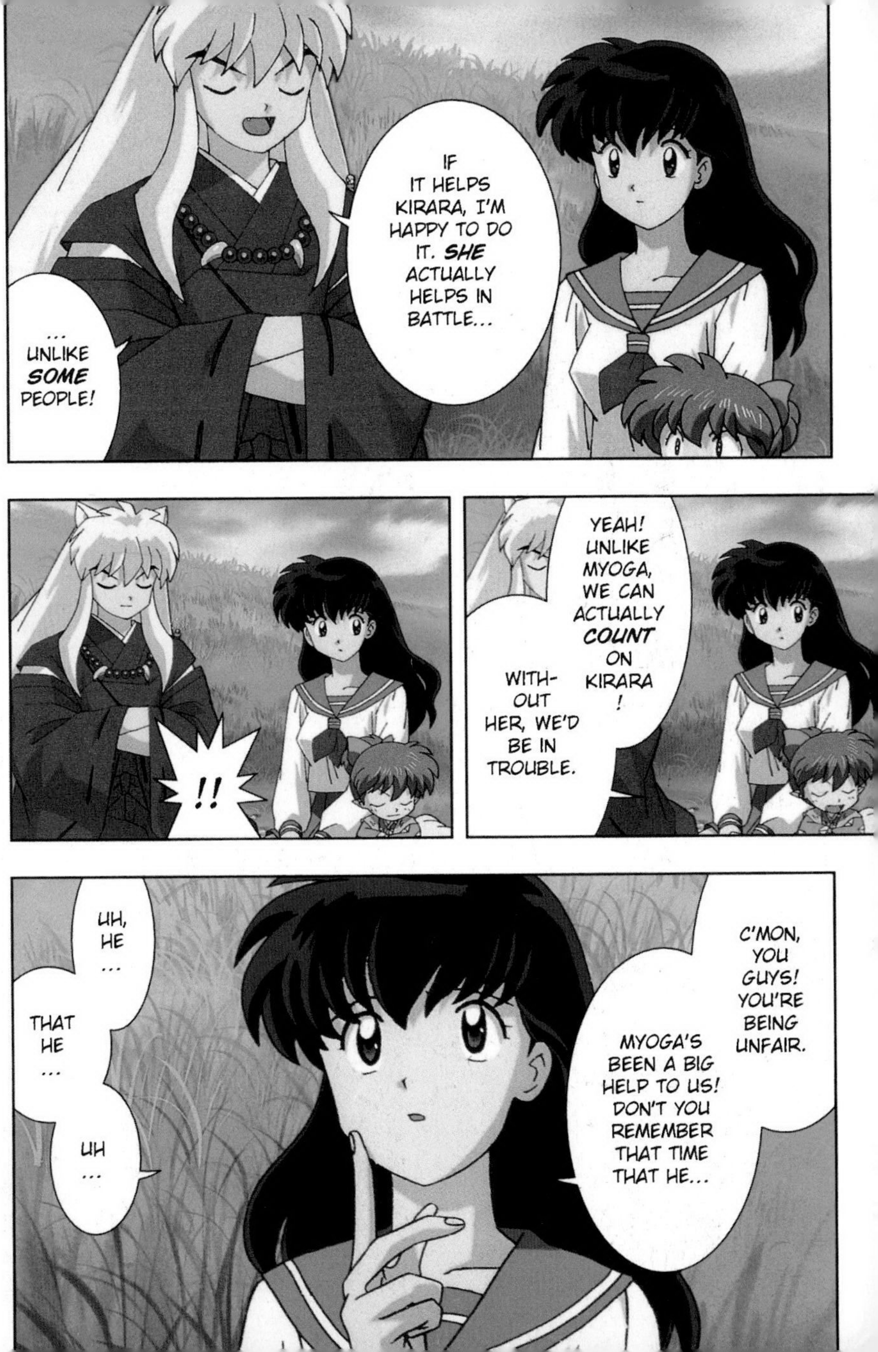
IF IT HELPS KIRARA, I'M HAPPY TO DO IT. SHE ACTUALLY HELPS IN BATTLE...
...UNLIKE SOME PEOPLE!
YEAH! UNLIKE MYOGA, WE CAN ACTUALLY COUNT ON KIRARA!
WITH-OUT HER, WE'D BE IN TROUBLE.
!!
C'MON, YOU GUYS! YOU'RE BEING UNFAIR.
MYOGA'S BEEN A BIG HELP TO US! DON'T YOU REMEMBER THAT TIME THAT HE...
UH, HE ...
THAT HE ...
UH ...

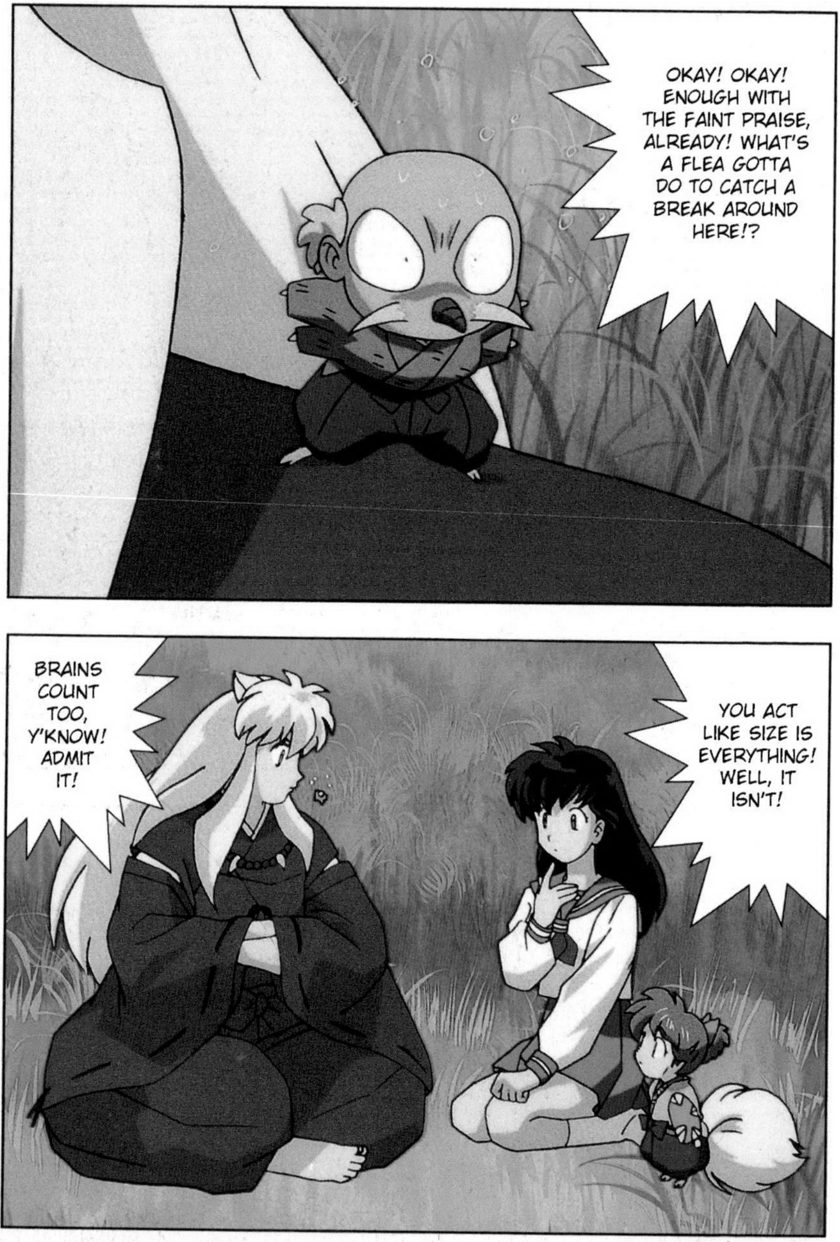
OKAY! OKAY! ENOUGH WITH THE FAINT PRAISE, ALREADY! WHAT'S A FLEA GOTTA DO TO CATCH A BREAK AROUND HERE!?
YOU ACT LIKE SIZE IS EVERYTHING! WELL, IT ISN'T!
BRAINS COUNT TOO, Y'KNOW! ADMIT IT!

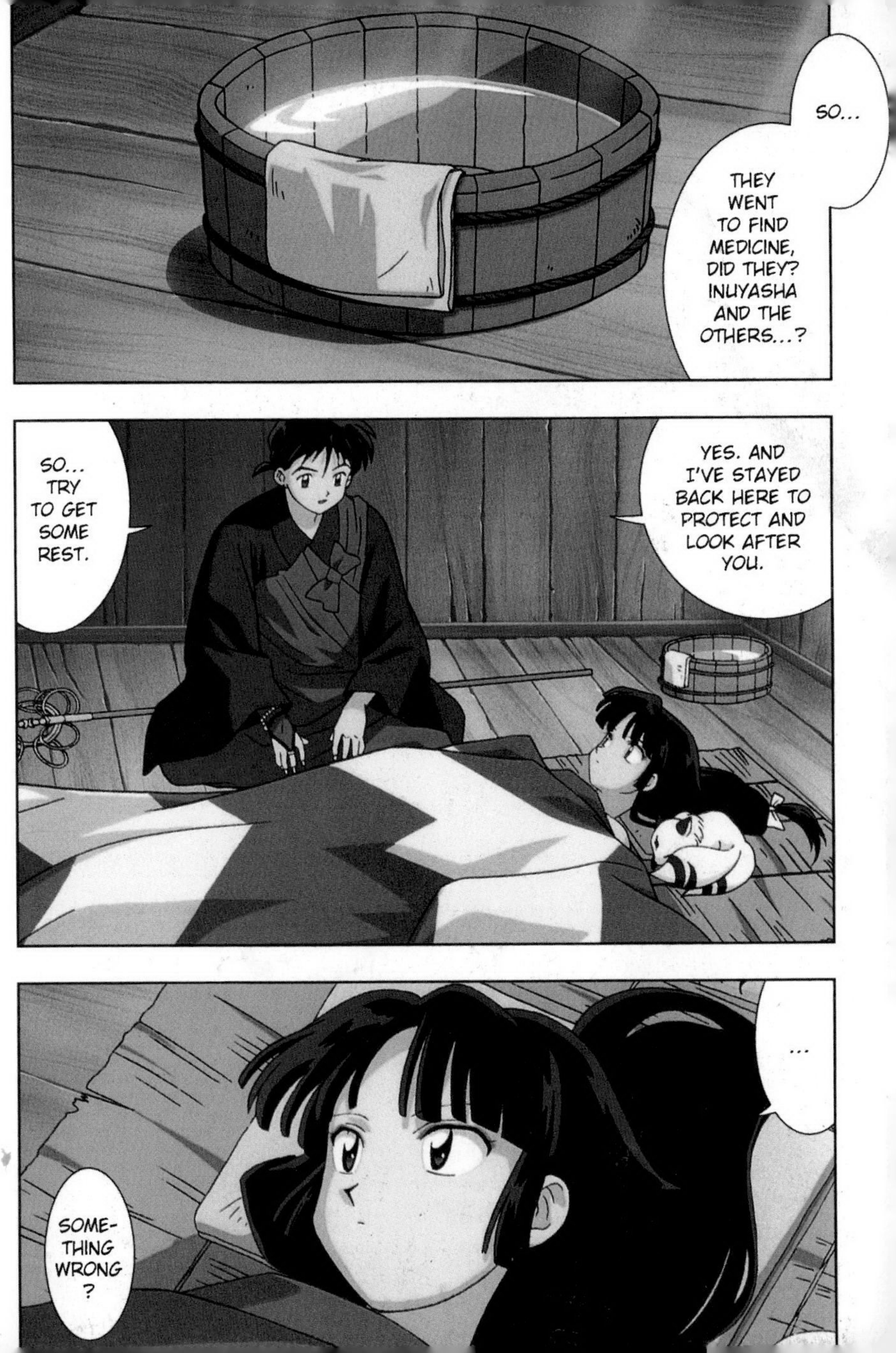
SO...
THEY WENT TO FIND MEDICINE, DID THEY? INUYASHA AND THE OTHERS...?
YES. AND I'VE STAYED BACK HERE TO PROTECT AND LOOK AFTER YOU.
SO... TRY TO GET SOME REST.
...
SOME-THING WRONG?

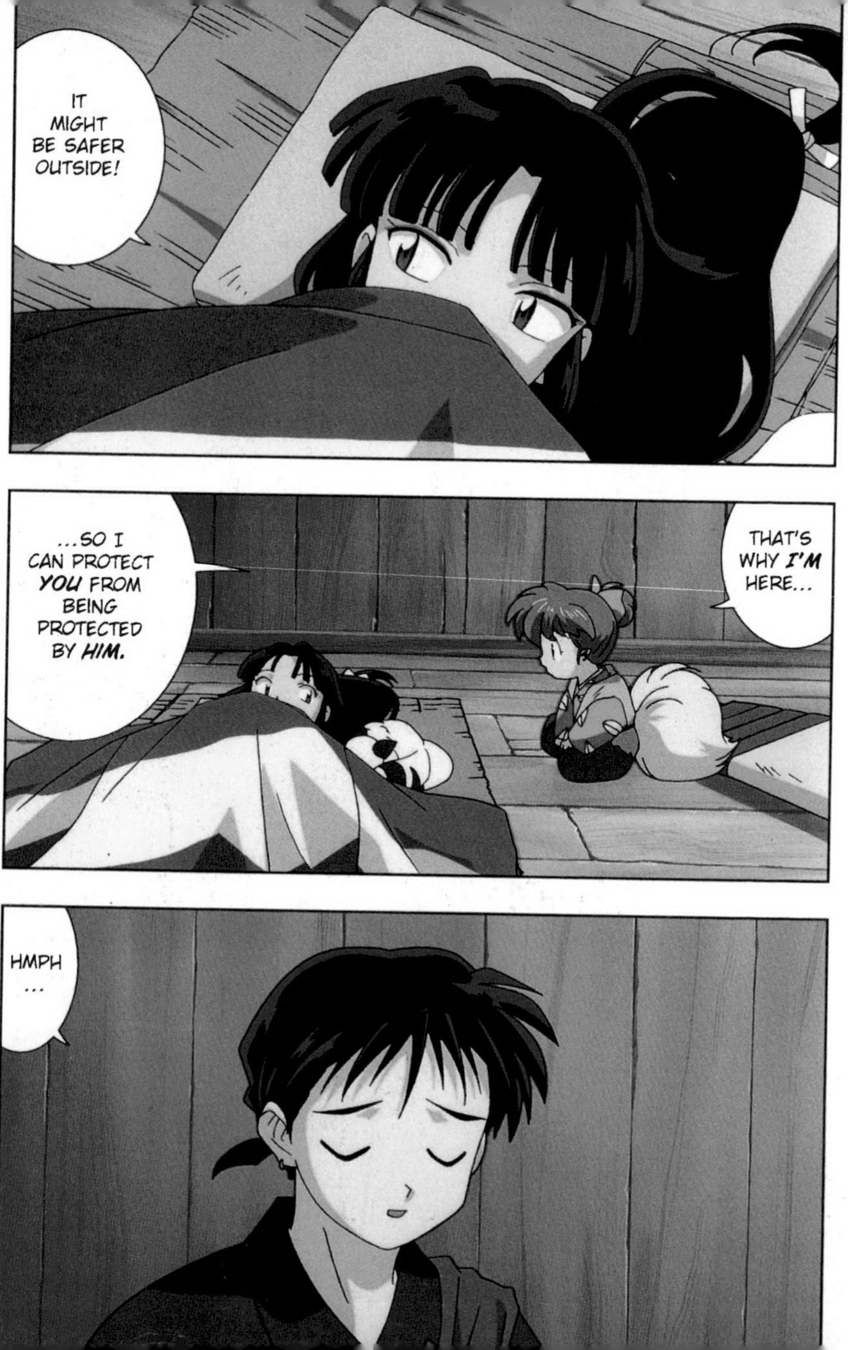
IT MIGHT BE SAFER OUTSIDE!
THAT'S WHY I'M HERE...
...SO I CAN PROTECT YOU FROM BEING PROTECTED BY HIM.
HMPH ...

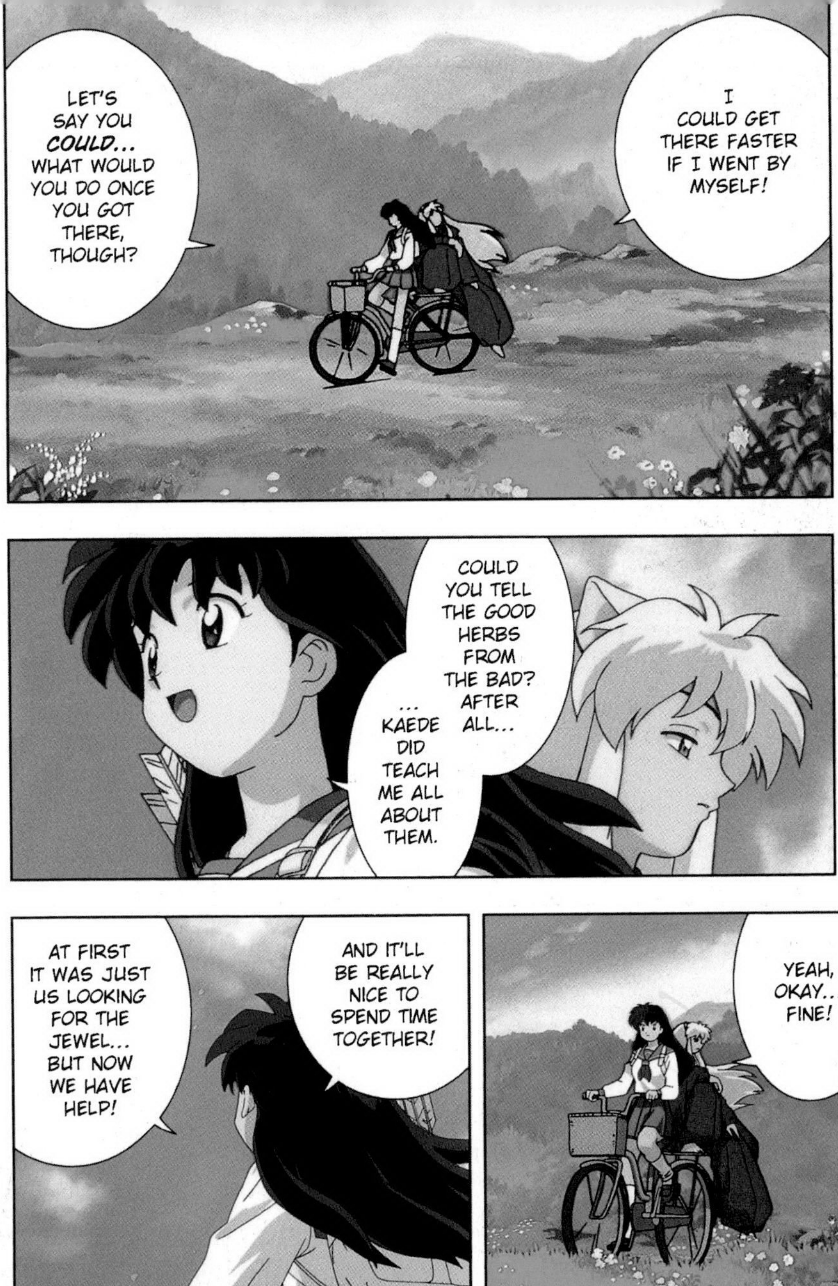
I COULD GET THERE FASTER IF I WENT BY MYSELF!
LET'S SAY YOU **COULD...** WHAT WOULD YOU DO ONCE YOU GOT THERE, THOUGH?
COULD YOU TELL THE GOOD HERBS FROM THE BAD? AFTER ALL...
...KAEDE DID TEACH ME ALL ABOUT THEM.
YEAH, OKAY... FINE!
AND IT'LL BE REALLY NICE TO SPEND TIME TOGETHER!
AT FIRST IT WAS JUST US LOOKING FOR THE JEWEL... BUT NOW WE HAVE HELP!

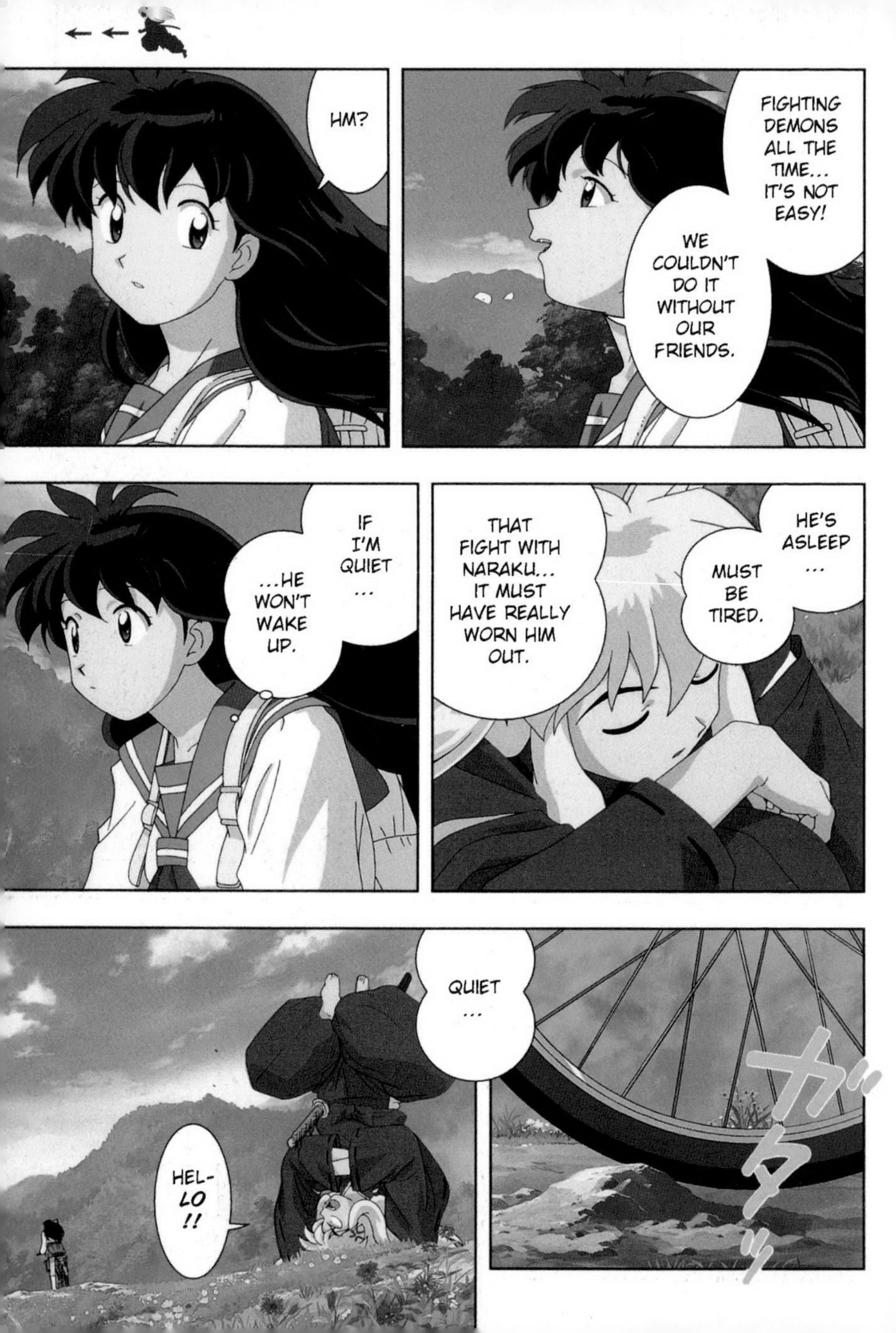
FIGHTING DEMONS ALL THE TIME... IT'S NOT EASY!
WE COULDN'T DO IT WITHOUT OUR FRIENDS.
HM?
HE'S ASLEEP...
MUST BE TIRED.
THAT FIGHT WITH NARAKU... IT MUST HAVE REALLY WORN HIM OUT.
IF I'M QUIET...
...HE WON'T WAKE UP.
ガタッ
QUIET...
HEL-LO!!

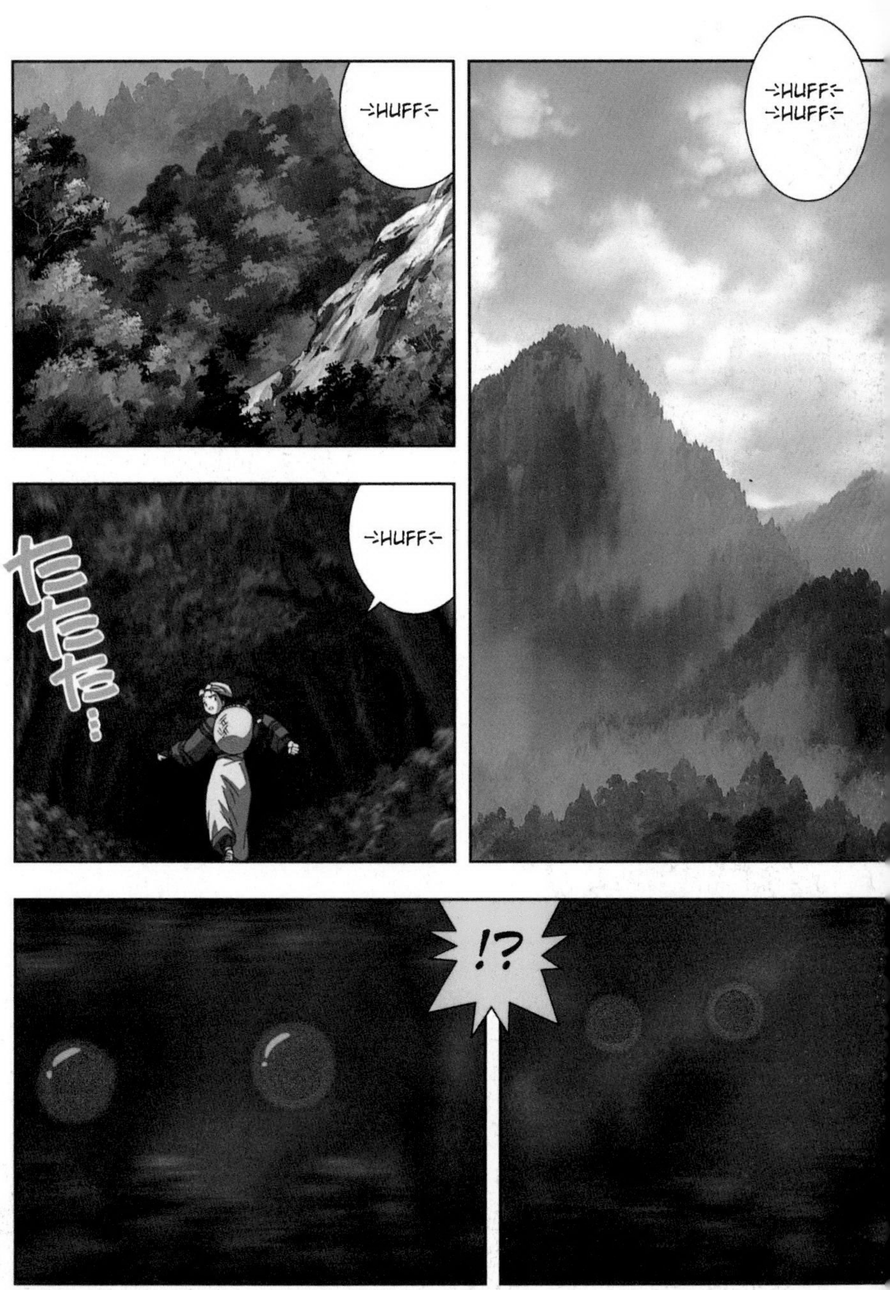
HUFF HUFF
HUFF
HUFF
たたた…
!?

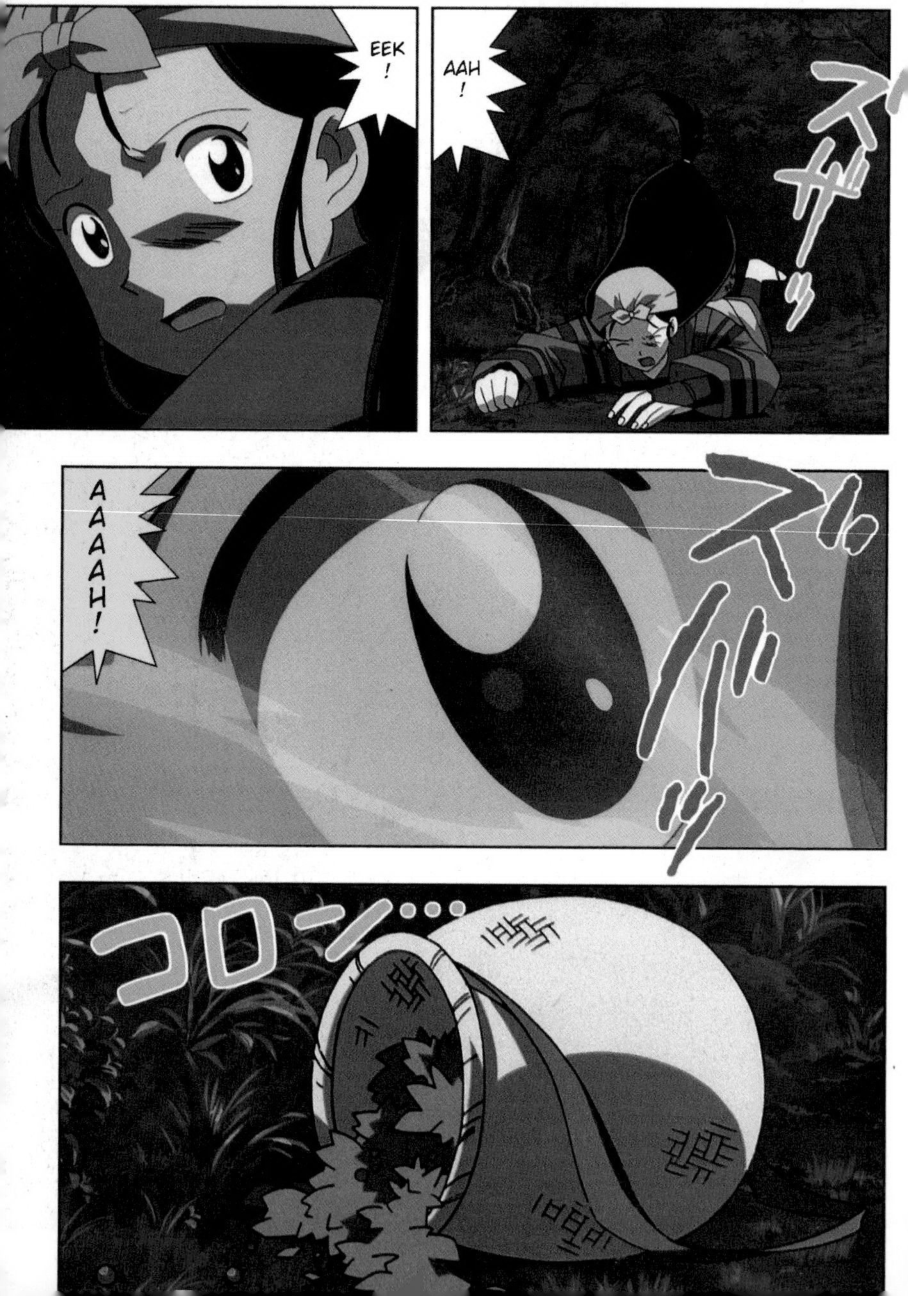
ズザーッ
AAH!
EEK!
AAAAAH!
コローン…

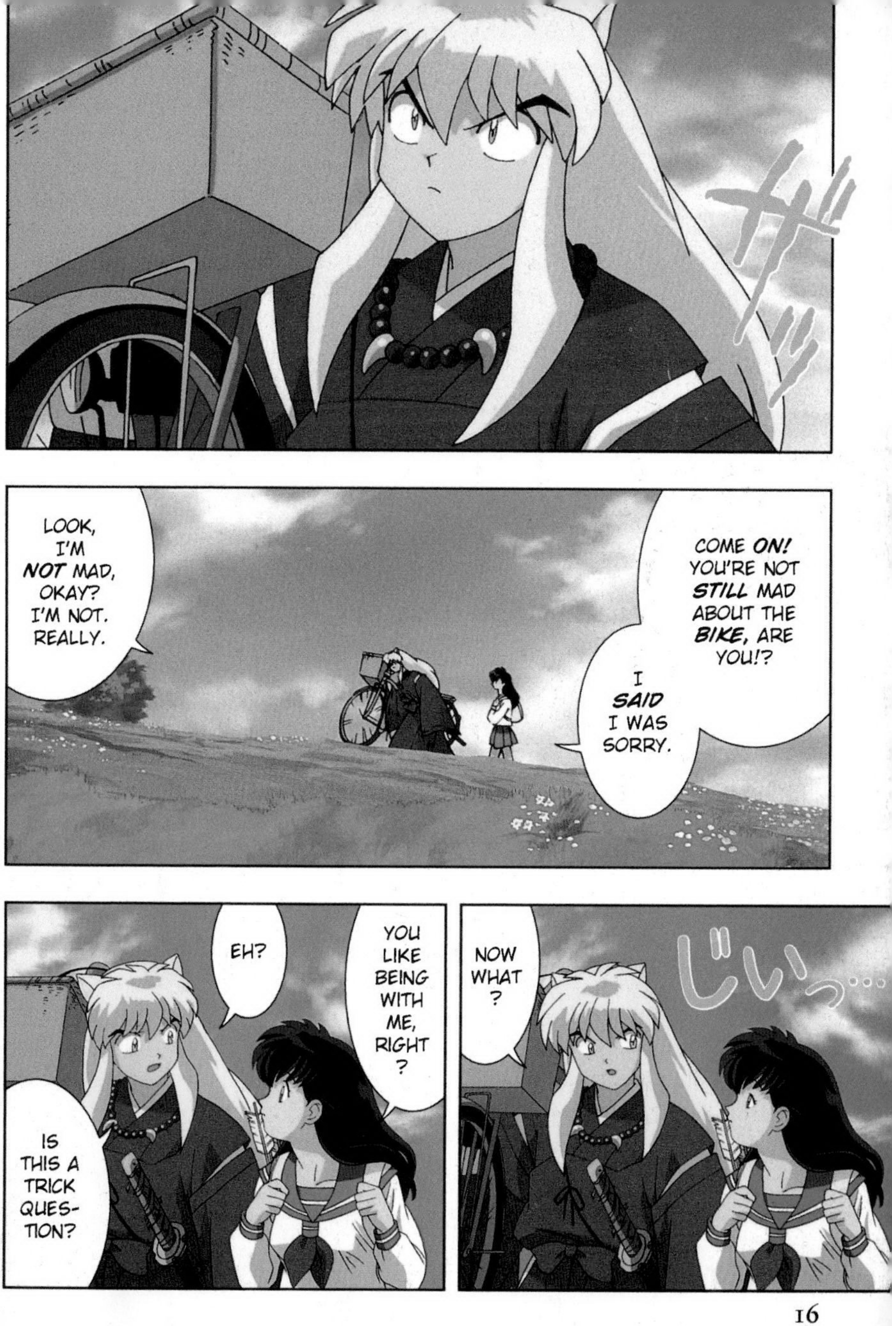
ザッ
COME ON! YOU'RE NOT STILL MAD ABOUT THE BIKE, ARE YOU!?
I SAID I WAS SORRY.
LOOK, I'M NOT MAD, OKAY? I'M NOT. REALLY.
じいっ…
NOW WHAT?
YOU LIKE BEING WITH ME, RIGHT?
EH?
IS THIS A TRICK QUES-TION?

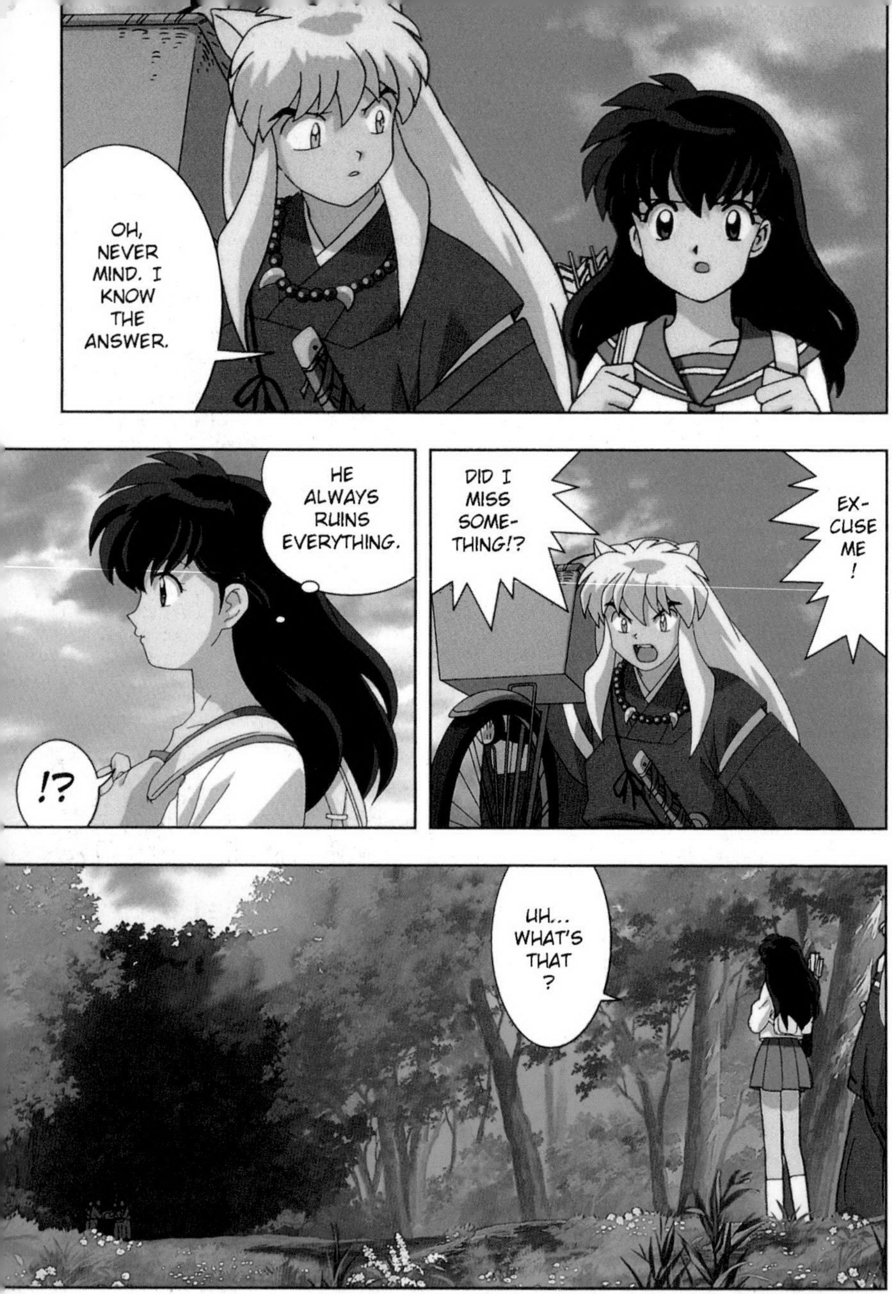
OH, NEVER MIND. I KNOW THE ANSWER.
EX-CUSE ME!
DID I MISS SOME-THING!?
HE ALWAYS RUINS EVERYTHING.
!?
UH... WHAT'S THAT?

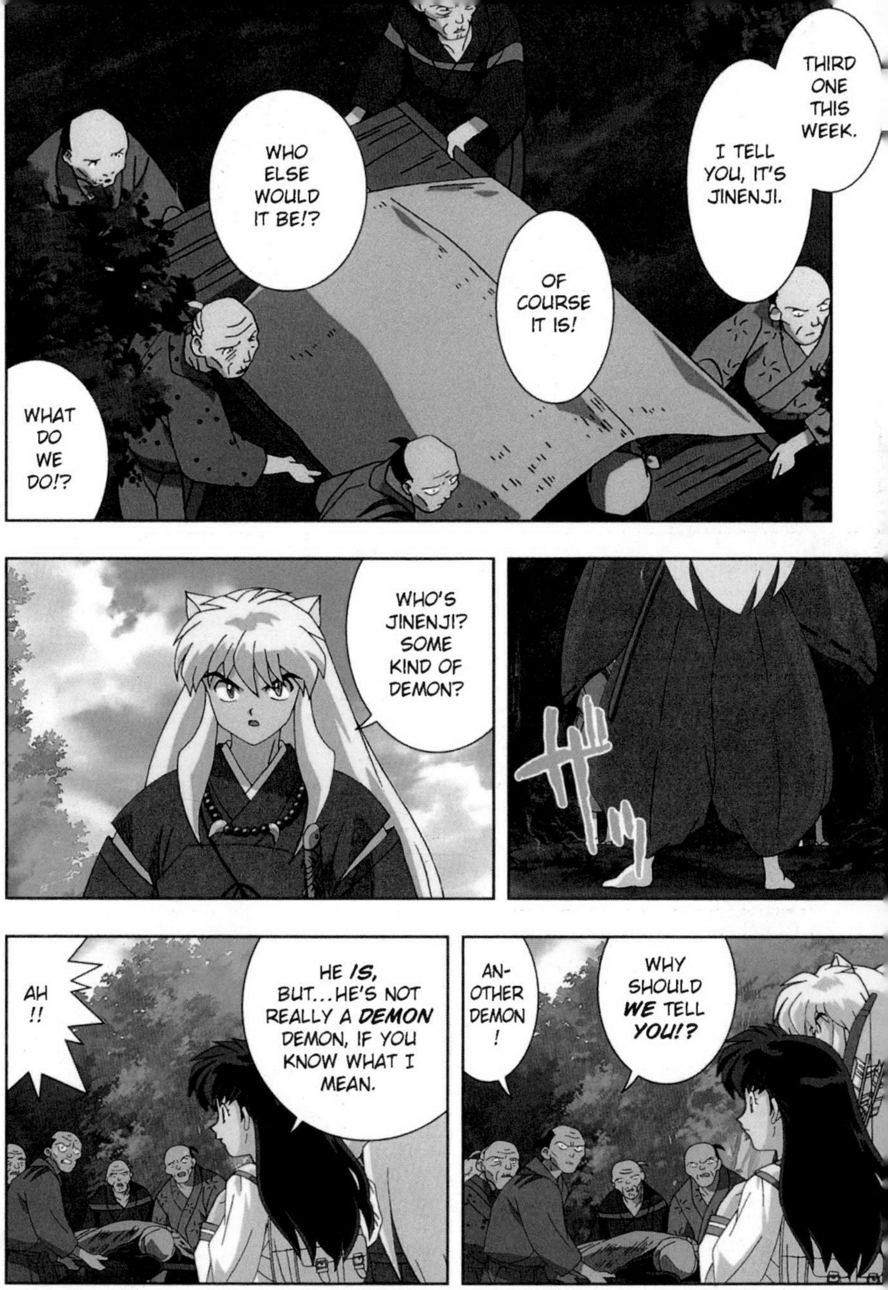
THIRD ONE THIS WEEK.
I TELL YOU, IT'S JINENJI.
OF COURSE IT IS!
WHO ELSE WOULD IT BE!?
WHAT DO WE DO!?
WHO'S JINENJI? SOME KIND OF DEMON?
WHY SHOULD WE TELL YOU!?
AN-OTHER DEMON!
HE IS, BUT...HE'S NOT REALLY A DEMON DEMON, IF YOU KNOW WHAT I MEAN.
AH!!

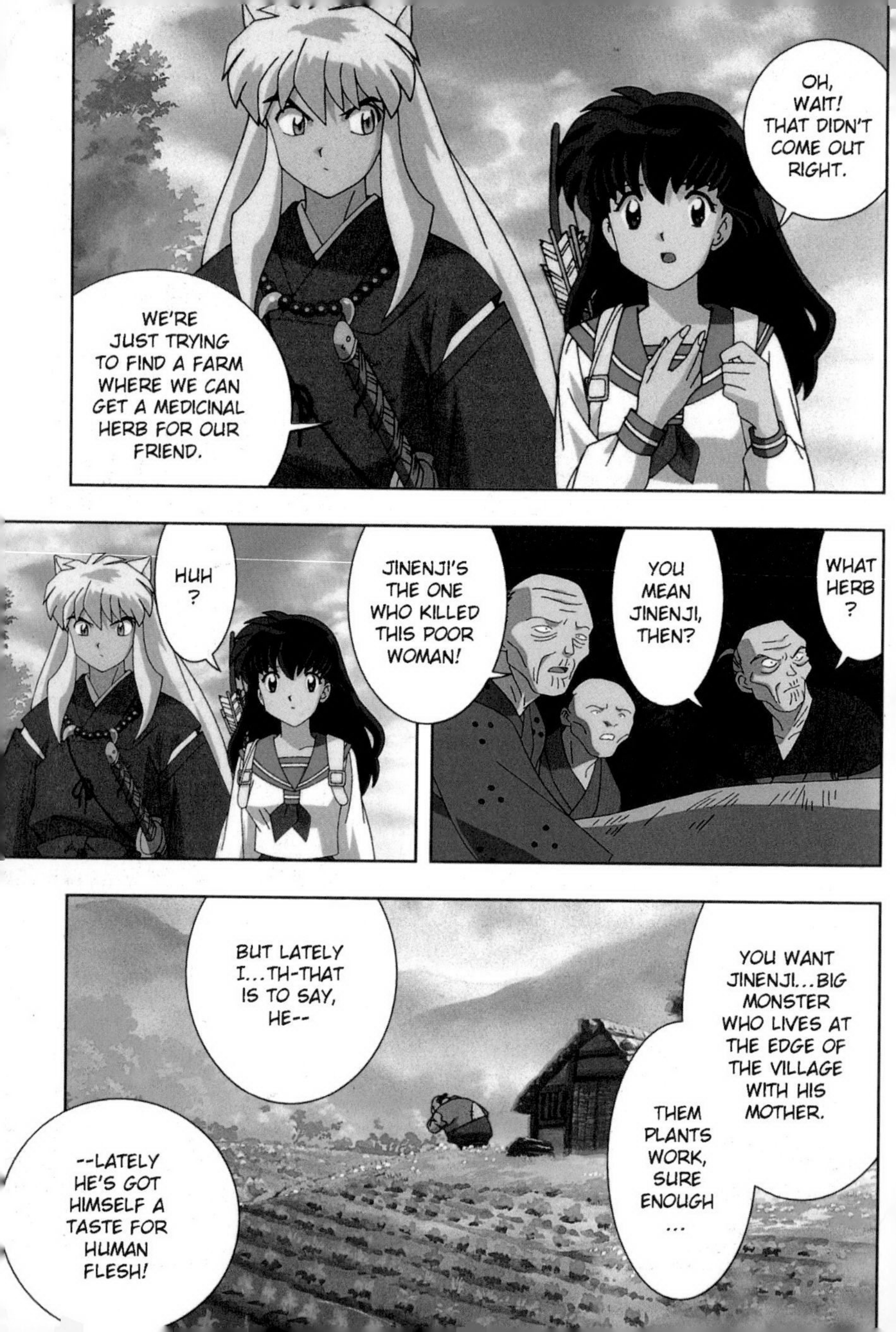
OH, WAIT! THAT DIDN'T COME OUT RIGHT.
WE'RE JUST TRYING TO FIND A FARM WHERE WE CAN GET A MEDICINAL HERB FOR OUR FRIEND.
WHAT HERB?
YOU MEAN JINENJI, THEN?
JINENJI'S THE ONE WHO KILLED THIS POOR WOMAN!
HUH?
YOU WANT JINENJI...BIG MONSTER WHO LIVES AT THE EDGE OF THE VILLAGE WITH HIS MOTHER.
THEM PLANTS WORK, SURE ENOUGH...
BUT LATELY I...TH-THAT IS TO SAY, HE--
--LATELY HE'S GOT HIMSELF A TASTE FOR HUMAN FLESH!

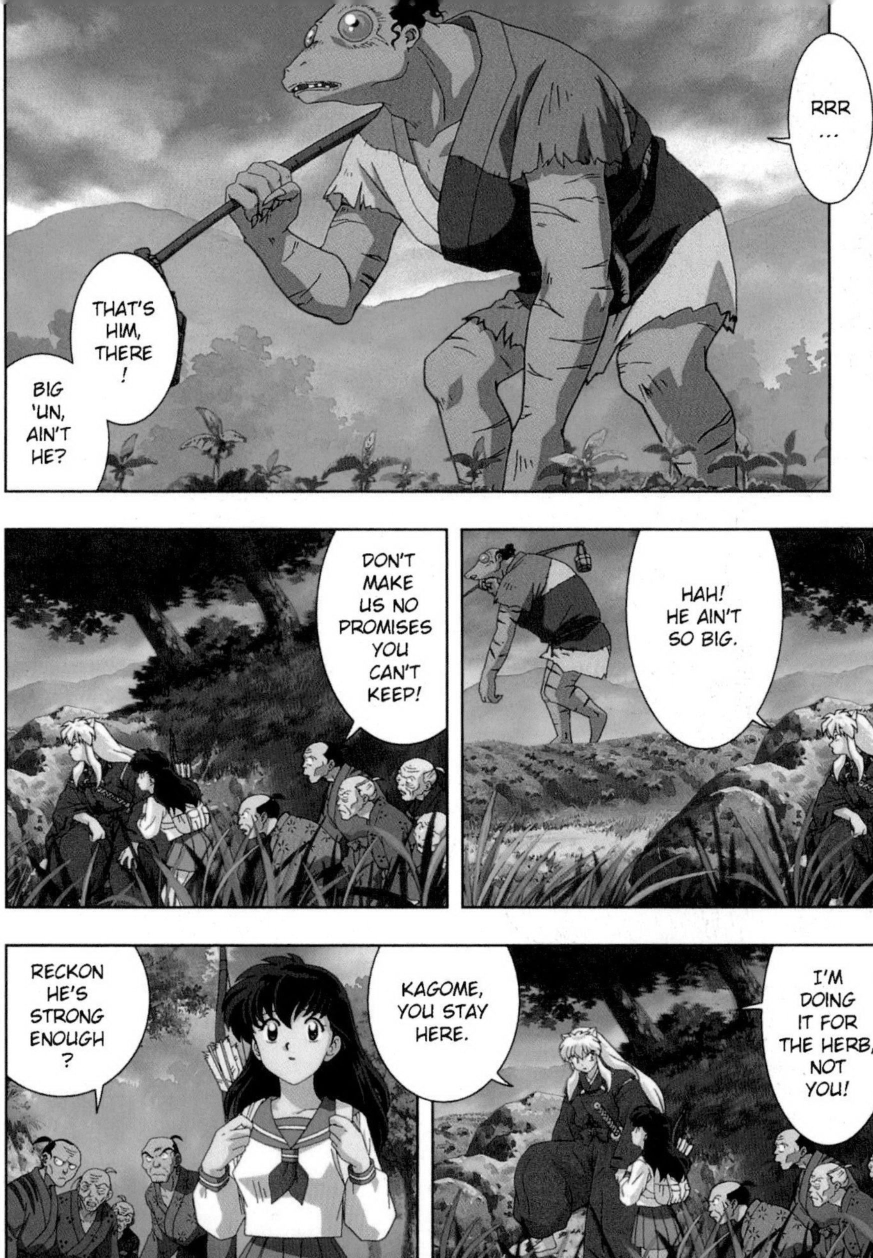
RRR...
THAT'S HIM, THERE!
BIG 'UN, AIN'T HE?
HAH! HE AIN'T SO BIG.
DON'T MAKE US NO PROMISES YOU CAN'T KEEP!
I'M DOING IT FOR THE HERB, NOT YOU!
KAGOME, YOU STAY HERE.
RECKON HE'S STRONG ENOUGH?

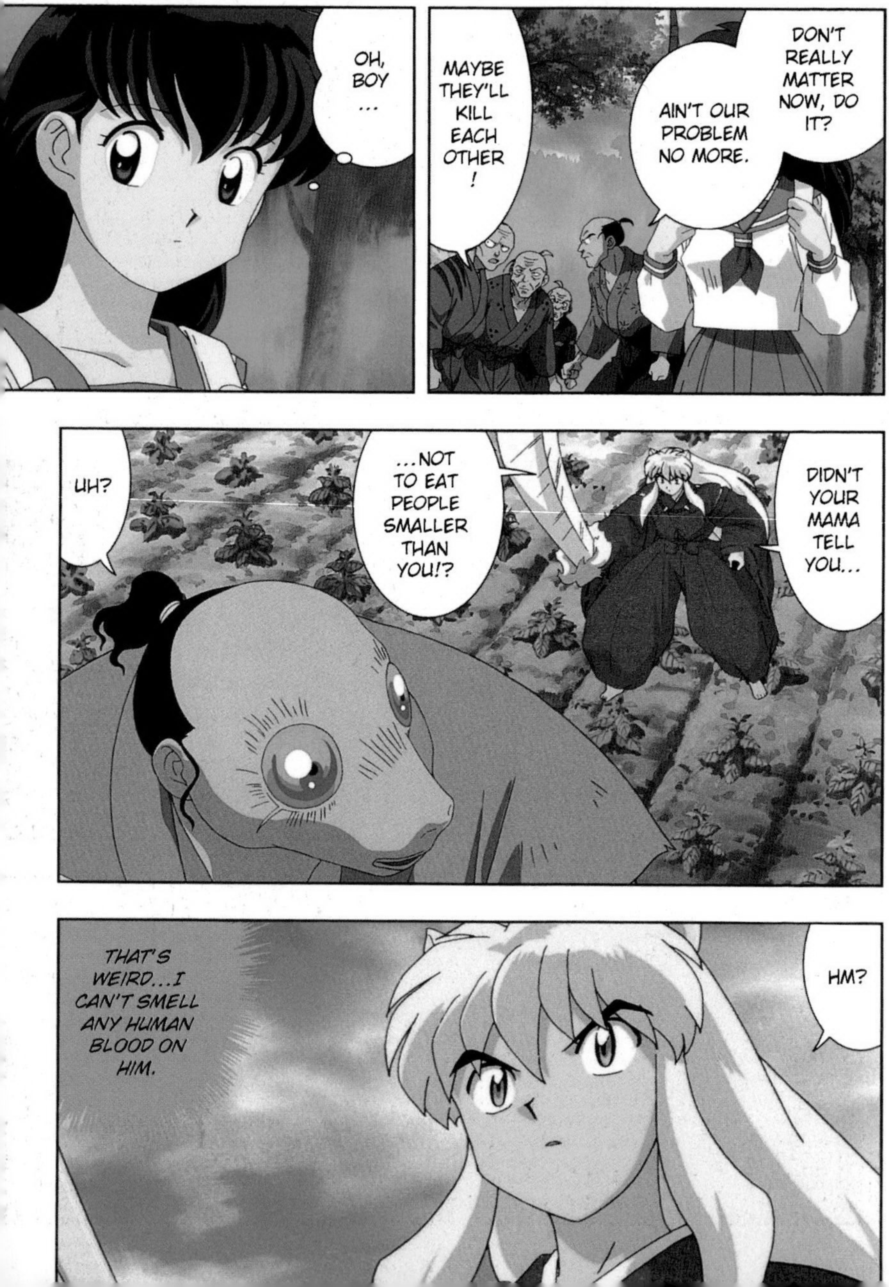
DON'T REALLY MATTER NOW, DO IT?
AIN'T OUR PROBLEM NO MORE.
MAYBE THEY'LL KILL EACH OTHER!
OH, BOY ...
DIDN'T YOUR MAMA TELL YOU...
...NOT TO EAT PEOPLE SMALLER THAN YOU!?
UH?
HM?
THAT'S WEIRD...I CAN'T SMELL ANY HUMAN BLOOD ON HIM.

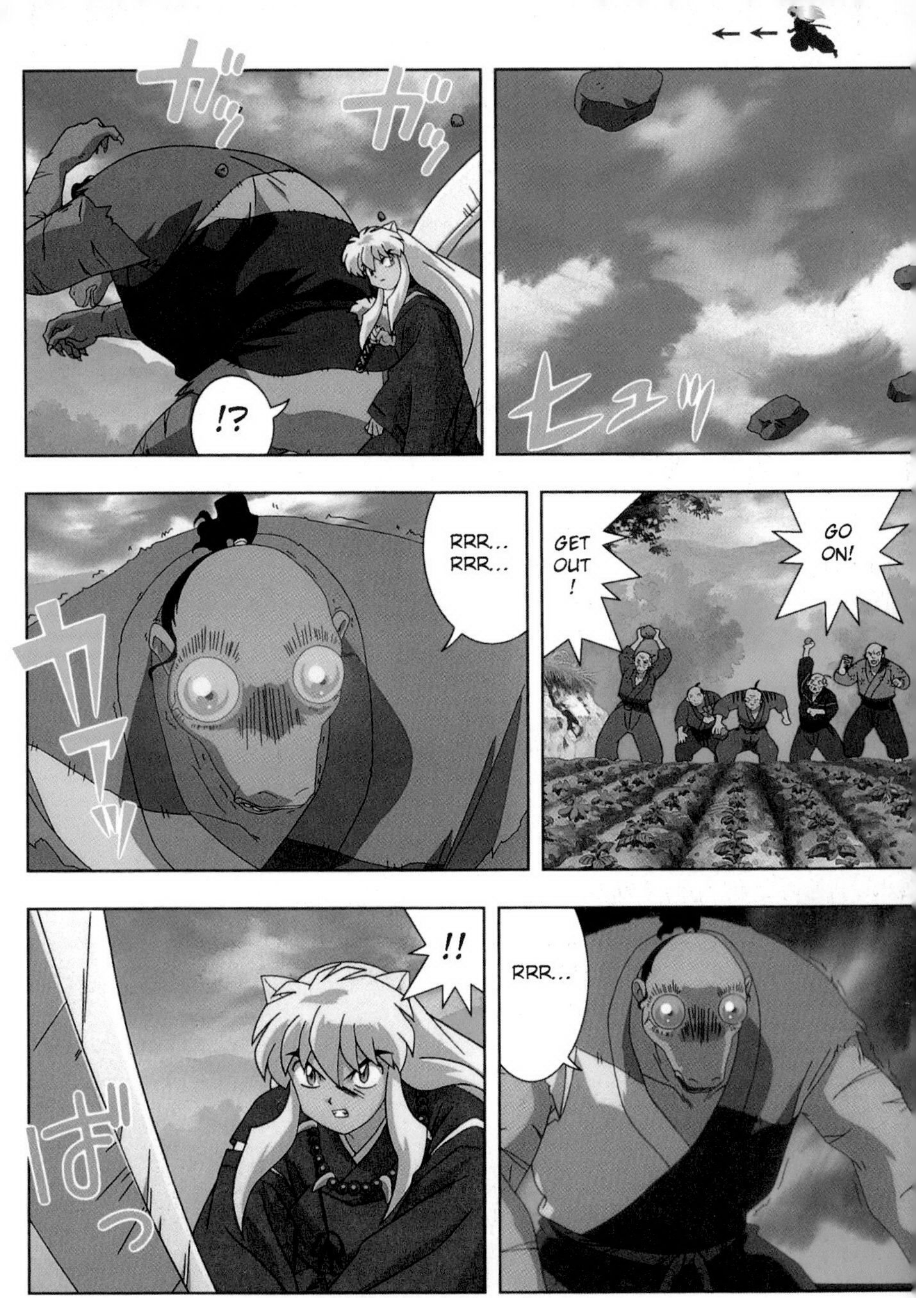
ヒュッ
ガッ
ガッ
!?
GO ON!
GET OUT!
RRR... RRR...
ヤァッ
RRR...
!!
ばっ

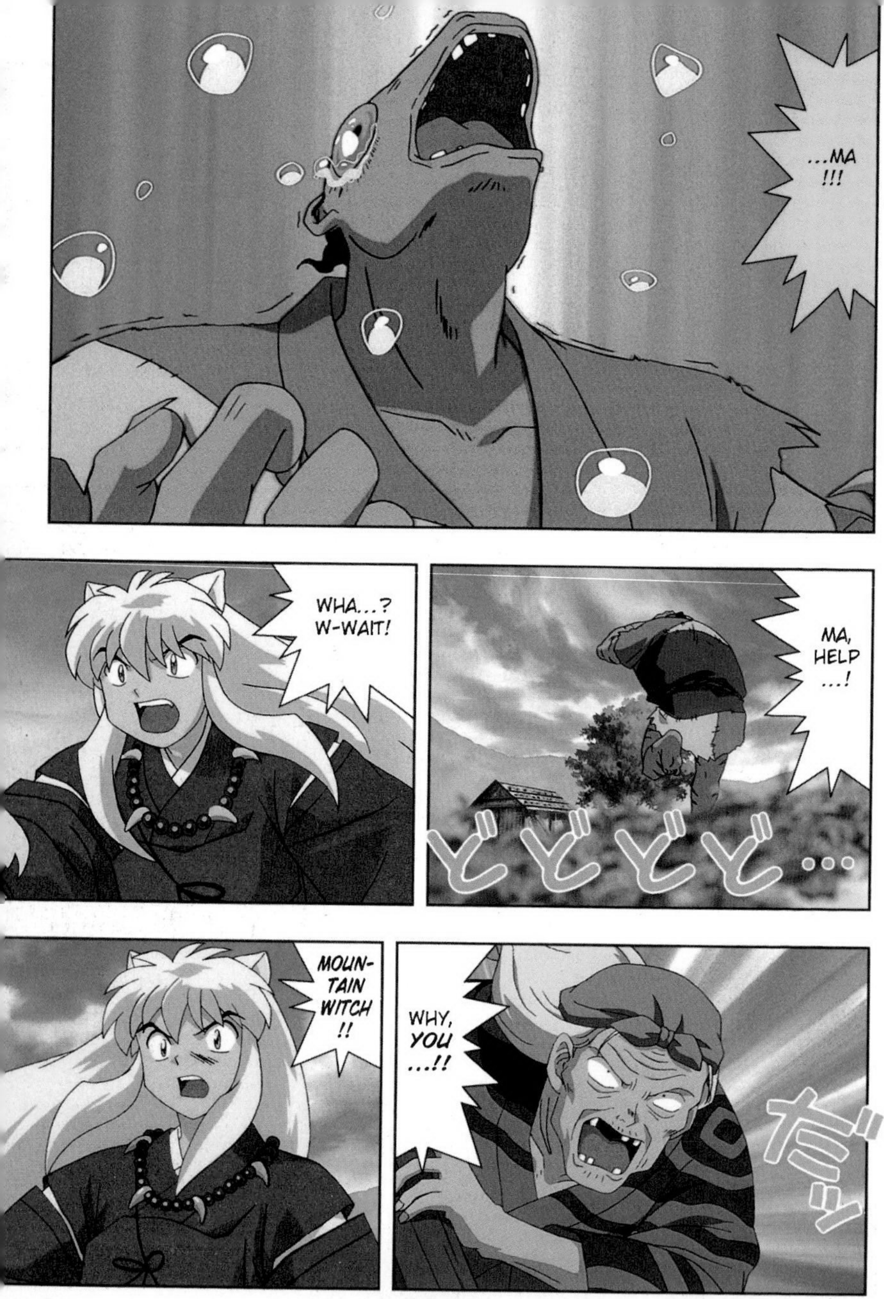
...MA !!!
MA, HELP ...!
どどどど...
WHA...? W-WAIT!
WHY, YOU ...!!
だッ
MOUN-TAIN WITCH !!

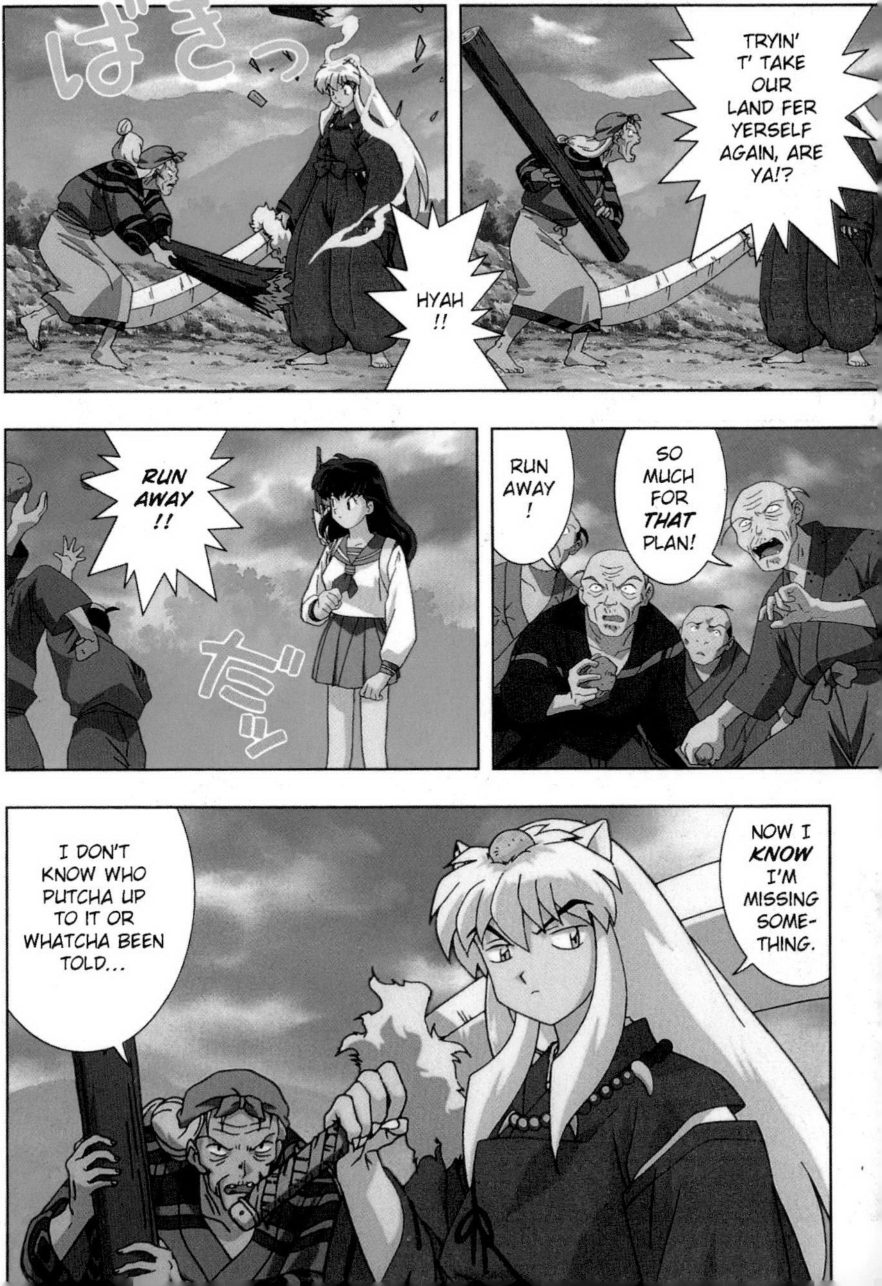
TRYIN' T' TAKE OUR LAND FER YERSELF AGAIN, ARE YA!?
ばきっ
HYAH!!
SO MUCH FOR THAT PLAN!
RUN AWAY!
RUN AWAY!!
だッ
NOW I KNOW I'M MISSING SOME-THING.
I DON'T KNOW WHO PUTCHA UP TO IT OR WHATCHA BEEN TOLD...

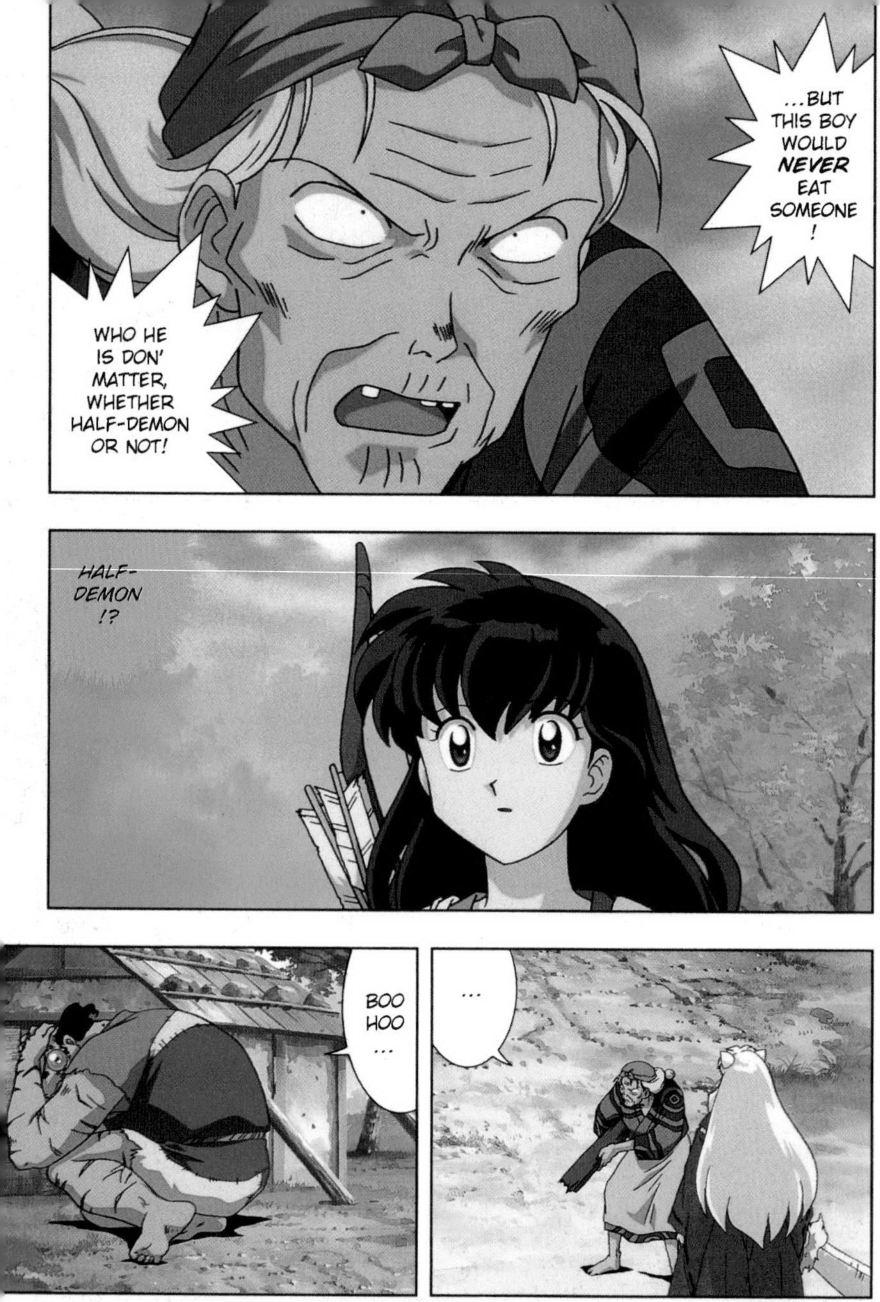
WHO HE IS DON' MATTER, WHETHER HALF-DEMON OR NOT!
...BUT THIS BOY WOULD **NEVER** EAT SOMEONE!
HALF-DEMON!?
...
BOO HOO...

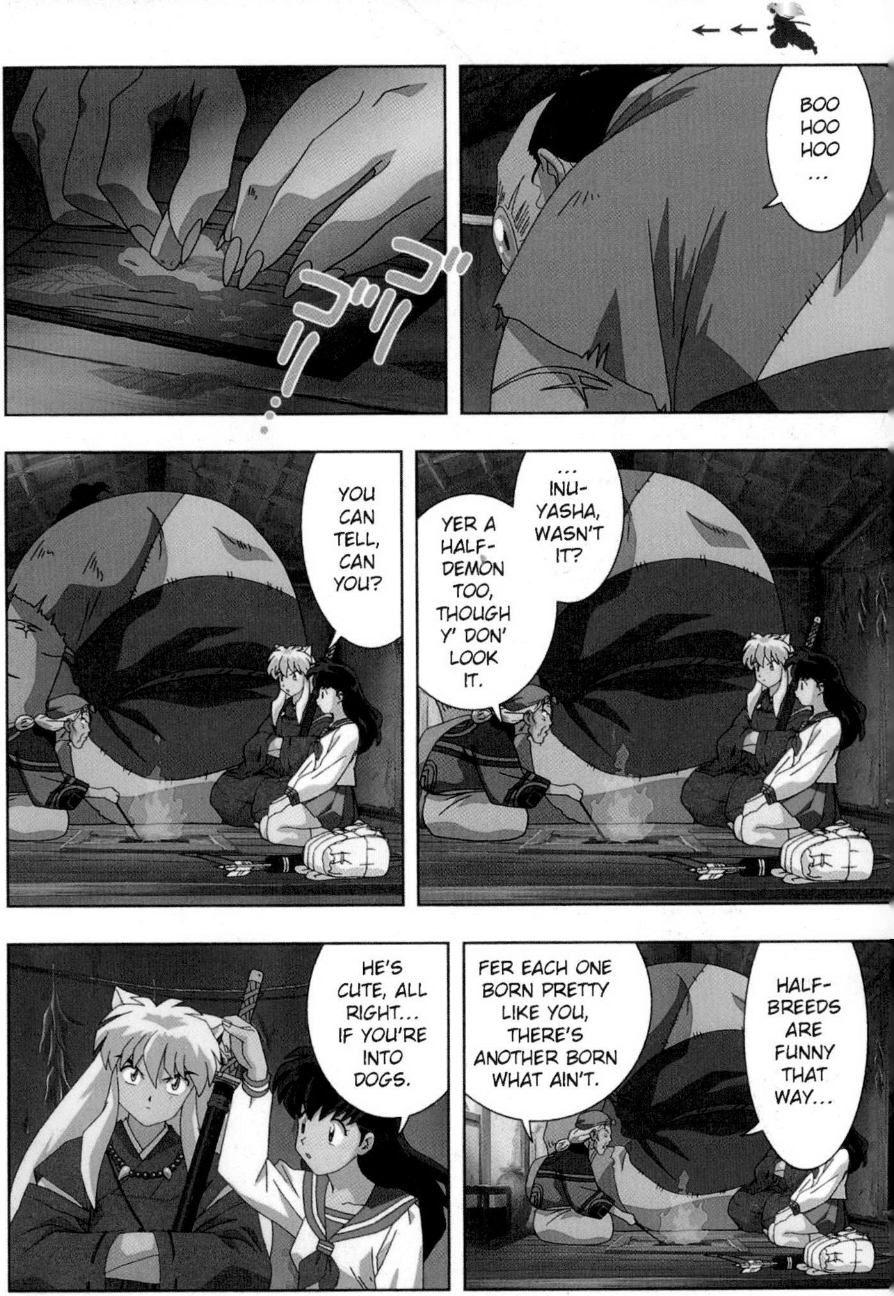
BOO HOO HOO ...
... INU-YASHA, WASN'T IT?
YER A HALF-DEMON TOO, THOUGH Y' DON' LOOK IT.
YOU CAN TELL, CAN YOU?
HALF-BREEDS ARE FUNNY THAT WAY...
FER EACH ONE BORN PRETTY LIKE YOU, THERE'S ANOTHER BORN WHAT AIN'T.
HE'S CUTE, ALL RIGHT... IF YOU'RE INTO DOGS.

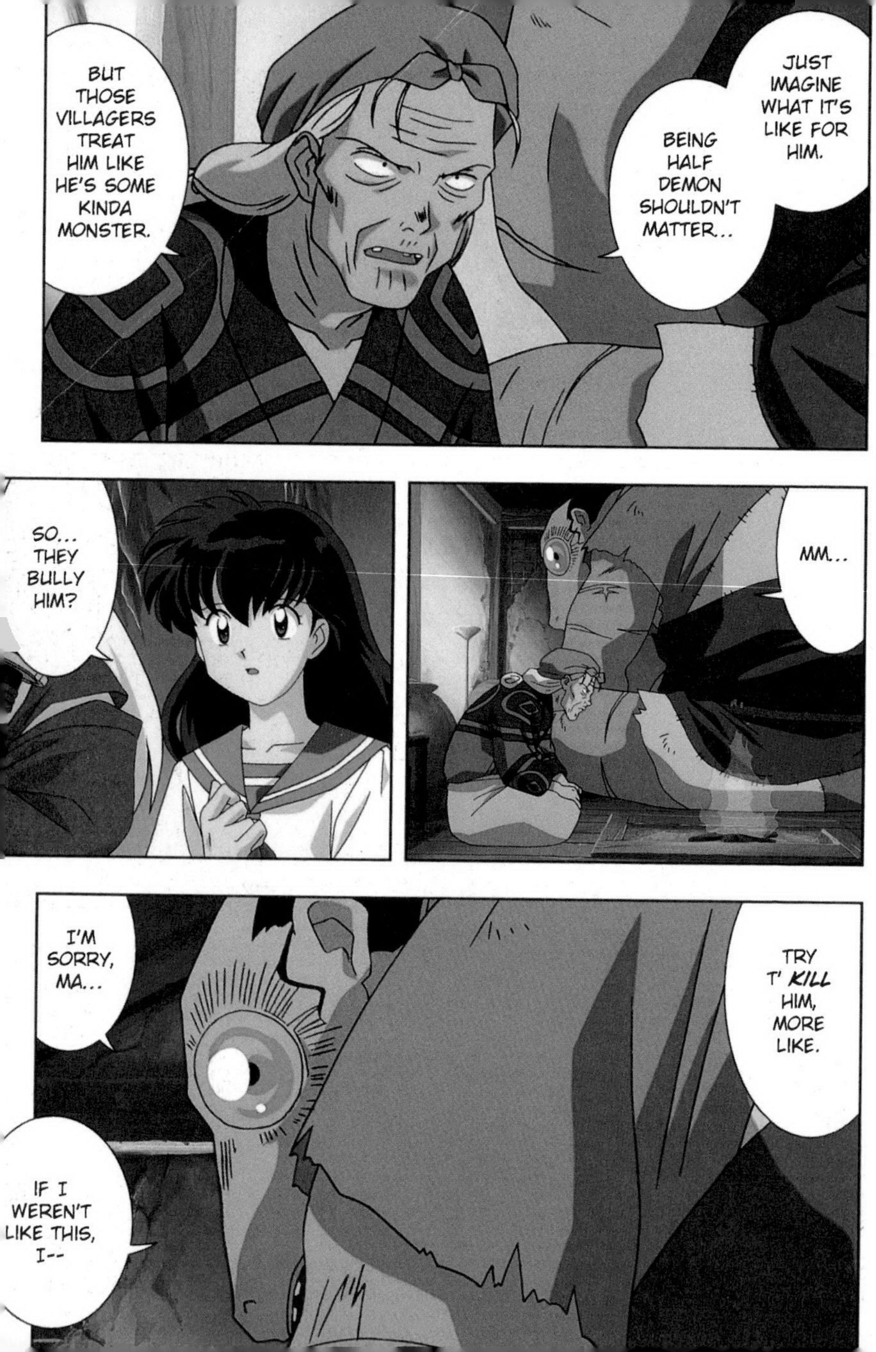
JUST IMAGINE WHAT IT'S LIKE FOR HIM.
BEING HALF DEMON SHOULDN'T MATTER...
BUT THOSE VILLAGERS TREAT HIM LIKE HE'S SOME KINDA MONSTER.
MM...
SO... THEY BULLY HIM?
TRY T' **KILL** HIM, MORE LIKE.
I'M SORRY, MA...
IF I WEREN'T LIKE THIS, I--

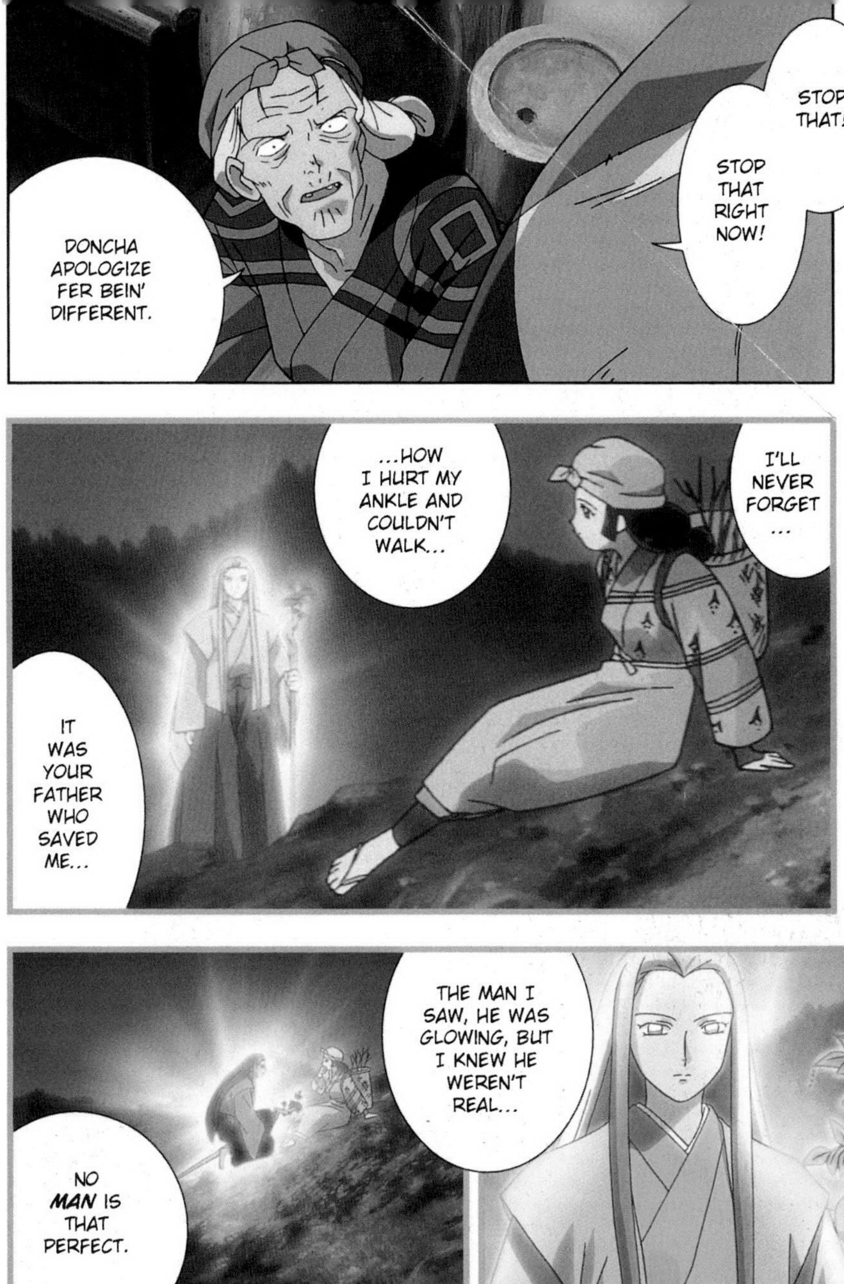
STOP THAT!
STOP THAT RIGHT NOW!
DONCHA APOLOGIZE FER BEIN' DIFFERENT.
I'LL NEVER FORGET...
...HOW I HURT MY ANKLE AND COULDN'T WALK...
IT WAS YOUR FATHER WHO SAVED ME...
THE MAN I SAW, HE WAS GLOWING, BUT I KNEW HE WEREN'T REAL...
NO *MAN* IS THAT PERFECT.

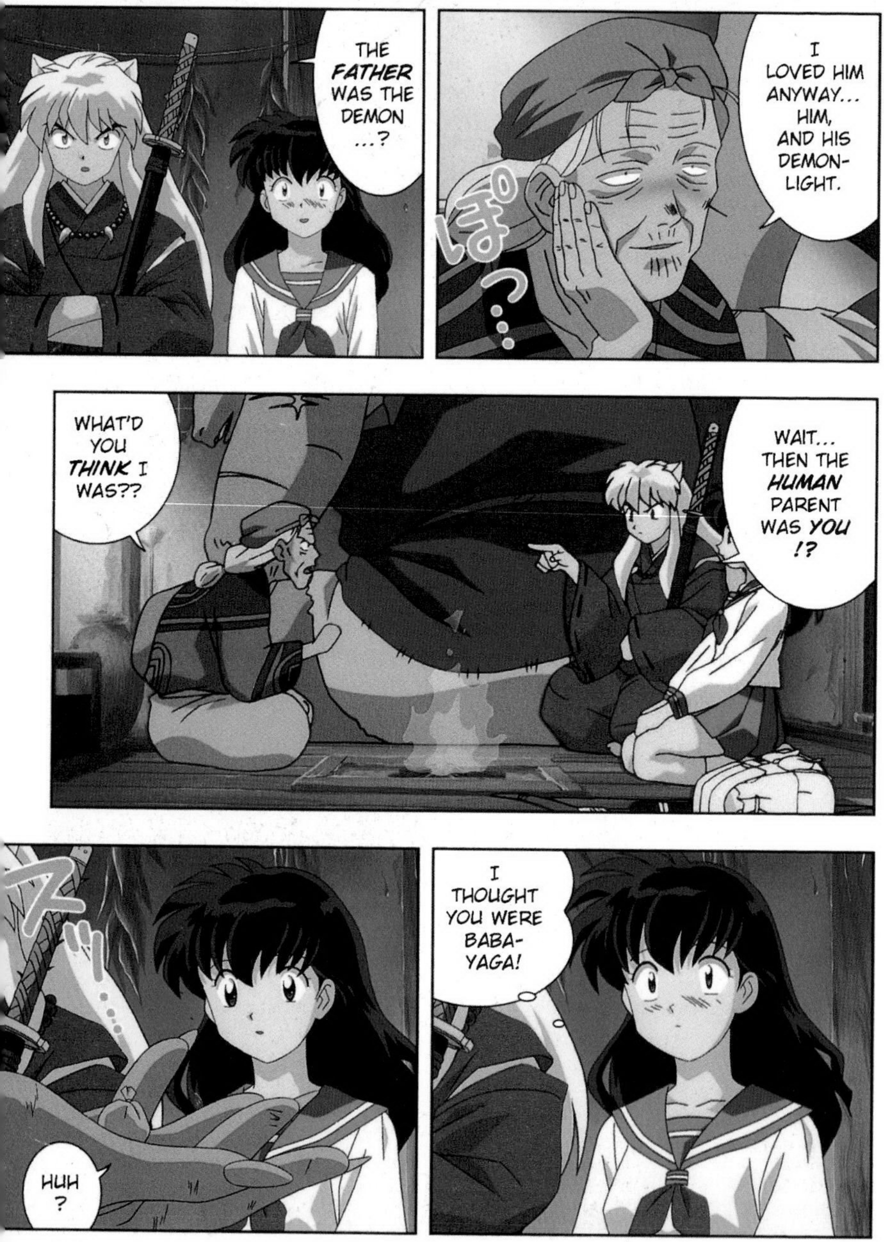
I LOVED HIM ANYWAY... HIM, AND HIS DEMON-LIGHT.
ぽっ…
THE *FATHER* WAS THE DEMON ...?
WAIT... THEN THE *HUMAN* PARENT WAS *YOU* !?
WHAT'D YOU *THINK* I WAS??
I THOUGHT YOU WERE BABA-YAGA!
HUH ?

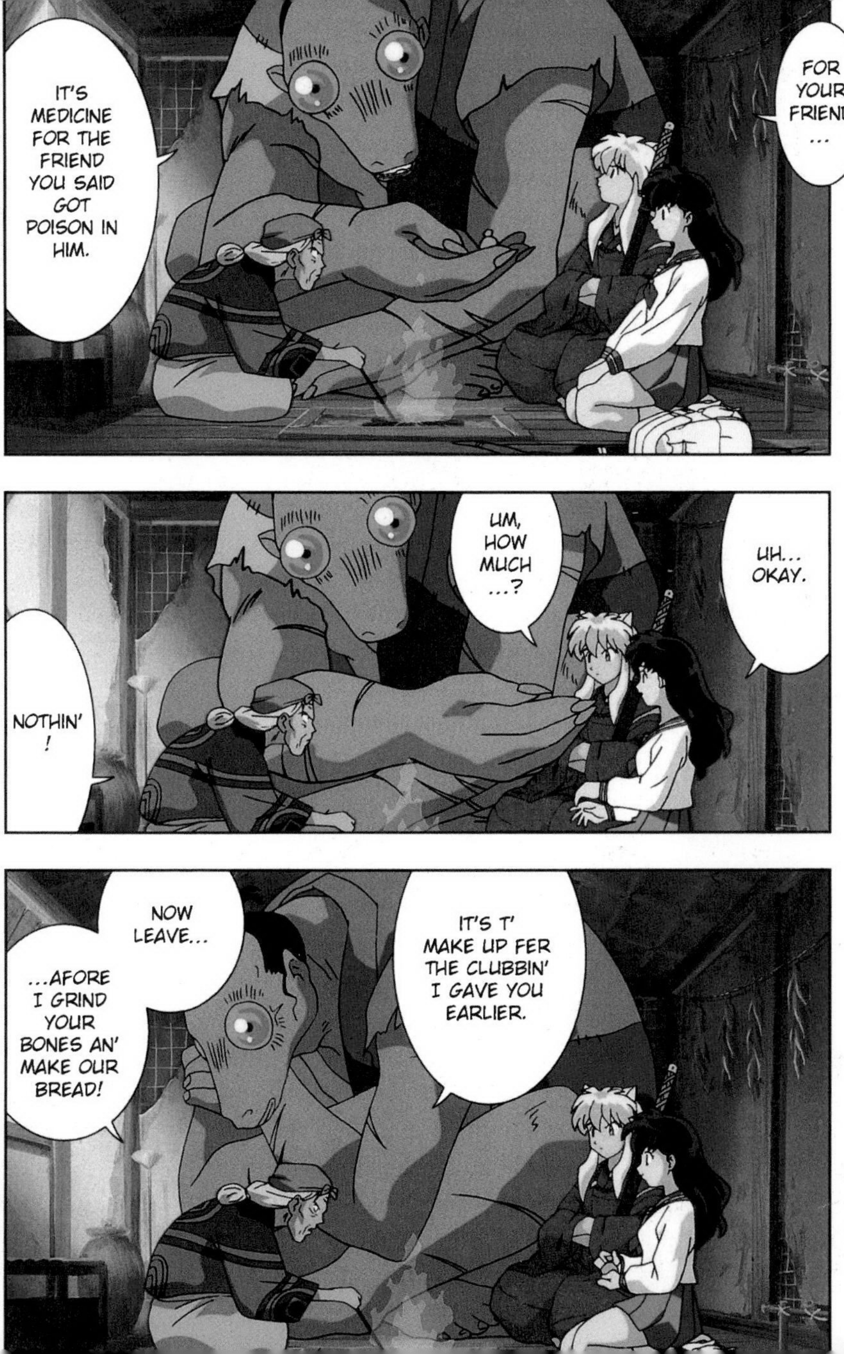
FOR YOUR FRIEND ...
IT'S MEDICINE FOR THE FRIEND YOU SAID GOT POISON IN HIM.
UH... OKAY.
UM, HOW MUCH ...?
NOTHIN' !
IT'S T' MAKE UP FER THE CLUBBIN' I GAVE YOU EARLIER.
NOW LEAVE...
...AFORE I GRIND YOUR BONES AN' MAKE OUR BREAD!

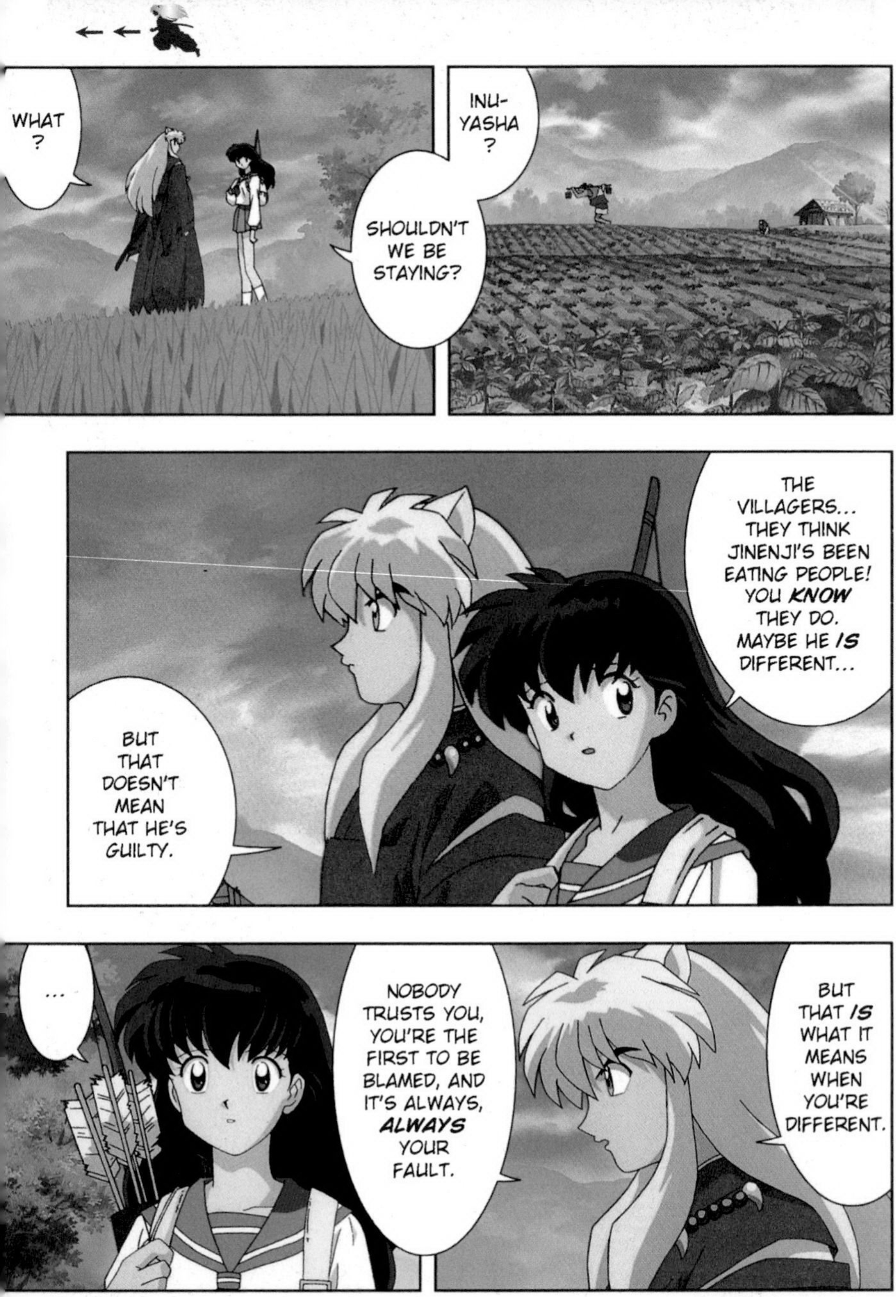
INU-YASHA?
SHOULDN'T WE BE STAYING?
WHAT?
THE VILLAGERS... THEY THINK JINENJI'S BEEN EATING PEOPLE! YOU *KNOW* THEY DO. MAYBE HE *IS* DIFFERENT...
BUT THAT DOESN'T MEAN THAT HE'S GUILTY.
BUT THAT *IS* WHAT IT MEANS WHEN YOU'RE DIFFERENT.
NOBODY TRUSTS YOU, YOU'RE THE FIRST TO BE BLAMED, AND IT'S ALWAYS, ***ALWAYS*** YOUR FAULT.
...

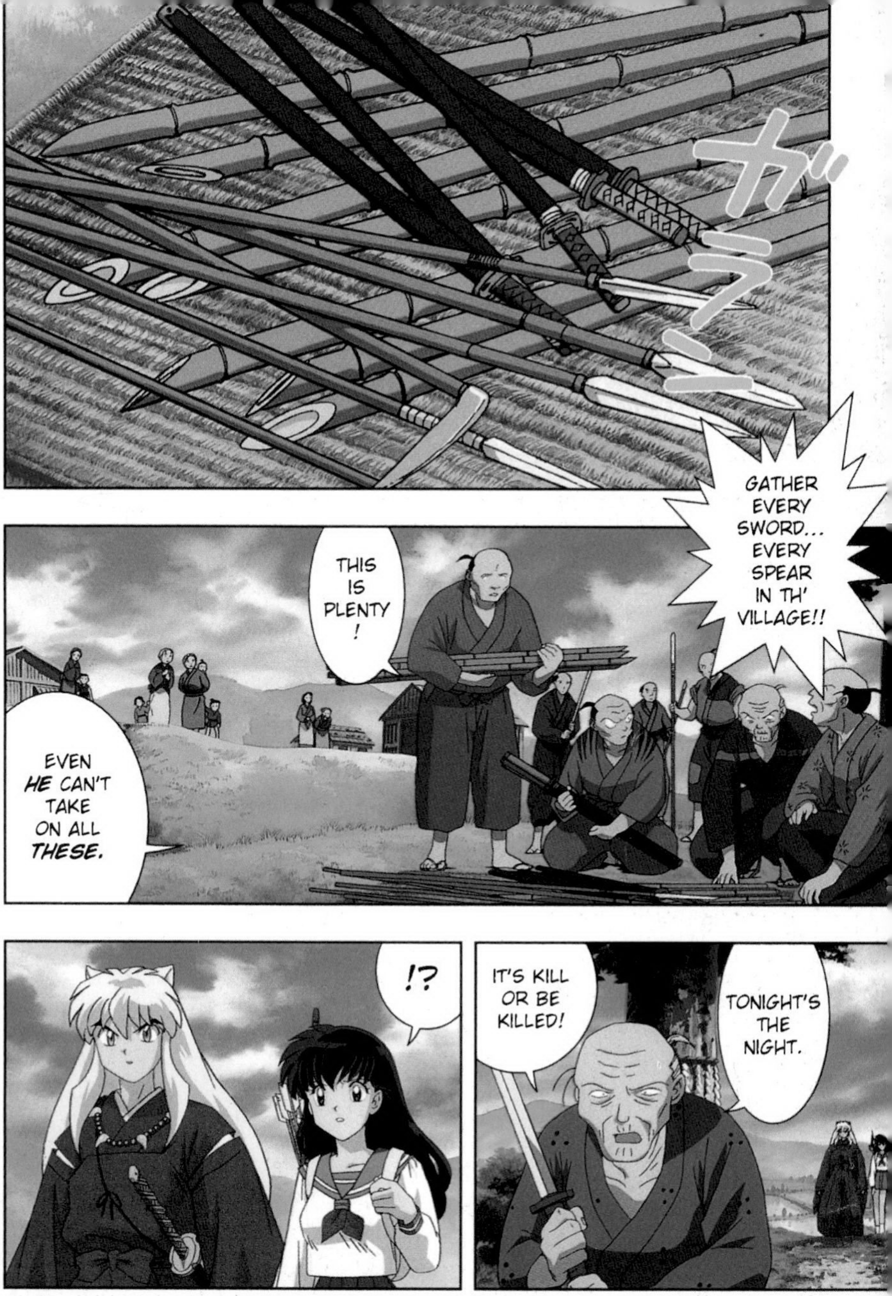
ガラン
GATHER EVERY SWORD... EVERY SPEAR IN TH' VILLAGE!!
THIS IS PLENTY!
EVEN *HE* CAN'T TAKE ON ALL *THESE.*
TONIGHT'S THE NIGHT.
IT'S KILL OR BE KILLED!
!?

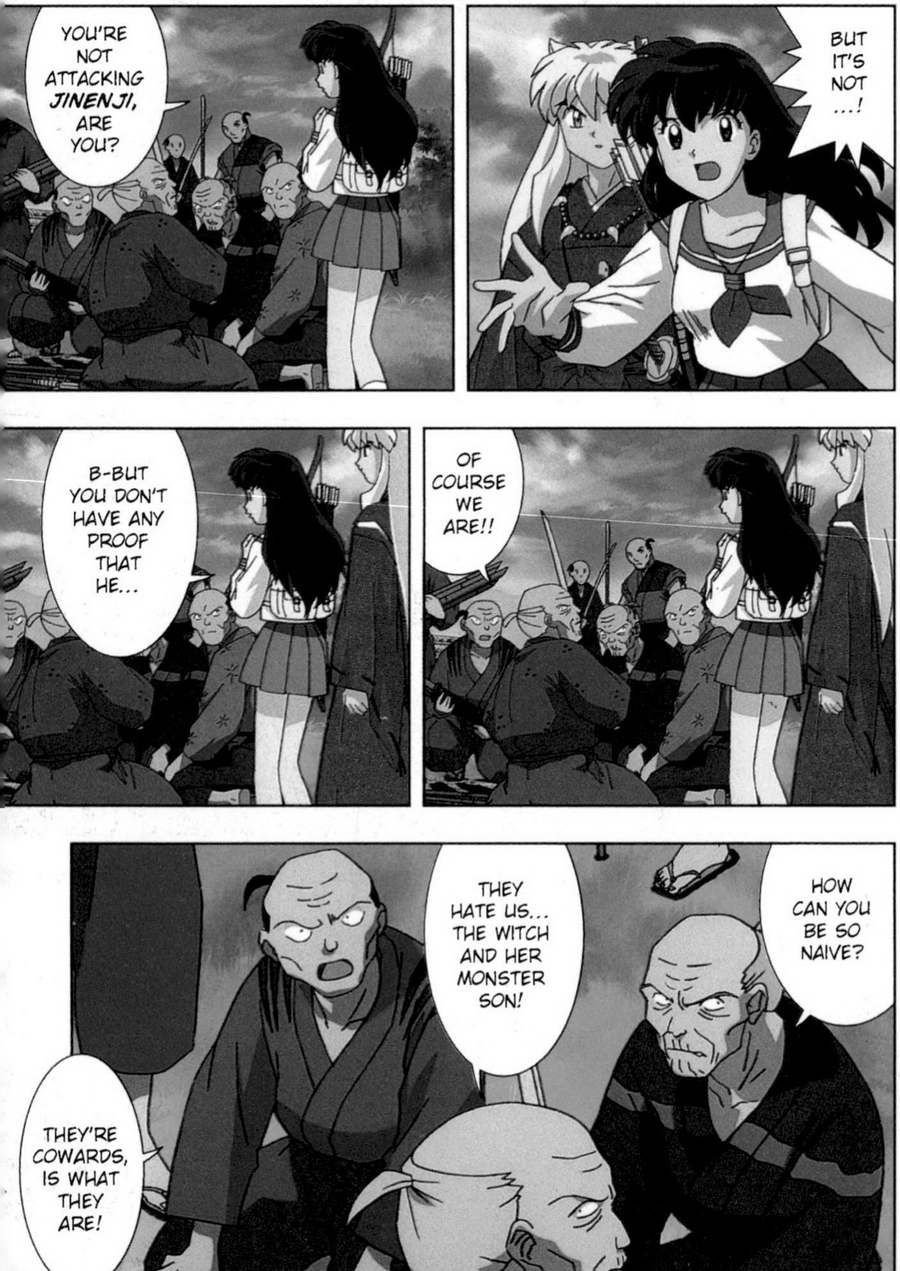
BUT IT'S NOT ...!
YOU'RE NOT ATTACKING *JINENJI*, ARE YOU?
OF COURSE WE ARE!!
B-BUT YOU DON'T HAVE ANY PROOF THAT HE...
HOW CAN YOU BE SO NAIVE?
THEY HATE US... THE WITCH AND HER MONSTER SON!
THEY'RE COWARDS, IS WHAT THEY ARE!

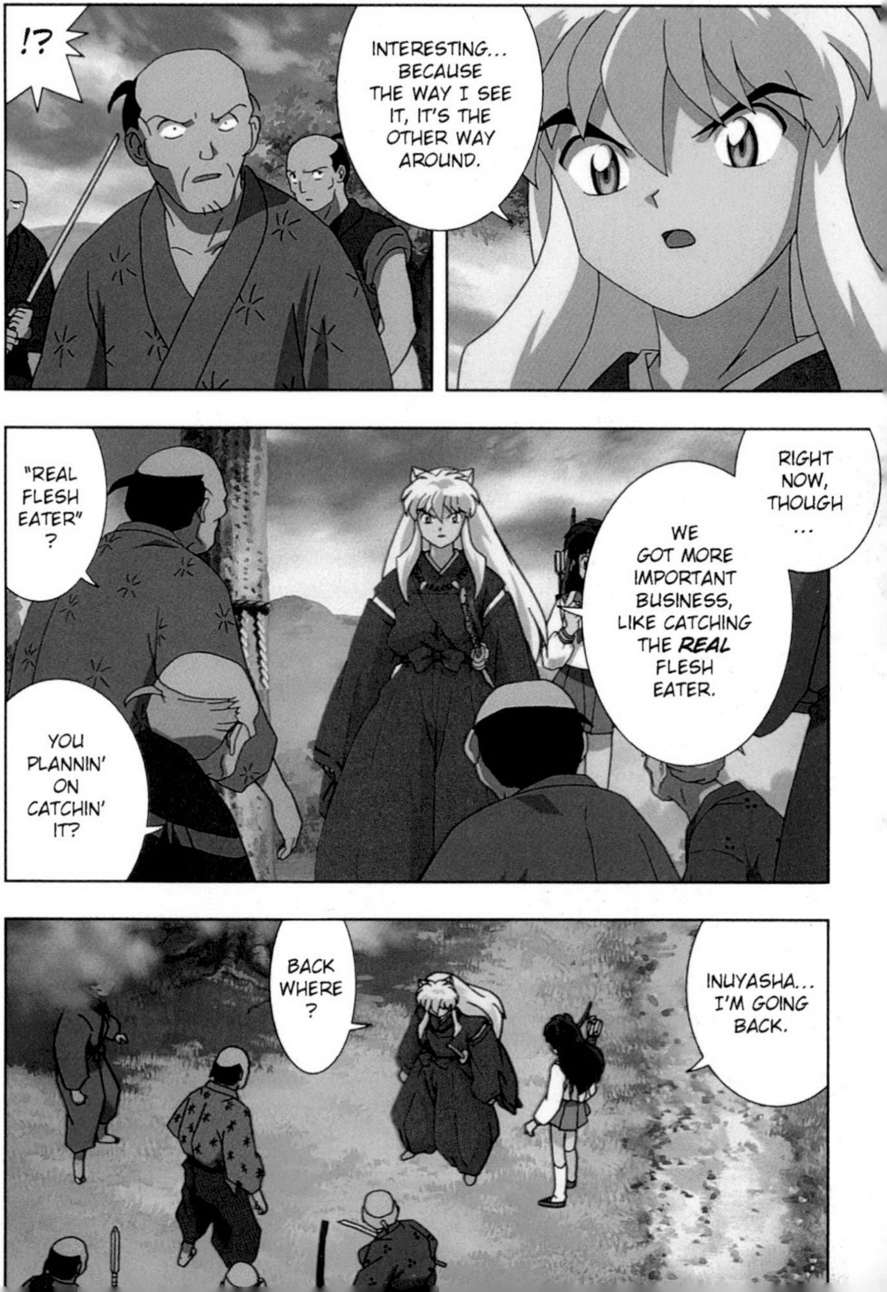
INTERESTING... BECAUSE THE WAY I SEE IT, IT'S THE OTHER WAY AROUND.
!?
RIGHT NOW, THOUGH...
WE GOT MORE IMPORTANT BUSINESS, LIKE CATCHING THE **REAL** FLESH EATER.
"REAL FLESH EATER"?
YOU PLANNIN' ON CATCHIN' IT?
INUYASHA... I'M GOING BACK.
BACK WHERE?

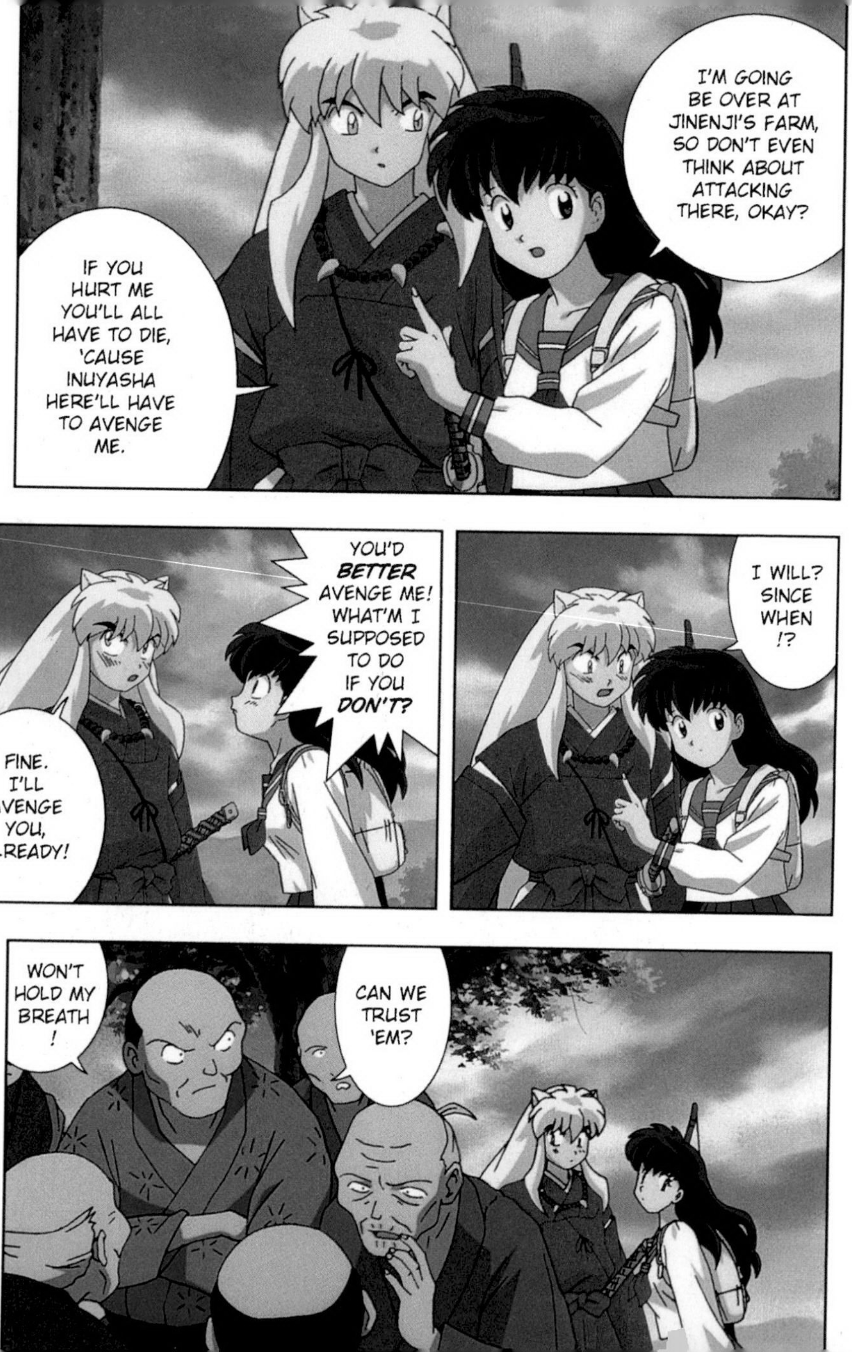
I'M GOING BE OVER AT JINENJI'S FARM, SO DON'T EVEN THINK ABOUT ATTACKING THERE, OKAY?
IF YOU HURT ME YOU'LL ALL HAVE TO DIE, 'CAUSE INUYASHA HERE'LL HAVE TO AVENGE ME.
I WILL? SINCE WHEN !?
YOU'D **BETTER** AVENGE ME! WHAT'M I SUPPOSED TO DO IF YOU ***DON'T?***
FINE. I'LL AVENGE YOU, ALREADY!
CAN WE TRUST 'EM?
WON'T HOLD MY BREATH !

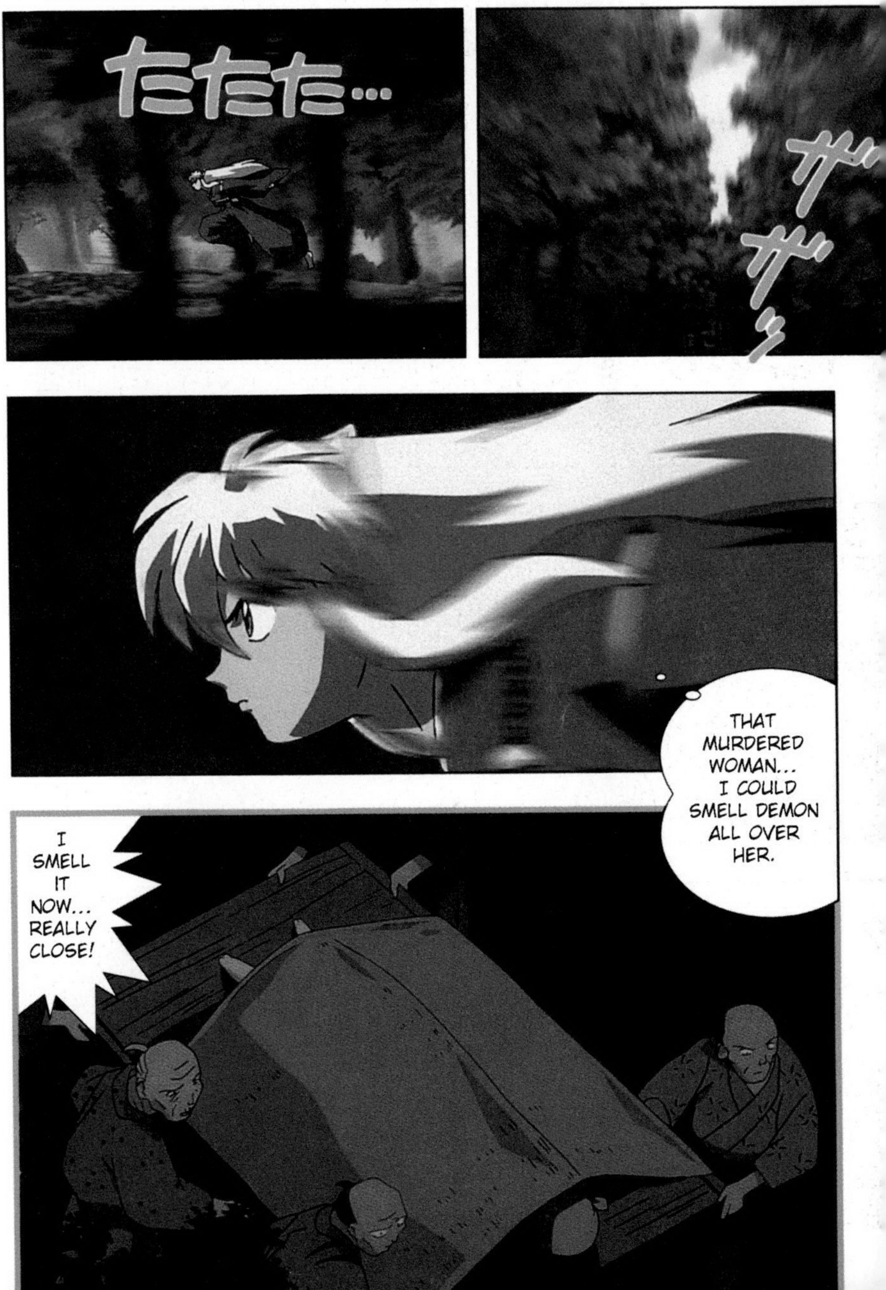
ザザッ
たたた…
THAT MURDERED WOMAN... I COULD SMELL DEMON ALL OVER HER.
I SMELL IT NOW... REALLY CLOSE!

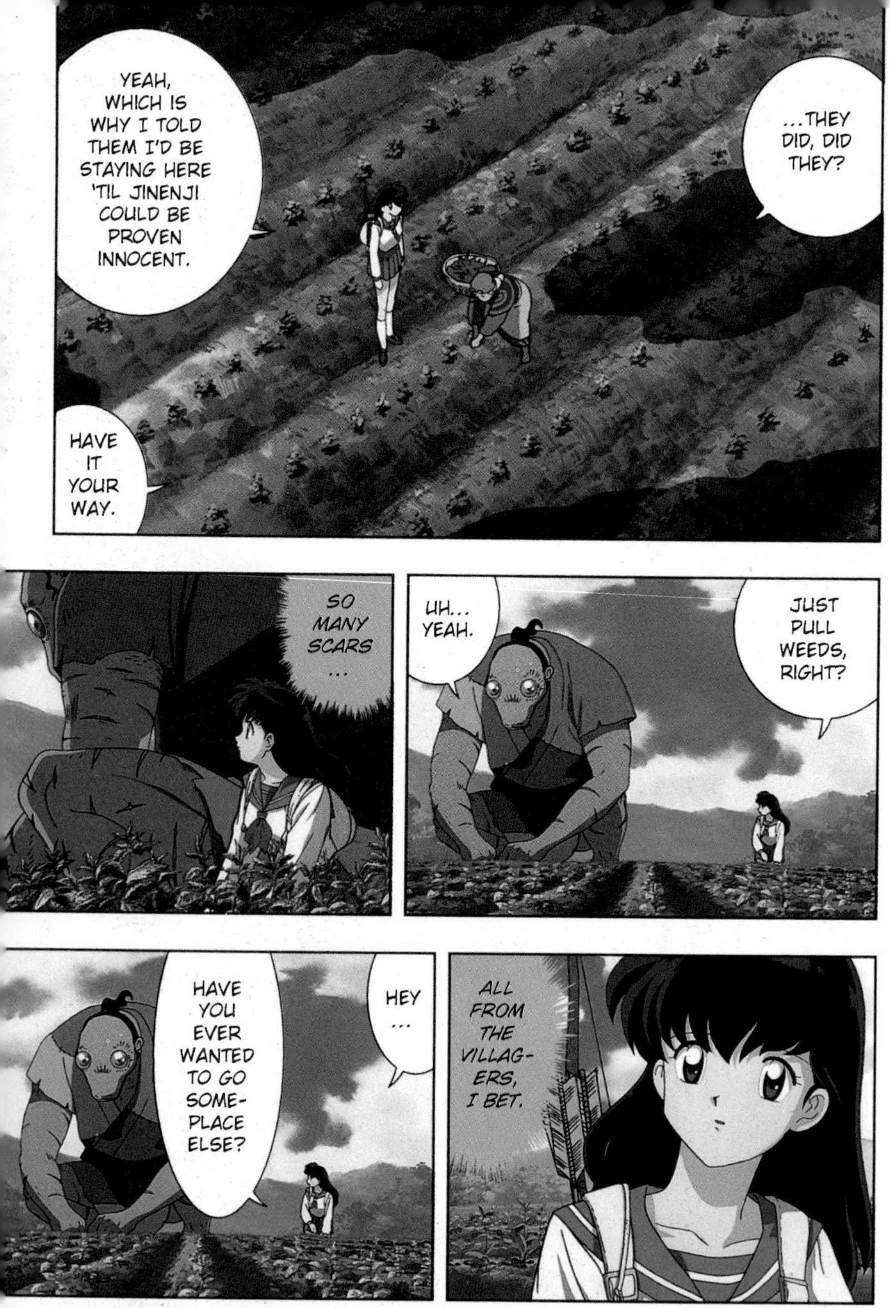
...THEY DID, DID THEY?
YEAH, WHICH IS WHY I TOLD THEM I'D BE STAYING HERE 'TIL JINENJI COULD BE PROVEN INNOCENT.
HAVE IT YOUR WAY.
JUST PULL WEEDS, RIGHT?
UH... YEAH.
SO MANY SCARS ...
ALL FROM THE VILLAG-ERS, I BET.
HEY ...
HAVE YOU EVER WANTED TO GO SOME-PLACE ELSE?

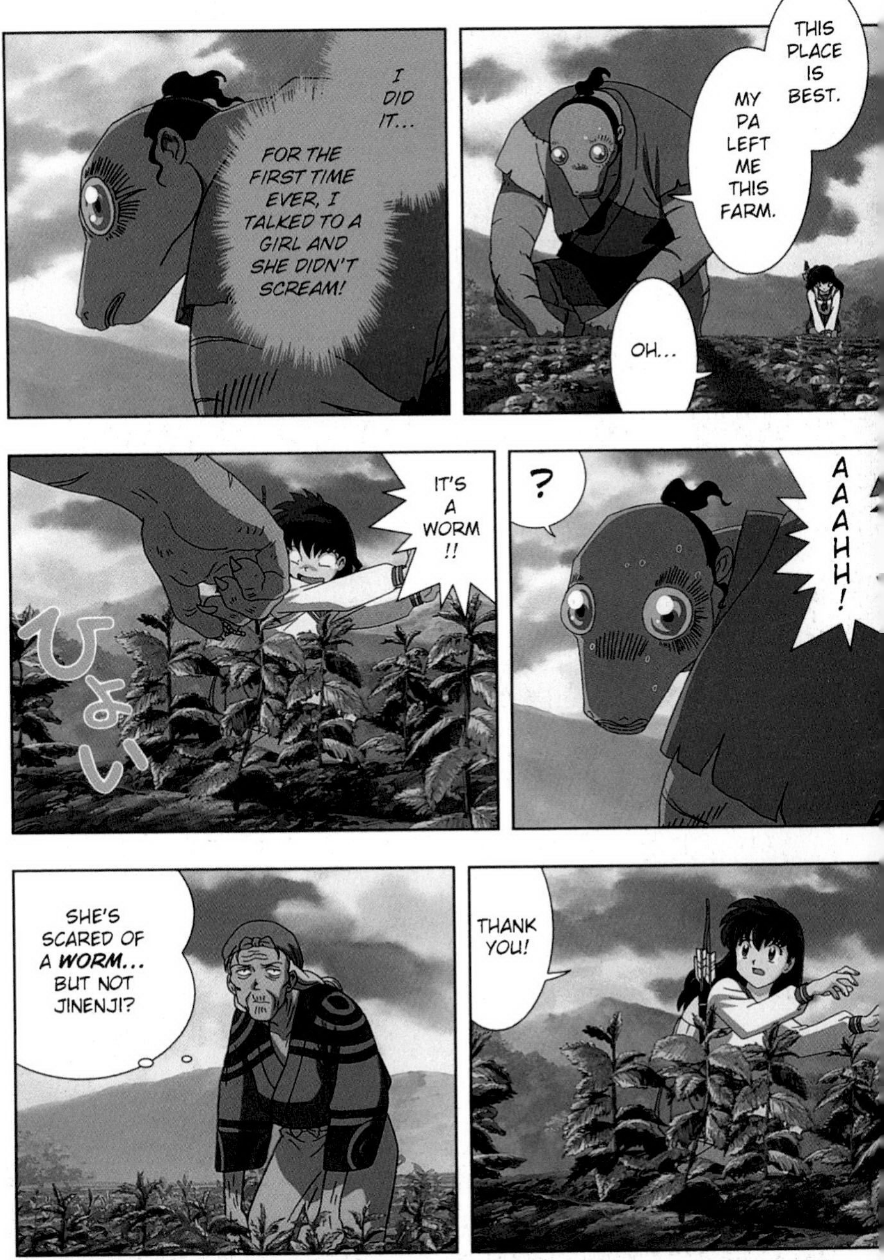
THIS PLACE IS BEST.
MY PA LEFT ME THIS FARM.
OH...
I DID IT...
FOR THE FIRST TIME EVER, I TALKED TO A GIRL AND SHE DIDN'T SCREAM!
AAAAHH!
?
IT'S A WORM!!
ひょい
THANK YOU!
SHE'S SCARED OF A ***WORM...*** BUT NOT JINENJI?

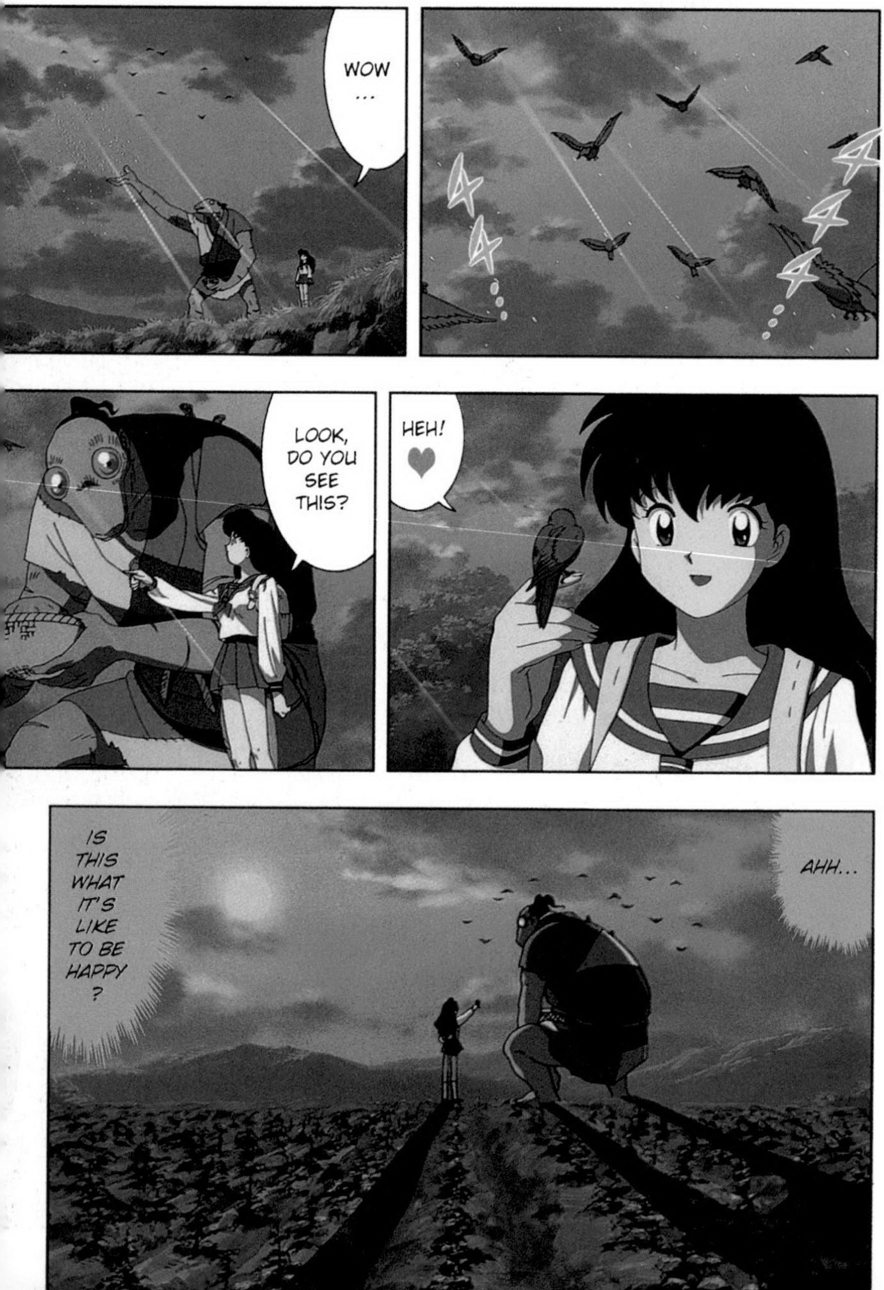
WOW ...
HEH! ♥
LOOK, DO YOU SEE THIS?
AHH...
IS THIS WHAT IT'S LIKE TO BE HAPPY?

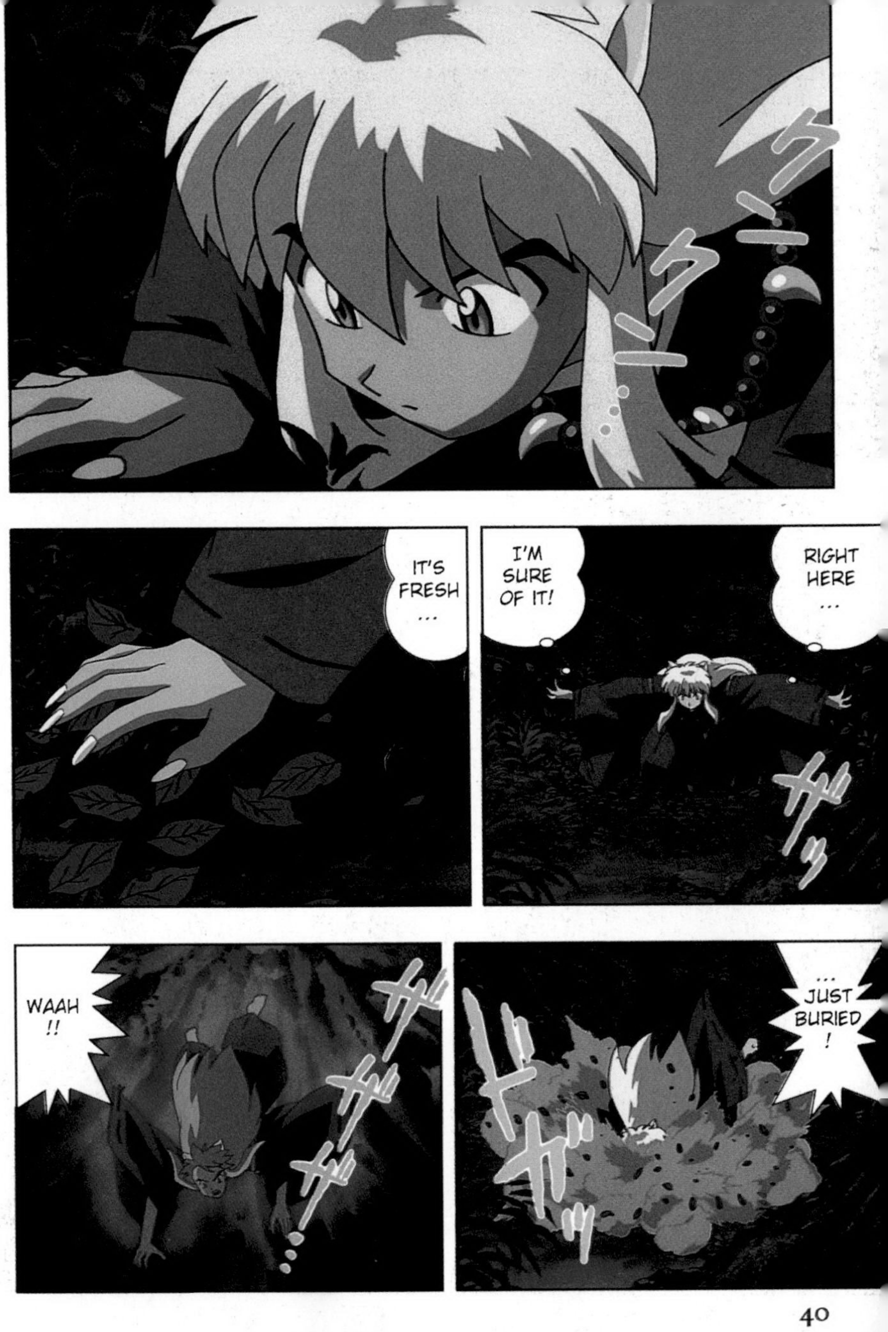
RIGHT HERE ...
I'M SURE OF IT!
IT'S FRESH ...
... JUST BURIED !
WAAH !!

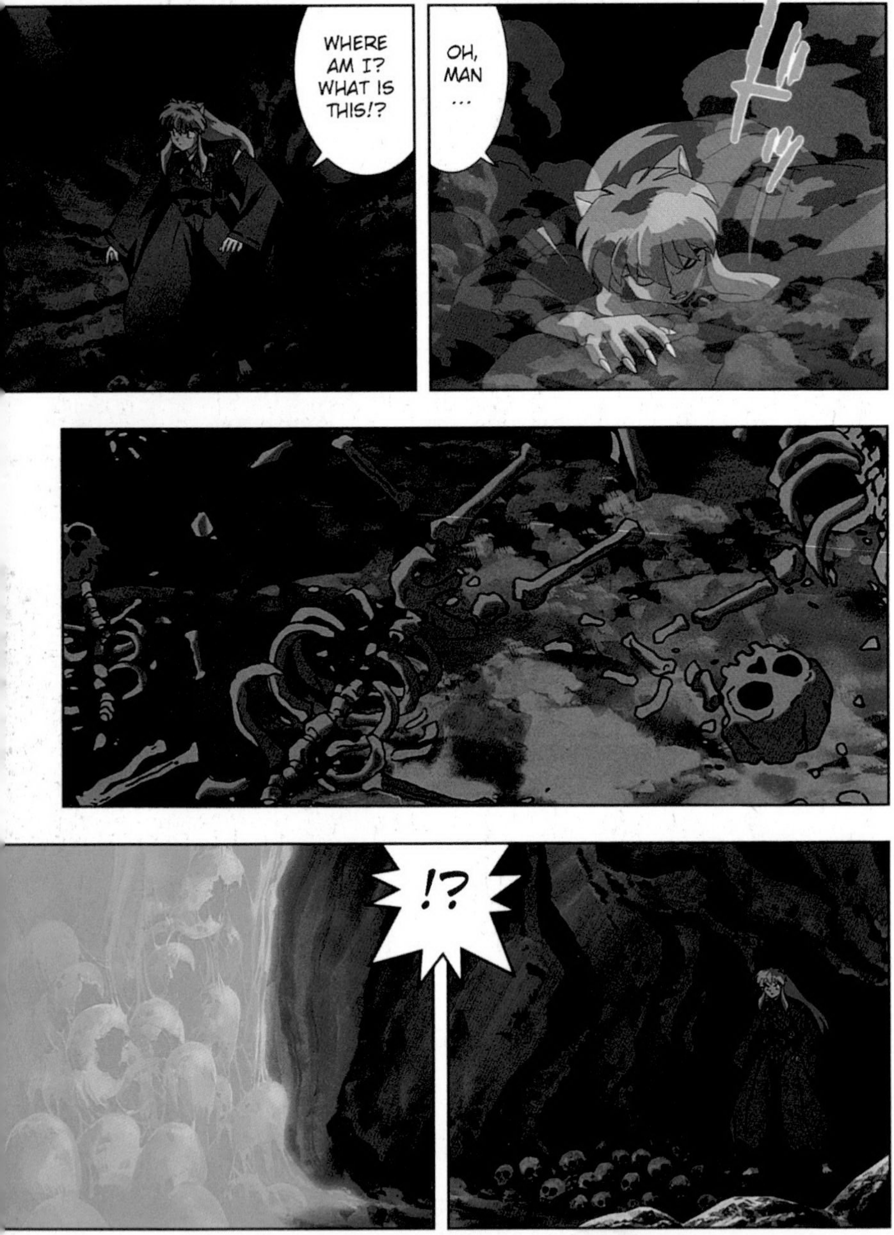

OH, MAN ...
WHERE AM I? WHAT IS THIS!?
!?

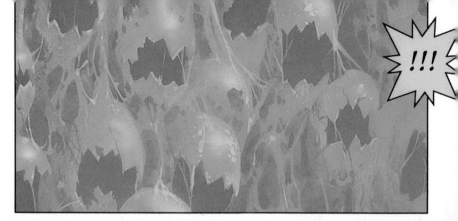

!!!

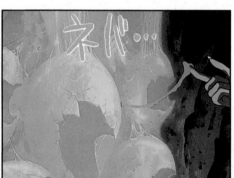

ネバ…

...

...AND
THEY'VE JUST
HATCHED.

THEY'RE
EGGS...

THIS
IS
DEFINITELY
THEIR
NEST!

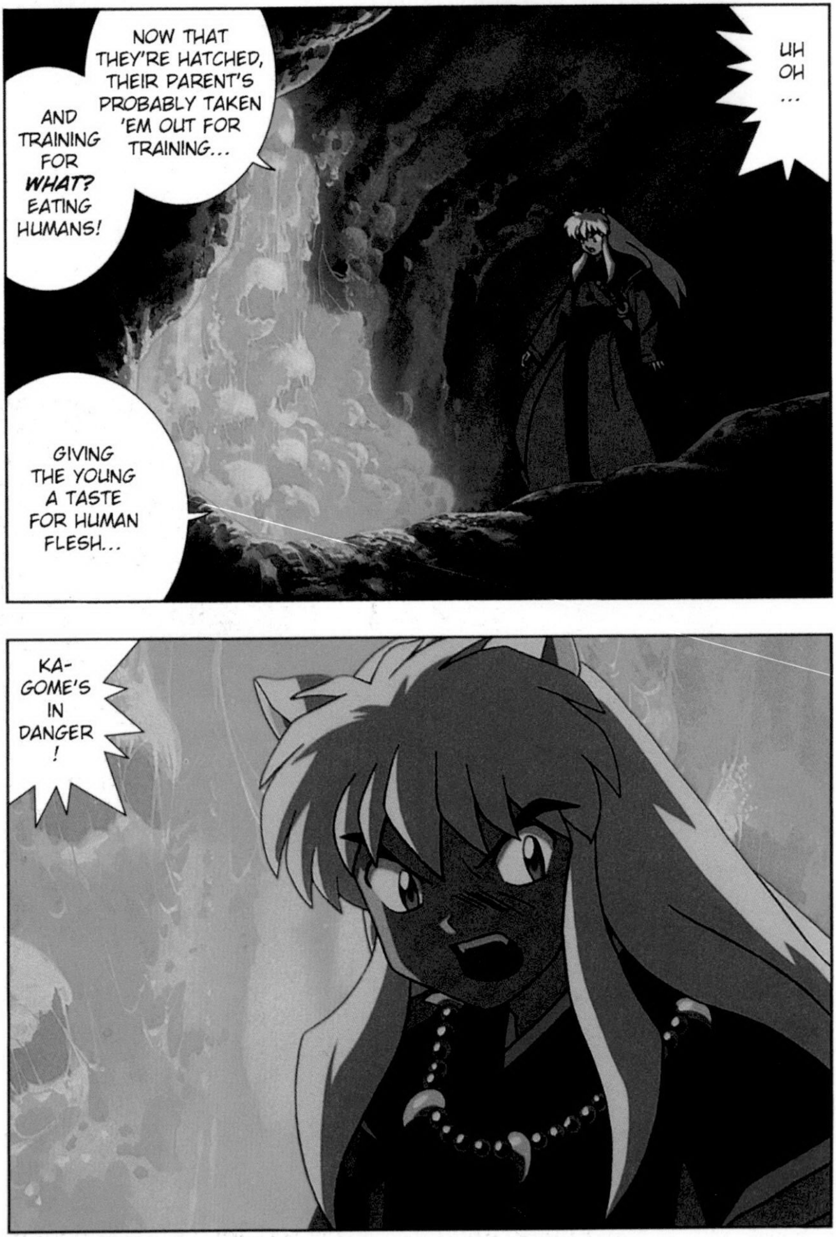
UH OH...
NOW THAT THEY'RE HATCHED, THEIR PARENT'S PROBABLY TAKEN 'EM OUT FOR TRAINING...
AND TRAINING FOR ***WHAT?*** EATING HUMANS!
GIVING THE YOUNG A TASTE FOR HUMAN FLESH...
KA-GOME'S IN DANGER!

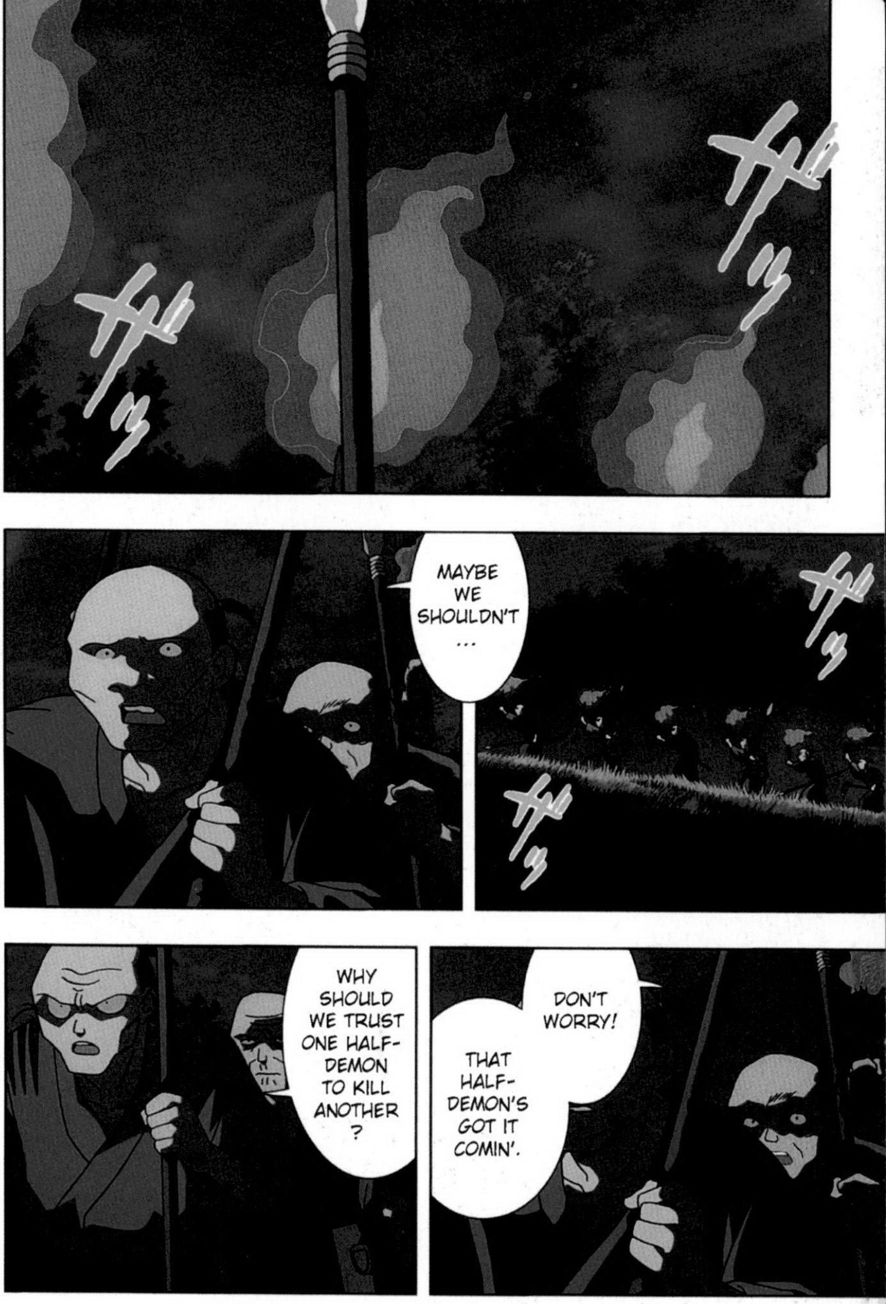
ザワ
ザワ
ザワ
ザワ
MAYBE WE SHOULDN'T ...
DON'T WORRY!
THAT HALF-DEMON'S GOT IT COMIN'.
WHY SHOULD WE TRUST ONE HALF-DEMON TO KILL ANOTHER?

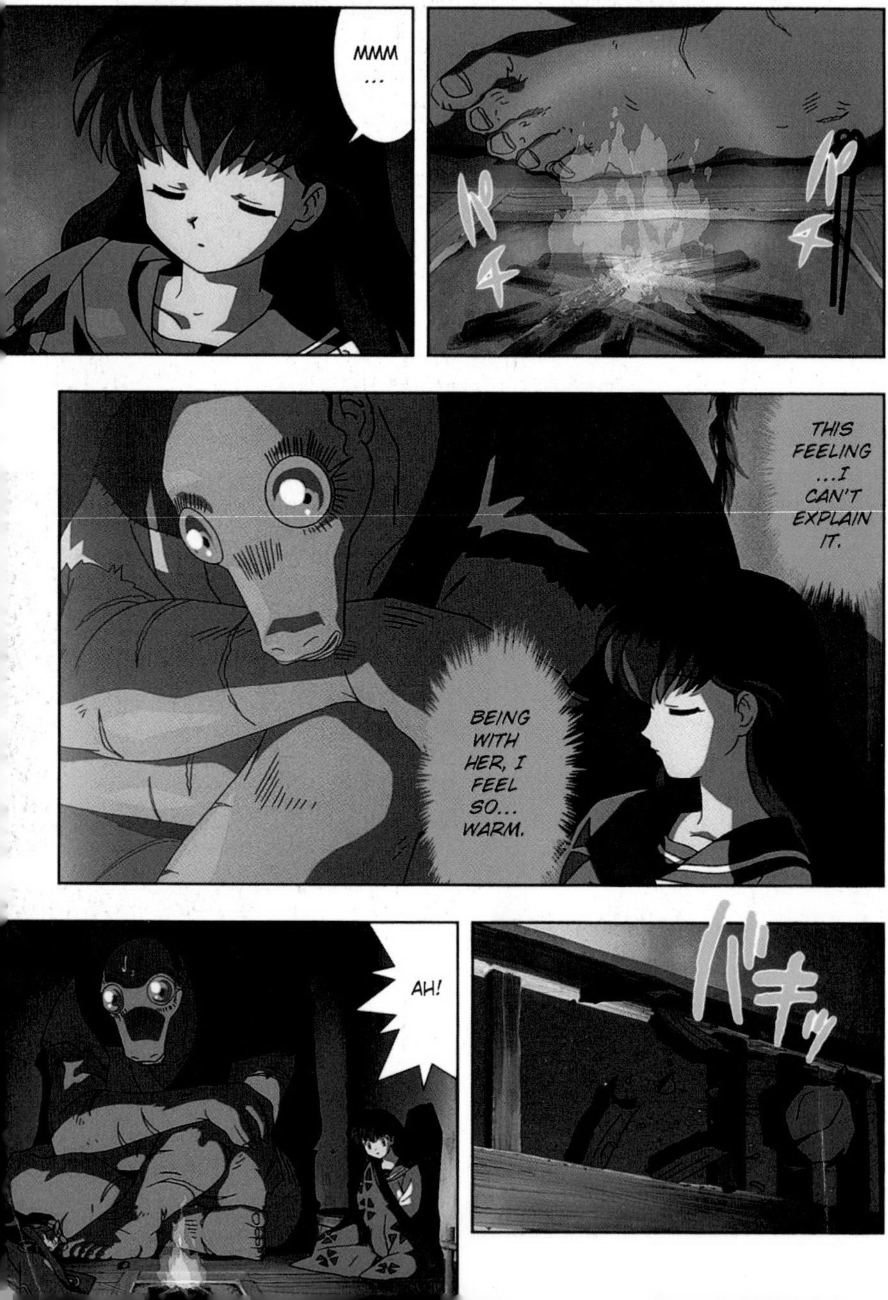
パチ
パチ
MMM ...
THIS FEELING ...I CAN'T EXPLAIN IT.
BEING WITH HER, I FEEL SO... WARM.
バキッ
AH!

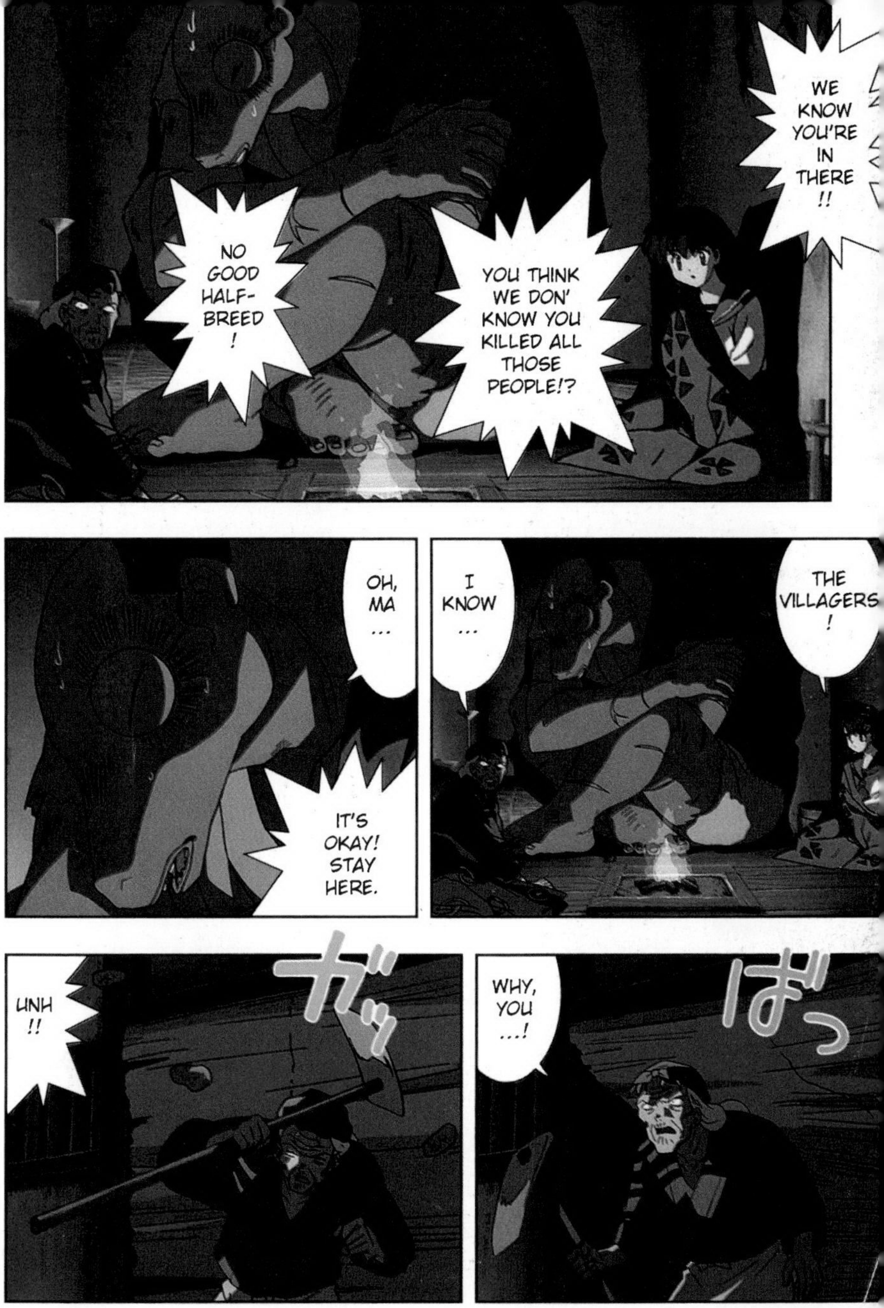
WE KNOW YOU'RE IN THERE!!
YOU THINK WE DON' KNOW YOU KILLED ALL THOSE PEOPLE!?
NO GOOD HALF-BREED!
THE VILLAGERS!
I KNOW...
OH, MA...
IT'S OKAY! STAY HERE.
ぱっ
WHY, YOU...!
ガッ
UNH!!

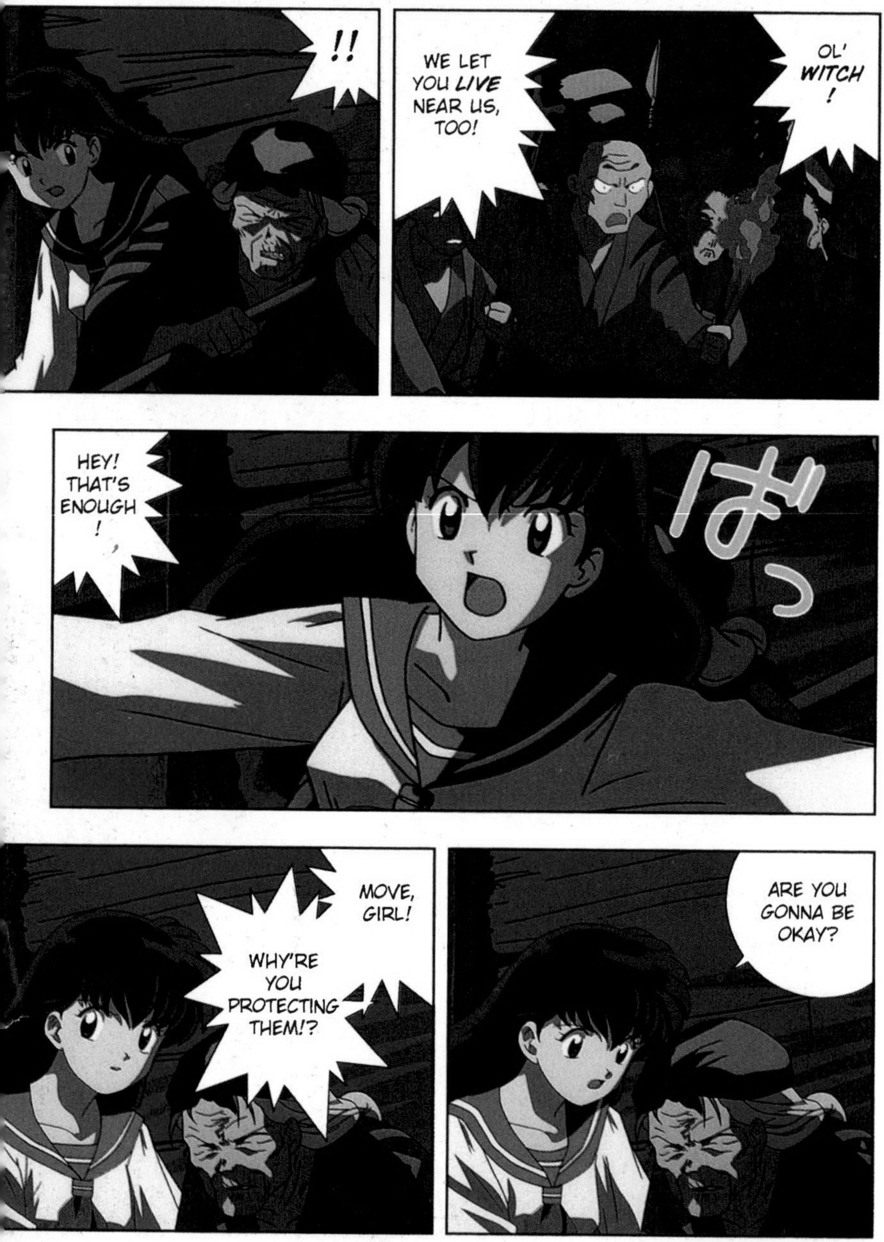
OL' WITCH!
WE LET YOU LIVE NEAR US, TOO!
!!
ぱっ
HEY! THAT'S ENOUGH!
ARE YOU GONNA BE OKAY?
MOVE, GIRL!
WHY'RE YOU PROTECTING THEM!?

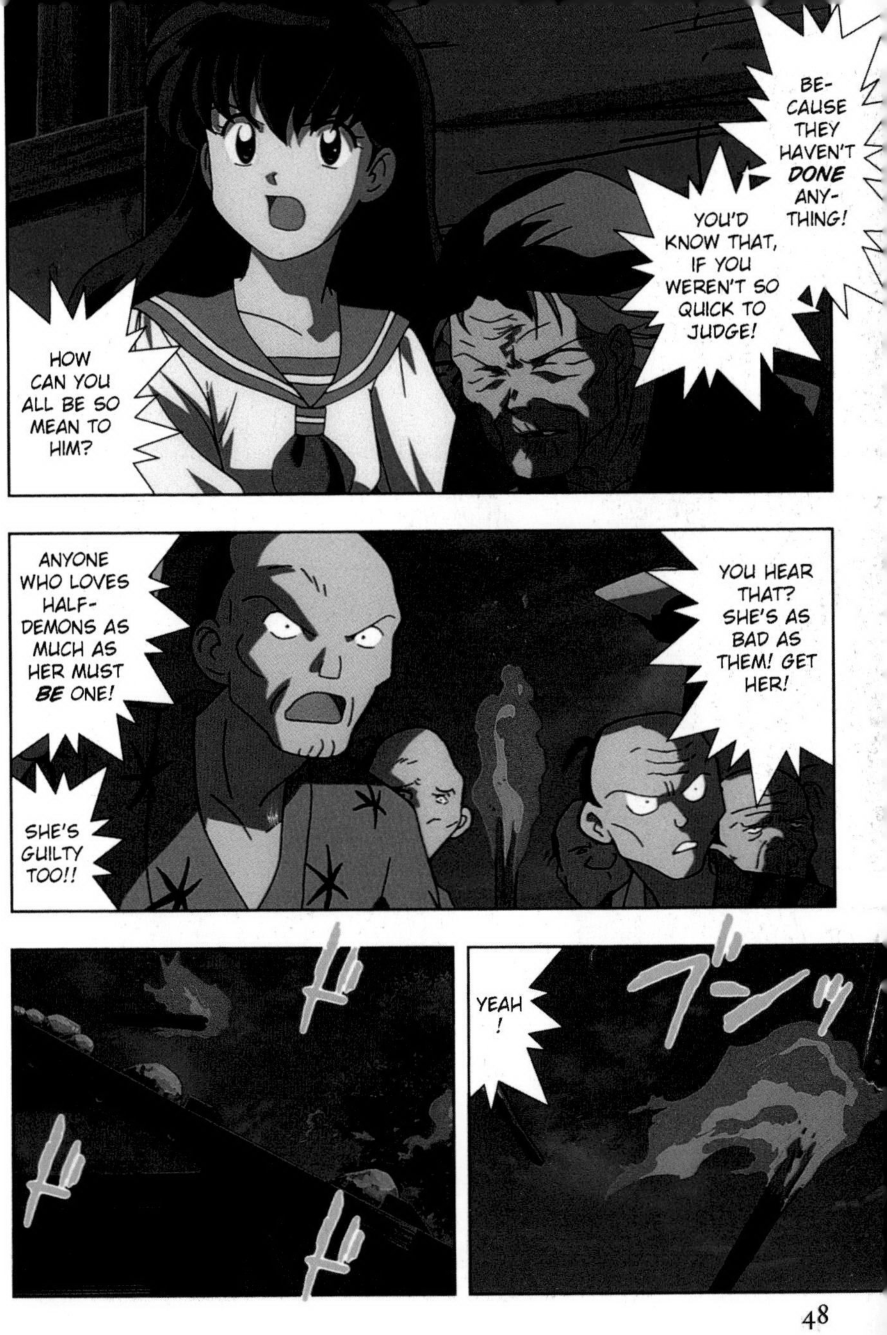
BE-CAUSE THEY HAVEN'T **DONE** ANY-THING!
YOU'D KNOW THAT, IF YOU WEREN'T SO QUICK TO JUDGE!
HOW CAN YOU ALL BE SO MEAN TO HIM?
YOU HEAR THAT? SHE'S AS BAD AS THEM! GET HER!
ANYONE WHO LOVES HALF-DEMONS AS MUCH AS HER MUST **BE** ONE!
SHE'S GUILTY TOO!!
ブンッ
YEAH!
ド
ド
ド
ド

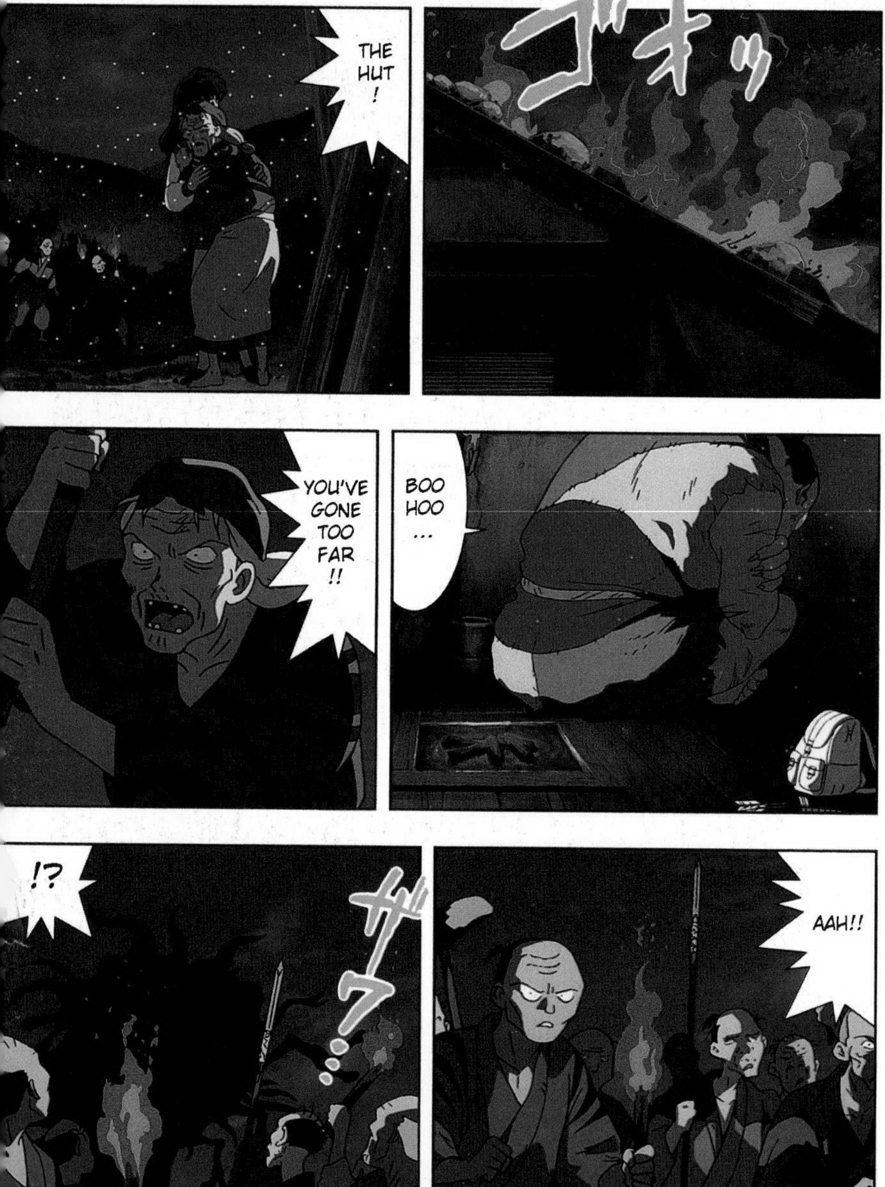
ゴオッ
THE HUT!
BOO HOO...
YOU'VE GONE TOO FAR!!
AAH!!
!?
ザワ…

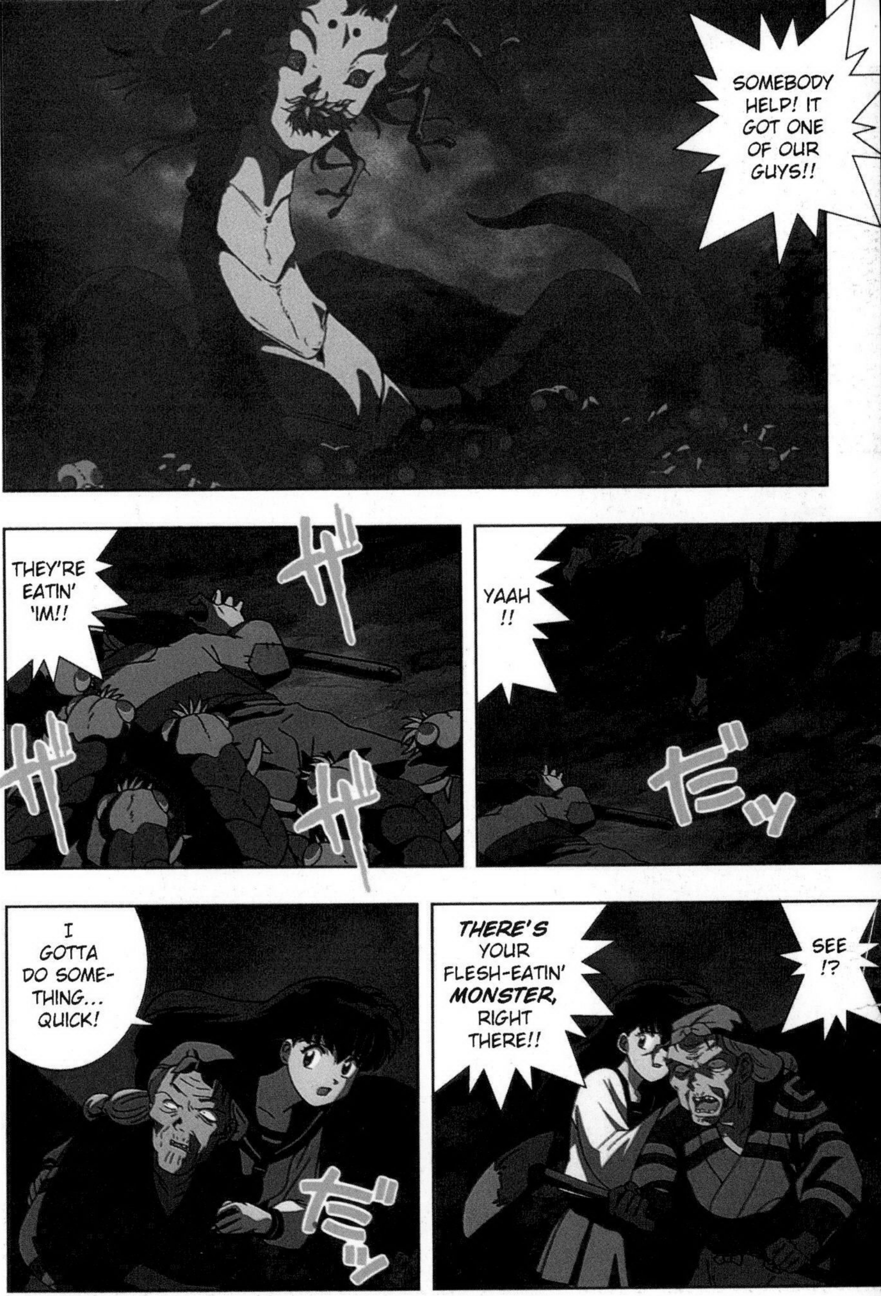

SOMEBODY HELP! IT GOT ONE OF OUR GUYS!!
YAAH !!
だッ
THEY'RE EATIN' 'IM!!
ザ
ザ
ザ
SEE !?
THERE'S YOUR FLESH-EATIN' *MONSTER,* RIGHT THERE!!
I GOTTA DO SOME-THING... QUICK!
だッ

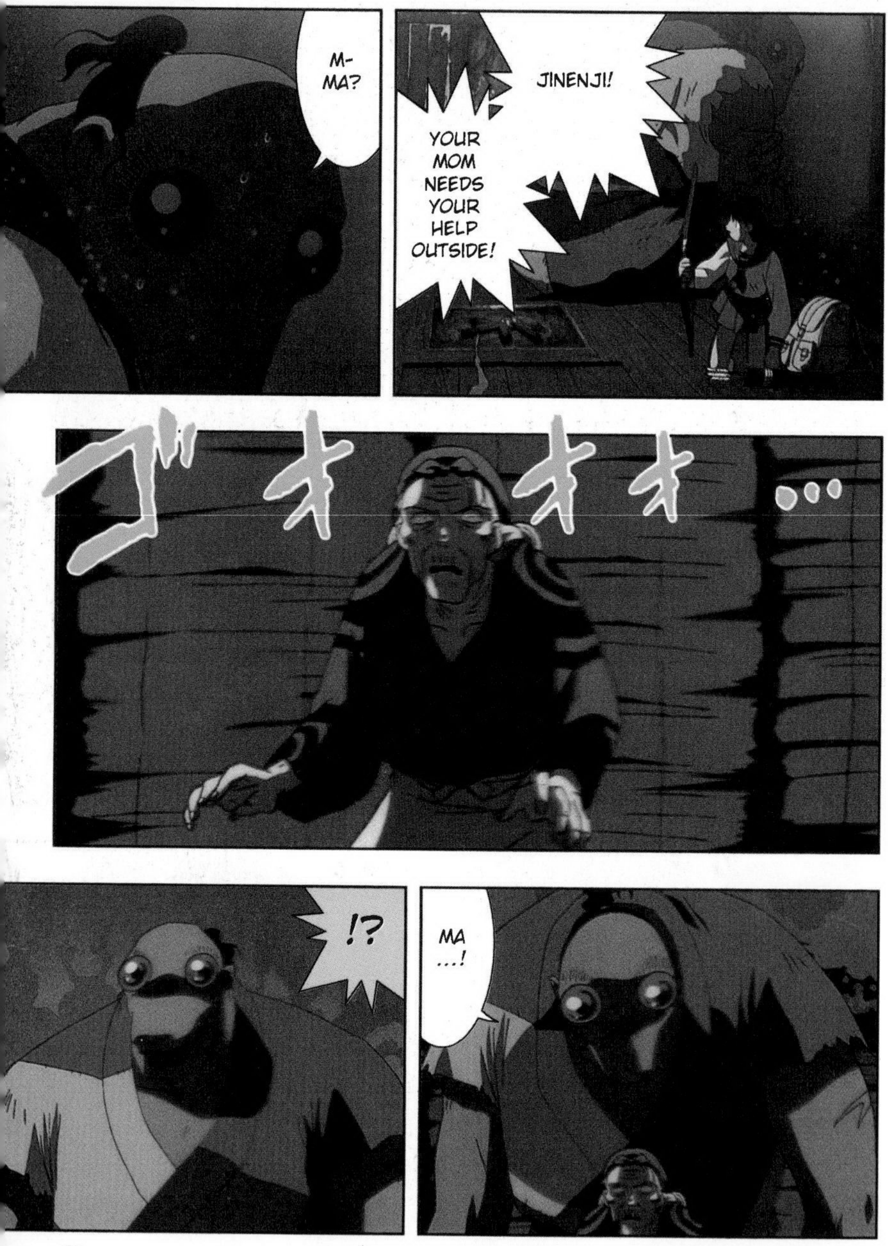
JINENJI!
YOUR MOM NEEDS YOUR HELP OUTSIDE!
M-MA?
ゴオオオ…
MA ...!
!?

GRAAH!

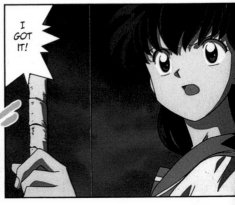

I GOT IT!

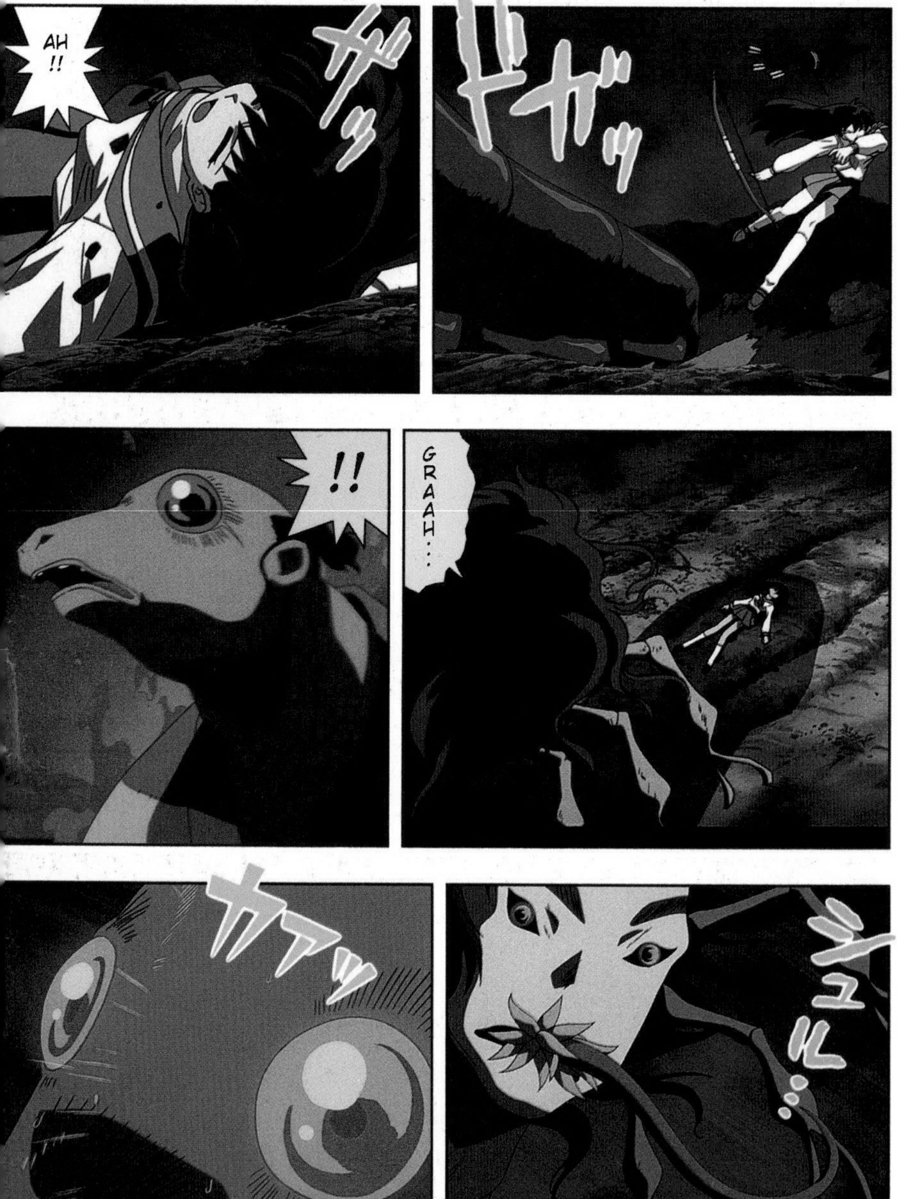
ドガッ
AH !!
ガッ
GRAAH...
!!
シュル…
カァッ

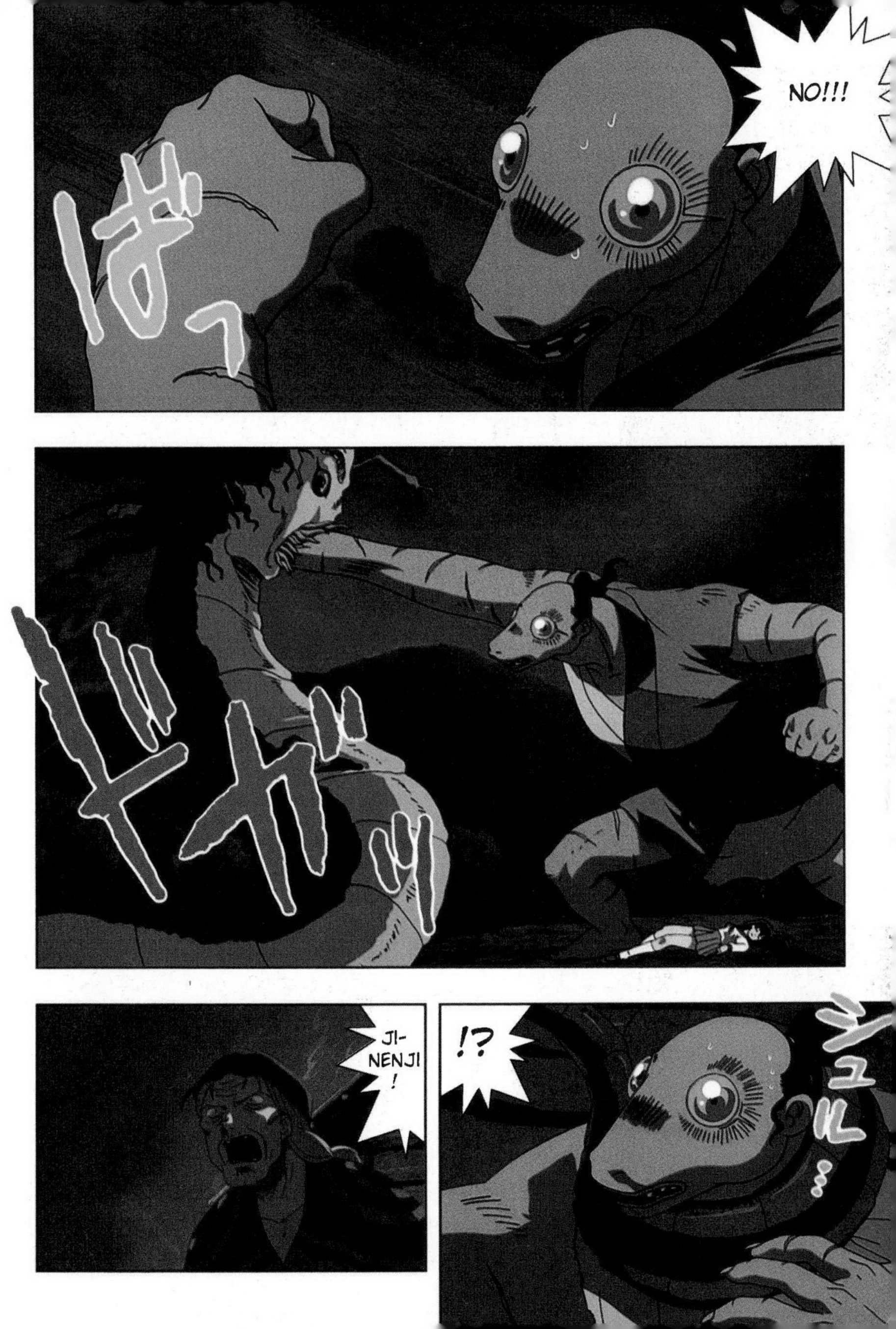
NO!!!
ぱっ
ドガッ
シュル…
!?
JI-NENJI!

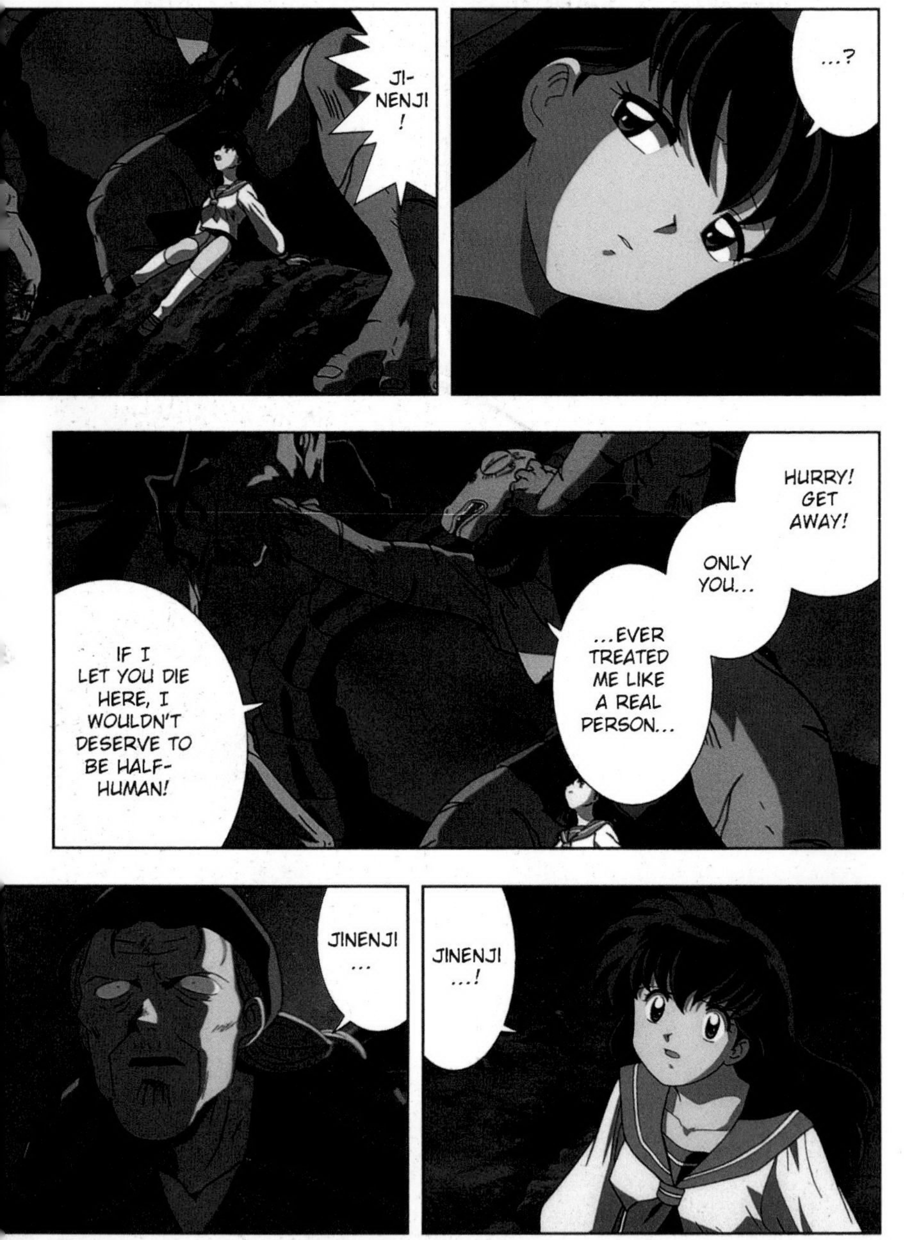
...?
JI-NENJI!
HURRY! GET AWAY!
ONLY YOU...
...EVER TREATED ME LIKE A REAL PERSON...
IF I LET YOU DIE HERE, I WOULDN'T DESERVE TO BE HALF-HUMAN!
JINENJI ...!
JINENJI ...

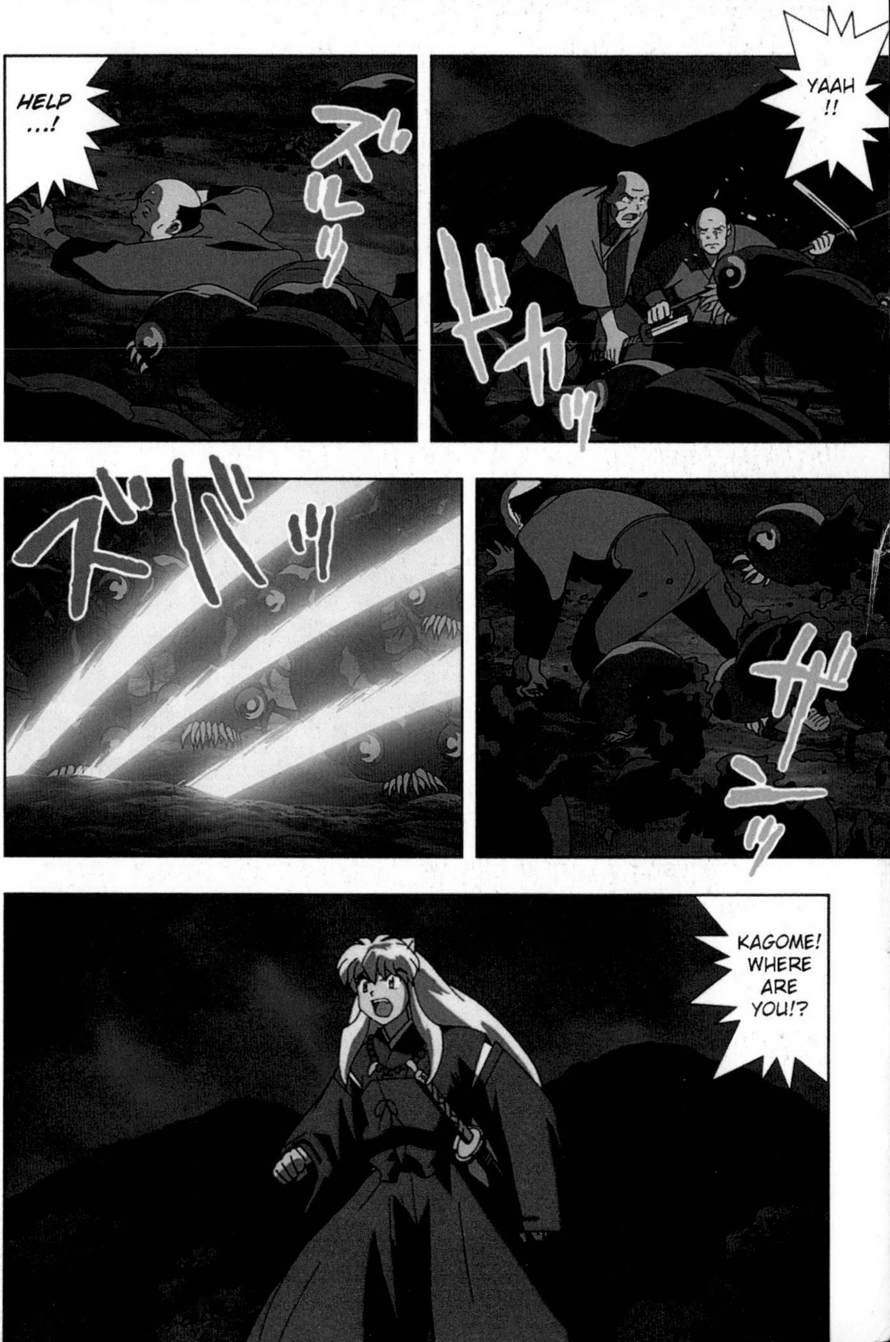
YAAH !!
ドカッ
HELP ...!
ズルッ
ザシュッ
ズバッ
KAGOME! WHERE ARE YOU!?

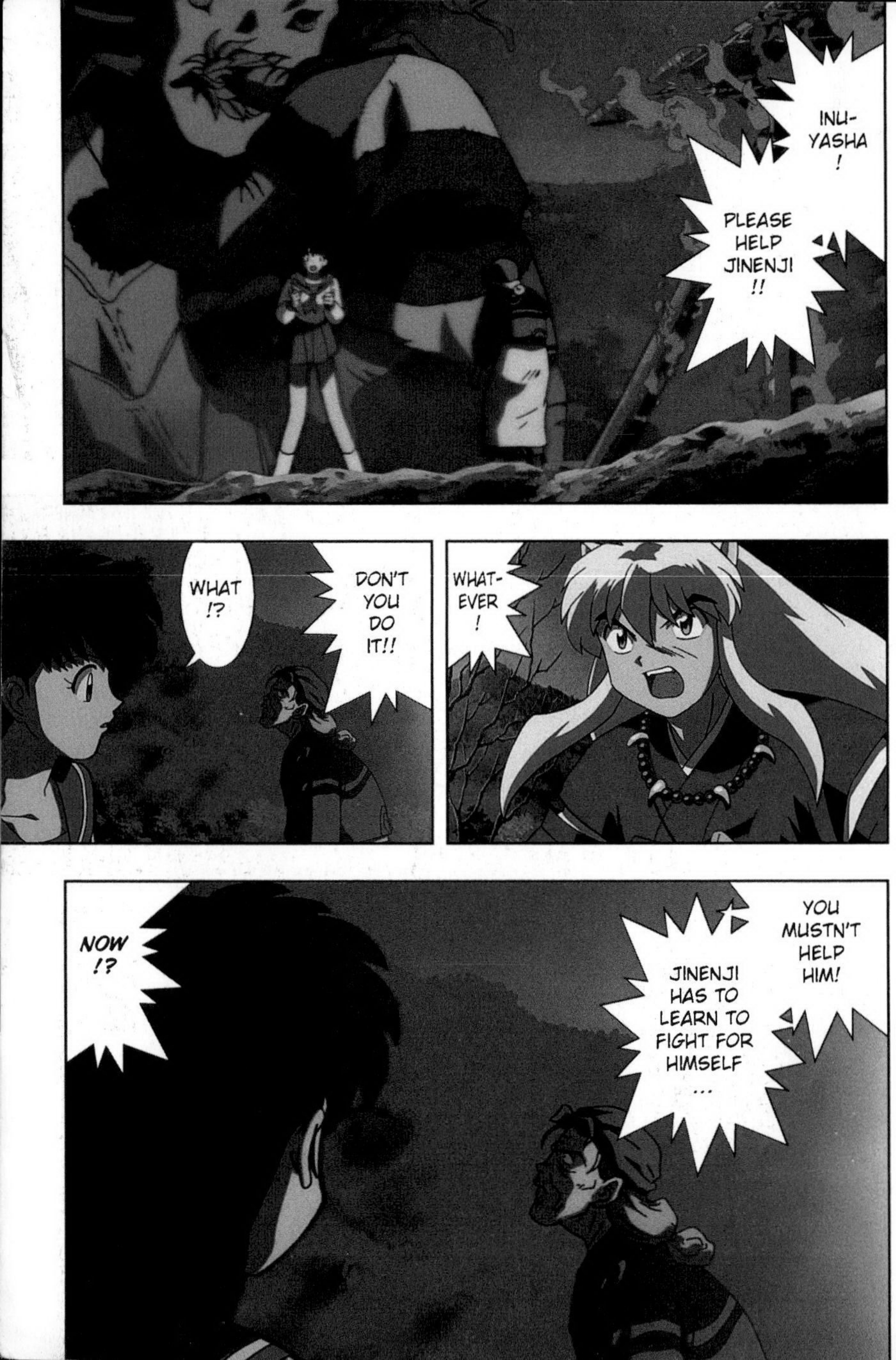
INU-YASHA!
PLEASE HELP JINENJI!!
WHAT-EVER!
DON'T YOU DO IT!!
WHAT!?
YOU MUSTN'T HELP HIM!
JINENJI HAS TO LEARN TO FIGHT FOR HIMSELF...
NOW!?

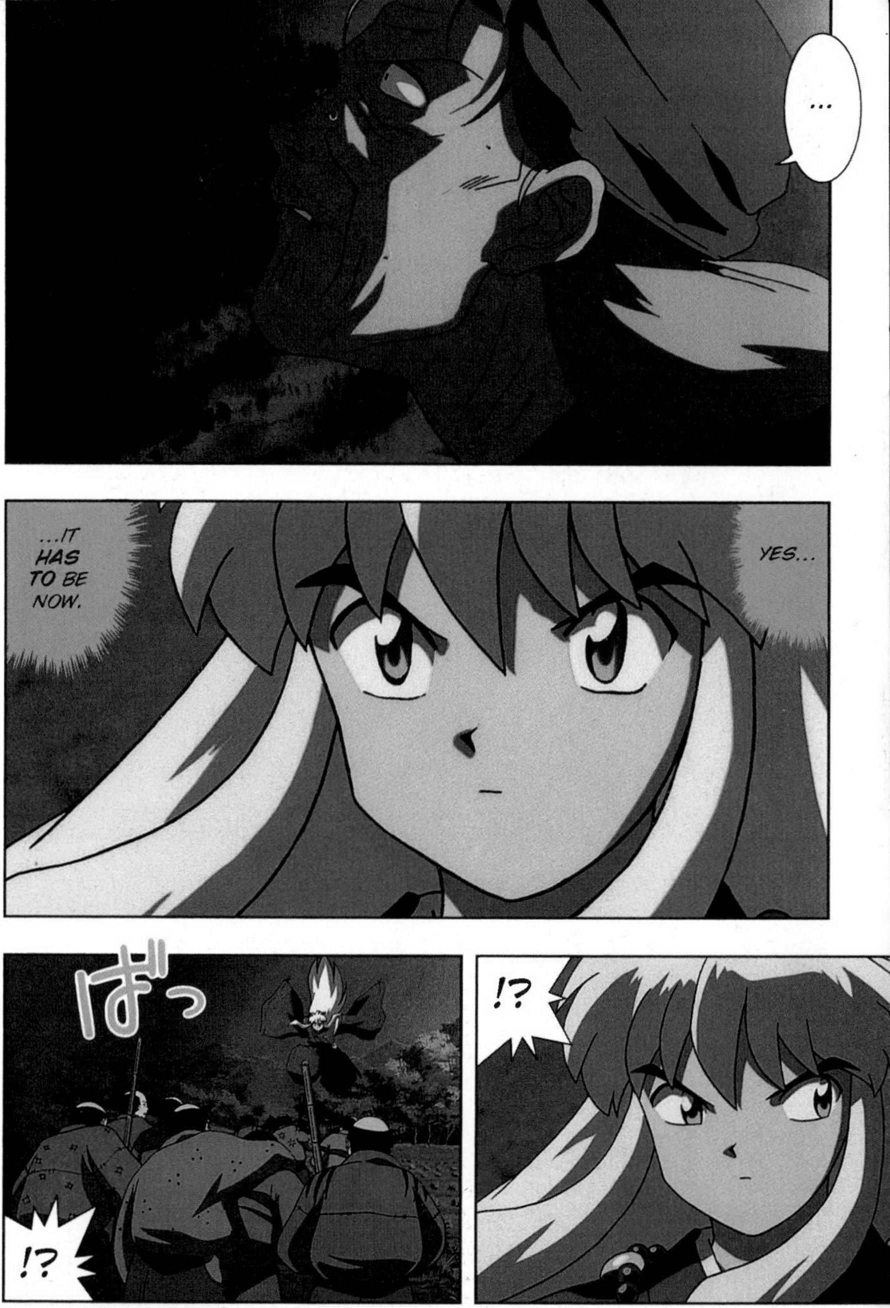
...
YES...
...IT HAS TO BE NOW.
!?
ばっ
!?

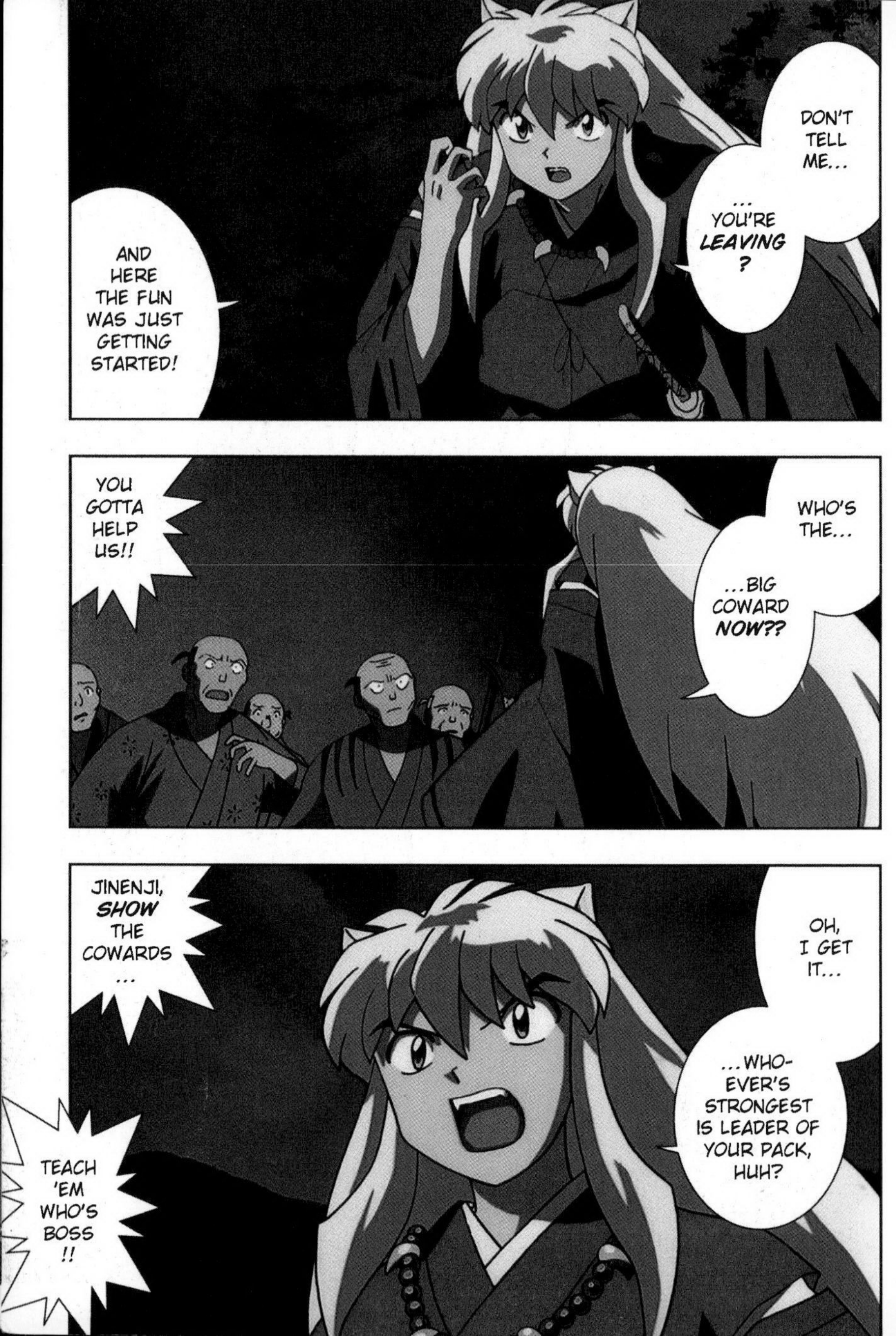
DON'T TELL ME...
...YOU'RE *LEAVING*?
AND HERE THE FUN WAS JUST GETTING STARTED!
WHO'S THE...
...BIG COWARD *NOW??*
YOU GOTTA HELP US!!
OH, I GET IT...
...WHO-EVER'S STRONGEST IS LEADER OF YOUR PACK, HUH?
JINENJI, *SHOW* THE COWARDS...
TEACH 'EM WHO'S BOSS!!

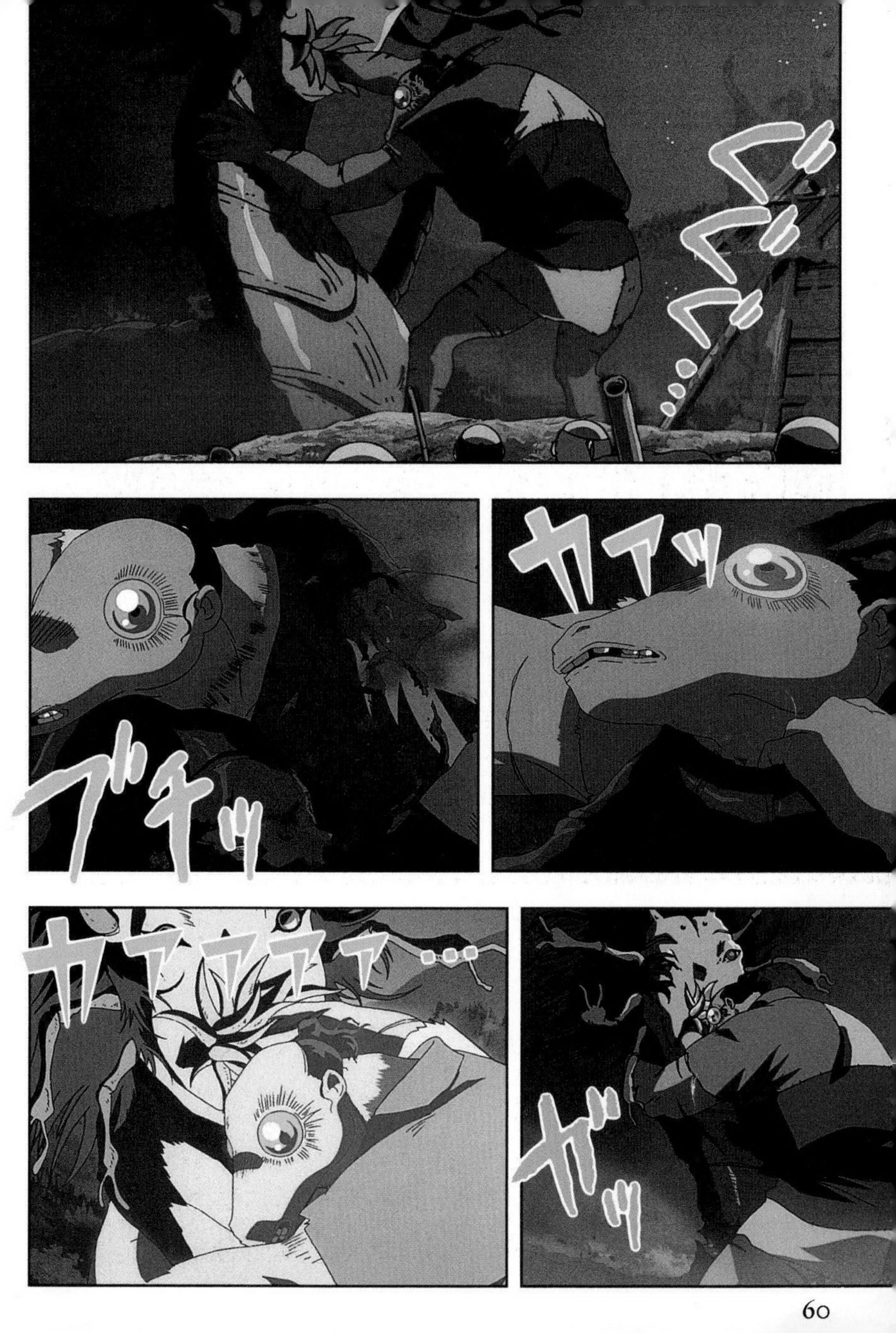
ぐぐぐ…
カァッ
ブチッ
ガッ
カァァァァ…

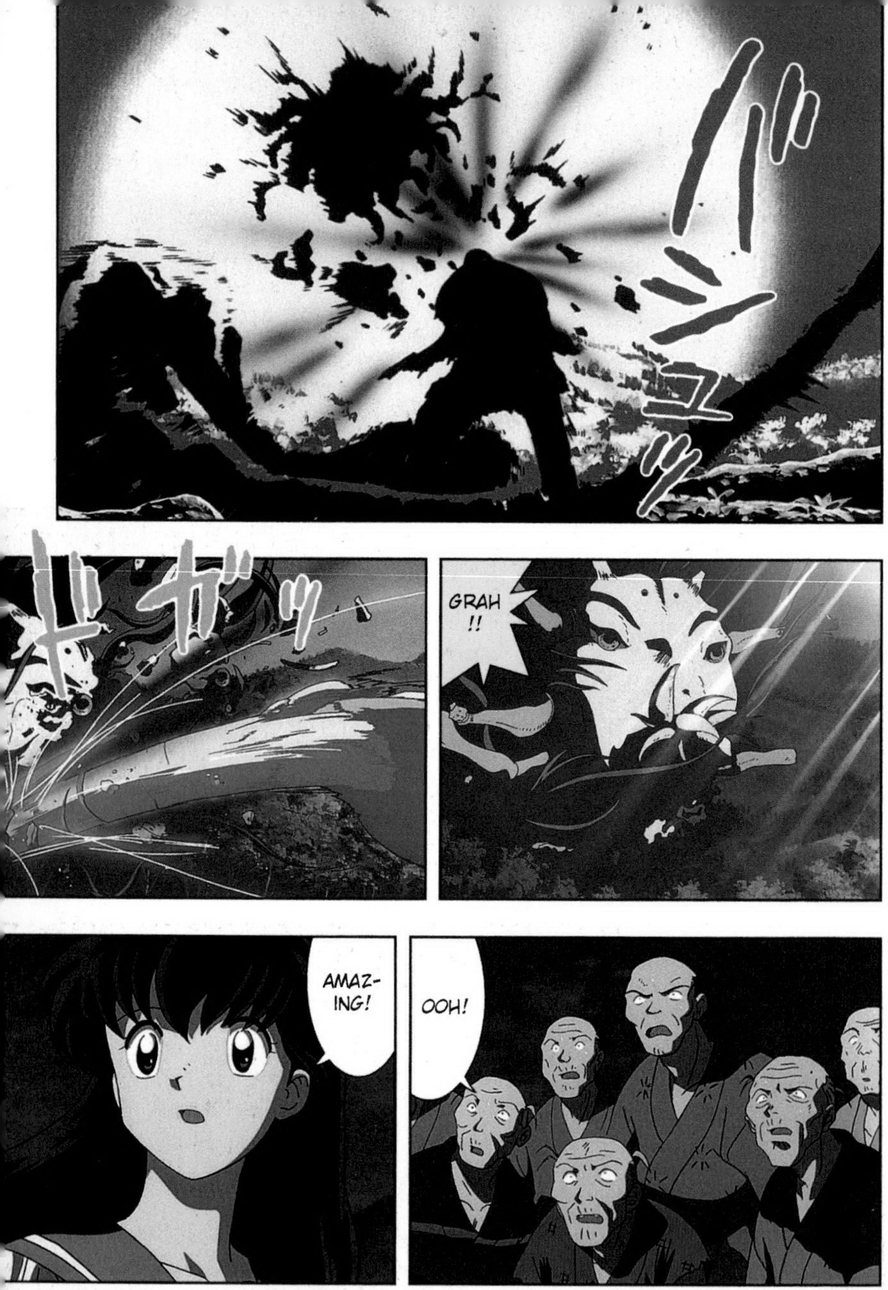
GRAH !!
ドガッ
OOH!
AMAZ-ING!

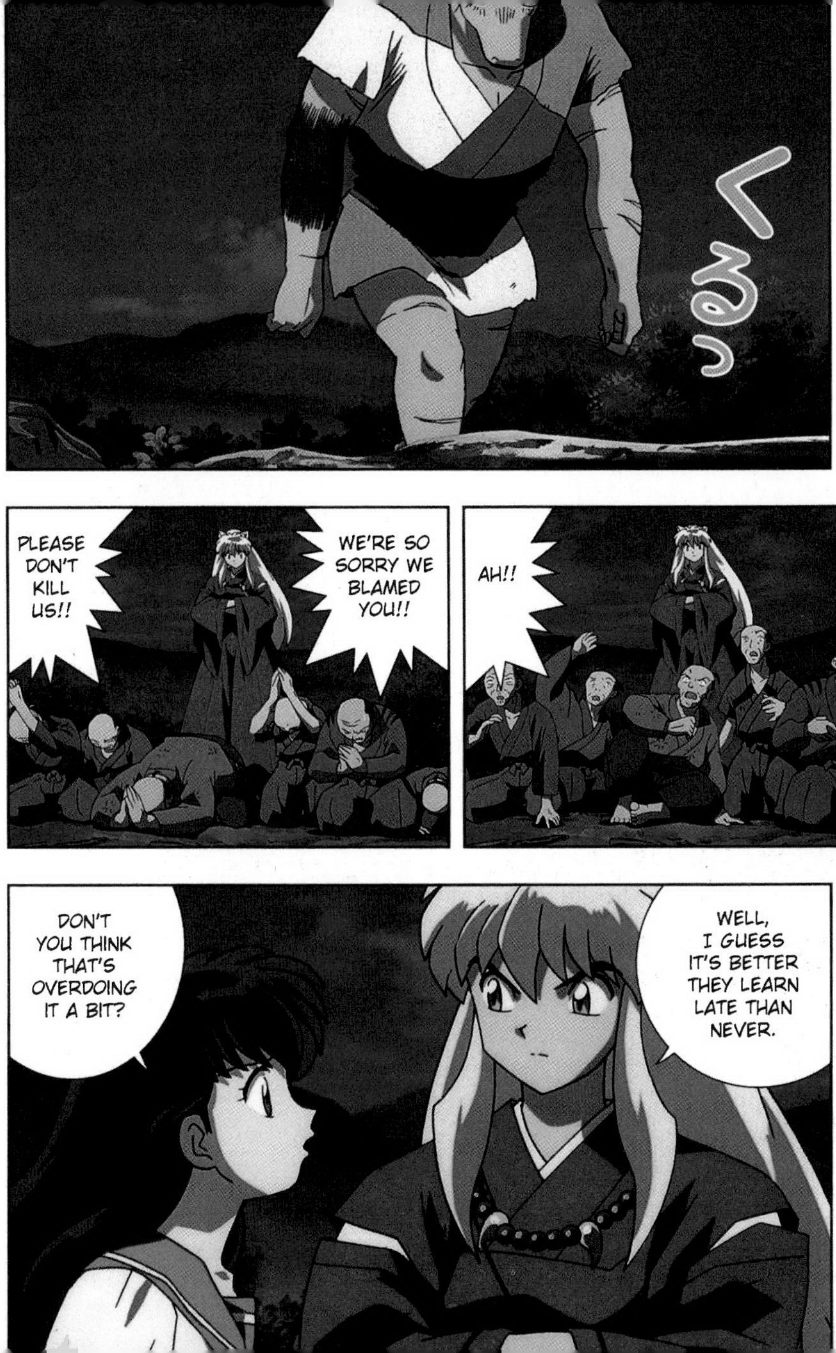
しるっ
AH!!
WE'RE SO SORRY WE BLAMED YOU!!
PLEASE DON'T KILL US!!
WELL, I GUESS IT'S BETTER THEY LEARN LATE THAN NEVER.
DON'T YOU THINK THAT'S OVERDOING IT A BIT?

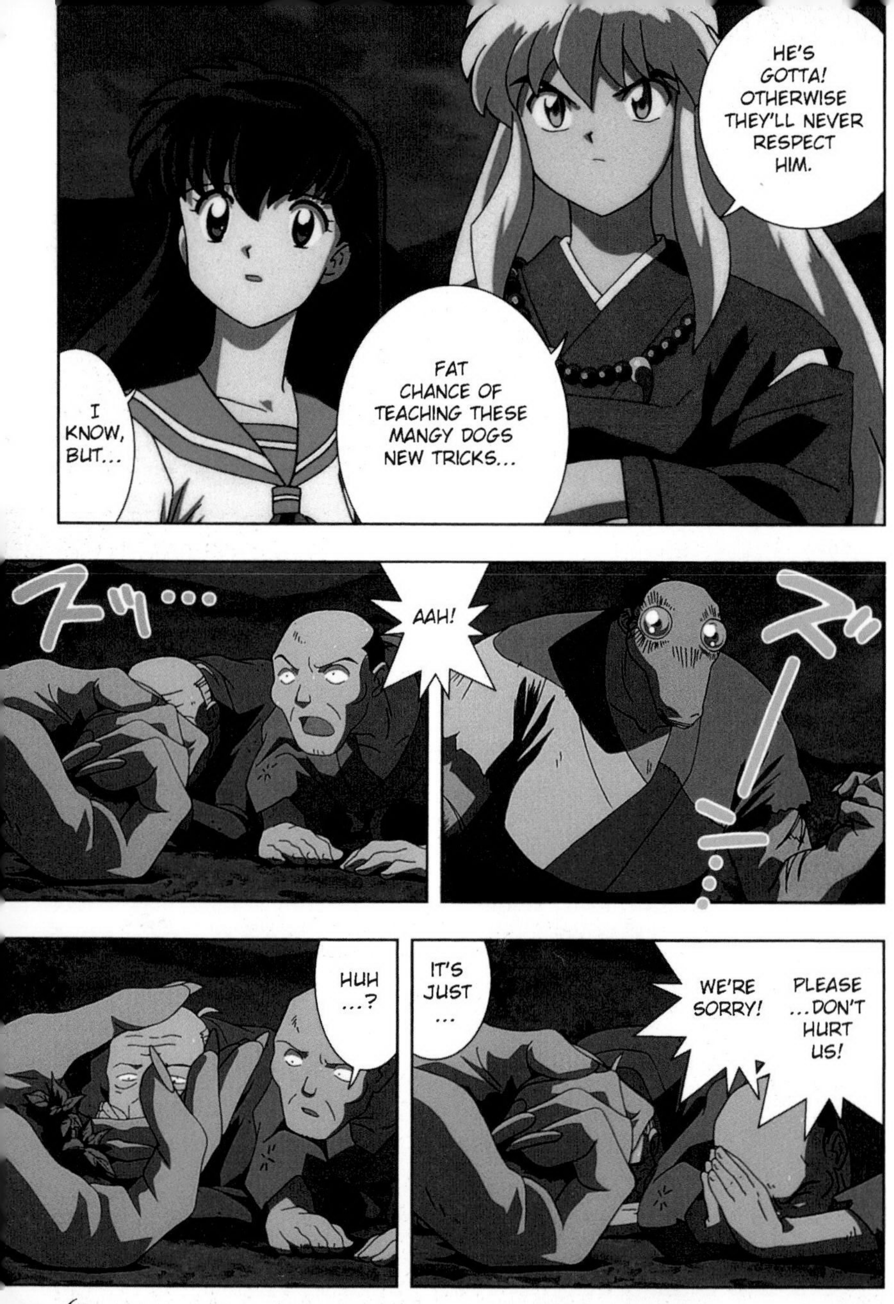
HE'S GOTTA! OTHERWISE THEY'LL NEVER RESPECT HIM.
FAT CHANCE OF TEACHING THESE MANGY DOGS NEW TRICKS...
I KNOW, BUT...
ズー…
AAH!
スッ…
PLEASE ...DON'T HURT US!
WE'RE SORRY!
IT'S JUST ...
HUH ...?

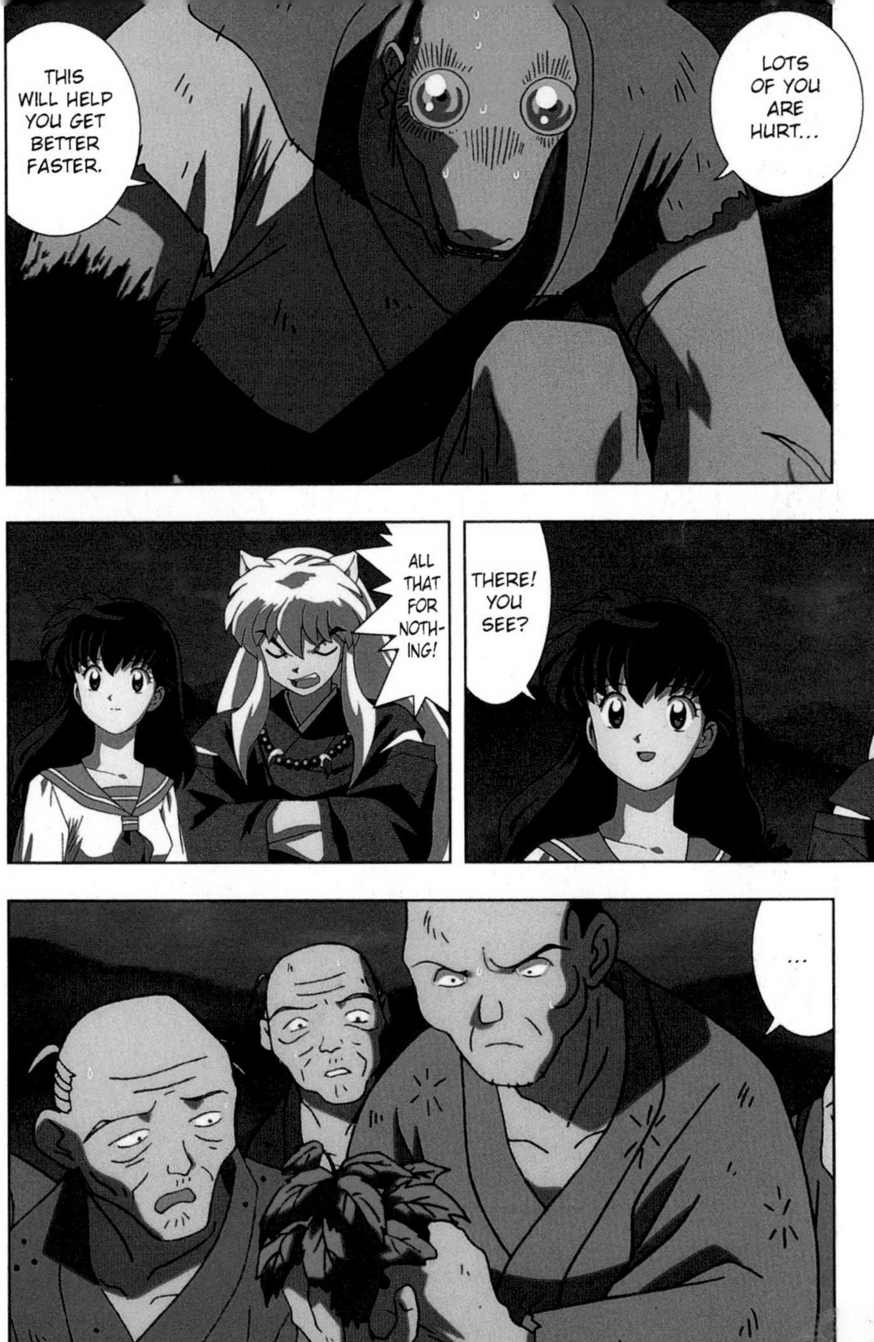
LOTS OF YOU ARE HURT...
THIS WILL HELP YOU GET BETTER FASTER.
THERE! YOU SEE?
ALL THAT FOR NOTH-ING!
...

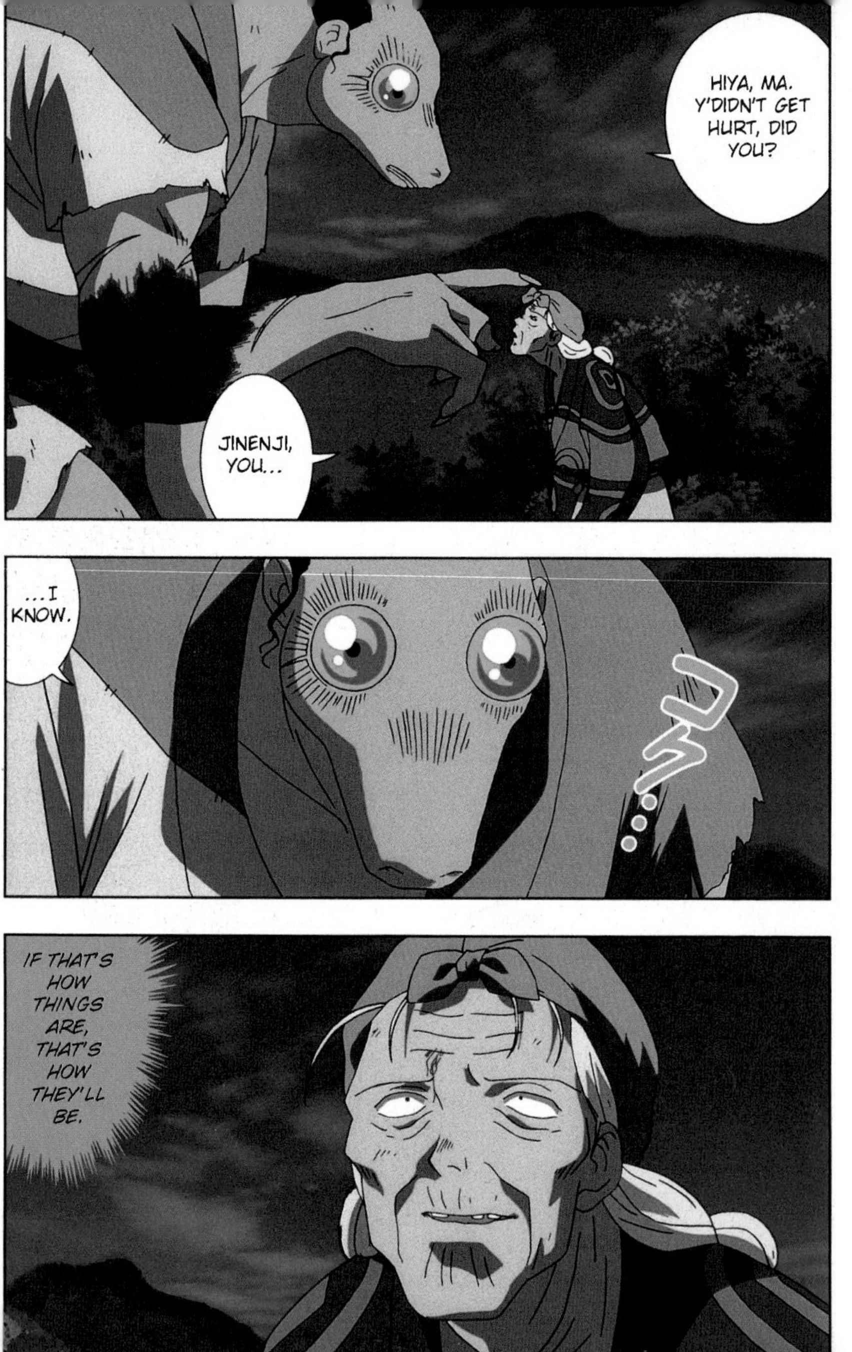
HIYA, MA. Y'DIDN'T GET HURT, DID YOU?
JINENJI, YOU...
...I KNOW.
IF THAT'S HOW THINGS ARE, THAT'S HOW THEY'LL BE.

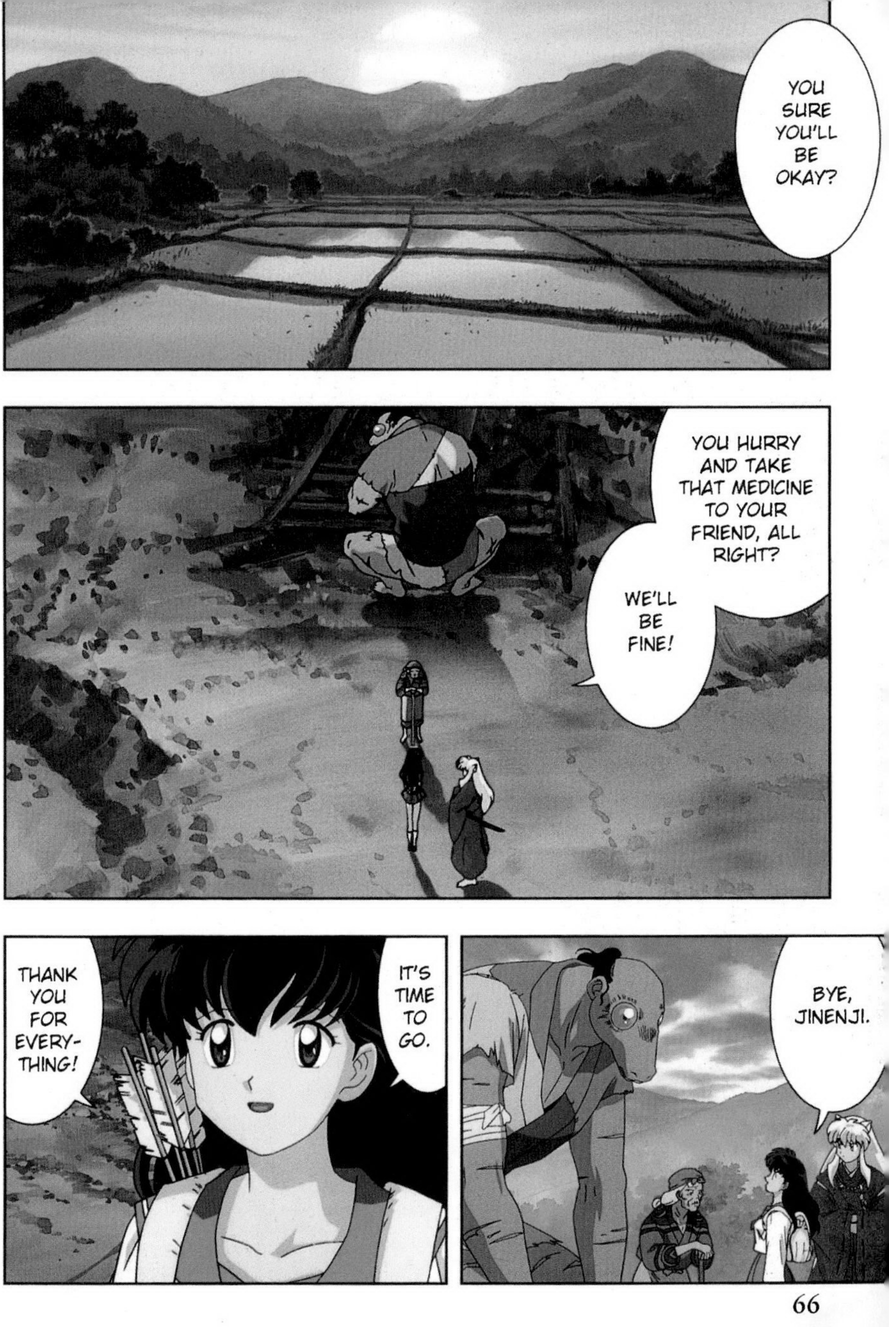
YOU SURE YOU'LL BE OKAY?
YOU HURRY AND TAKE THAT MEDICINE TO YOUR FRIEND, ALL RIGHT?
WE'LL BE FINE!
BYE, JINENJI.
IT'S TIME TO GO.
THANK YOU FOR EVERY-THING!

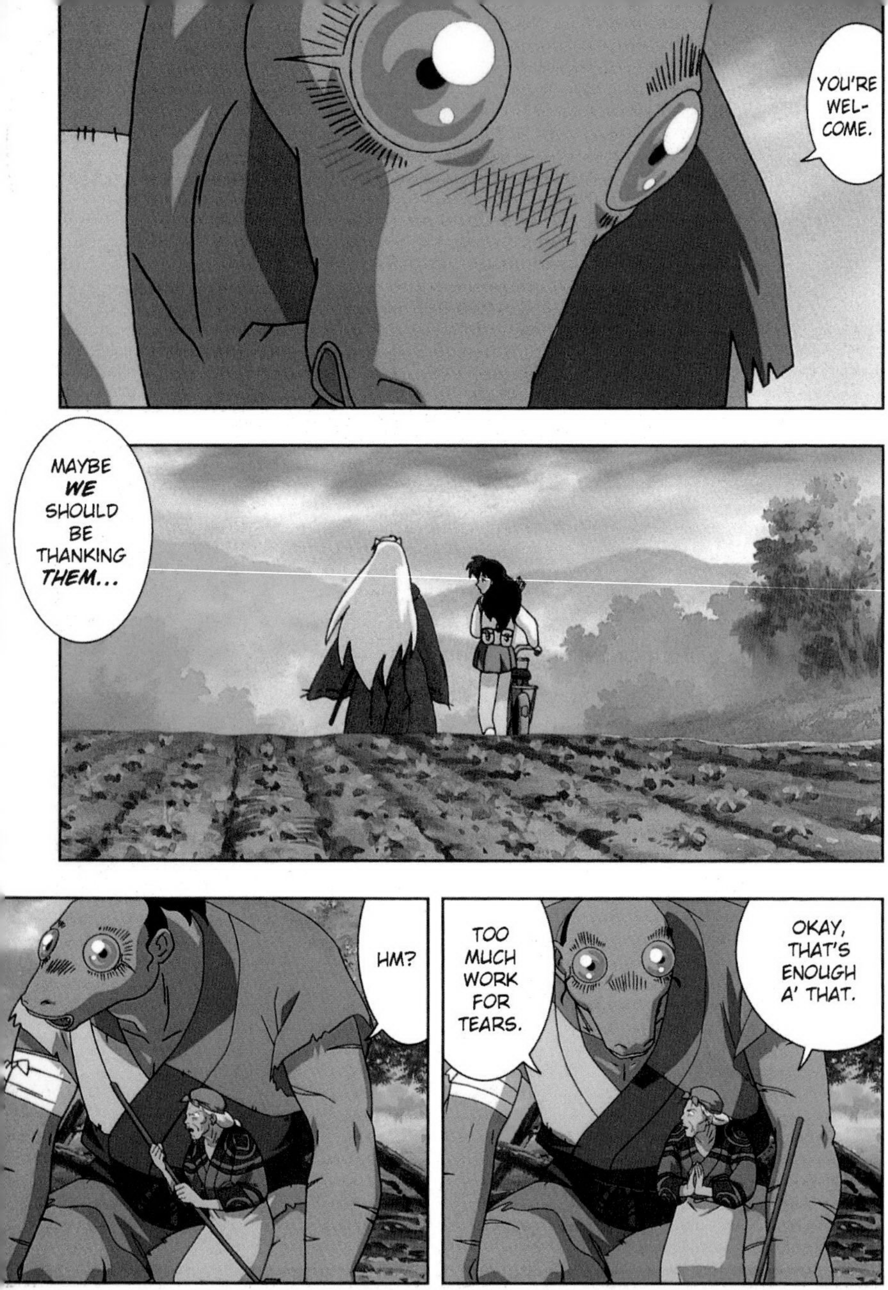
YOU'RE WEL-COME.
MAYBE WE SHOULD BE THANKING THEM...
OKAY, THAT'S ENOUGH A' THAT.
TOO MUCH WORK FOR TEARS.
HM?

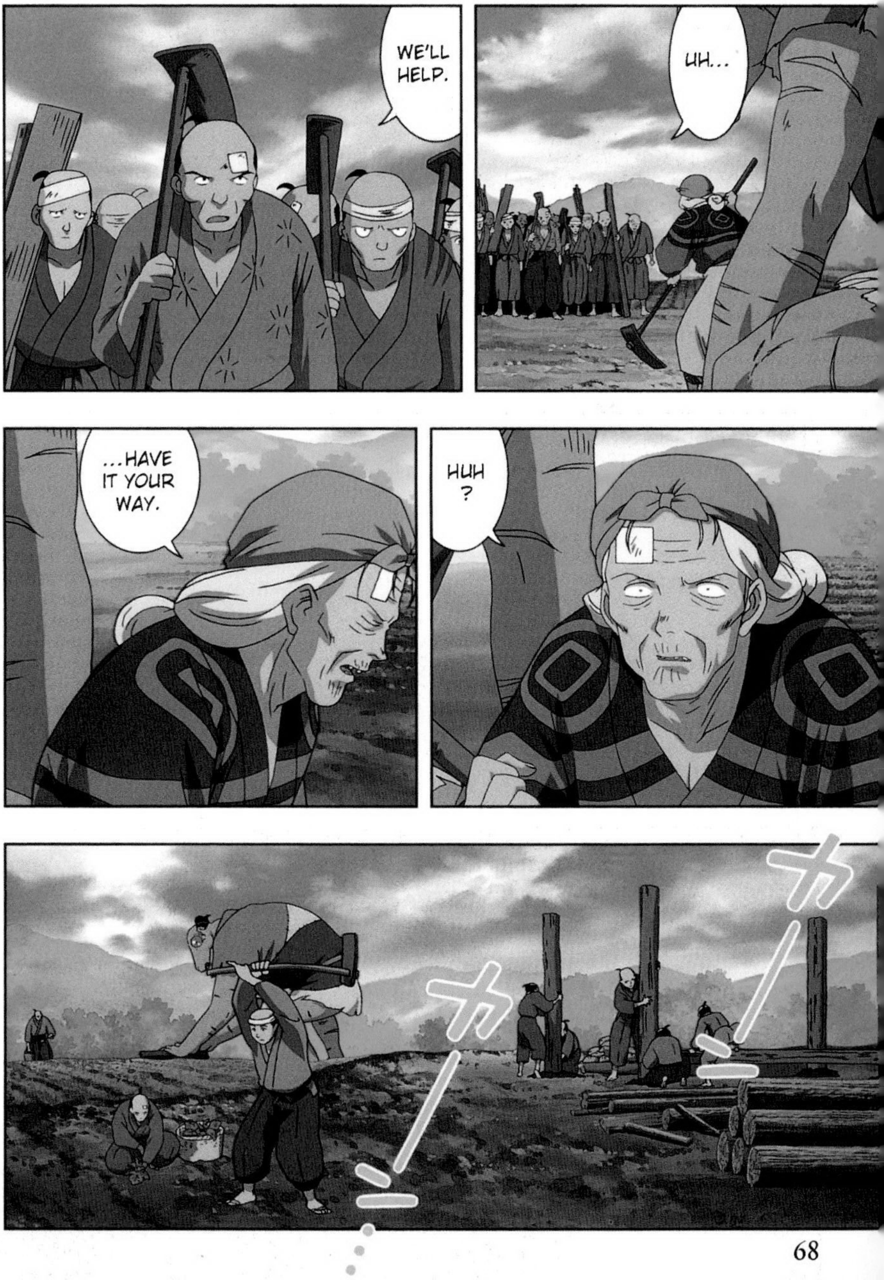
UH...
WE'LL HELP.
HUH ?
...HAVE IT YOUR WAY.

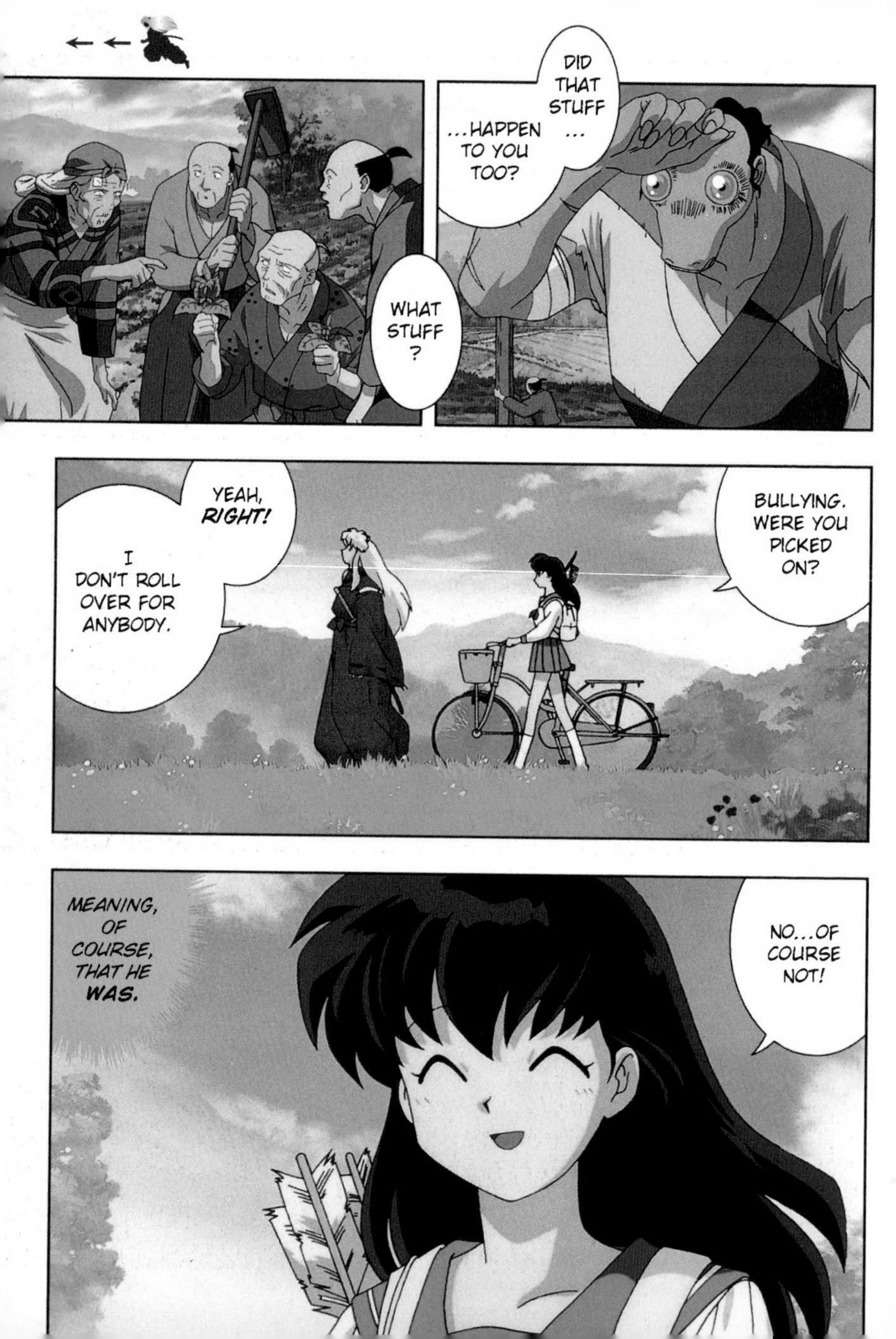
DID THAT STUFF ...
...HAPPEN TO YOU TOO?
WHAT STUFF ?
BULLYING. WERE YOU PICKED ON?
YEAH, *RIGHT!*
I DON'T ROLL OVER FOR ANYBODY.
NO...OF COURSE NOT!
MEANING, OF COURSE, THAT HE *WAS.*

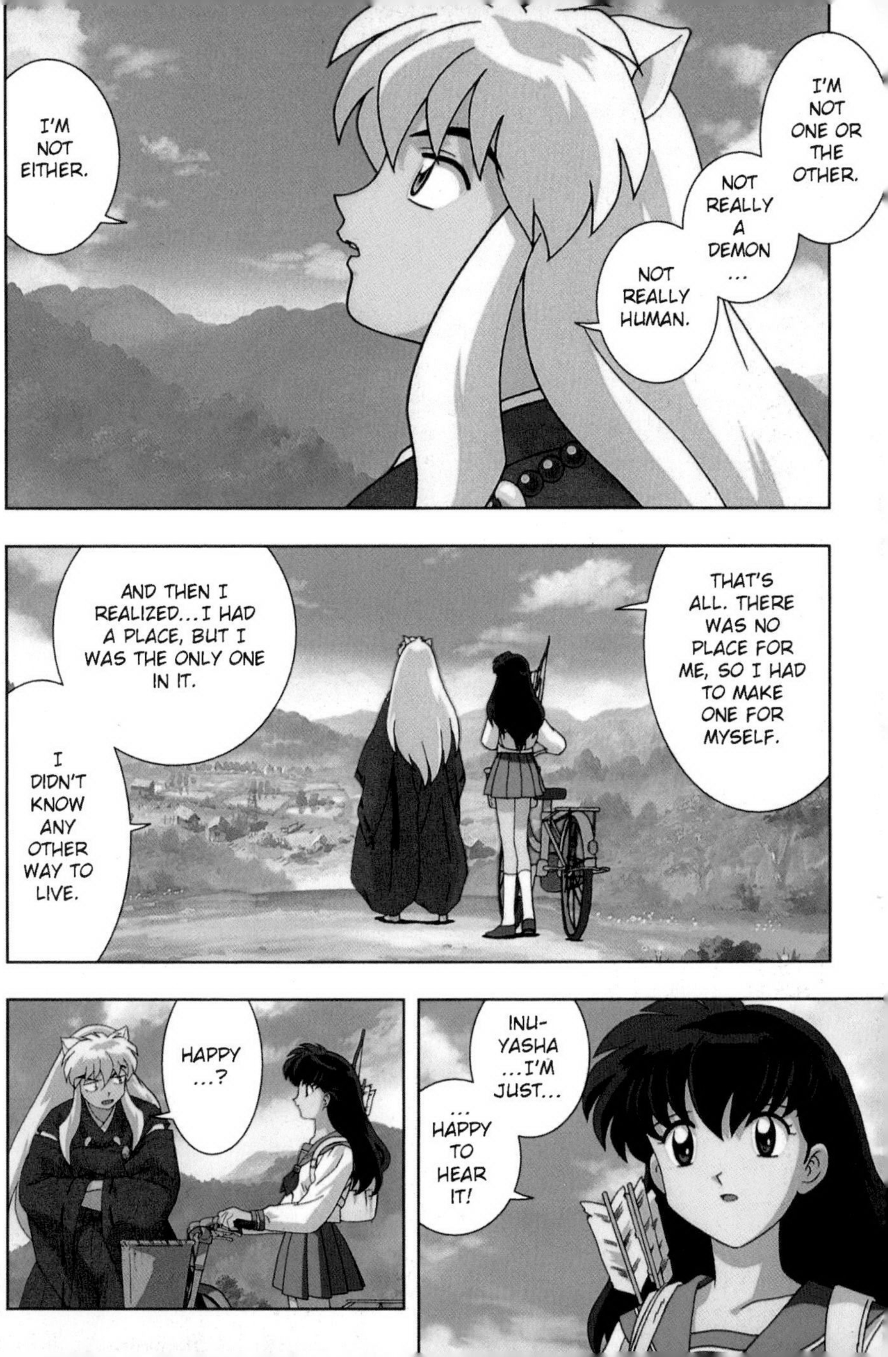
I'M NOT ONE OR THE OTHER.
NOT REALLY A DEMON...
NOT REALLY HUMAN.
I'M NOT EITHER.
THAT'S ALL. THERE WAS NO PLACE FOR ME, SO I HAD TO MAKE ONE FOR MYSELF.
AND THEN I REALIZED...I HAD A PLACE, BUT I WAS THE ONLY ONE IN IT.
I DIDN'T KNOW ANY OTHER WAY TO LIVE.
INU-YASHA ...I'M JUST...
...HAPPY TO HEAR IT!
HAPPY ...?

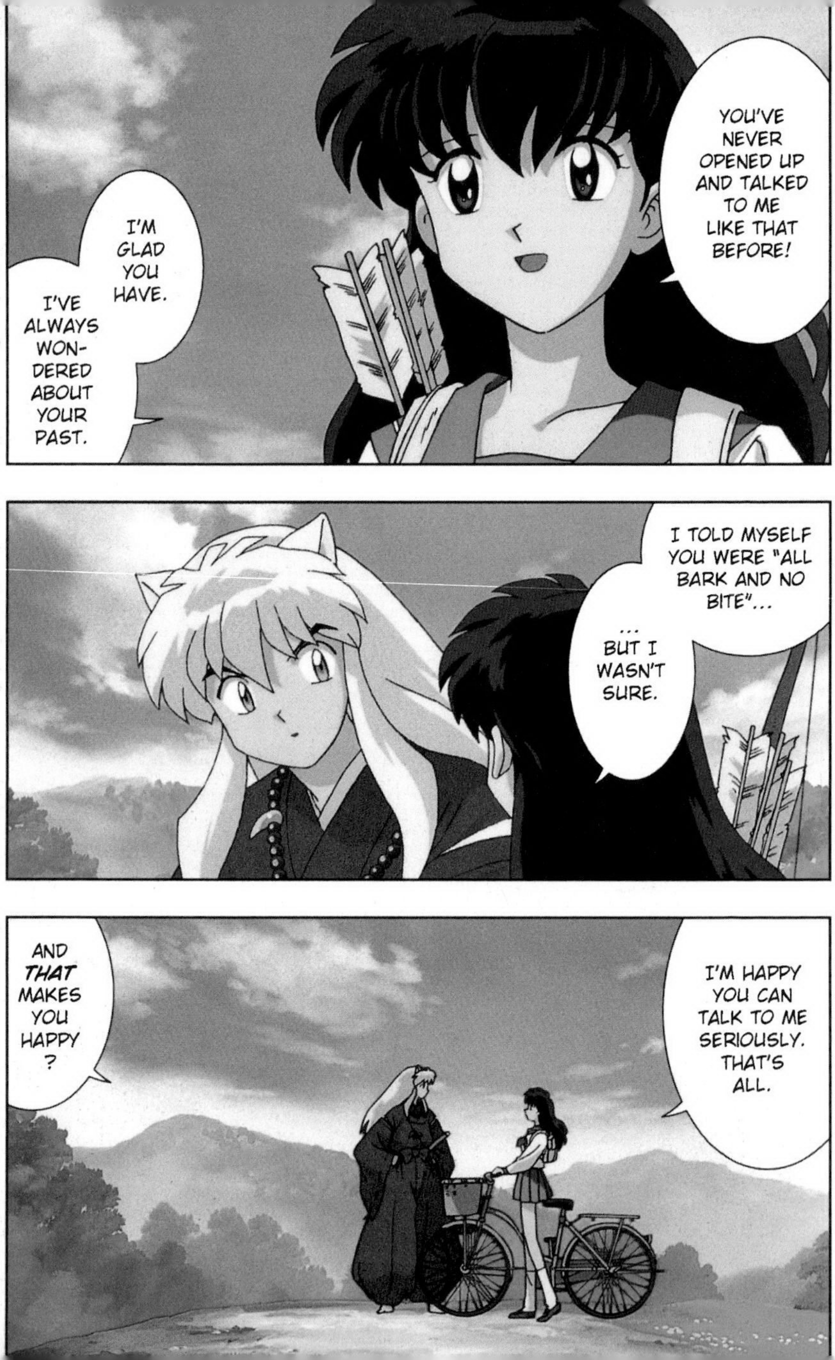
YOU'VE NEVER OPENED UP AND TALKED TO ME LIKE THAT BEFORE!
I'M GLAD YOU HAVE.
I'VE ALWAYS WON-DERED ABOUT YOUR PAST.
I TOLD MYSELF YOU WERE "ALL BARK AND NO BITE"...
... BUT I WASN'T SURE.
I'M HAPPY YOU CAN TALK TO ME SERIOUSLY. THAT'S ALL.
AND *THAT* MAKES YOU HAPPY?

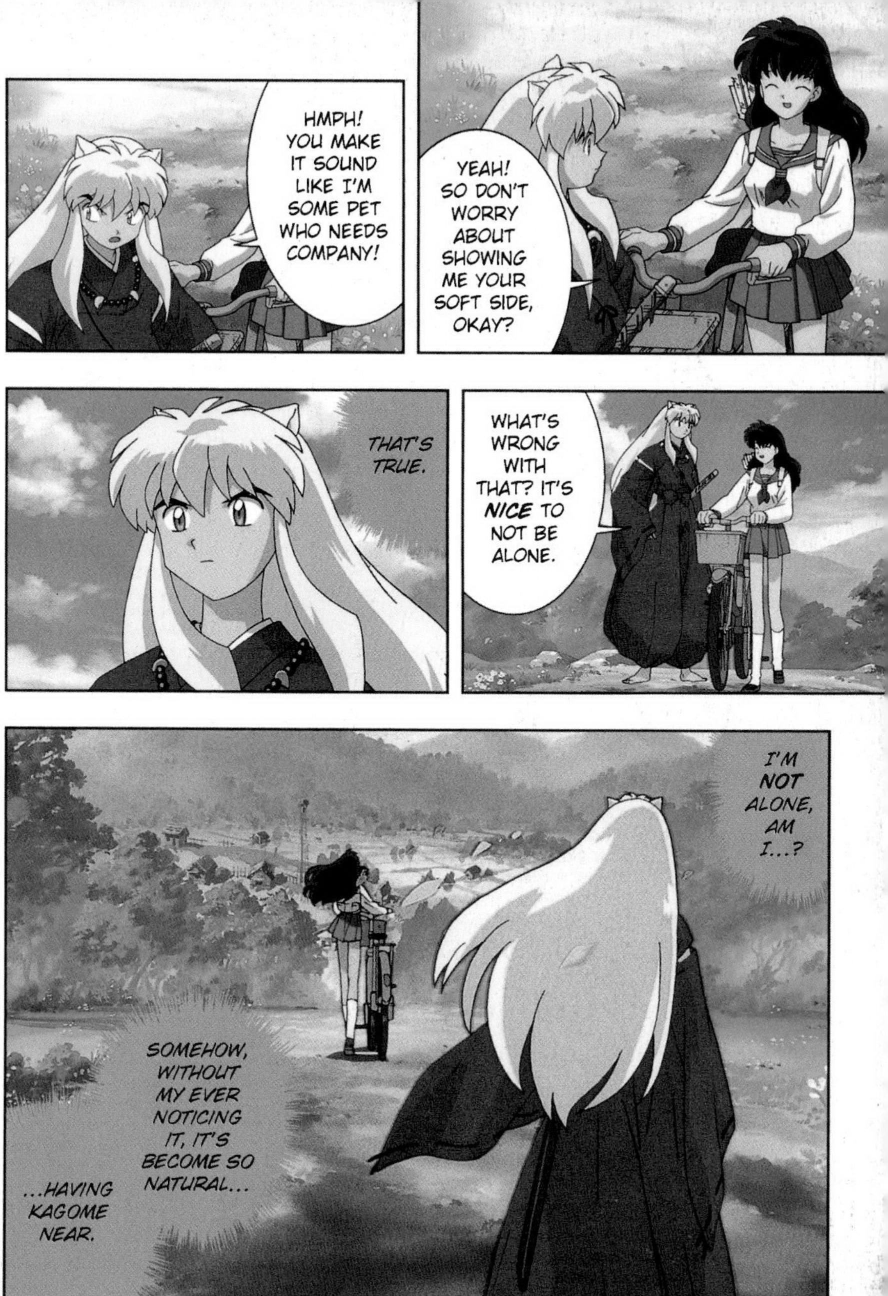
YEAH! SO DON'T WORRY ABOUT SHOWING ME YOUR SOFT SIDE, OKAY?
HMPH! YOU MAKE IT SOUND LIKE I'M SOME PET WHO NEEDS COMPANY!
WHAT'S WRONG WITH THAT? IT'S NICE TO NOT BE ALONE.
THAT'S TRUE.
I'M NOT ALONE, AM I...?
SOMEHOW, WITHOUT MY EVER NOTICING IT, IT'S BECOME SO NATURAL...
...HAVING KAGOME NEAR.

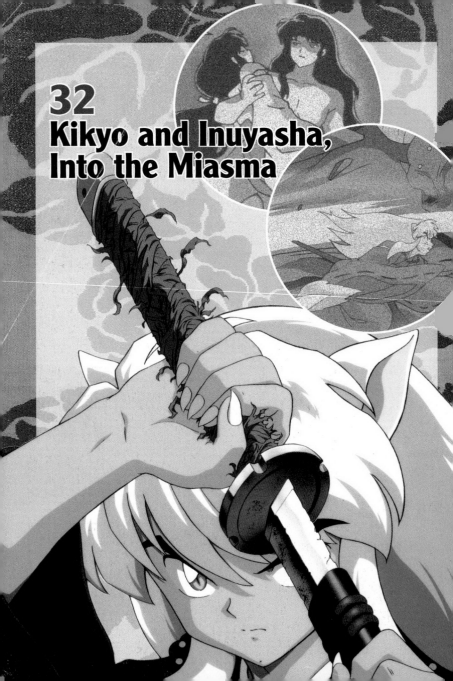

32
Kikyo and Inuyasha,
Into the Miasma

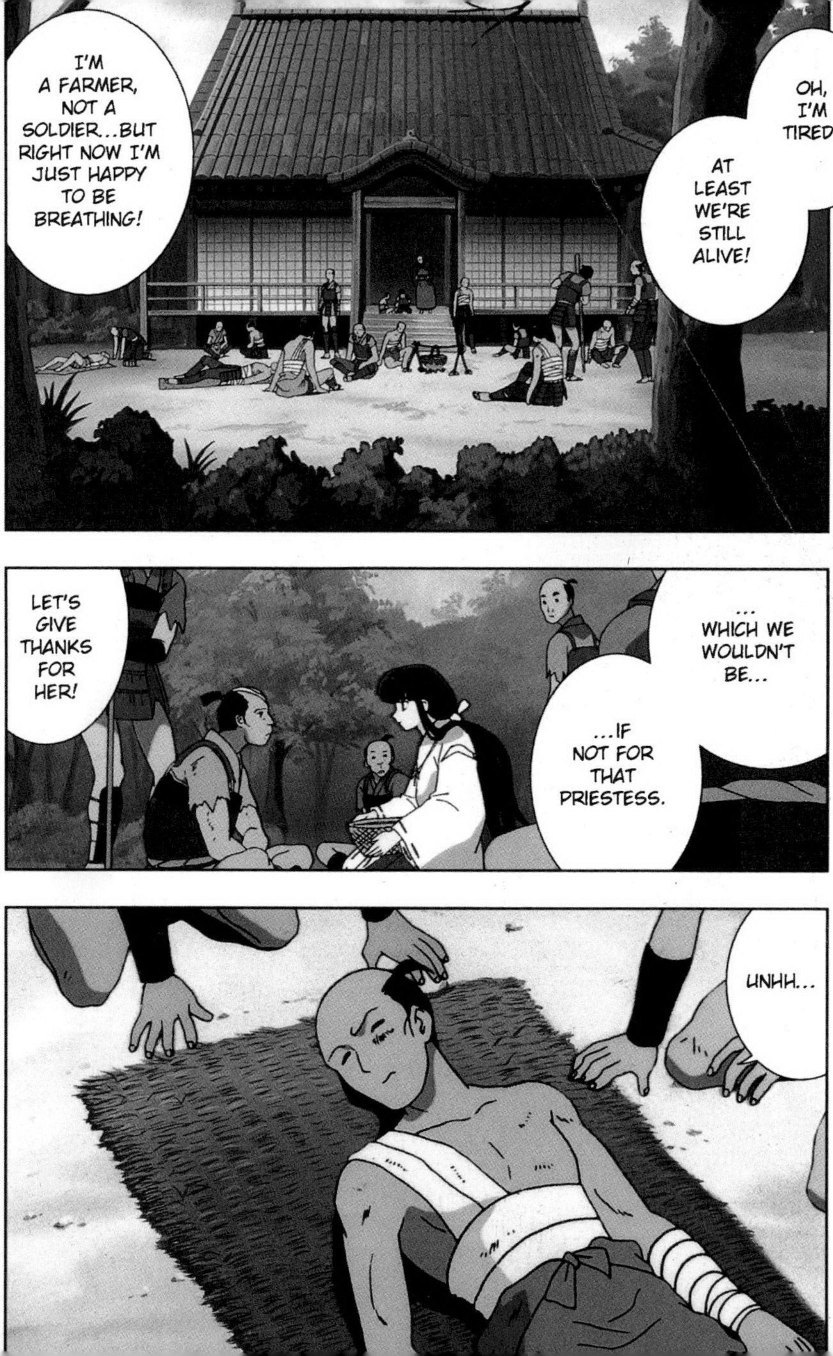
OH, I'M TIRED!
AT LEAST WE'RE STILL ALIVE!
I'M A FARMER, NOT A SOLDIER...BUT RIGHT NOW I'M JUST HAPPY TO BE BREATHING!
...WHICH WE WOULDN'T BE...
...IF NOT FOR THAT PRIESTESS.
LET'S GIVE THANKS FOR HER!
UNHH...

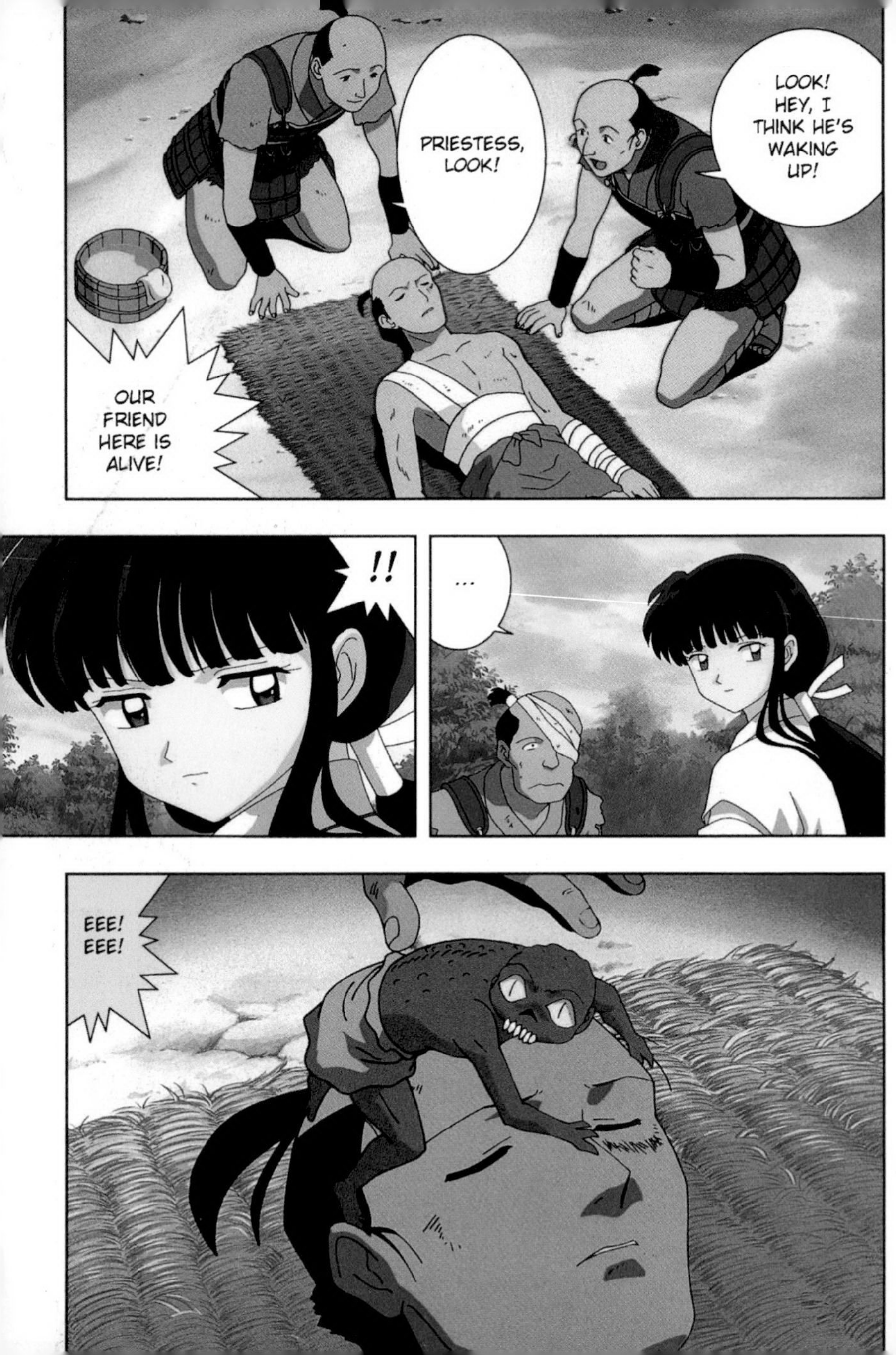
LOOK! HEY, I THINK HE'S WAKING UP!
PRIESTESS, LOOK!
OUR FRIEND HERE IS ALIVE!
...
!!
EEE! EEE!

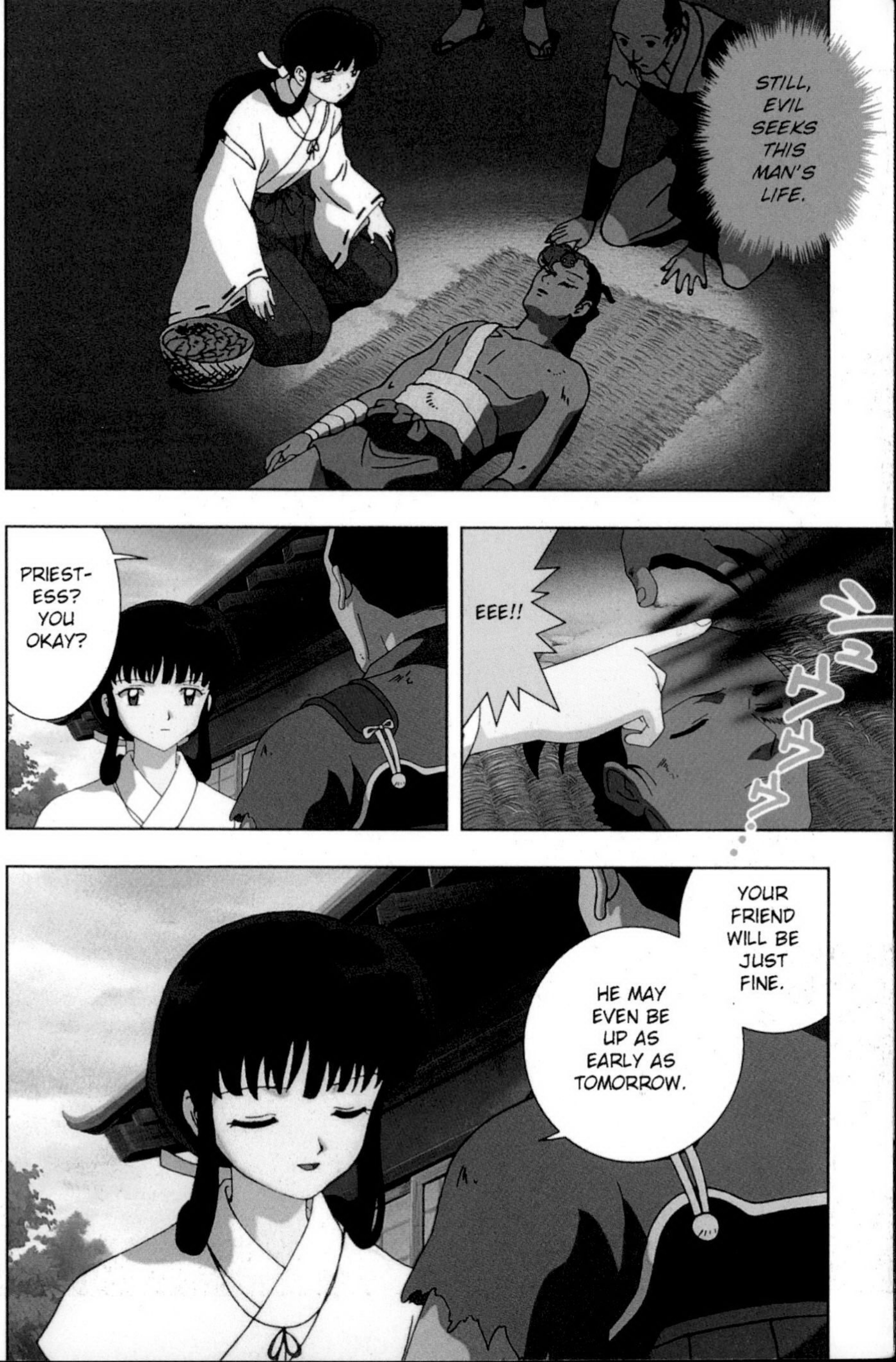
STILL, EVIL SEEKS THIS MAN'S LIFE.
EEE!!
PRIEST-ESS? YOU OKAY?
YOUR FRIEND WILL BE JUST FINE.
HE MAY EVEN BE UP AS EARLY AS TOMORROW.

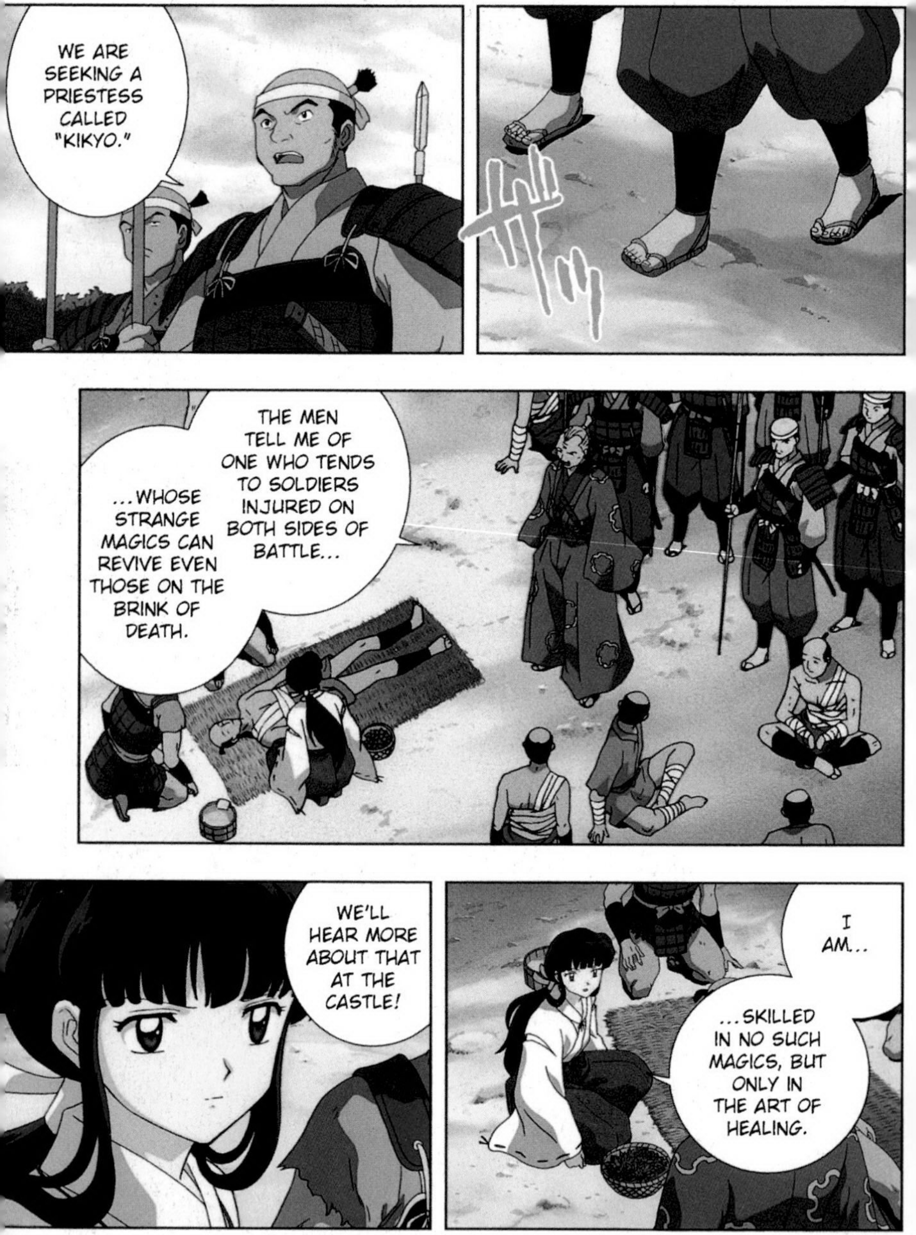
WE ARE SEEKING A PRIESTESS CALLED "KIKYO."
THE MEN TELL ME OF ONE WHO TENDS TO SOLDIERS INJURED ON BOTH SIDES OF BATTLE...
...WHOSE STRANGE MAGICS CAN REVIVE EVEN THOSE ON THE BRINK OF DEATH.
I AM...
...SKILLED IN NO SUCH MAGICS, BUT ONLY IN THE ART OF HEALING.
WE'LL HEAR MORE ABOUT THAT AT THE CASTLE!

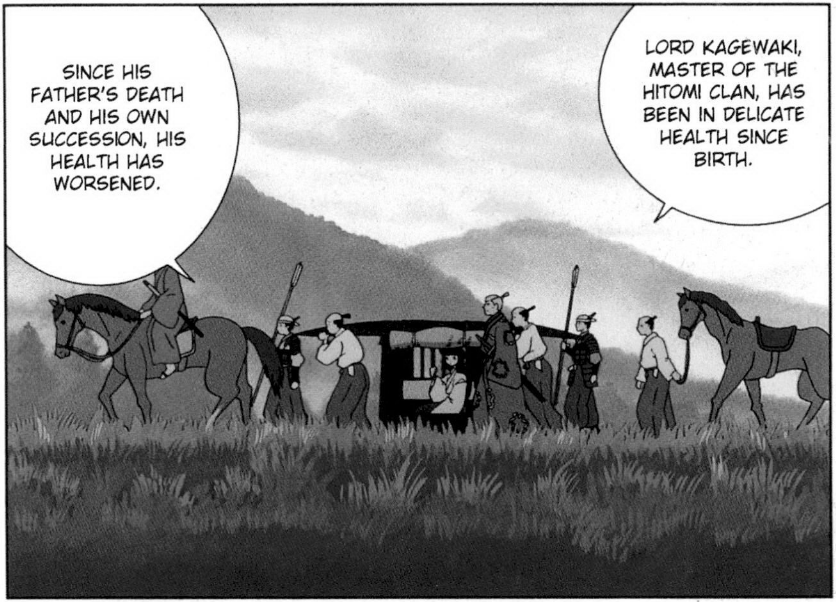
LORD KAGEWAKI, MASTER OF THE HITOMI CLAN, HAS BEEN IN DELICATE HEALTH SINCE BIRTH.
SINCE HIS FATHER'S DEATH AND HIS OWN SUCCESSION, HIS HEALTH HAS WORSENED.

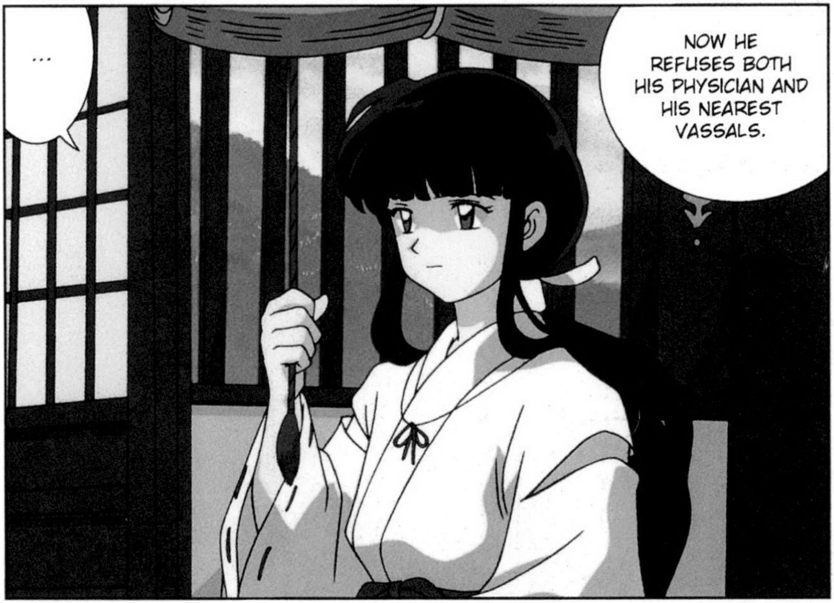
NOW HE REFUSES BOTH HIS PHYSICIAN AND HIS NEAREST VASSALS.
...

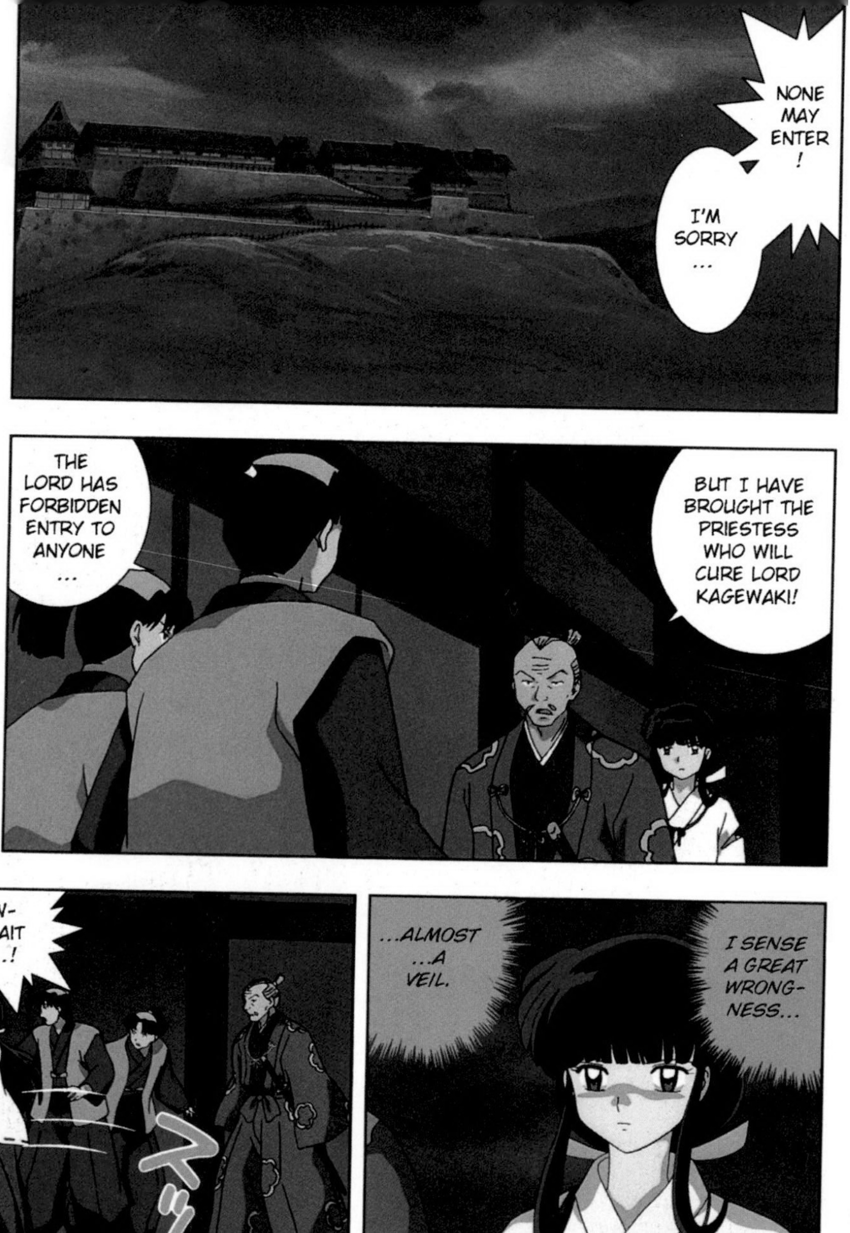
NONE MAY ENTER!
I'M SORRY...
BUT I HAVE BROUGHT THE PRIESTESS WHO WILL CURE LORD KAGEWAKI!
THE LORD HAS FORBIDDEN ENTRY TO ANYONE...
I SENSE A GREAT WRONG-NESS...
...ALMOST ...A VEIL.
W-WAIT...!
スッ

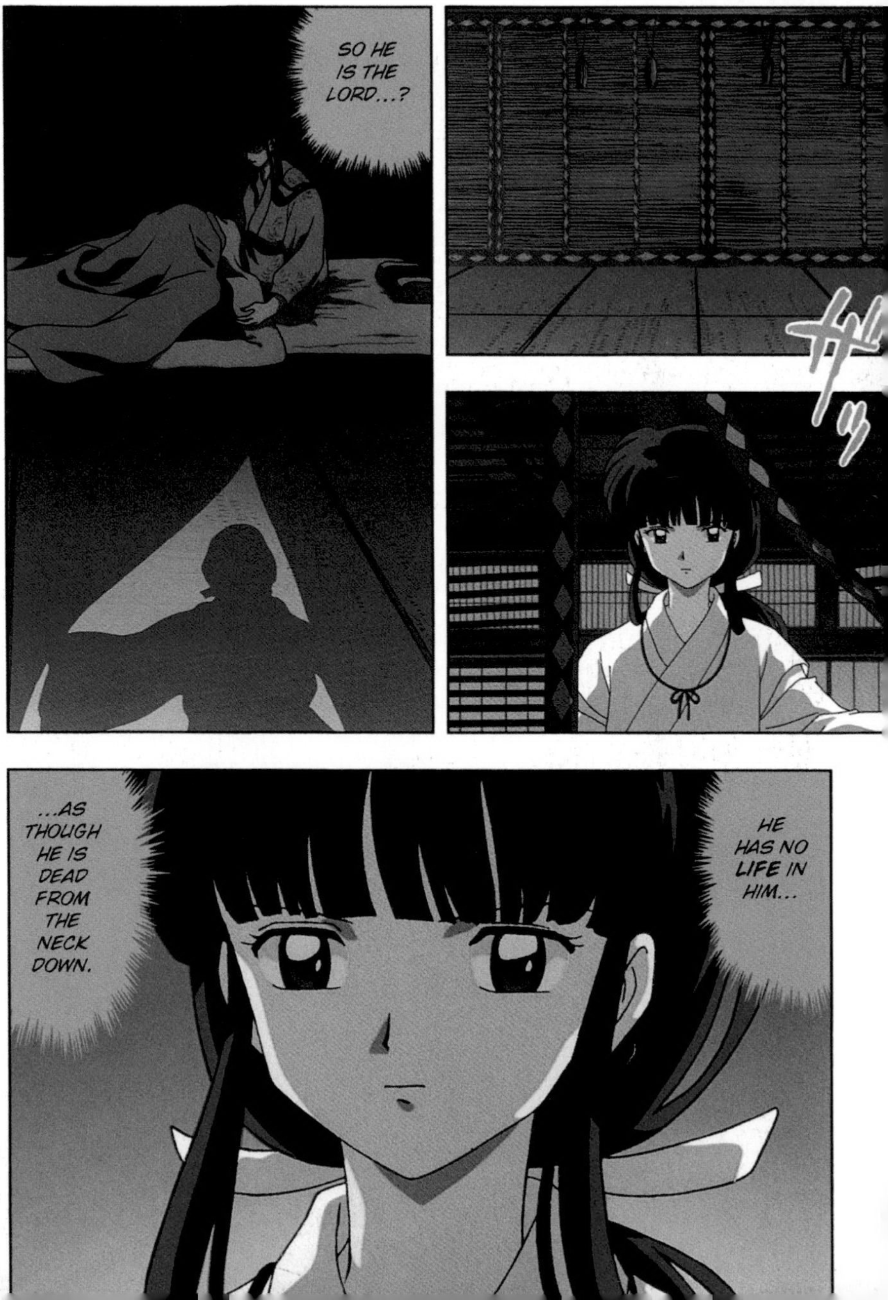
ザッ
SO HE IS THE LORD...?
HE HAS NO LIFE IN HIM...
...AS THOUGH HE IS DEAD FROM THE NECK DOWN.

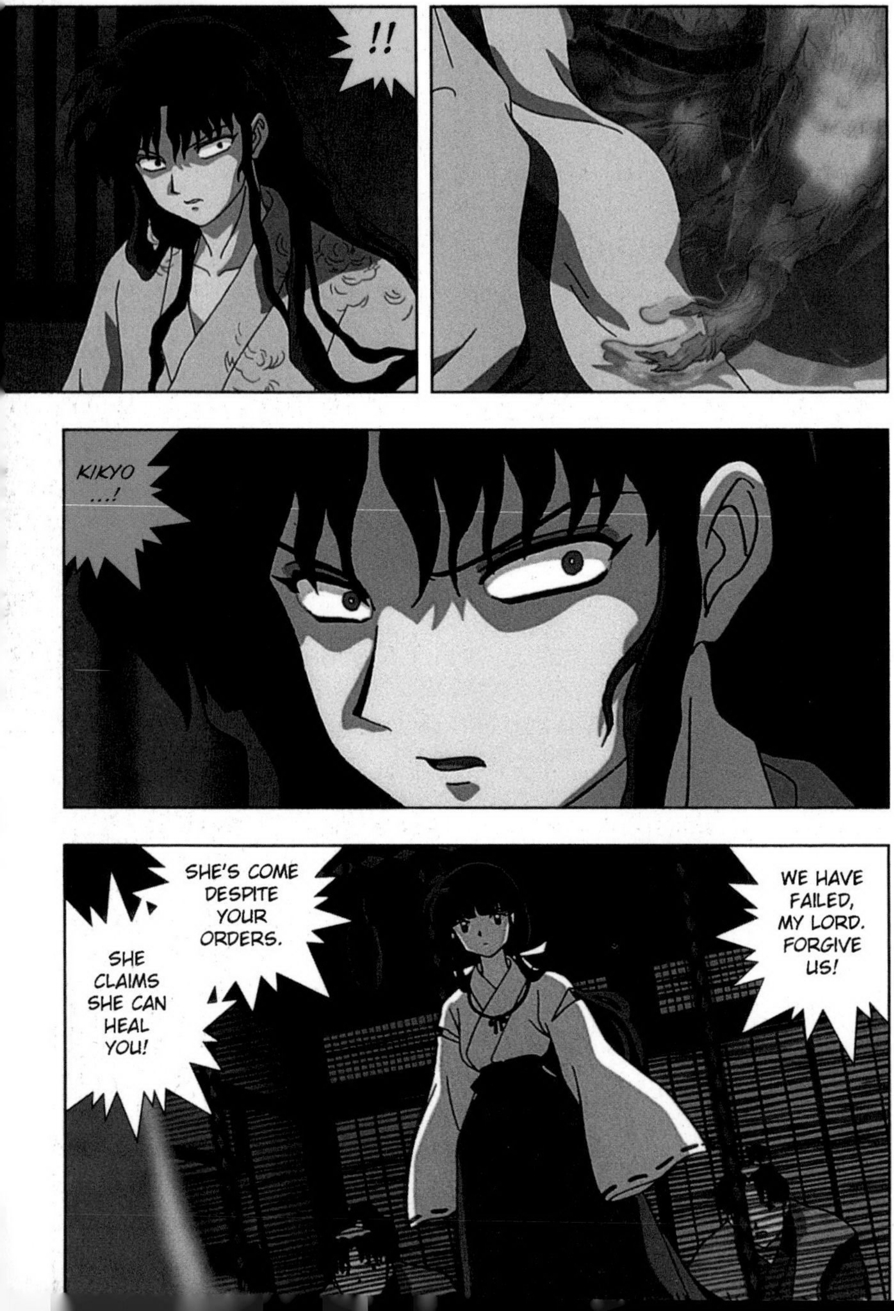
!!
KIKYO ...!
WE HAVE FAILED, MY LORD. FORGIVE US!
SHE'S COME DESPITE YOUR ORDERS.
SHE CLAIMS SHE CAN HEAL YOU!

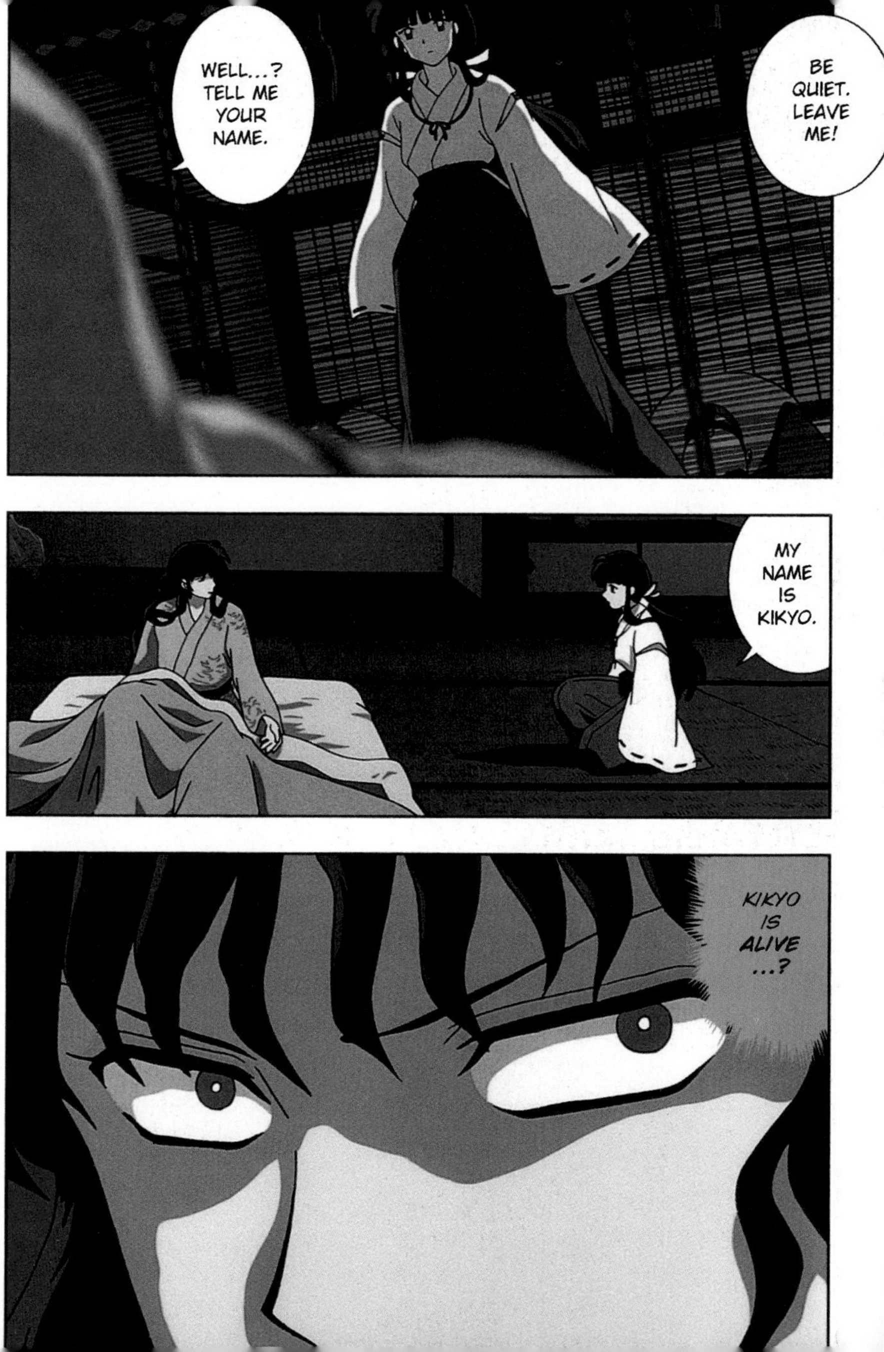
BE QUIET. LEAVE ME!
WELL...? TELL ME YOUR NAME.
MY NAME IS KIKYO.
KIKYO IS ALIVE ...?

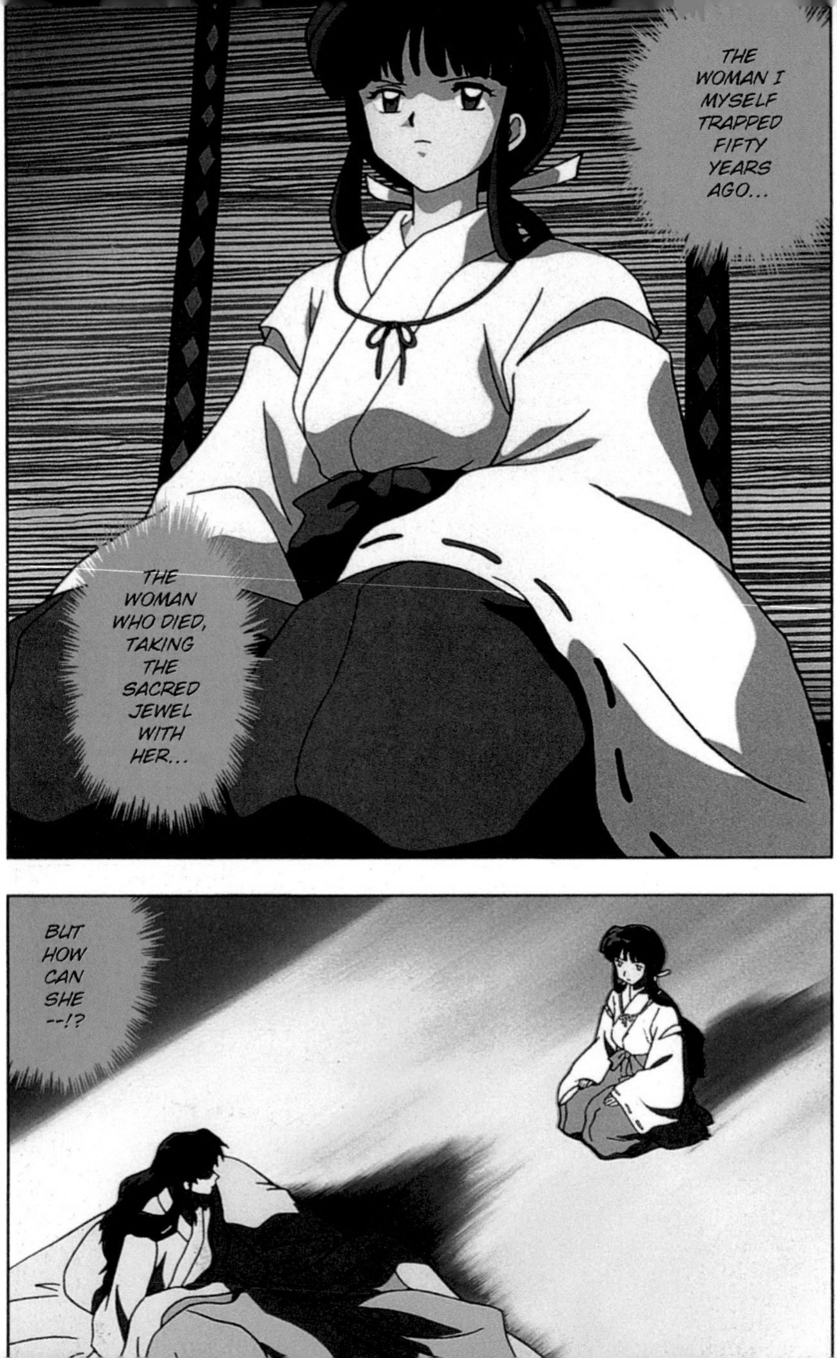
THE WOMAN I MYSELF TRAPPED FIFTY YEARS AGO...
THE WOMAN WHO DIED, TAKING THE SACRED JEWEL WITH HER...
BUT HOW CAN SHE --!?

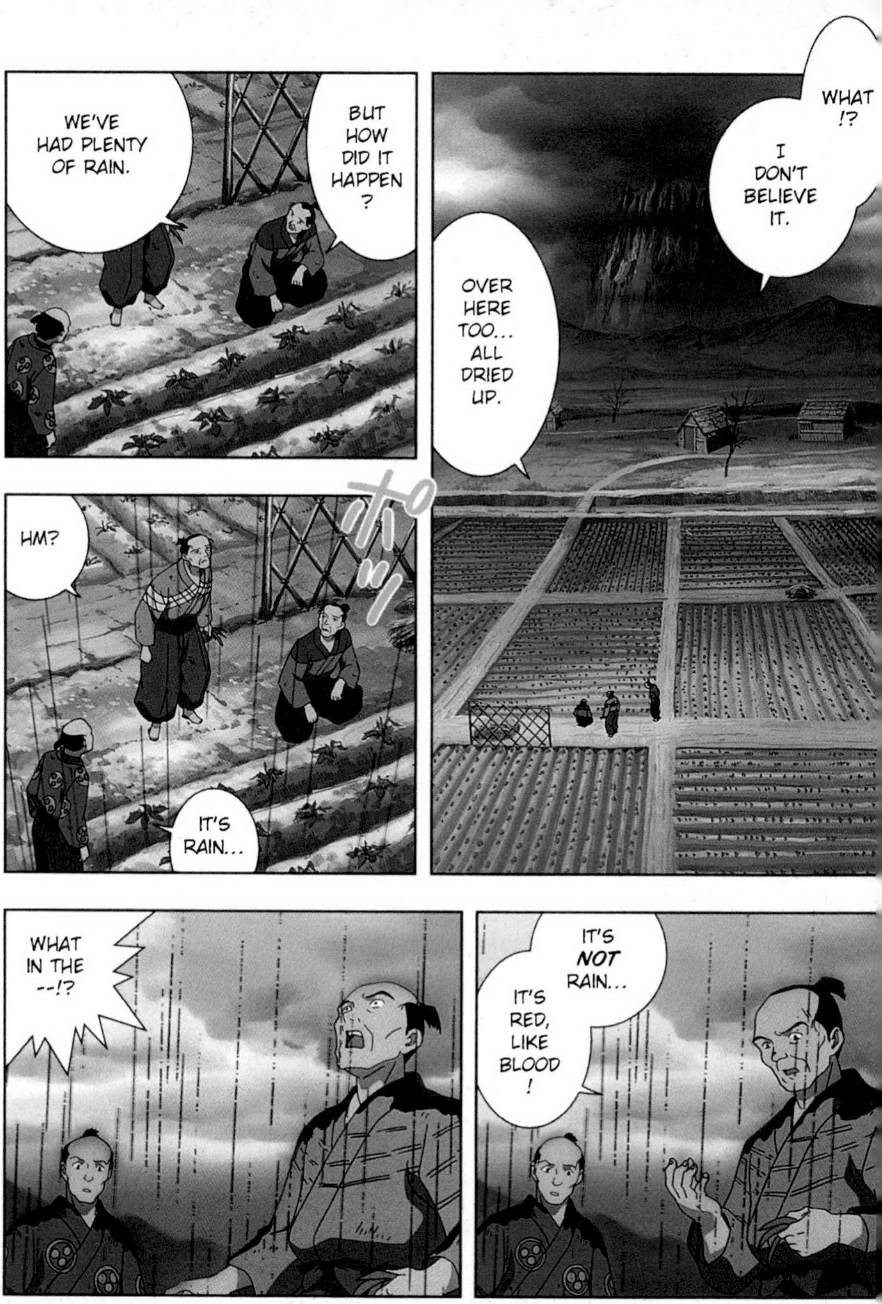
WHAT !?
I DON'T BELIEVE IT.
OVER HERE TOO... ALL DRIED UP.
BUT HOW DID IT HAPPEN ?
WE'VE HAD PLENTY OF RAIN.
HM?
IT'S RAIN...
IT'S **NOT** RAIN...
IT'S RED, LIKE BLOOD !
WHAT IN THE --!?

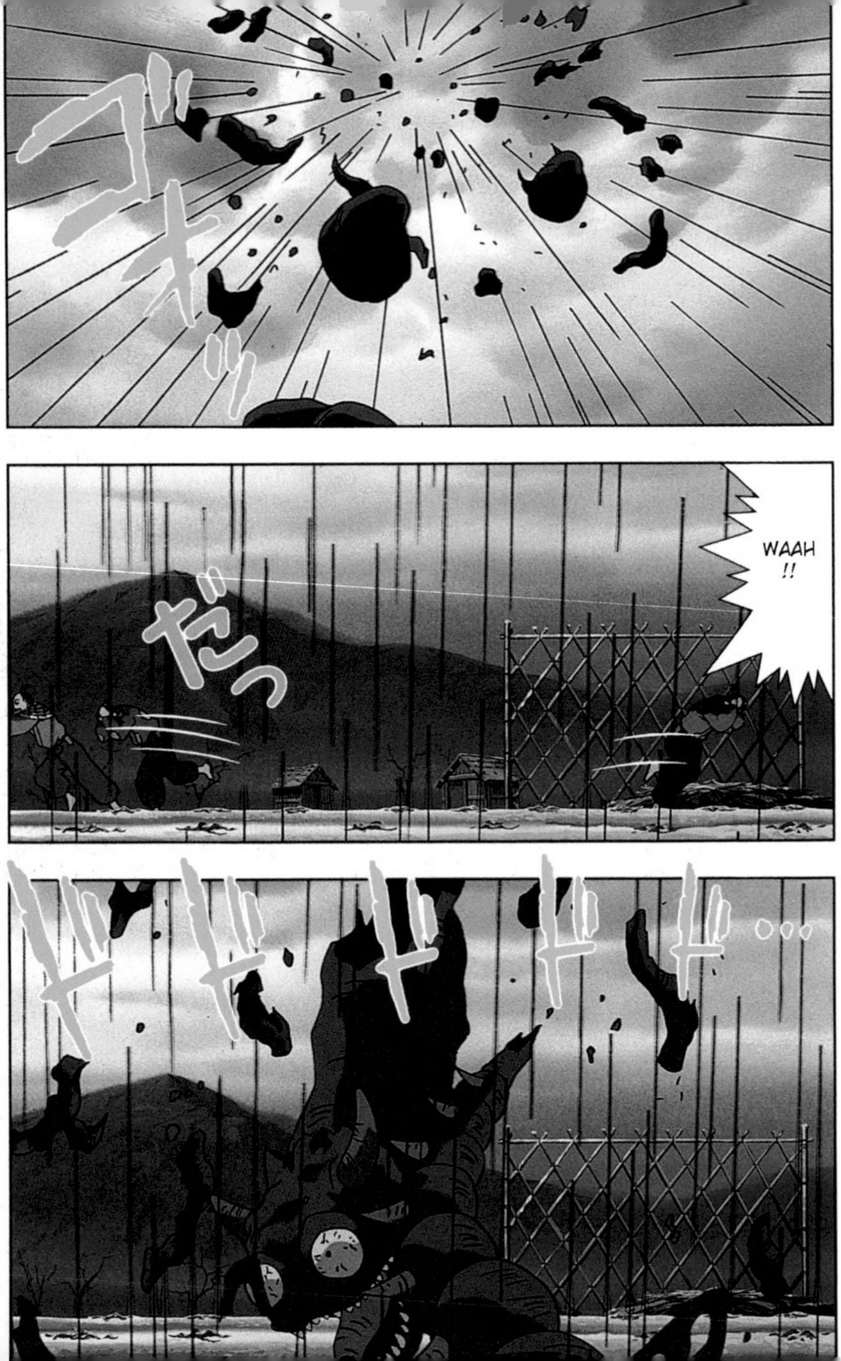
ゴォッ
WAAH !!
だっ
ドドドドド...

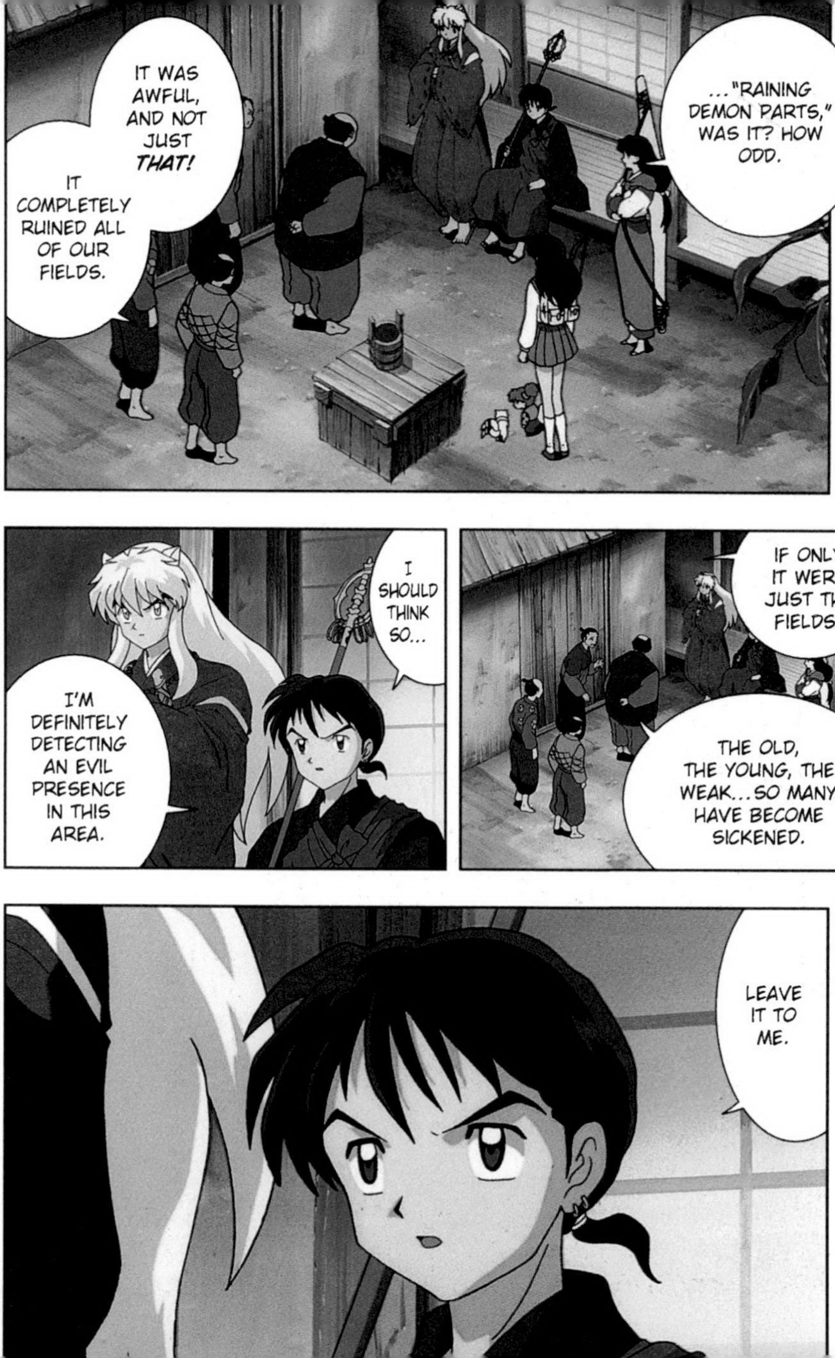
..."RAINING DEMON PARTS," WAS IT? HOW ODD.
IT WAS AWFUL, AND NOT JUST *THAT!*
IT COMPLETELY RUINED ALL OF OUR FIELDS.
IF ONLY IT WERE JUST THE FIELDS!
THE OLD, THE YOUNG, THE WEAK...SO MANY HAVE BECOME SICKENED.
I SHOULD THINK SO...
I'M DEFINITELY DETECTING AN EVIL PRESENCE IN THIS AREA.
LEAVE IT TO ME.

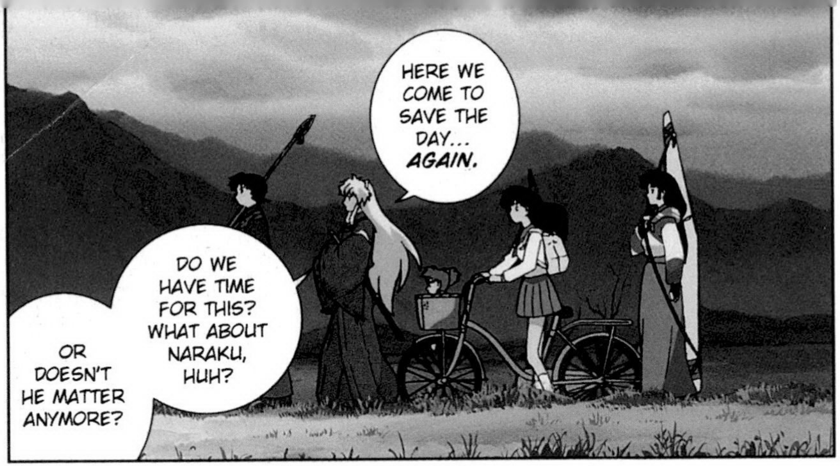
HERE WE COME TO SAVE THE DAY... AGAIN.
DO WE HAVE TIME FOR THIS? WHAT ABOUT NARAKU, HUH?
OR DOESN'T HE MATTER ANYMORE?
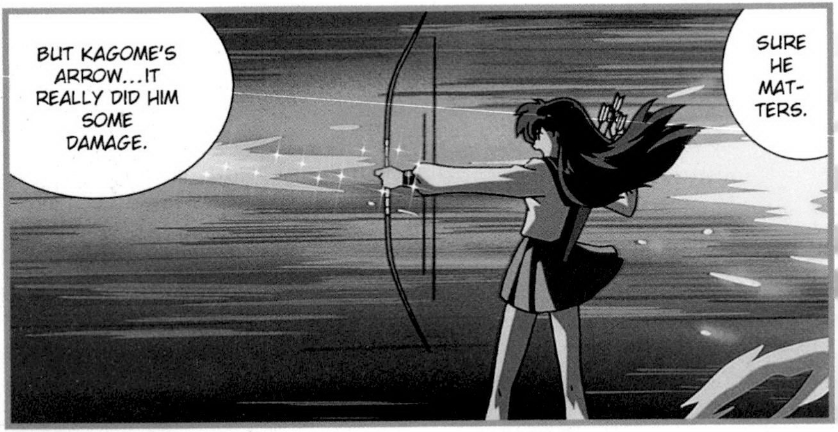
SURE HE MAT-TERS.
BUT KAGOME'S ARROW...IT REALLY DID HIM SOME DAMAGE.
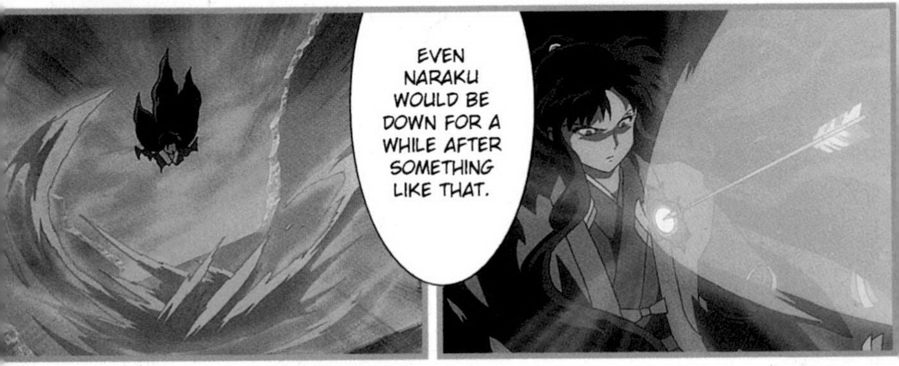
EVEN NARAKU WOULD BE DOWN FOR A WHILE AFTER SOMETHING LIKE THAT.

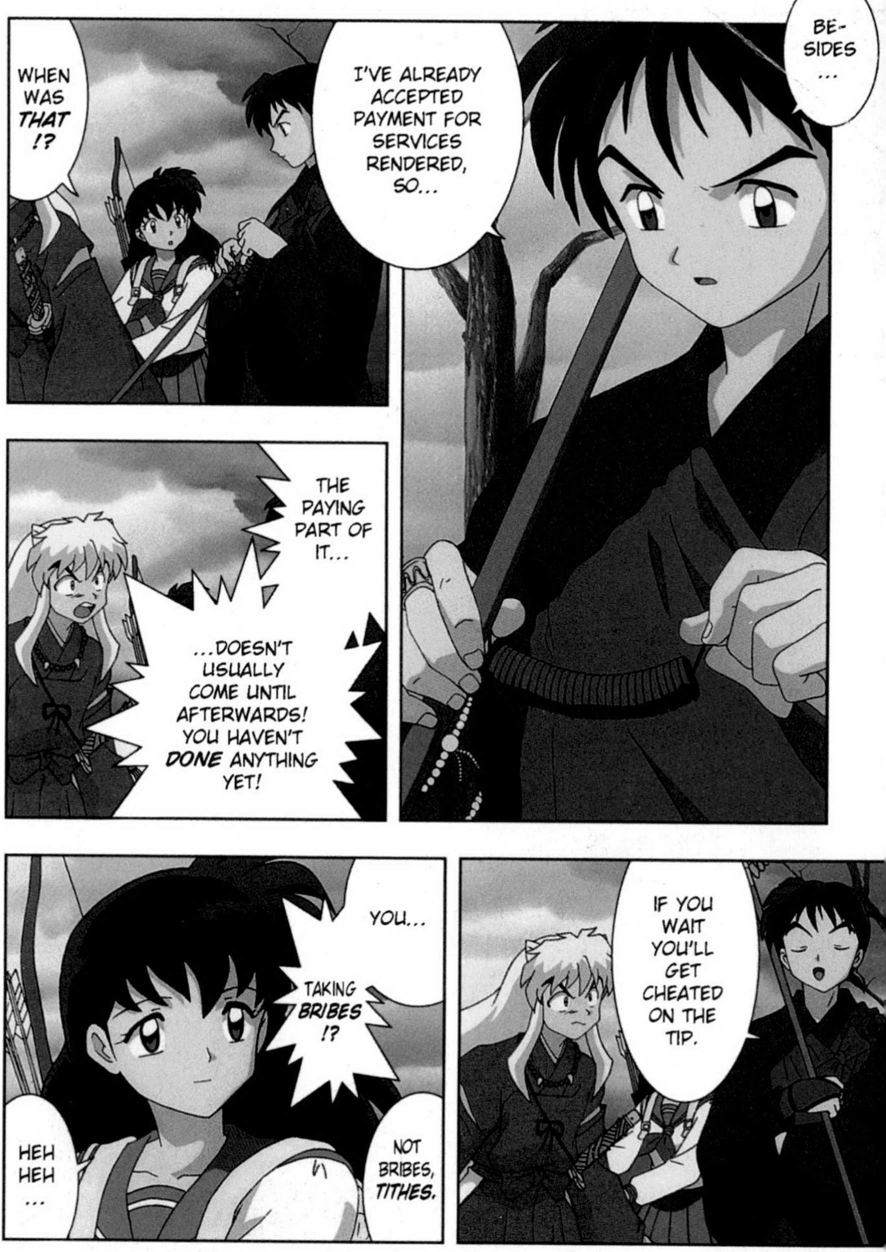

BE-SIDES...
I'VE ALREADY ACCEPTED PAYMENT FOR SERVICES RENDERED, SO...
WHEN WAS *THAT* !?
THE PAYING PART OF IT...
...DOESN'T USUALLY COME UNTIL AFTERWARDS! YOU HAVEN'T *DONE* ANYTHING YET!
IF YOU WAIT YOU'LL GET CHEATED ON THE TIP.
YOU...
TAKING *BRIBES* !?
NOT BRIBES, *TITHES.*
HEH HEH ...

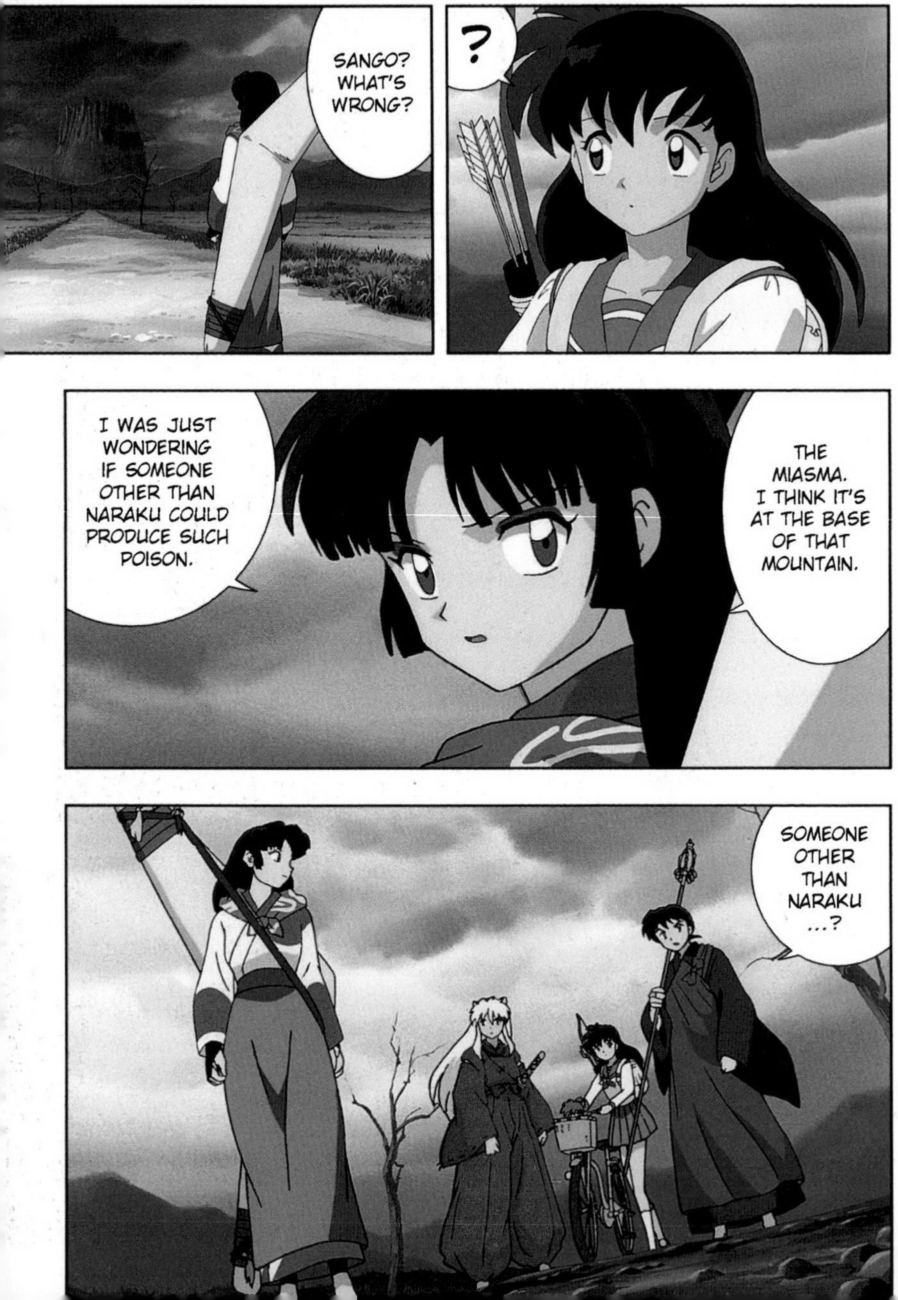
?
SANGO? WHAT'S WRONG?
THE MIASMA. I THINK IT'S AT THE BASE OF THAT MOUNTAIN.
I WAS JUST WONDERING IF SOMEONE OTHER THAN NARAKU COULD PRODUCE SUCH POISON.
SOMEONE OTHER THAN NARAKU ...?

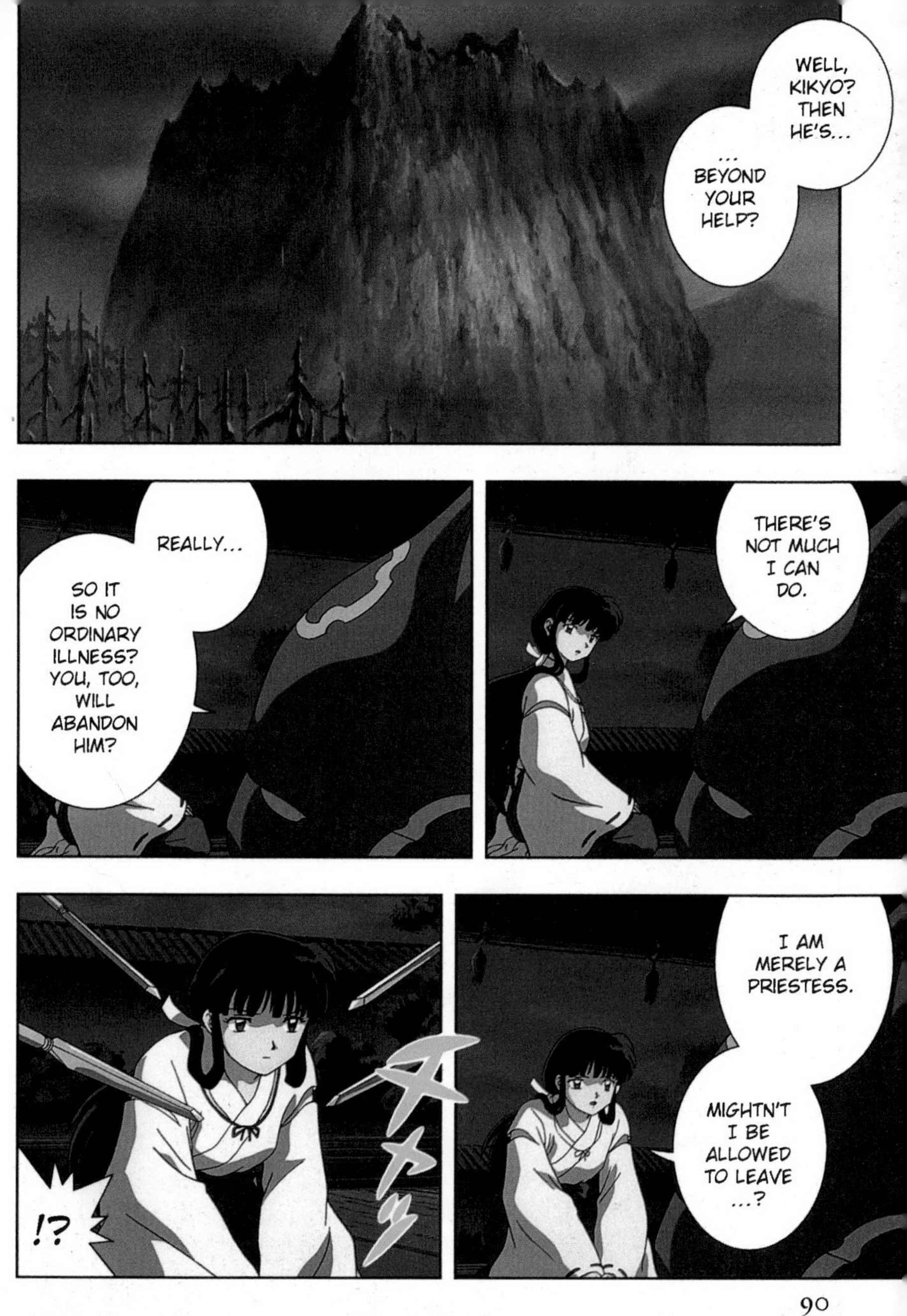
WELL, KIKYO? THEN HE'S...
... BEYOND YOUR HELP?
THERE'S NOT MUCH I CAN DO.
REALLY...
SO IT IS NO ORDINARY ILLNESS? YOU, TOO, WILL ABANDON HIM?
I AM MERELY A PRIESTESS.
MIGHTN'T I BE ALLOWED TO LEAVE ...?
!?

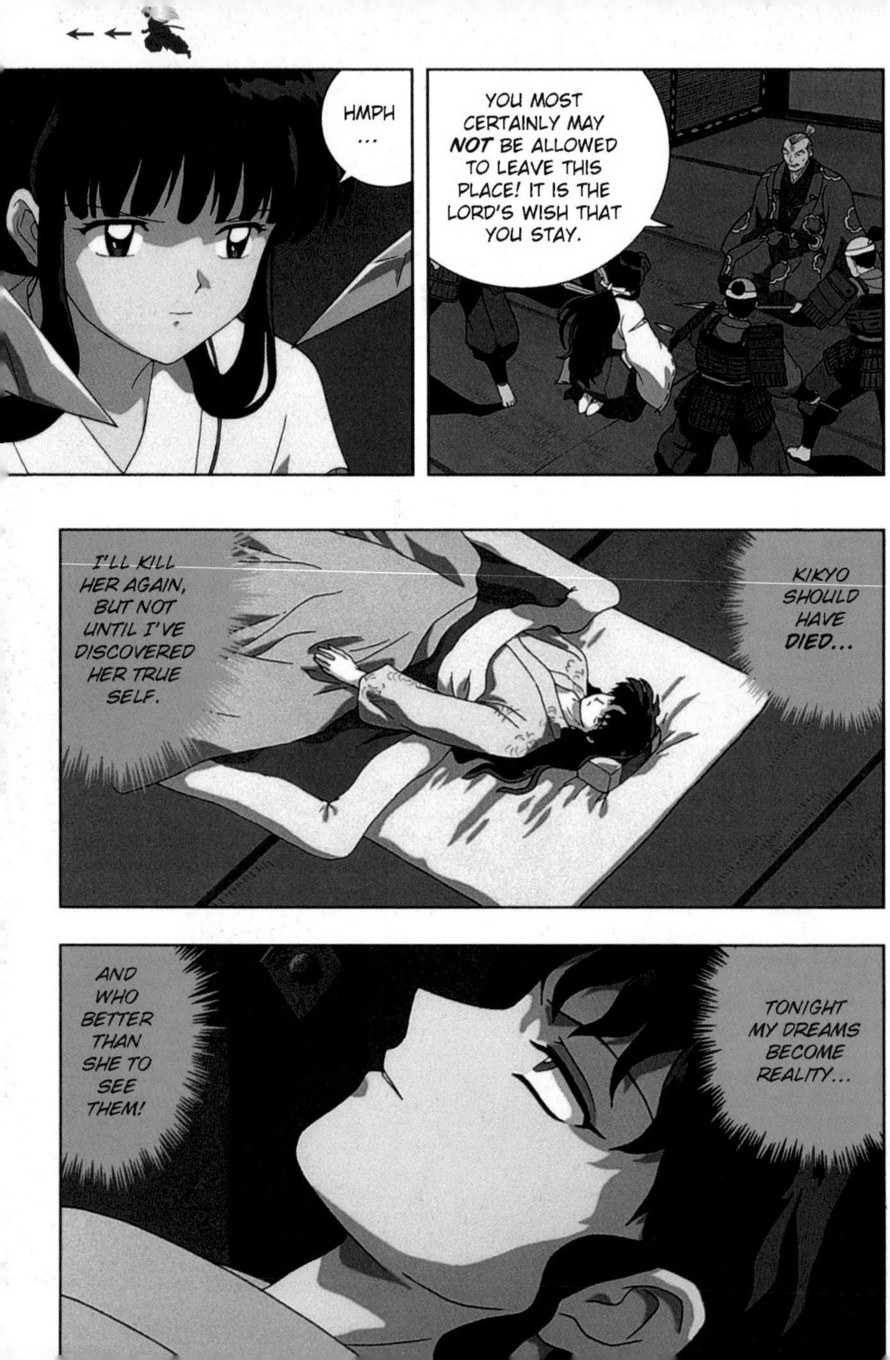
YOU MOST CERTAINLY MAY **NOT** BE ALLOWED TO LEAVE THIS PLACE! IT IS THE LORD'S WISH THAT YOU STAY.
HMPH ...
KIKYO SHOULD HAVE **DIED**...
I'LL KILL HER AGAIN, BUT NOT UNTIL I'VE DISCOVERED HER TRUE SELF.
TONIGHT MY DREAMS BECOME REALITY...
AND WHO BETTER THAN SHE TO SEE THEM!

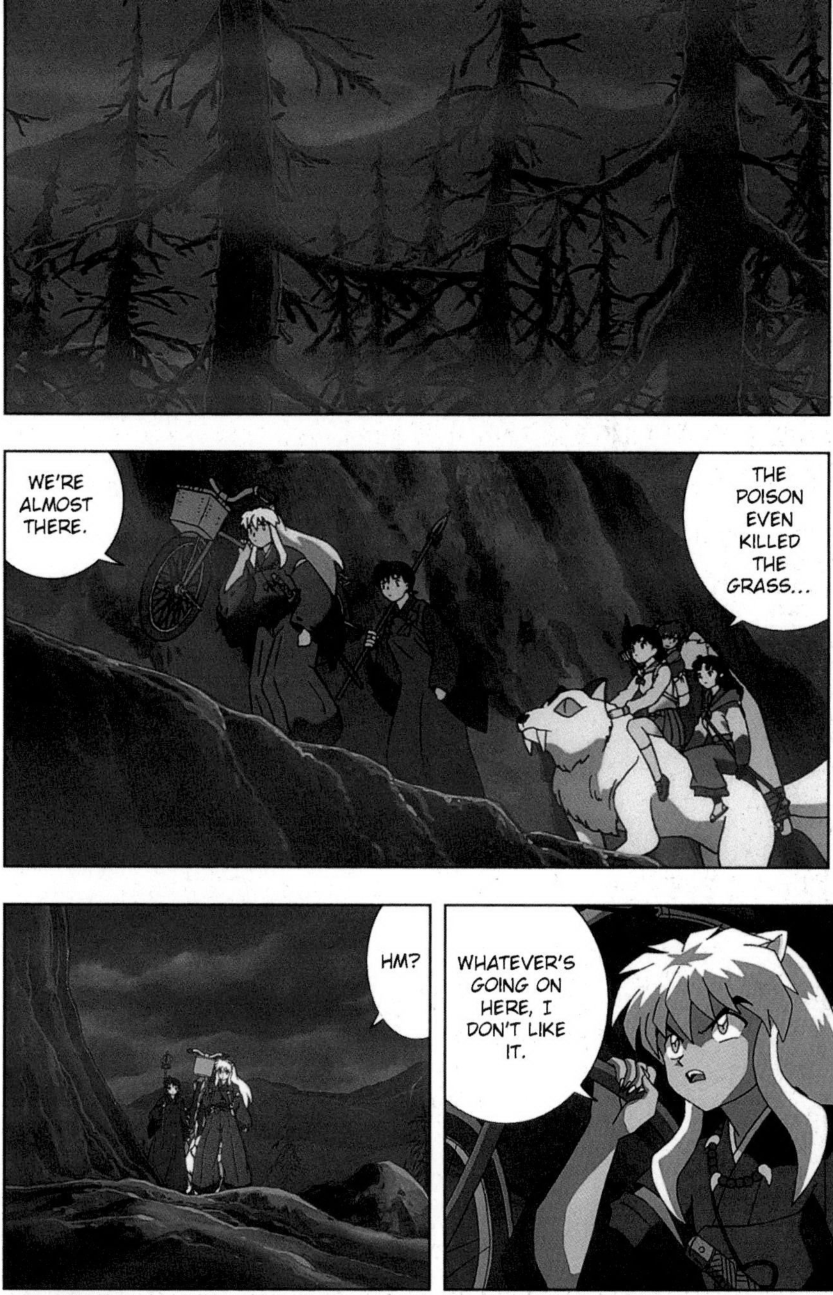
THE POISON EVEN KILLED THE GRASS...
WE'RE ALMOST THERE.
WHATEVER'S GOING ON HERE, I DON'T LIKE IT.
HM?

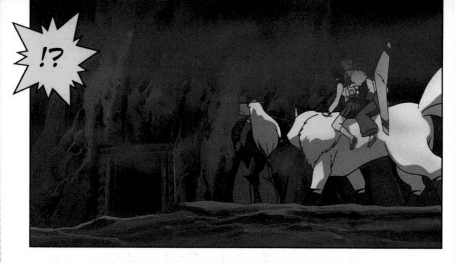

!?

...COMING FROM THAT CAVE?

THE MIASMA IS...

SANGO...!

-:KOFF:-
-:KOFF:-

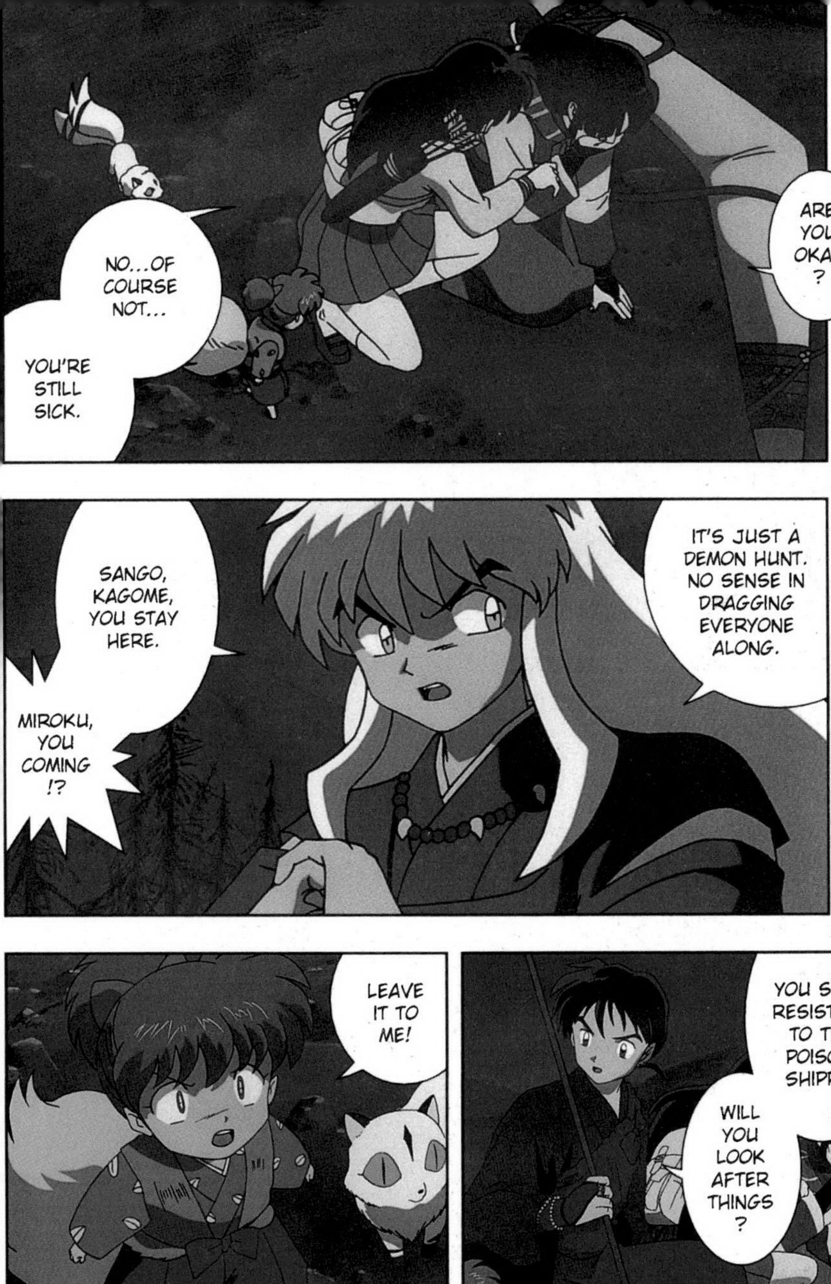
ARE YOU OKAY?
NO...OF COURSE NOT...
YOU'RE STILL SICK.
IT'S JUST A DEMON HUNT. NO SENSE IN DRAGGING EVERYONE ALONG.
SANGO, KAGOME, YOU STAY HERE.
MIROKU, YOU COMING!?
YOU SEEM RESISTANT TO THE POISON, SHIPPO.
WILL YOU LOOK AFTER THINGS?
LEAVE IT TO ME!

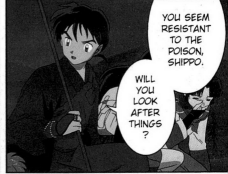

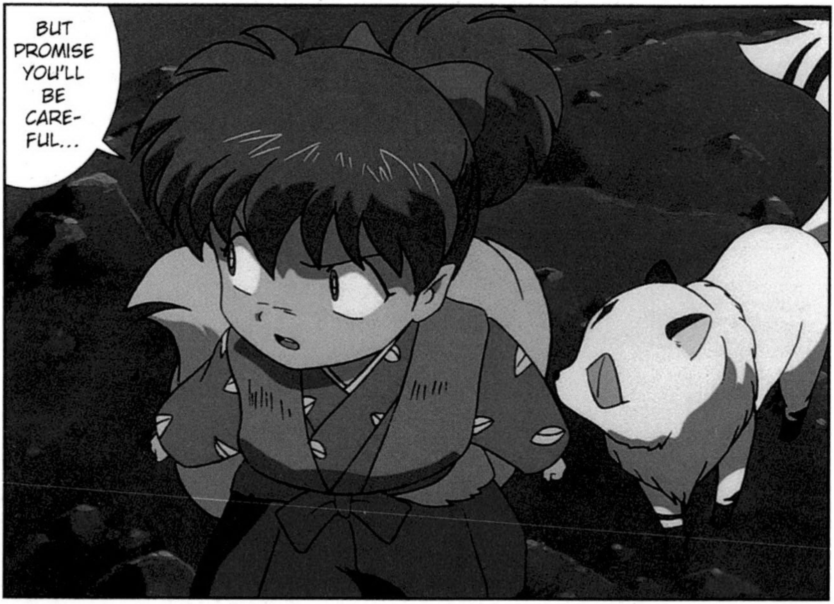
BUT PROMISE YOU'LL BE CARE-FUL...

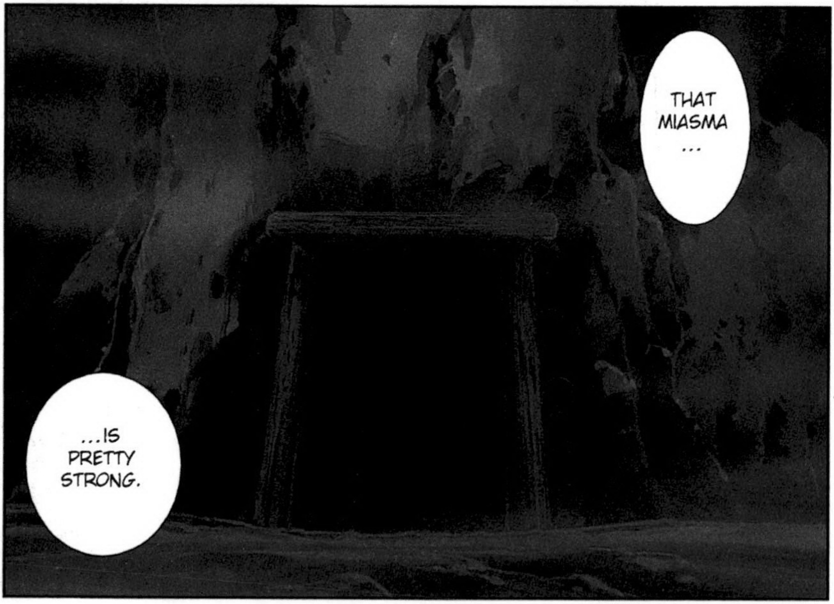
THAT MIASMA ...
...IS PRETTY STRONG.

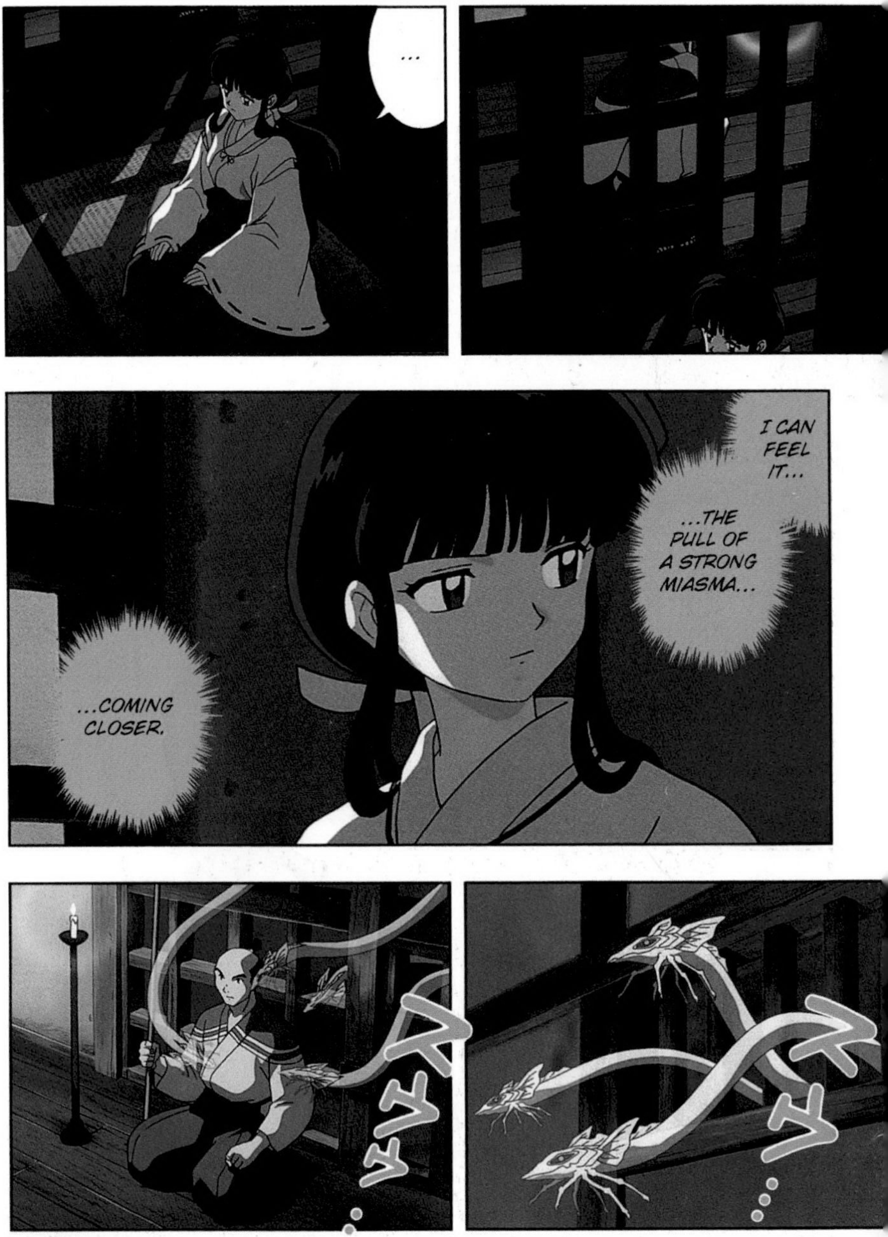
...
I CAN FEEL IT...
...THE PULL OF A STRONG MIASMA...
...COMING CLOSER.
スゥ…
スゥ…

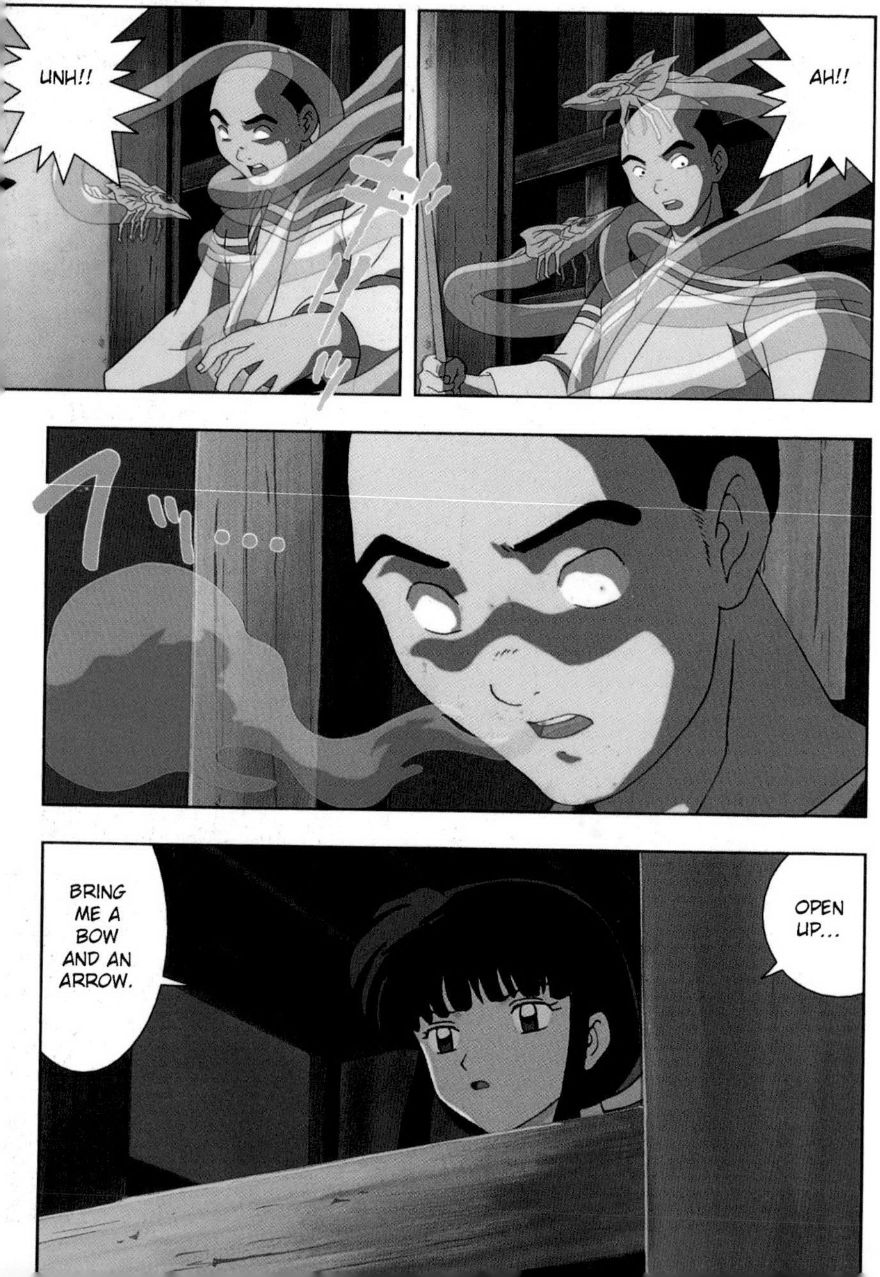
AH!!
UNH!!
OPEN UP...
BRING ME A BOW AND AN ARROW.

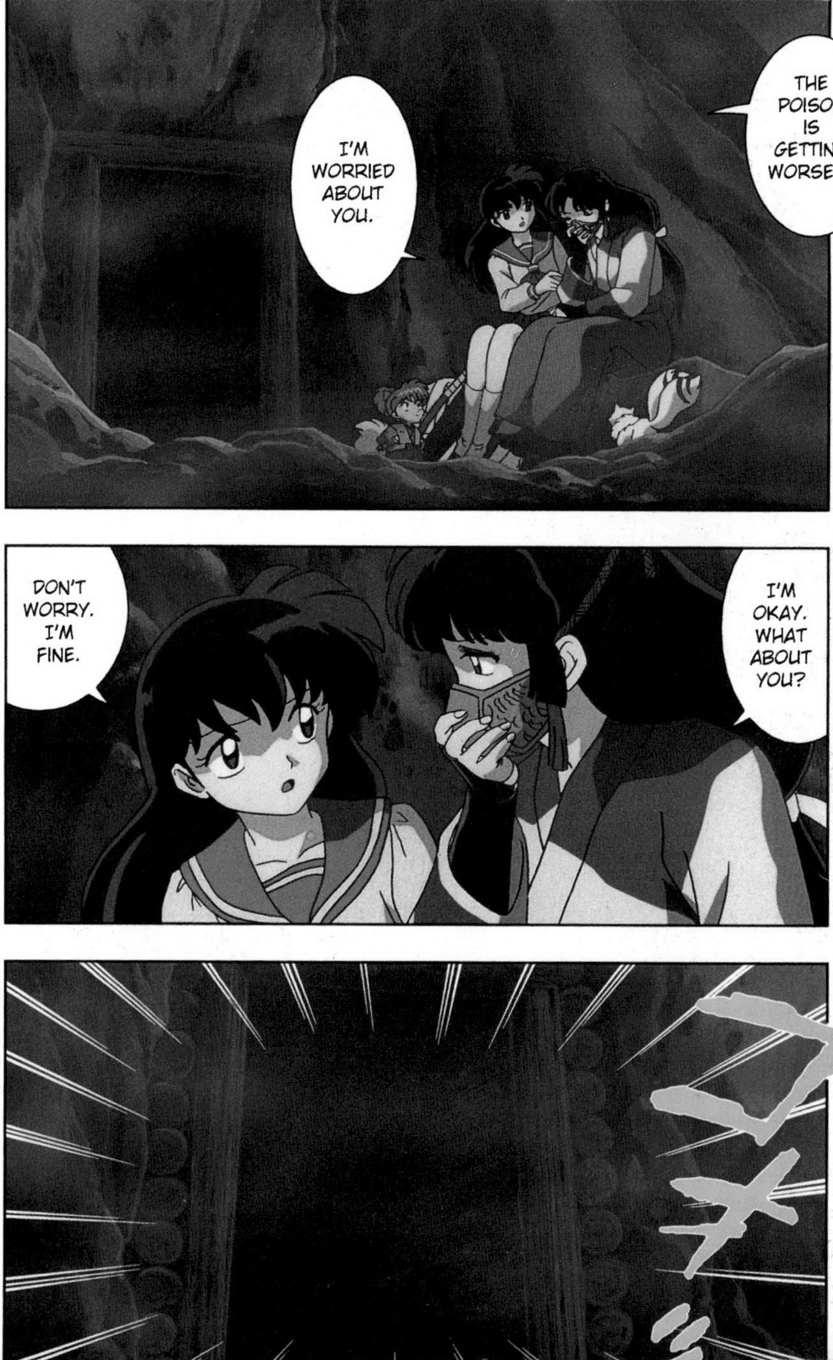
THE POISON IS GETTING WORSE...
I'M WORRIED ABOUT YOU.
I'M OKAY. WHAT ABOUT YOU?
DON'T WORRY. I'M FINE.

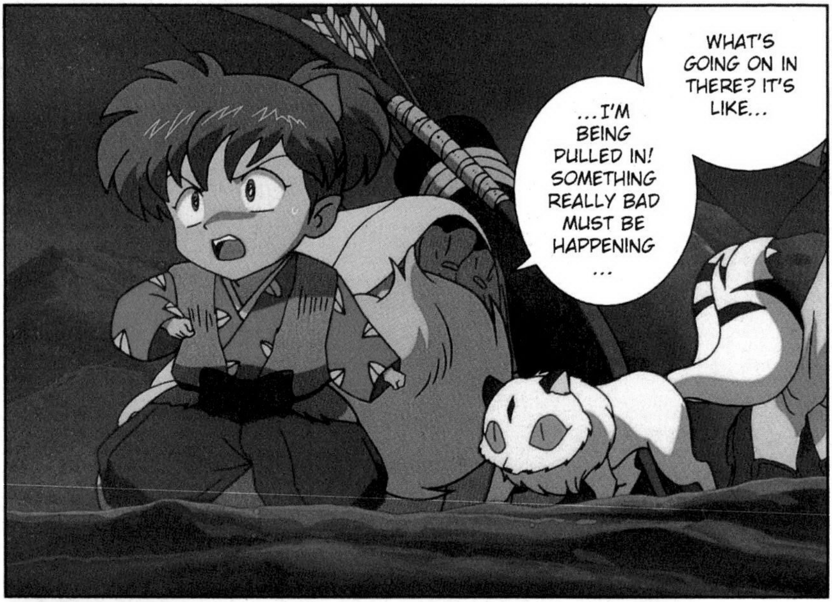
WHAT'S GOING ON IN THERE? IT'S LIKE...
...I'M BEING PULLED IN! SOMETHING REALLY BAD MUST BE HAPPENING ...

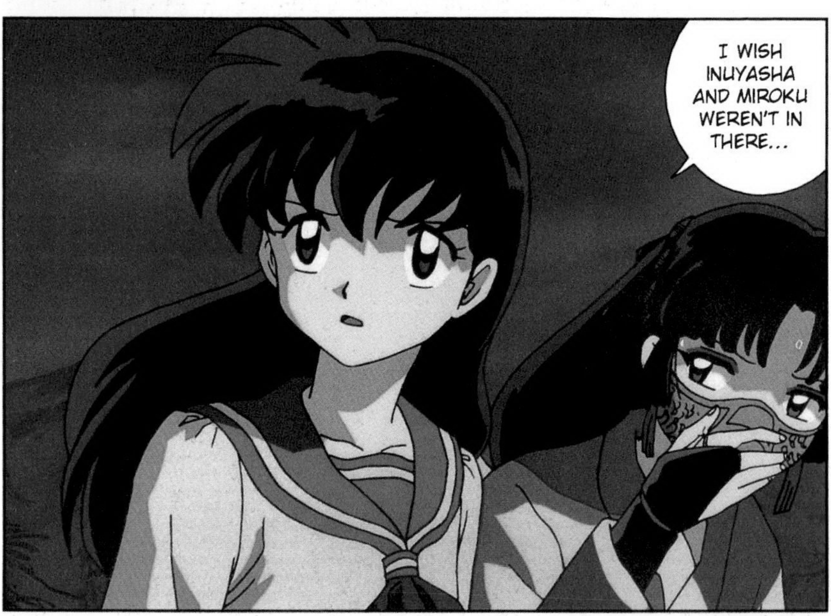
I WISH INUYASHA AND MIROKU WEREN'T IN THERE...

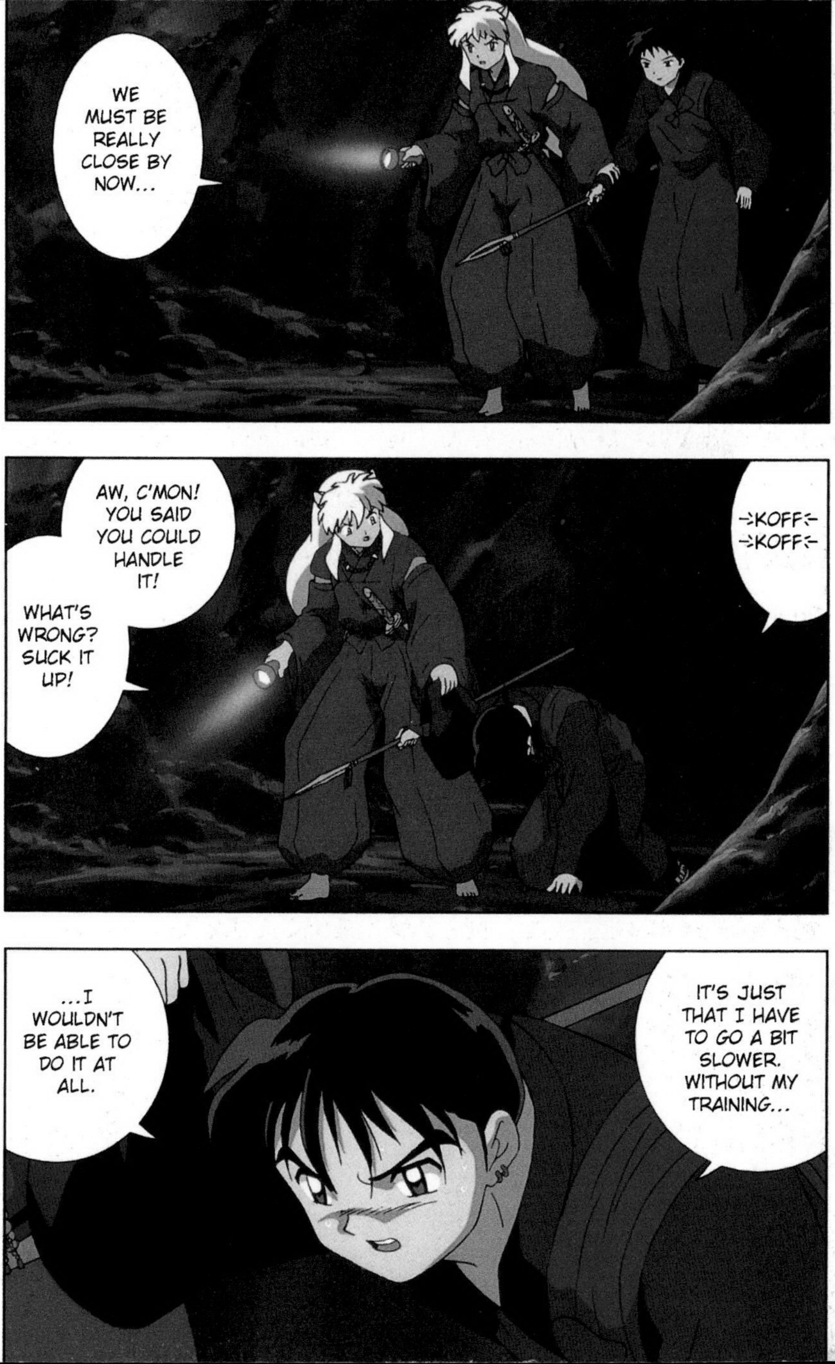
WE MUST BE REALLY CLOSE BY NOW...
-KOFF- -KOFF-
AW, C'MON! YOU SAID YOU COULD HANDLE IT!
WHAT'S WRONG? SUCK IT UP!
IT'S JUST THAT I HAVE TO GO A BIT SLOWER. WITHOUT MY TRAINING...
...I WOULDN'T BE ABLE TO DO IT AT ALL.

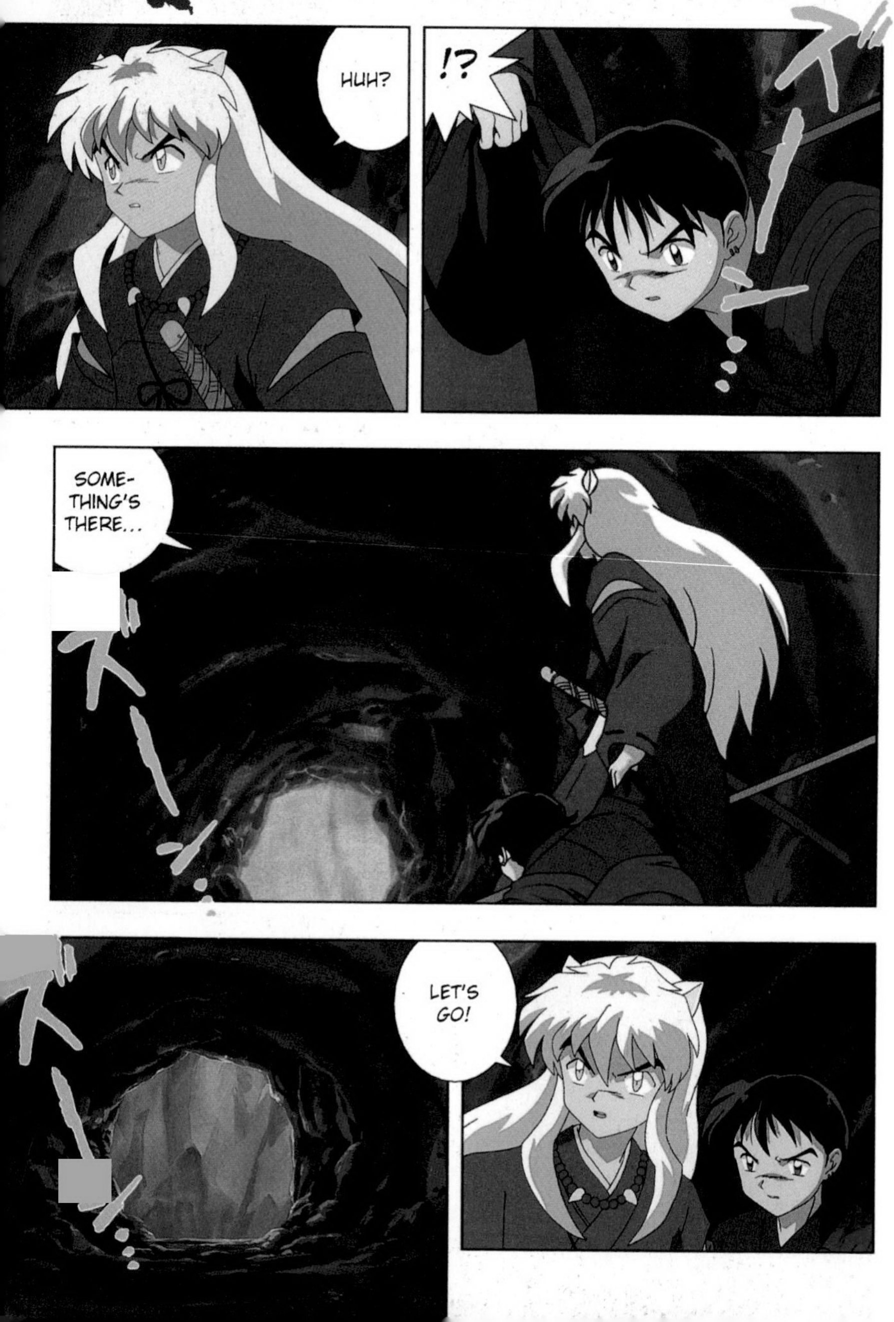
!?
HUH?
SOME-THING'S THERE...
LET'S GO!

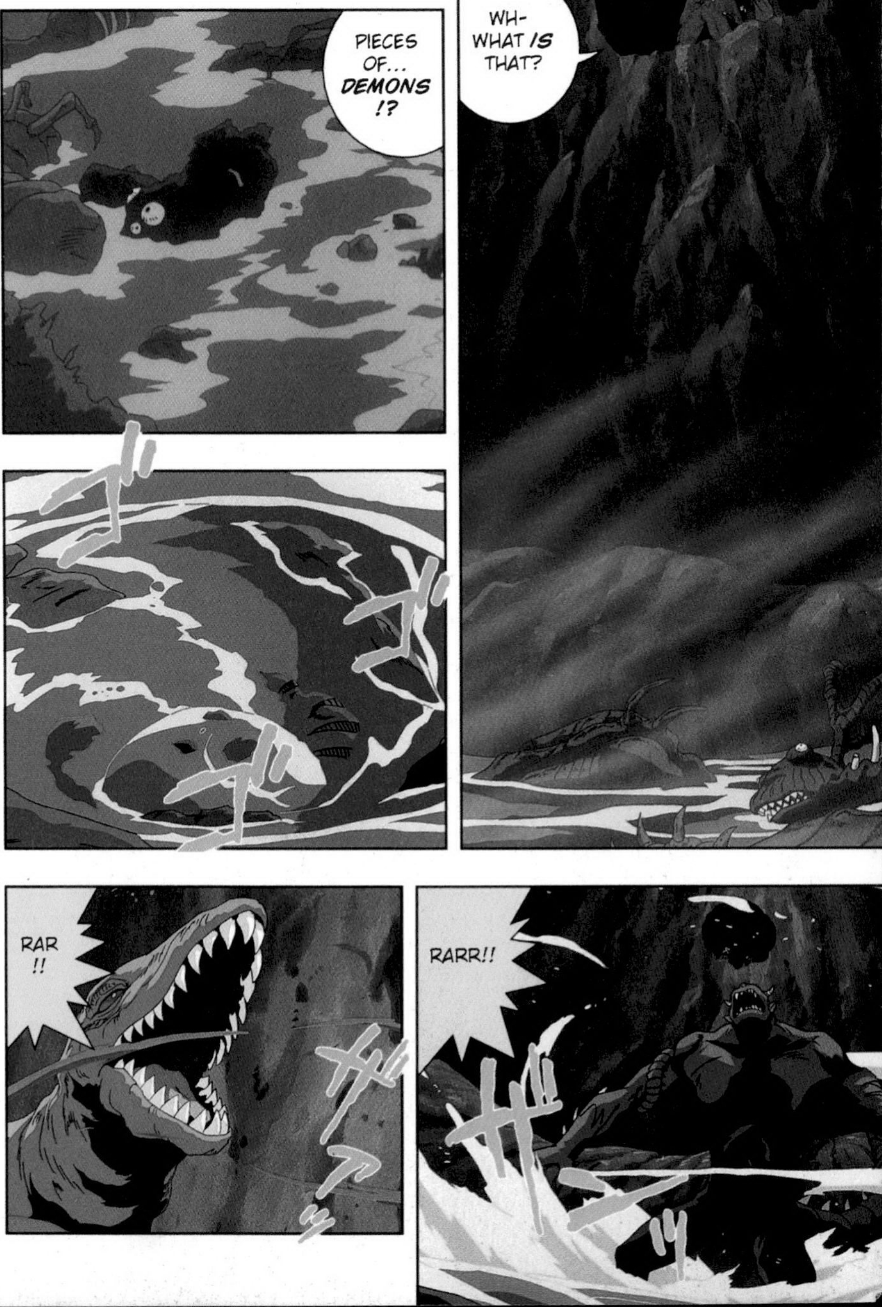

WH- WHAT *IS* THAT?
PIECES OF... ***DEMONS*** !?
RARR!!
RAR !!

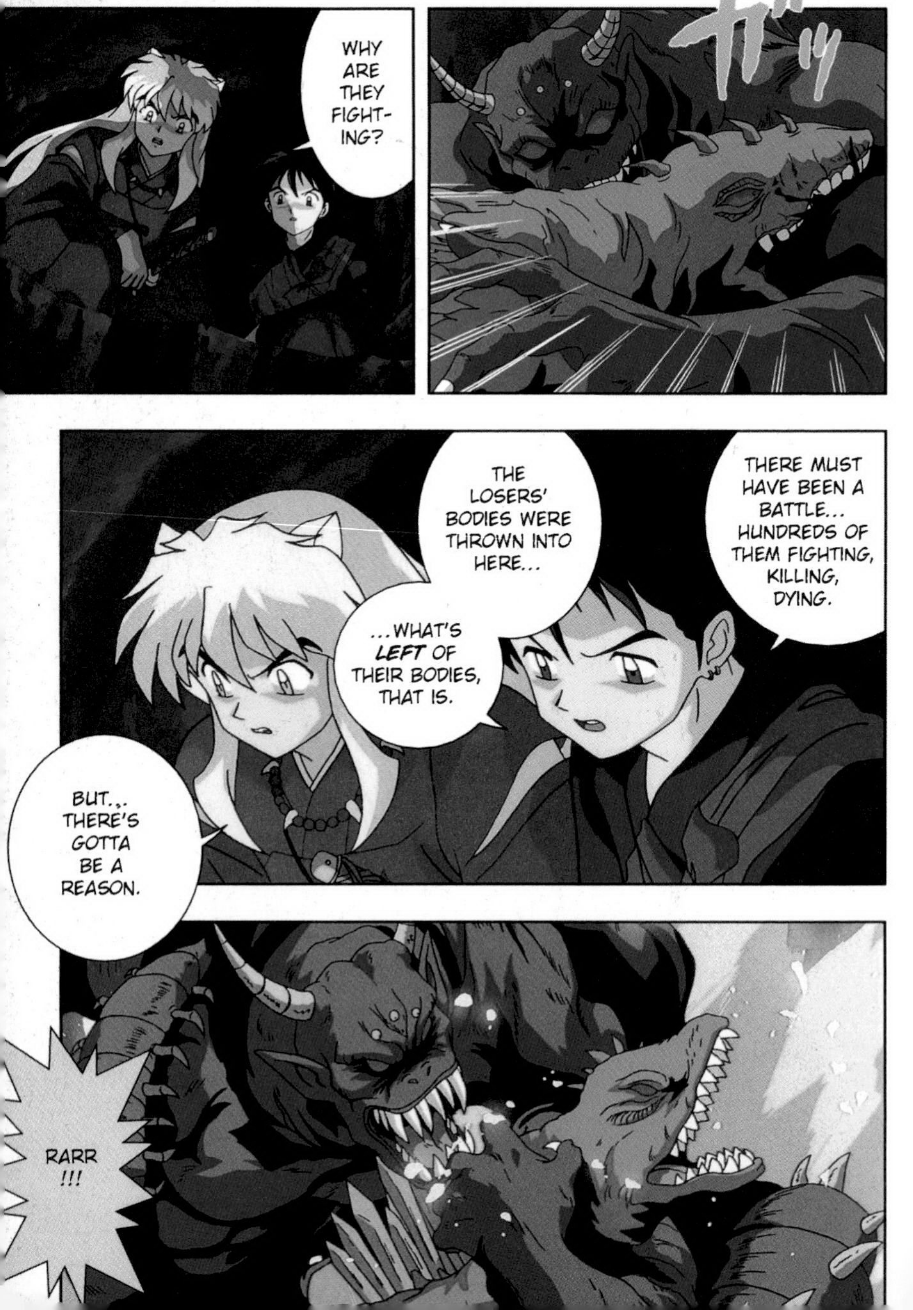
ガッ
WHY ARE THEY FIGHTING?
THERE MUST HAVE BEEN A BATTLE... HUNDREDS OF THEM FIGHTING, KILLING, DYING.
THE LOSERS' BODIES WERE THROWN INTO HERE...
...WHAT'S *LEFT* OF THEIR BODIES, THAT IS.
BUT... THERE'S GOTTA BE A REASON.
RARR !!!

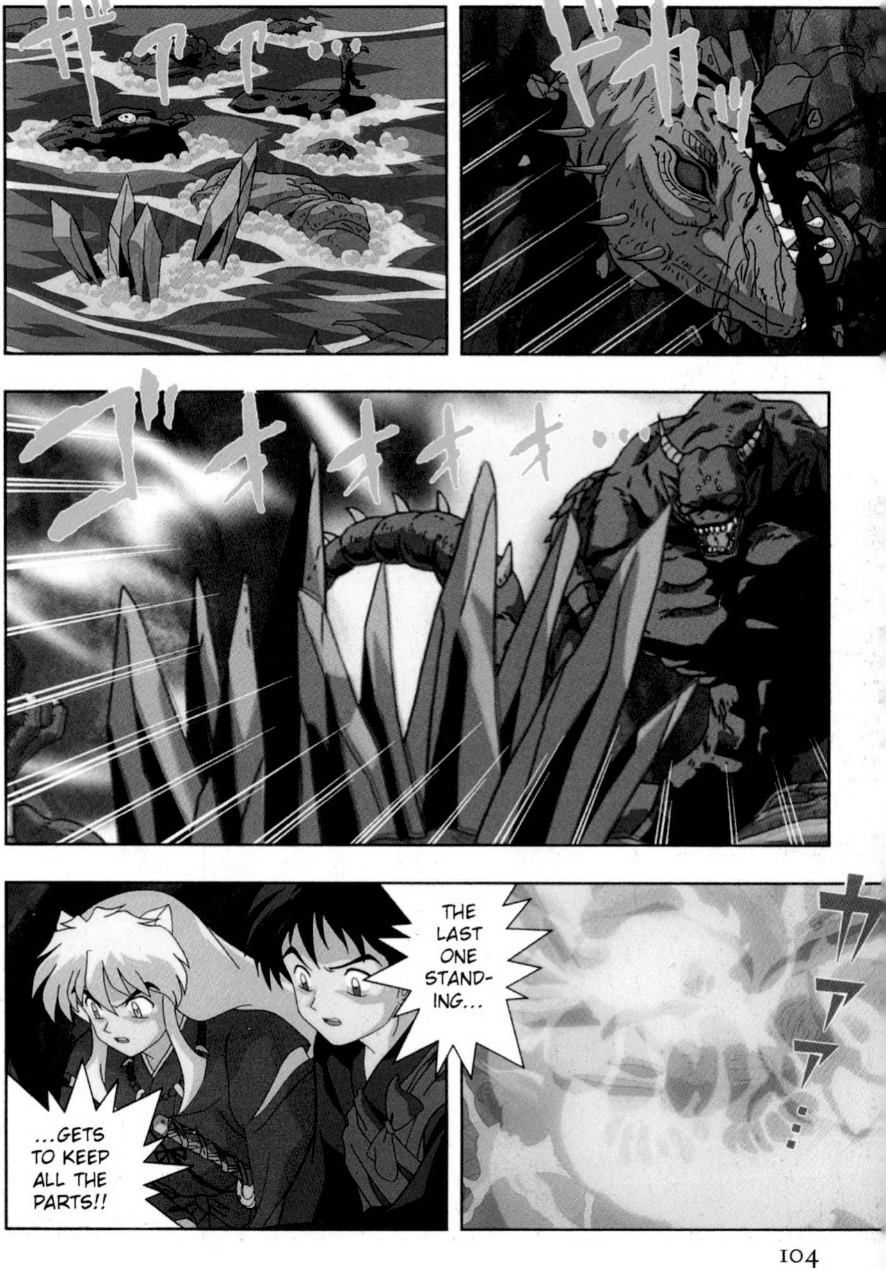
ドガッ
ザァァ…
ゴォォォォ…
ガァァ…
THE LAST ONE STANDING...
...GETS TO KEEP ALL THE PARTS!!

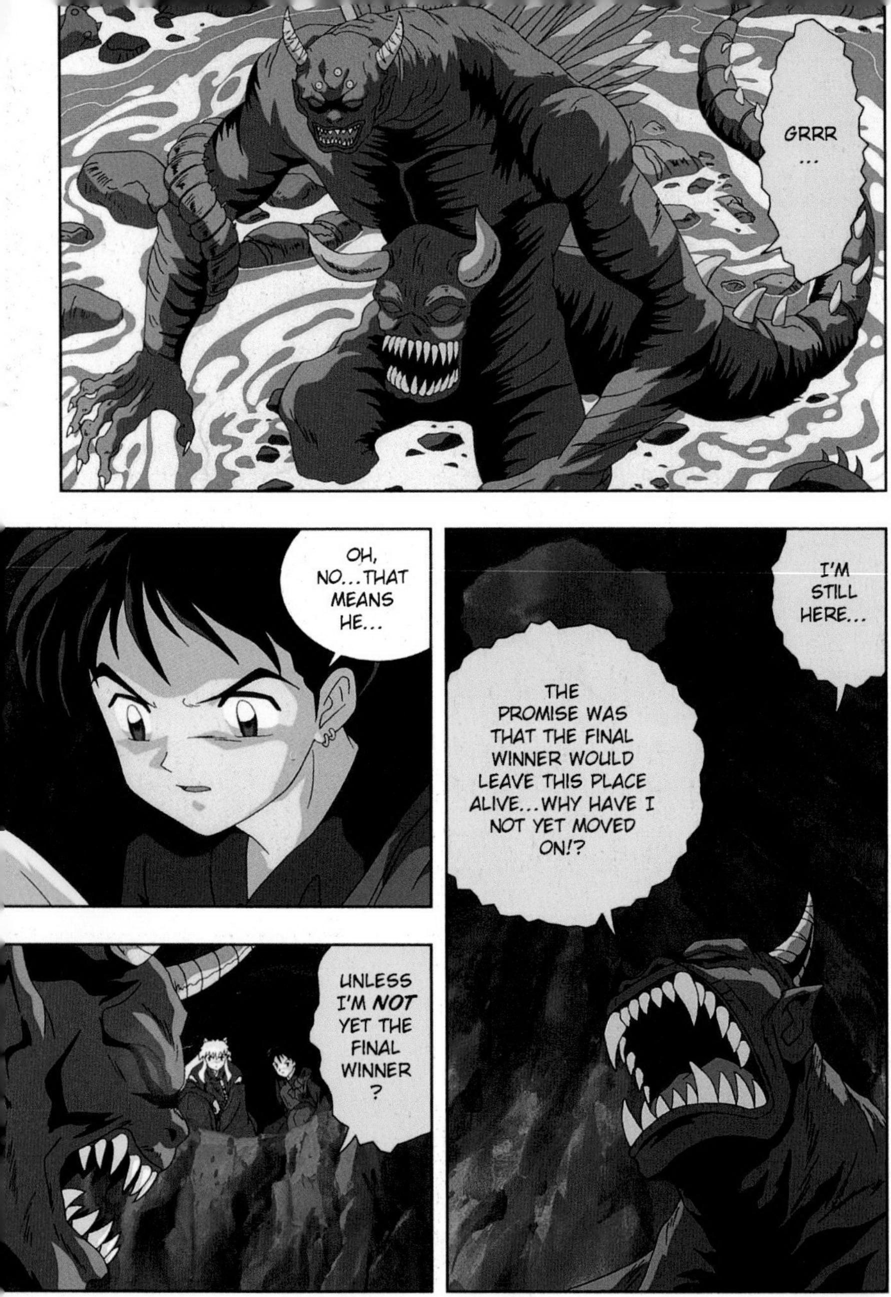
GRRR...
I'M STILL HERE...
THE PROMISE WAS THAT THE FINAL WINNER WOULD LEAVE THIS PLACE ALIVE...WHY HAVE I NOT YET MOVED ON!?
OH, NO...THAT MEANS HE...
UNLESS I'M ***NOT*** YET THE FINAL WINNER?

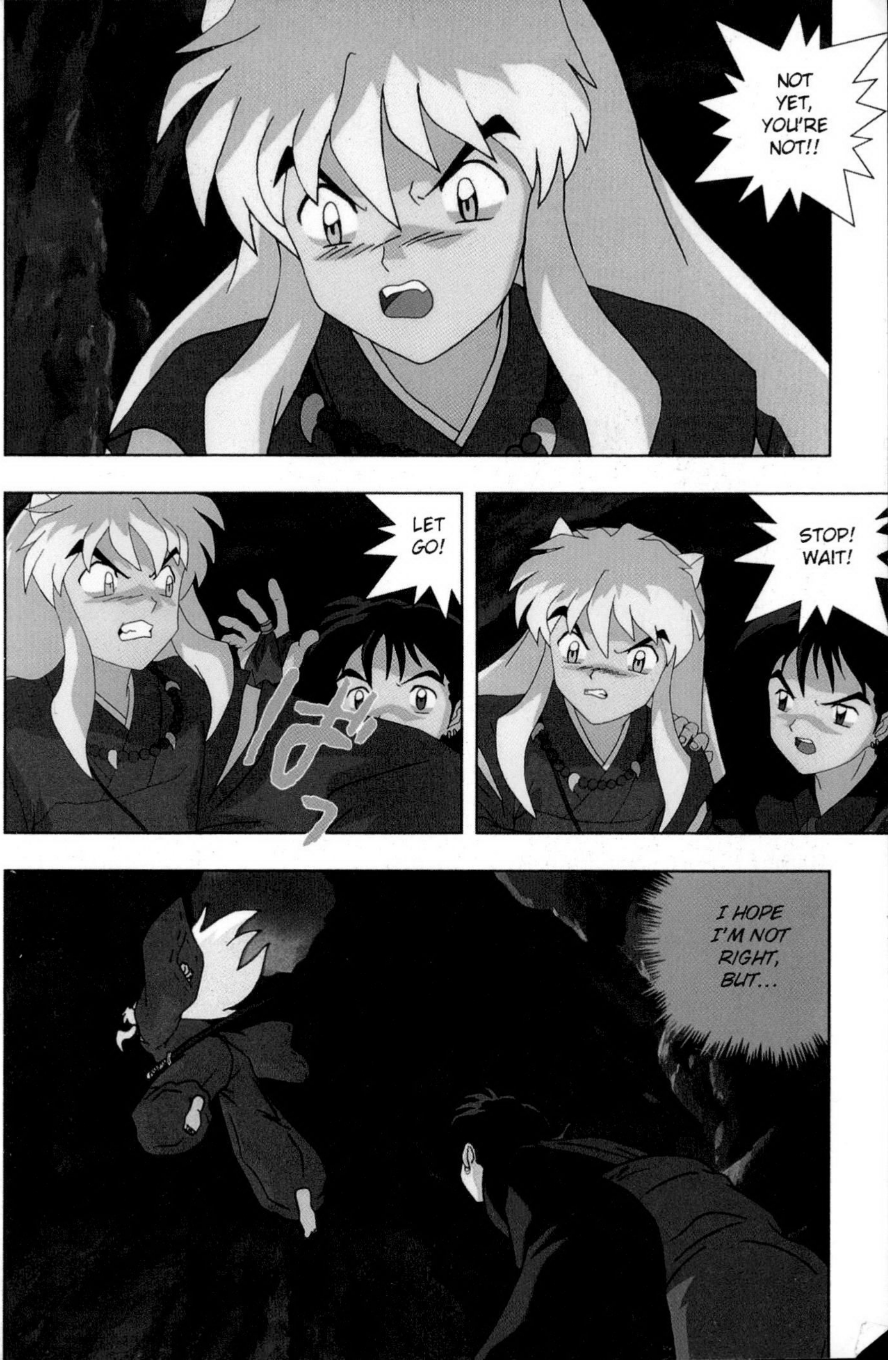
NOT YET, YOU'RE NOT!!
STOP! WAIT!
LET GO!
I HOPE I'M NOT RIGHT, BUT...

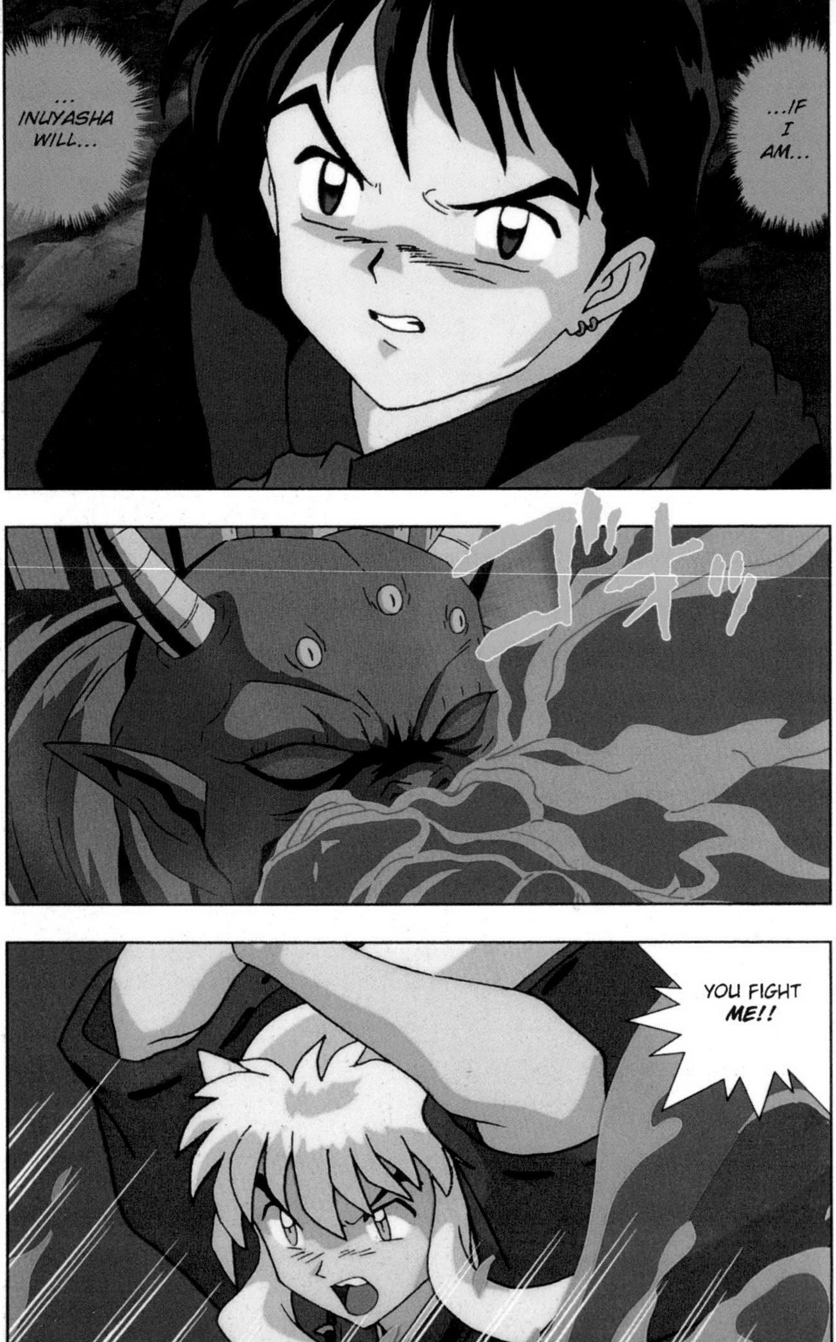
...IF I AM...
...INUYASHA WILL...
ゴオッ
YOU FIGHT ME!!

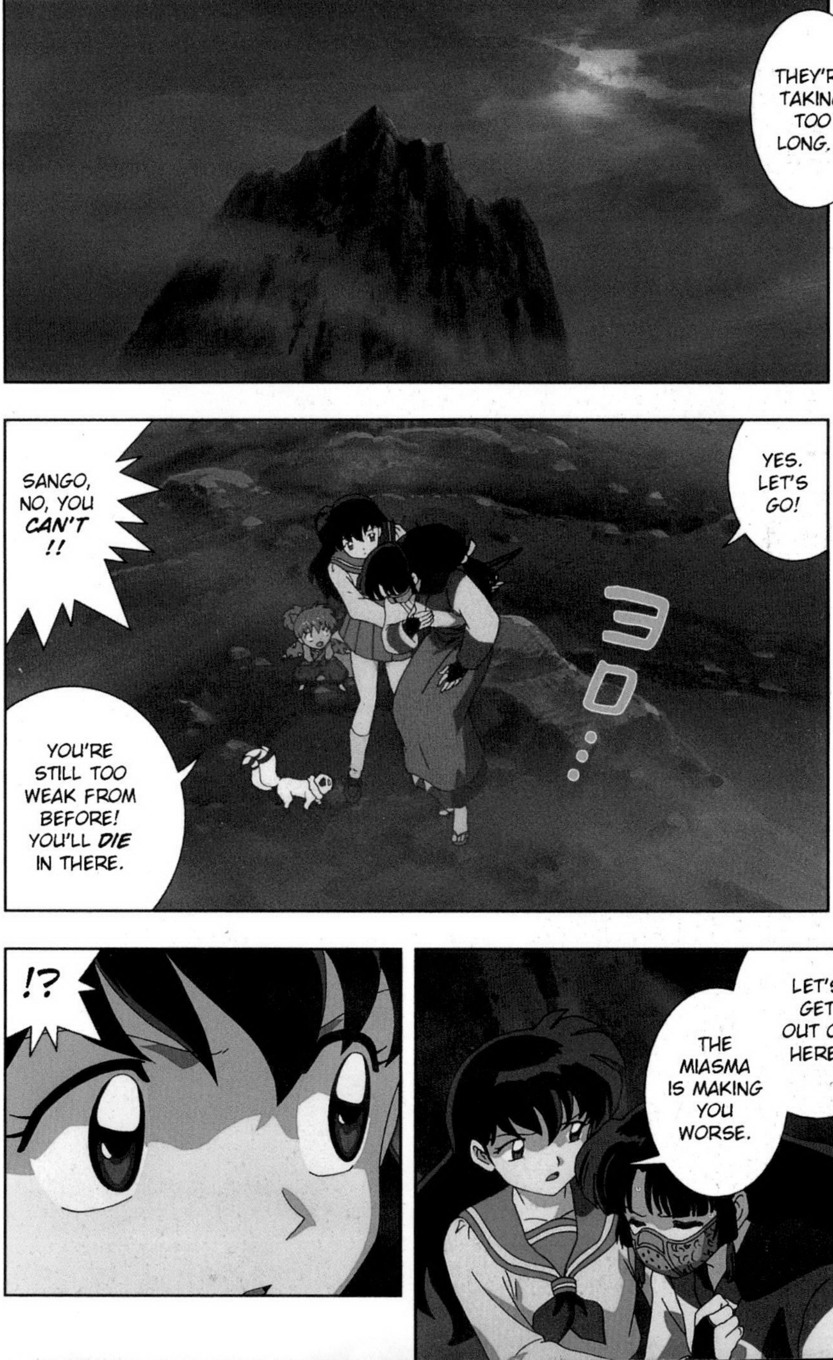
THEY'RE TAKING TOO LONG...
YES. LET'S GO!
ヨロ...
SANGO, NO, YOU *CAN'T* !!
YOU'RE STILL TOO WEAK FROM BEFORE! YOU'LL *DIE* IN THERE.
LET'S GET OUT OF HERE.
THE MIASMA IS MAKING YOU WORSE.
!?

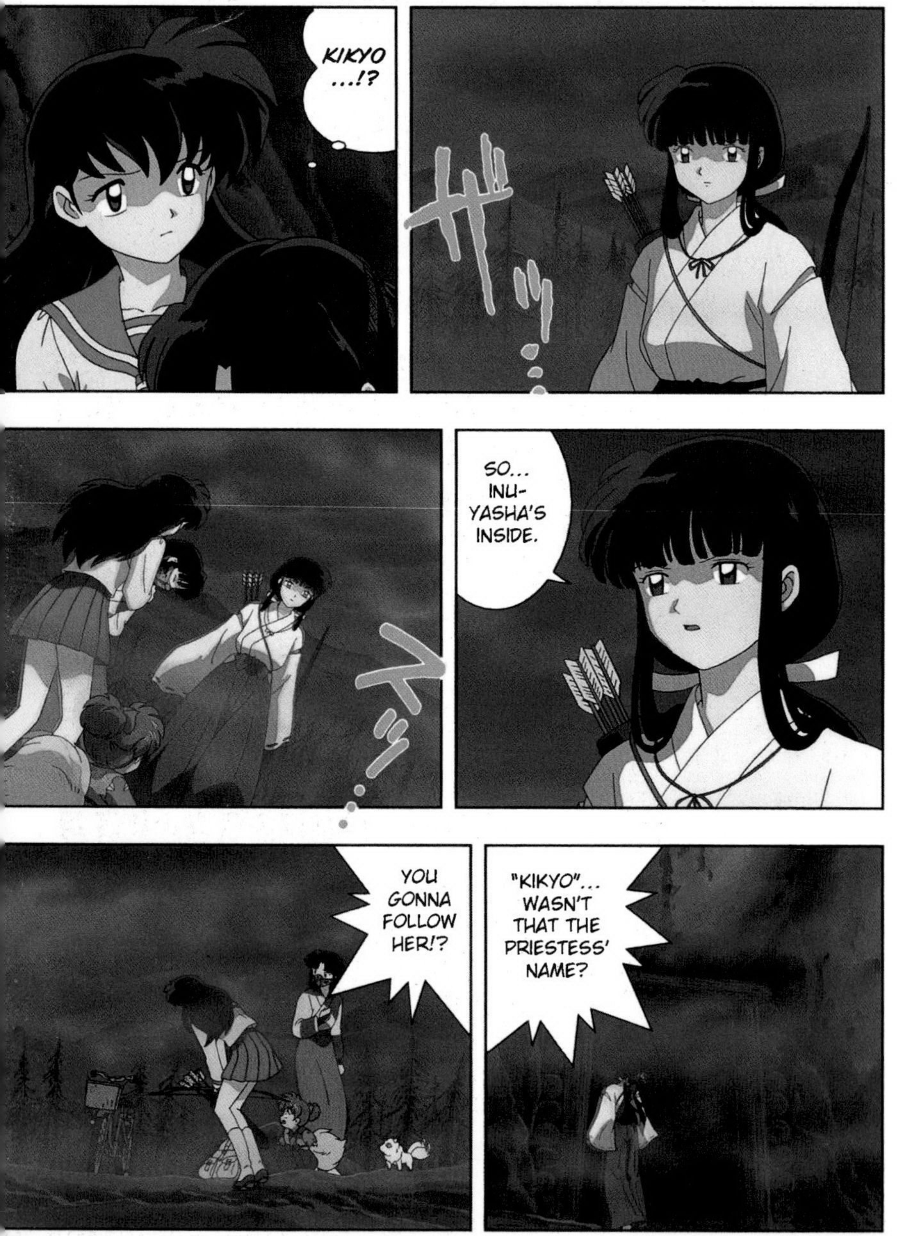
ザッ…
KIKYO ...!?
SO... INU-YASHA'S INSIDE.
スッ…
"KIKYO"... WASN'T THAT THE PRIESTESS' NAME?
YOU GONNA FOLLOW HER!?

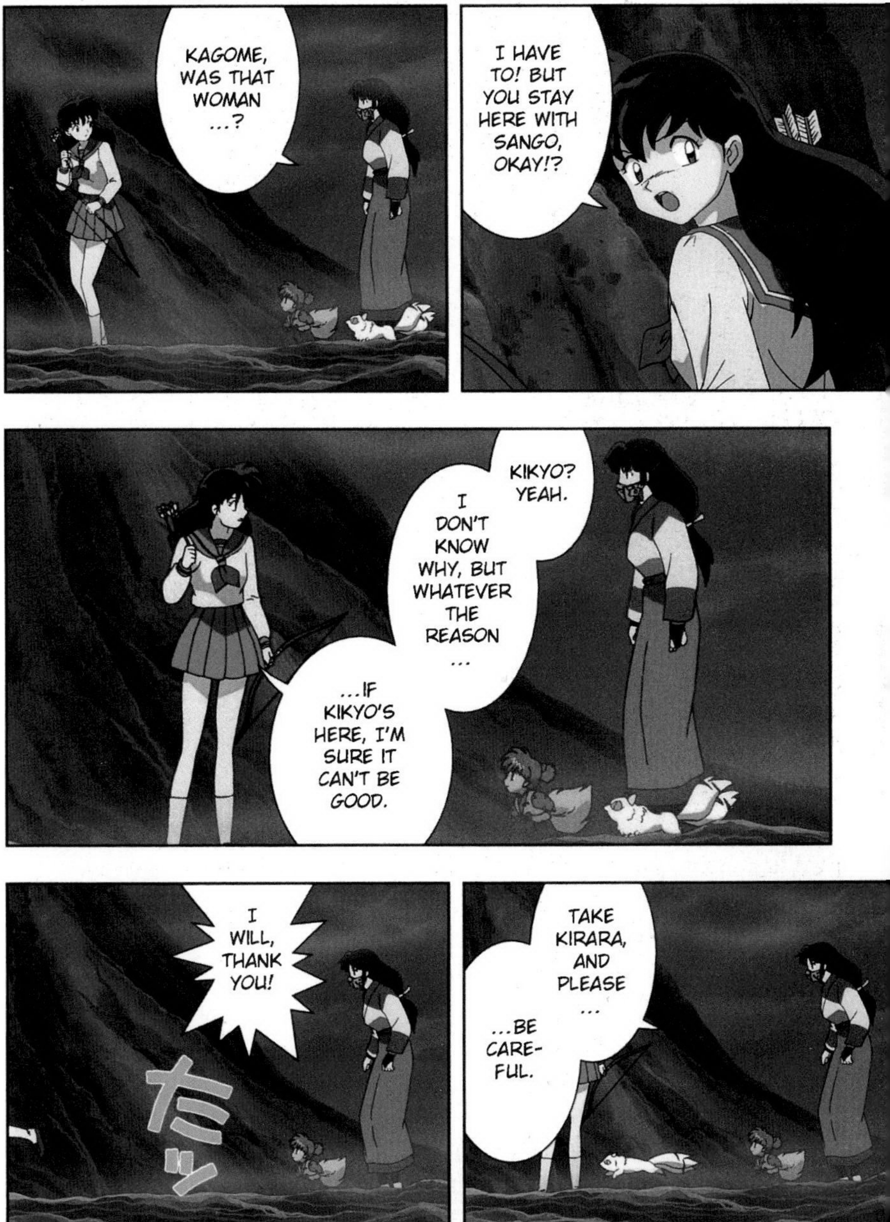
I HAVE TO! BUT YOU STAY HERE WITH SANGO, OKAY!?
KAGOME, WAS THAT WOMAN ...?
KIKYO? YEAH.
I DON'T KNOW WHY, BUT WHATEVER THE REASON ...
...IF KIKYO'S HERE, I'M SURE IT CAN'T BE GOOD.
TAKE KIRARA, AND PLEASE ...
...BE CARE-FUL.
I WILL, THANK YOU!
タッ

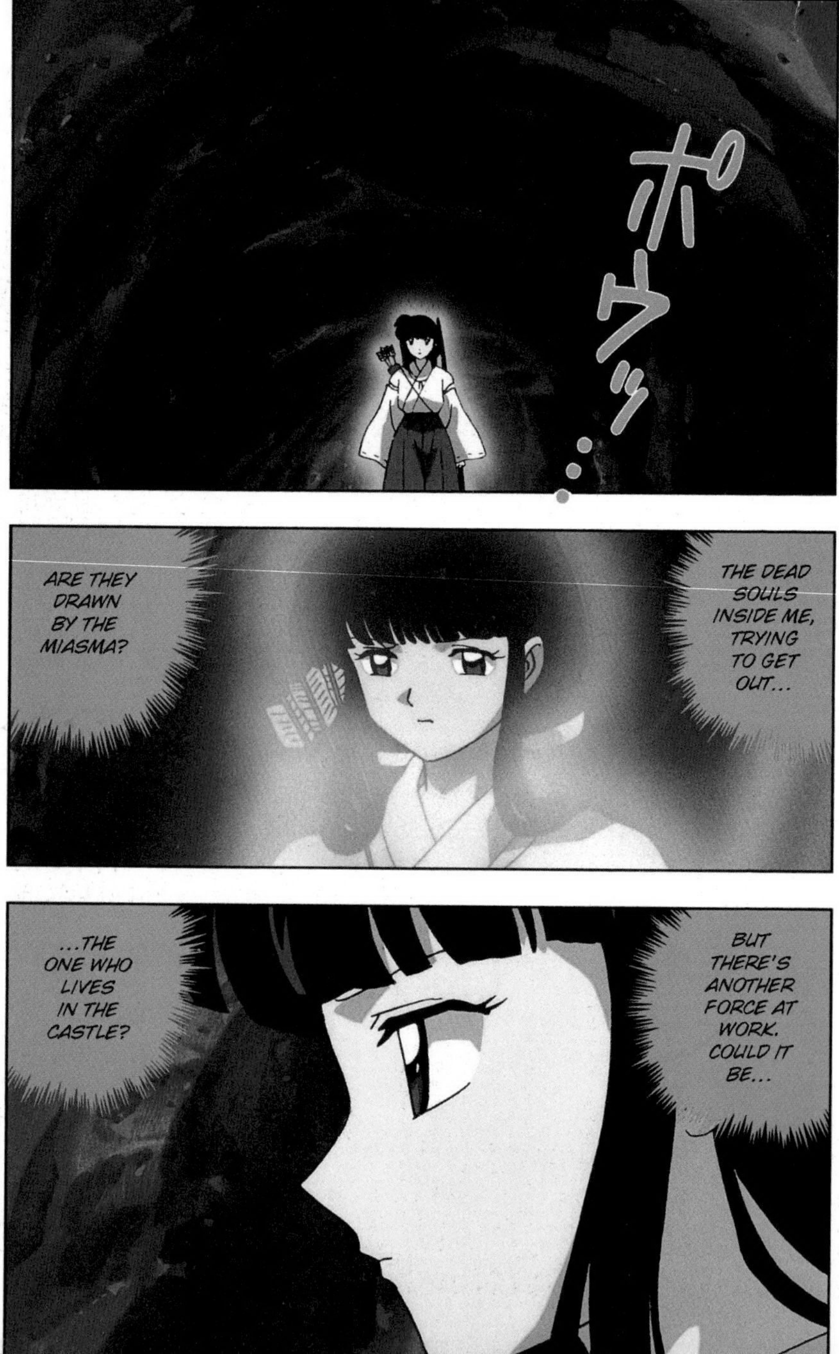
ポウッ…
THE DEAD SOULS INSIDE ME, TRYING TO GET OUT...
ARE THEY DRAWN BY THE MIASMA?
BUT THERE'S ANOTHER FORCE AT WORK. COULD IT BE...
...THE ONE WHO LIVES IN THE CASTLE?

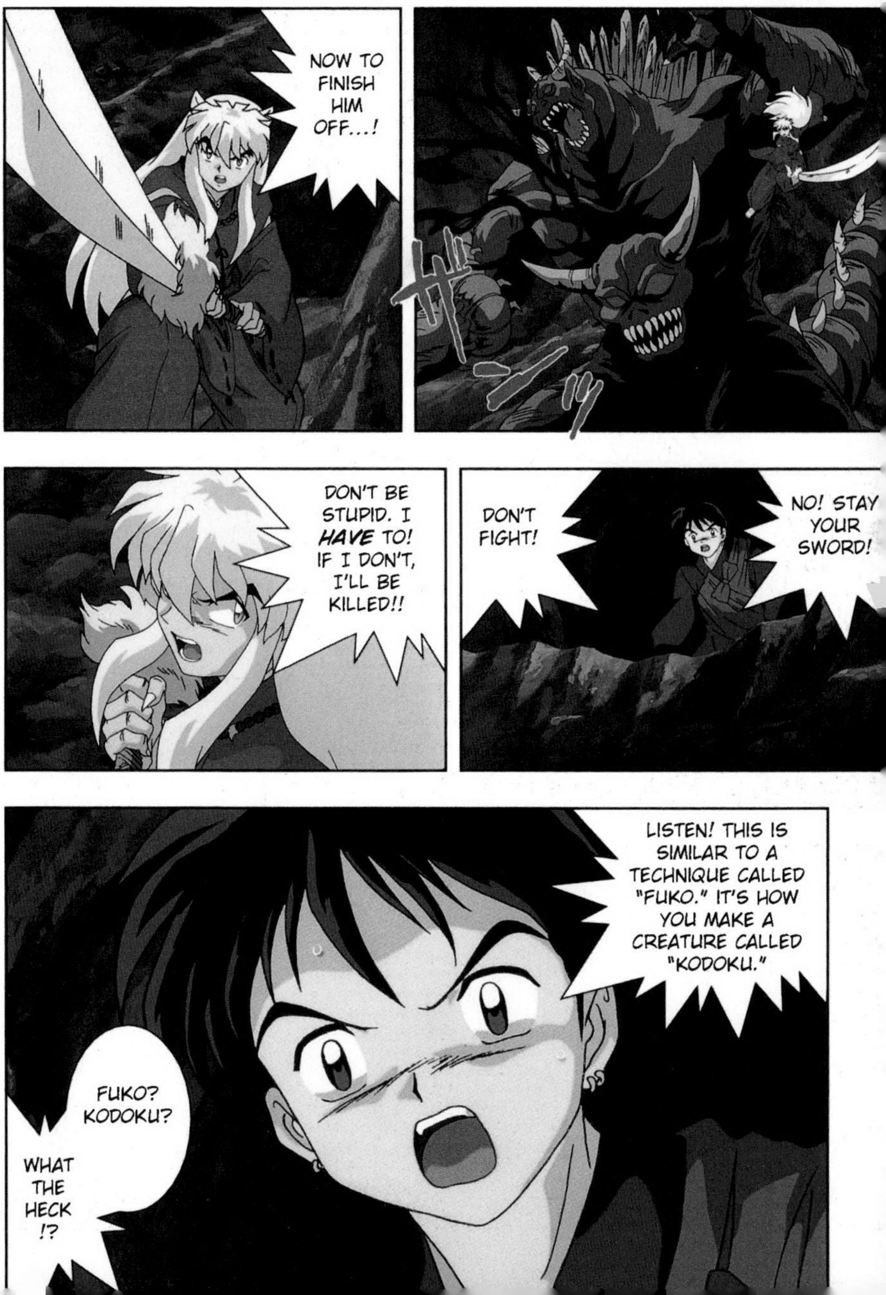
NOW TO FINISH HIM OFF...!
NO! STAY YOUR SWORD!
DON'T FIGHT!
DON'T BE STUPID. I *HAVE* TO! IF I DON'T, I'LL BE KILLED!!
LISTEN! THIS IS SIMILAR TO A TECHNIQUE CALLED "FUKO." IT'S HOW YOU MAKE A CREATURE CALLED "KODOKU."
FUKO? KODOKU?
WHAT THE HECK !?

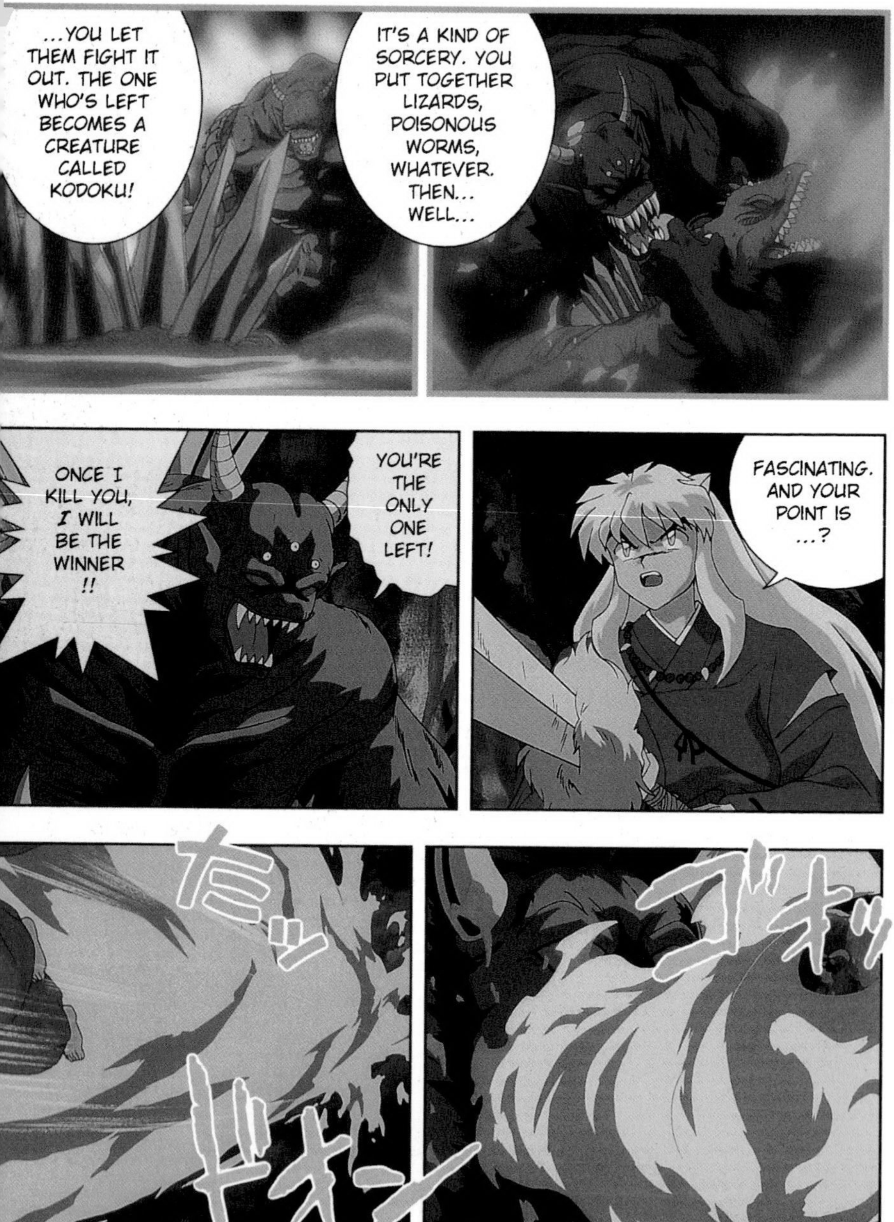
IT'S A KIND OF SORCERY. YOU PUT TOGETHER LIZARDS, POISONOUS WORMS, WHATEVER. THEN... WELL...
...YOU LET THEM FIGHT IT OUT. THE ONE WHO'S LEFT BECOMES A CREATURE CALLED KODOKU!
FASCINATING. AND YOUR POINT IS ...?
YOU'RE THE ONLY ONE LEFT!
ONCE I KILL YOU, *I* WILL BE THE WINNER !!
ゴオッ
だッ
ドオーン

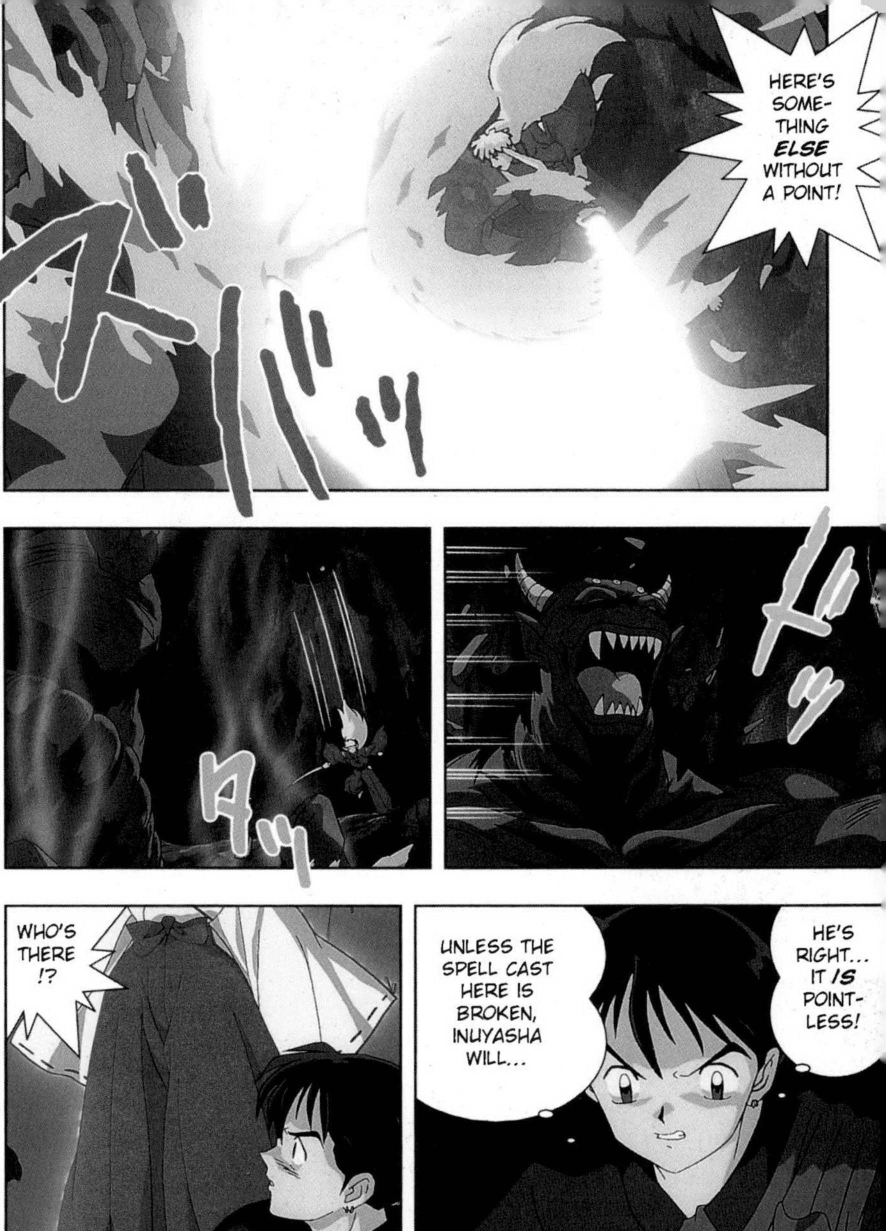
ズバッ
HERE'S SOME-THING *ELSE* WITHOUT A POINT!
ドッ
タッ
HE'S RIGHT... IT *IS* POINT-LESS!
UNLESS THE SPELL CAST HERE IS BROKEN, INUYASHA WILL...
WHO'S THERE !?

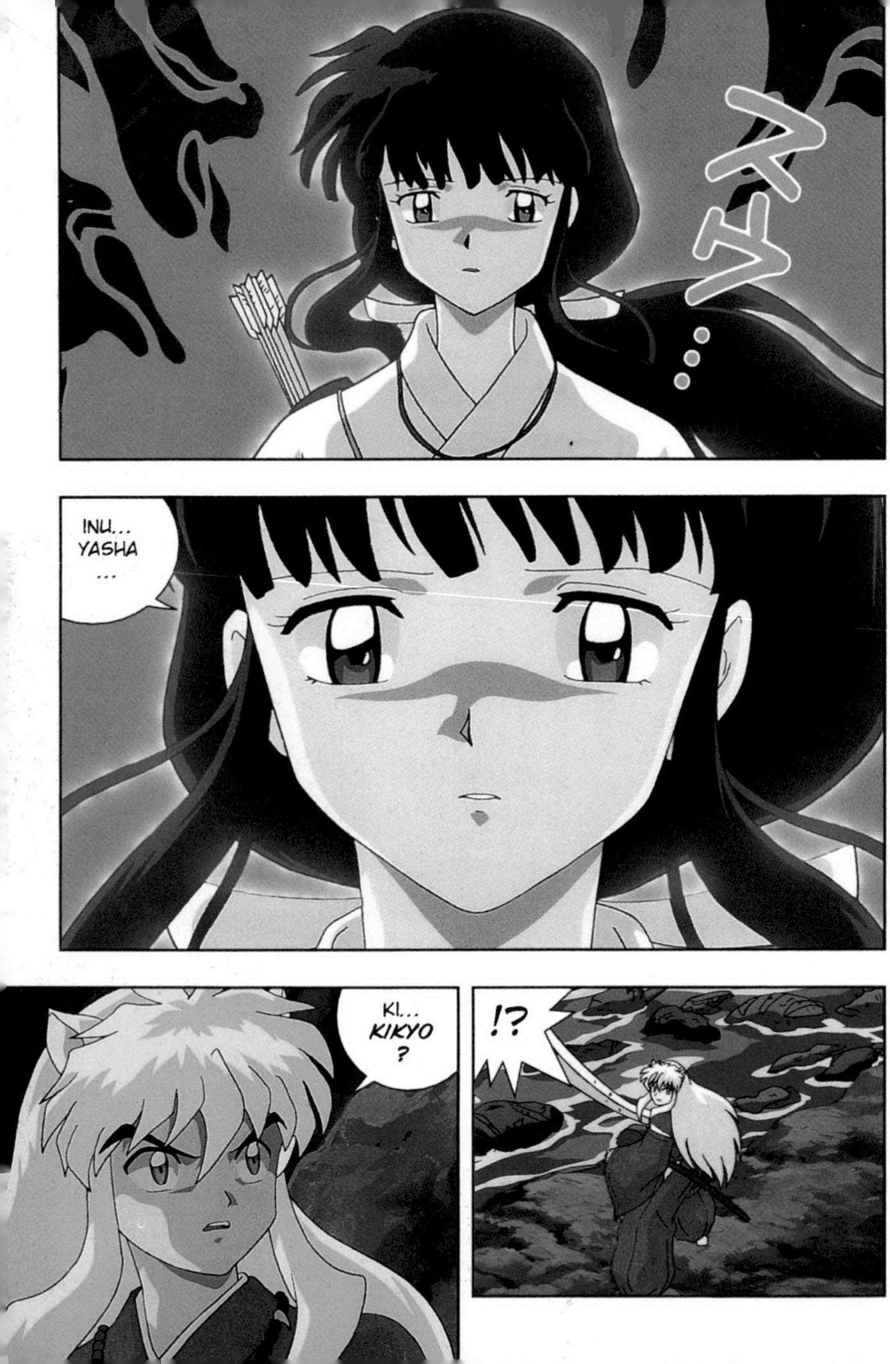
スッ…
INU... YASHA ...
!?
KI... KIKYO ?

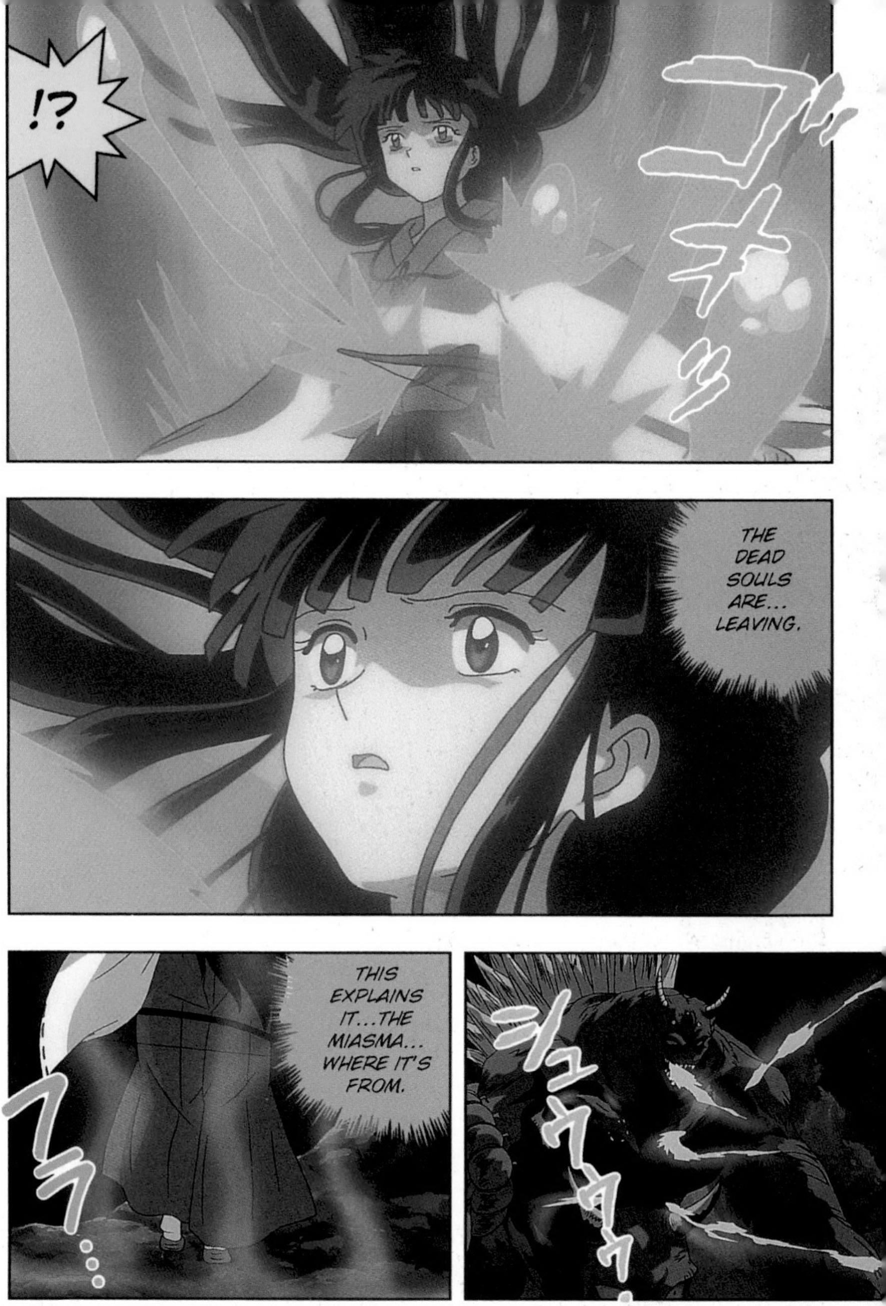
!?
THE DEAD SOULS ARE... LEAVING.
THIS EXPLAINS IT...THE MIASMA... WHERE IT'S FROM.
フラ...

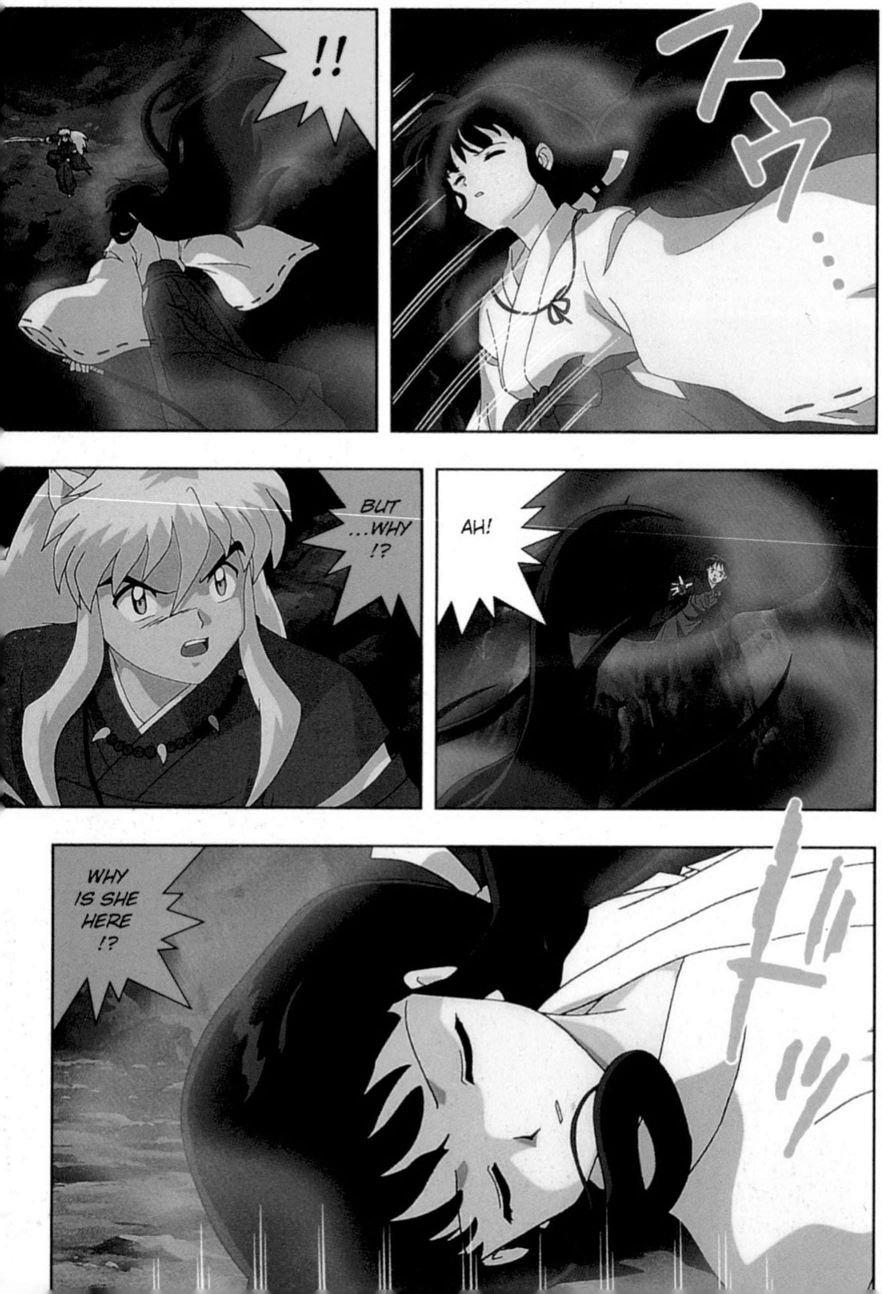
フゥ…
!!
AH!
BUT ...WHY !?
ドッ
WHY IS SHE HERE !?

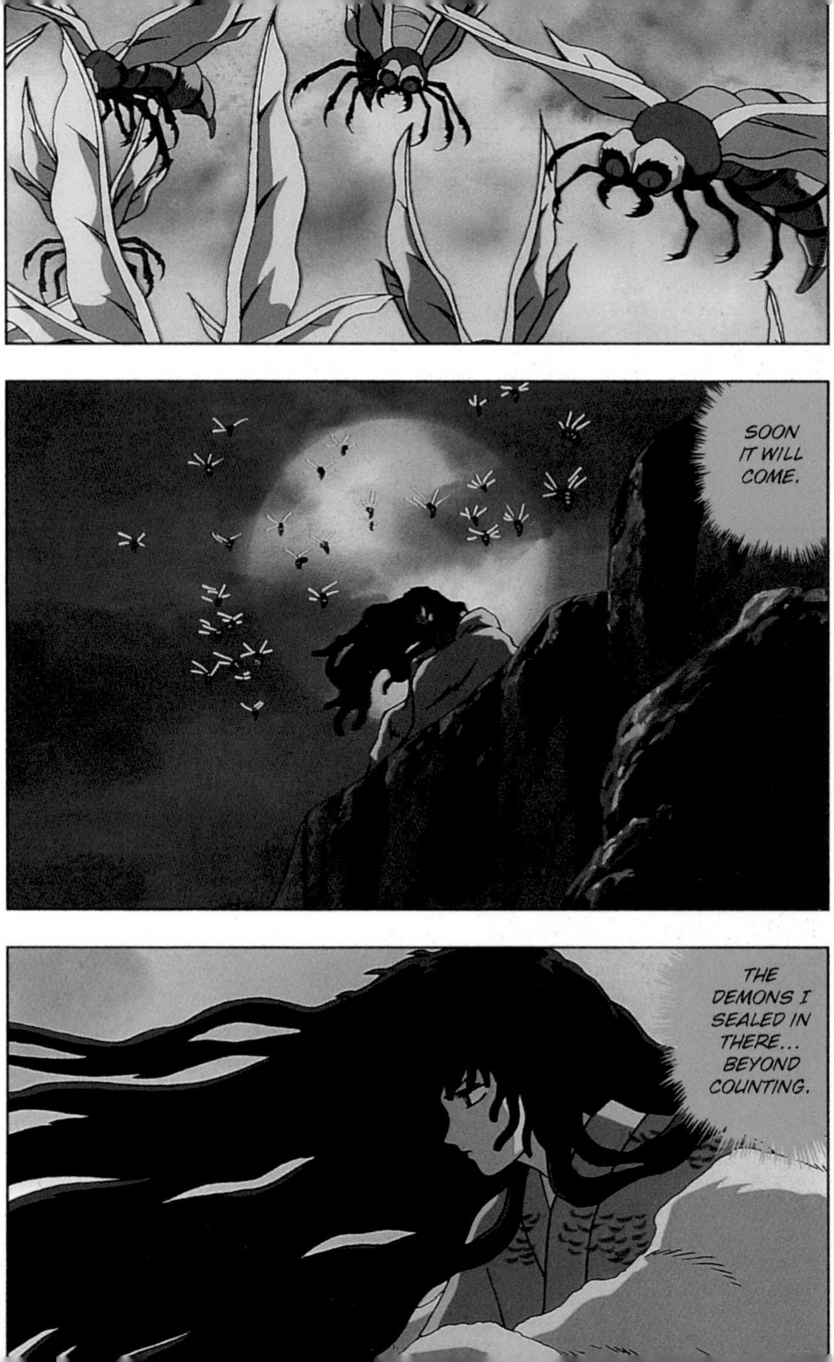
SOON IT WILL COME.
THE DEMONS I SEALED IN THERE... BEYOND COUNTING.

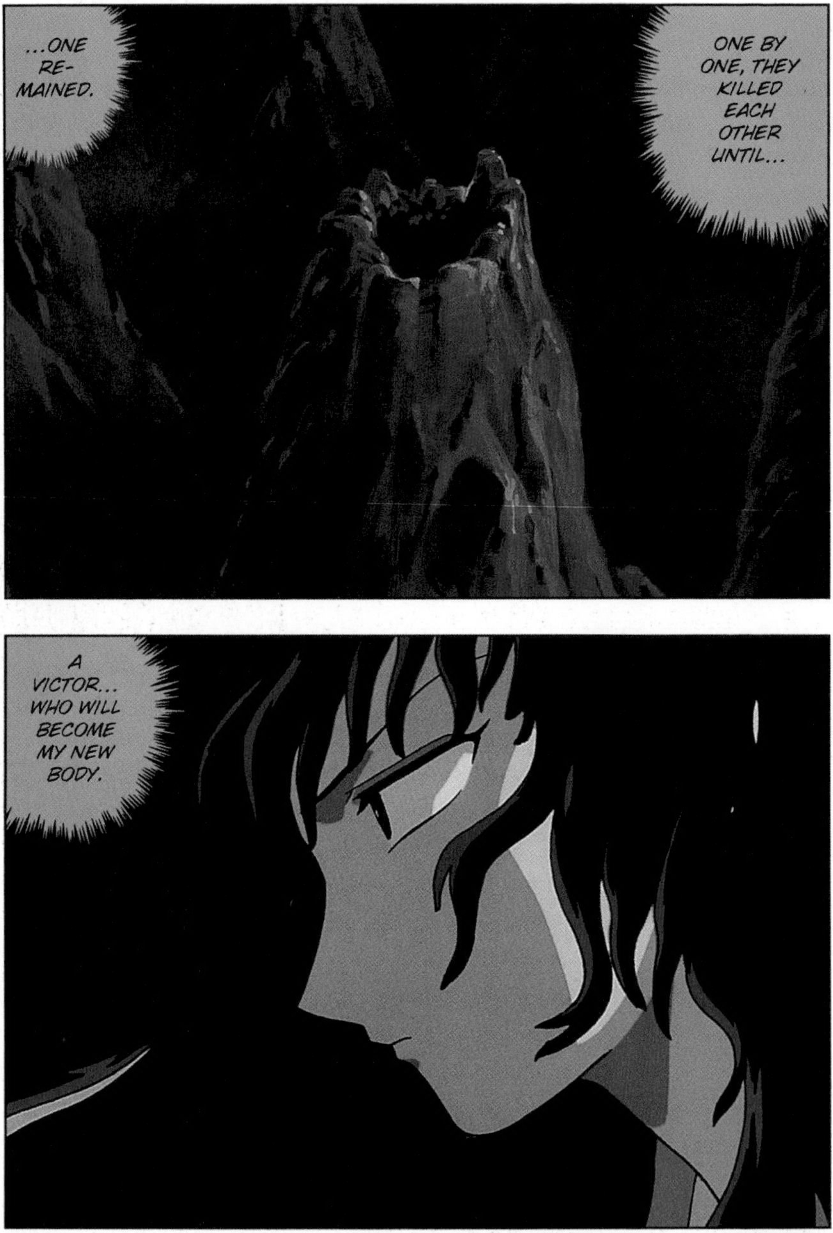
ONE BY ONE, THEY KILLED EACH OTHER UNTIL...
...ONE RE-MAINED.
A VICTOR... WHO WILL BECOME MY NEW BODY.

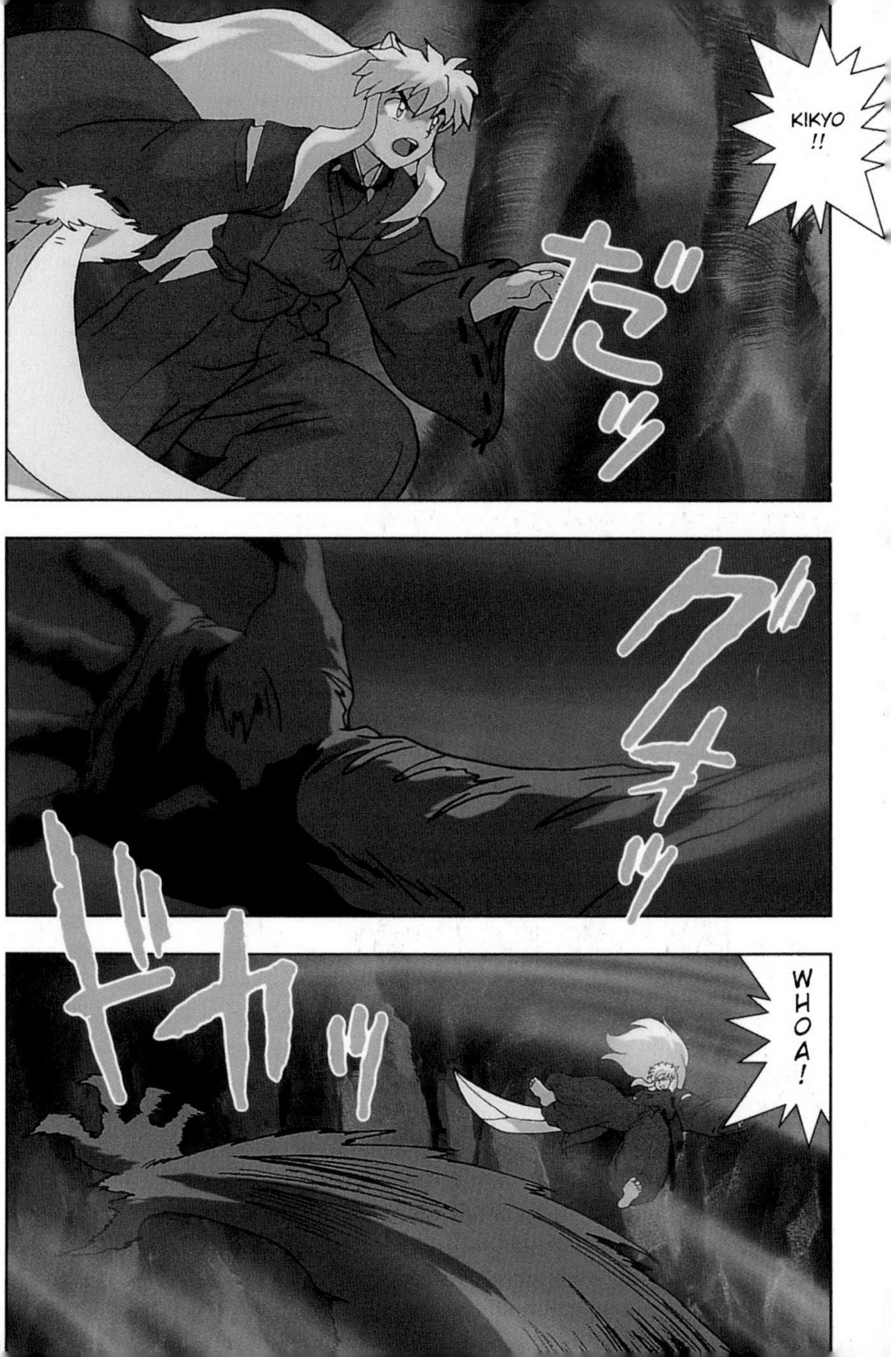
KIKYO !!
だッ
ドカッ
WHOA!

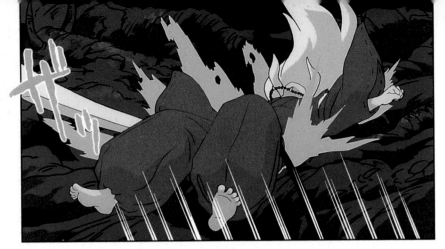

UNH
...

KIKYO
...!!

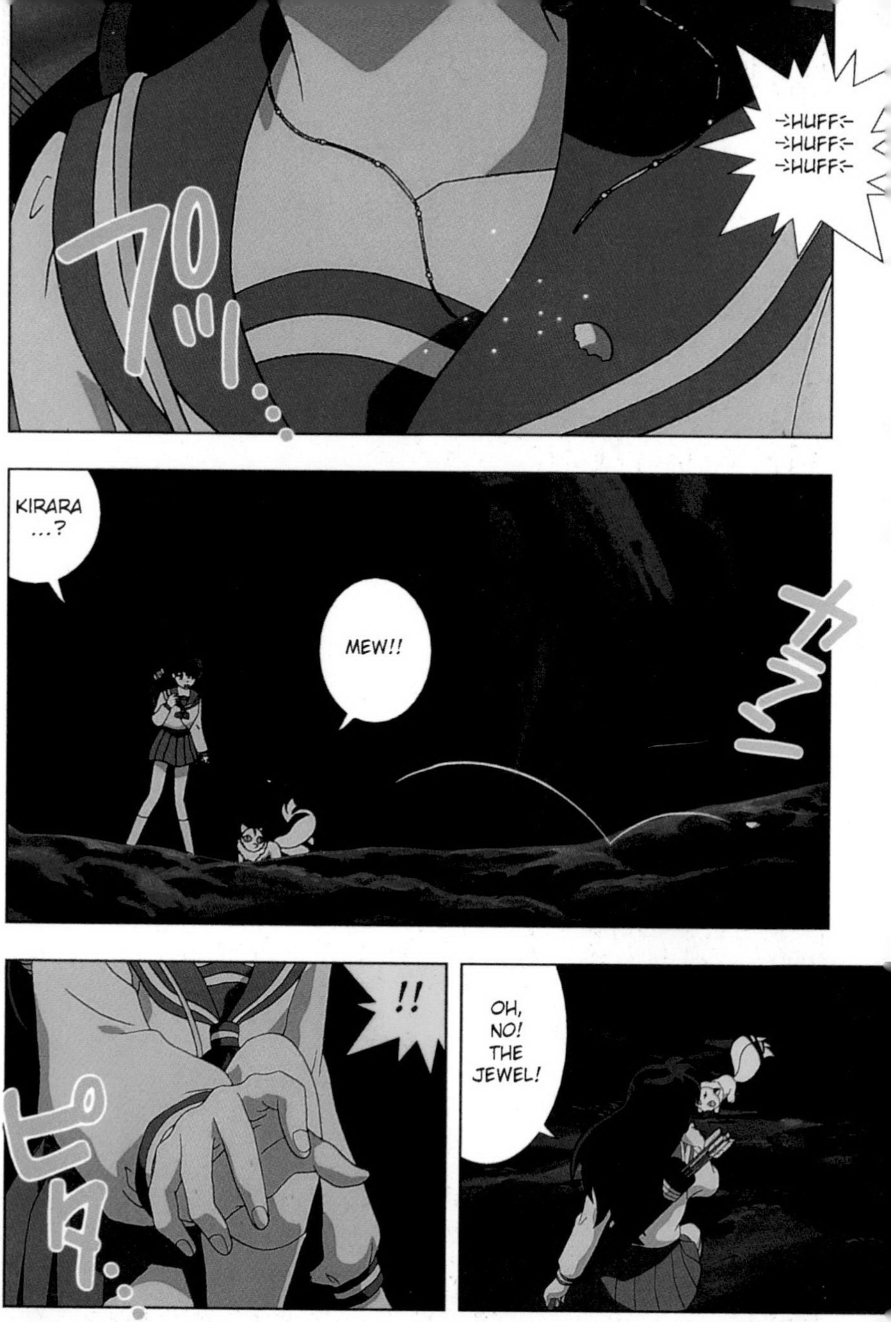
HUFF HUFF HUFF
KIRARA ...?
MEW!!
OH, NO! THE JEWEL!
!!

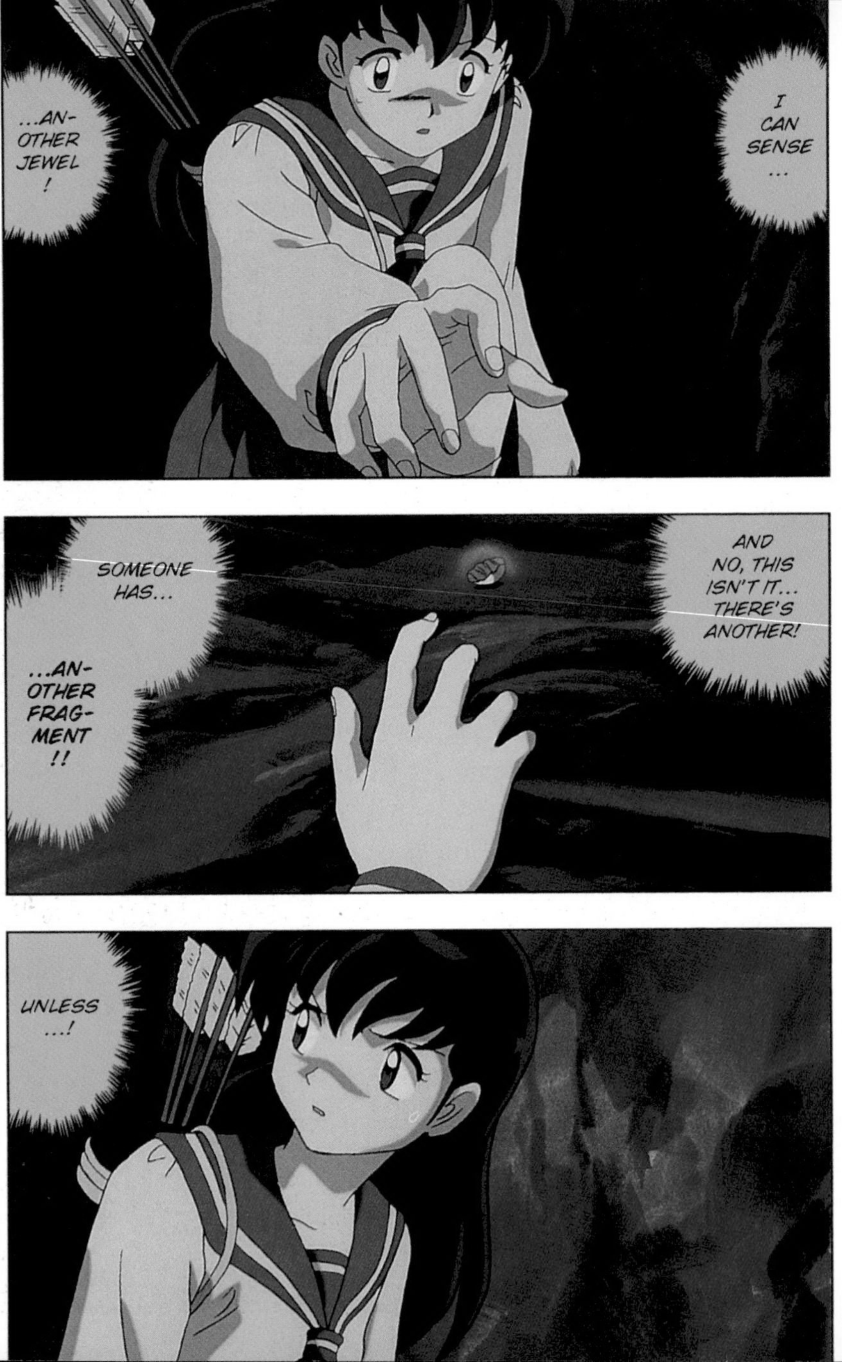
I CAN SENSE...
...ANOTHER JEWEL!
AND NO, THIS ISN'T IT... THERE'S ANOTHER!
SOMEONE HAS...
...ANOTHER FRAGMENT!!
UNLESS ...!

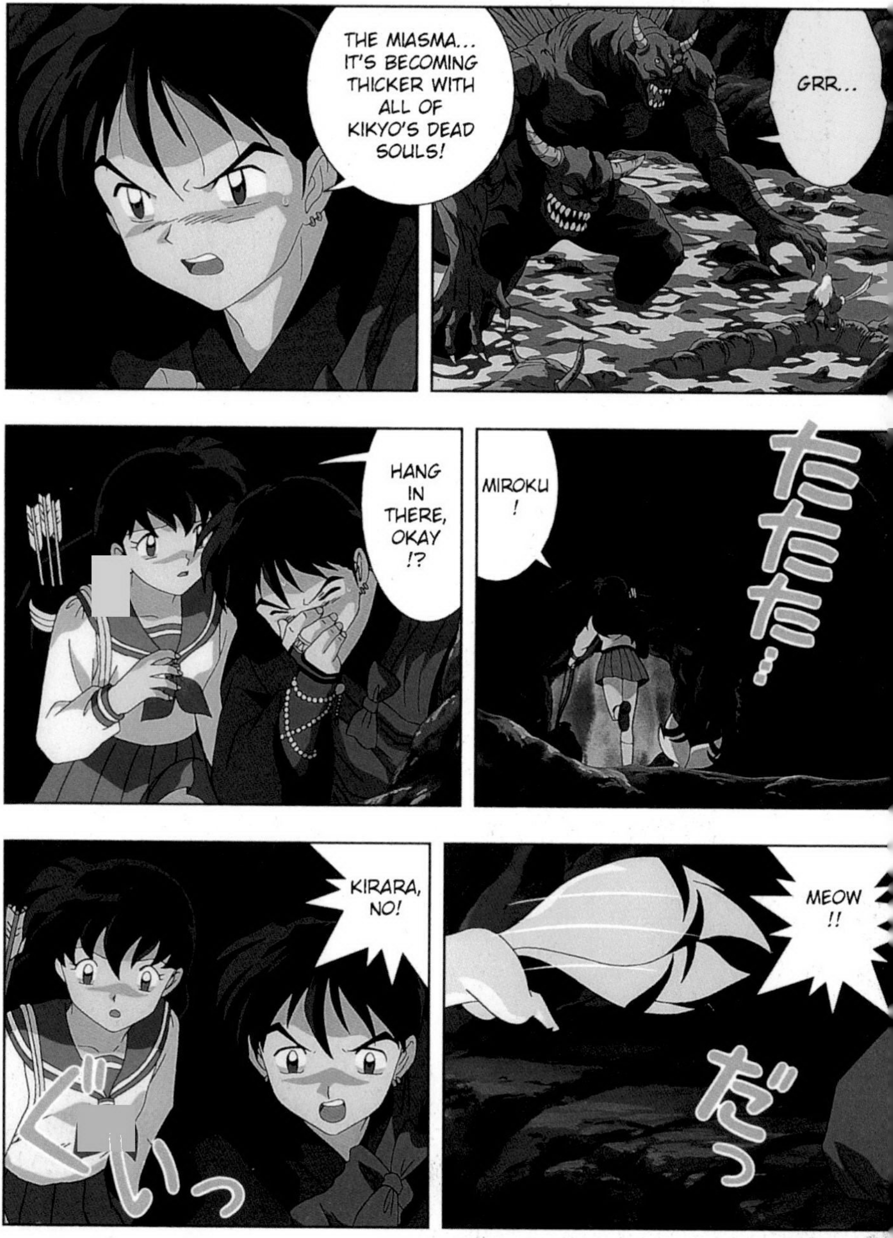
GRR...
THE MIASMA... IT'S BECOMING THICKER WITH ALL OF KIKYO'S DEAD SOULS!
たたた…
MIROKU!
HANG IN THERE, OKAY!?
MEOW!!
だっ
KIRARA, NO!
ぐいっ

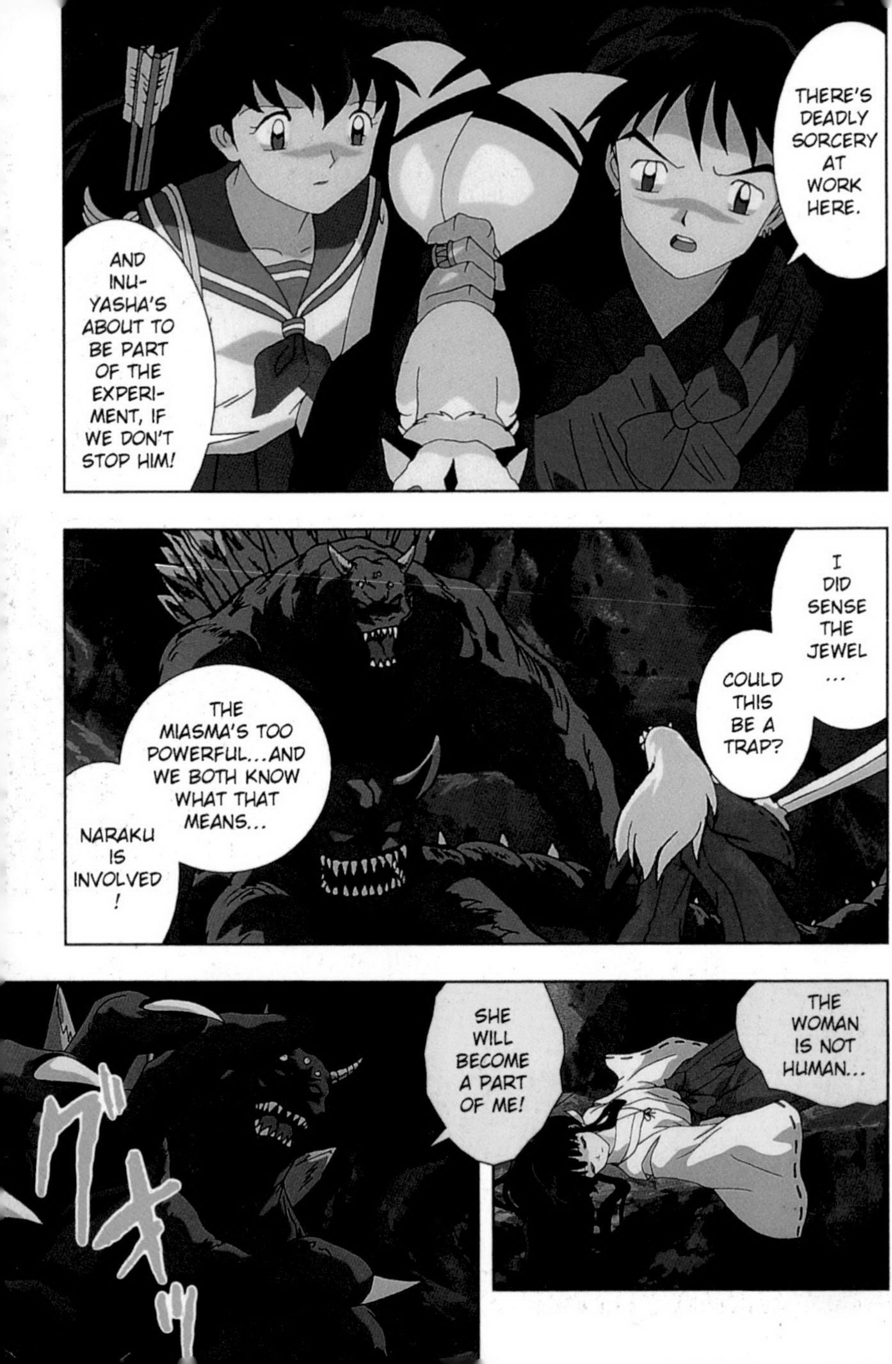
THERE'S DEADLY SORCERY AT WORK HERE.
AND INU-YASHA'S ABOUT TO BE PART OF THE EXPERI-MENT, IF WE DON'T STOP HIM!
I DID SENSE THE JEWEL...
COULD THIS BE A TRAP?
THE MIASMA'S TOO POWERFUL...AND WE BOTH KNOW WHAT THAT MEANS...
NARAKU IS INVOLVED!
THE WOMAN IS NOT HUMAN...
SHE WILL BECOME A PART OF ME!
グオッ

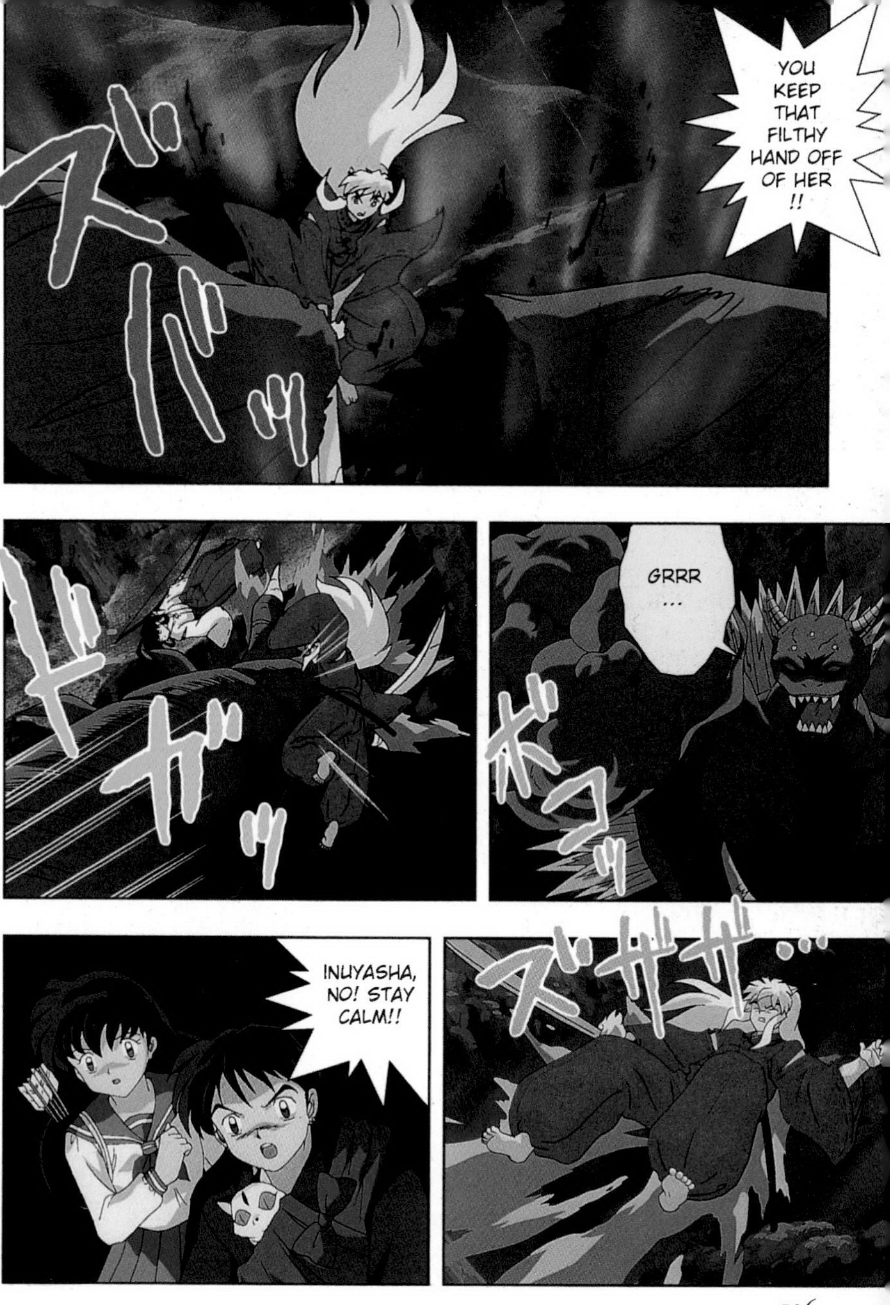
ズバッ
YOU KEEP THAT FILTHY HAND OFF OF HER !!
GRRR ...
ボコッ
ドガッ
ズザザ…
INUYASHA, NO! STAY CALM!!

I AM GOING TO PROTECT KIKYO!!

NO, I WILL NOT...

... "STAY CALM"!

KAGOME ...

...!!

HYAH!!

WHAT...!?

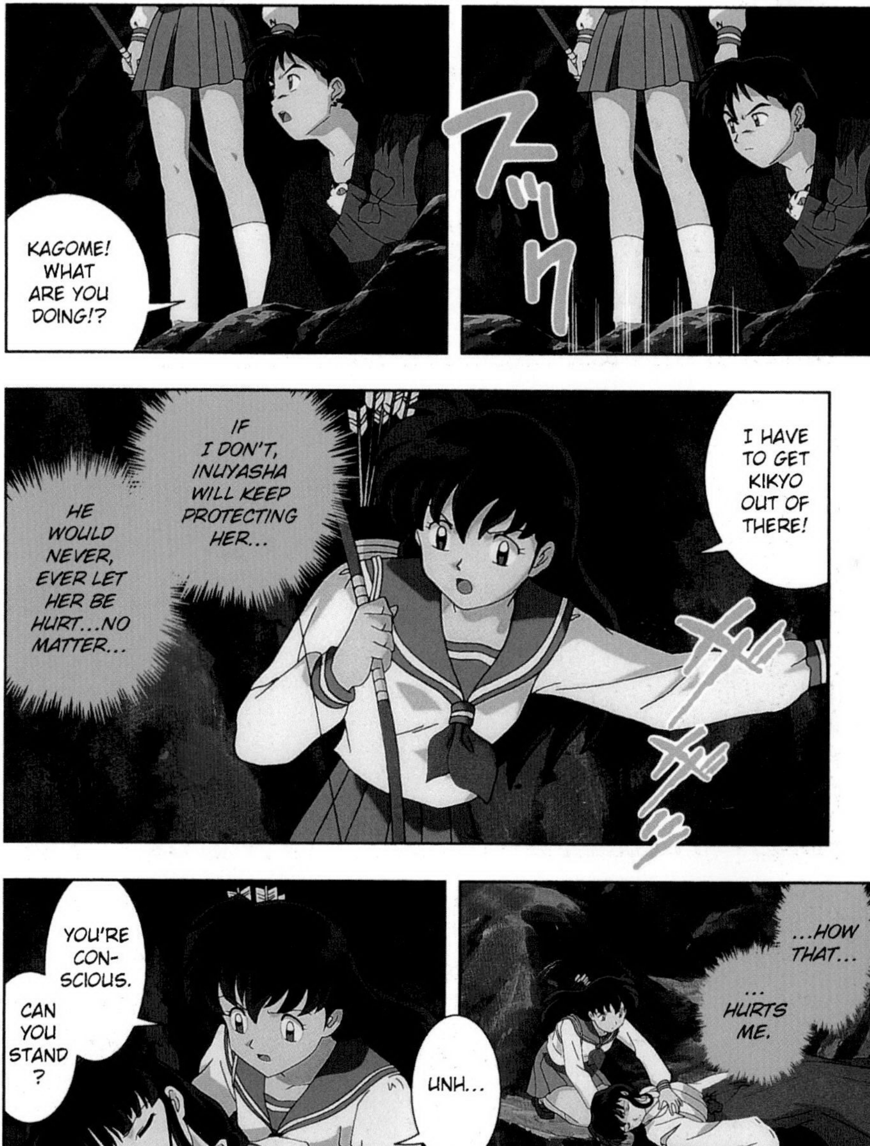
スック
KAGOME! WHAT ARE YOU DOING!?
I HAVE TO GET KIKYO OUT OF THERE!
IF I DON'T, INUYASHA WILL KEEP PROTECTING HER...
HE WOULD NEVER, EVER LET HER BE HURT...NO MATTER...
...HOW THAT...
...HURTS ME.
YOU'RE CON-SCIOUS.
CAN YOU STAND?
UNH...

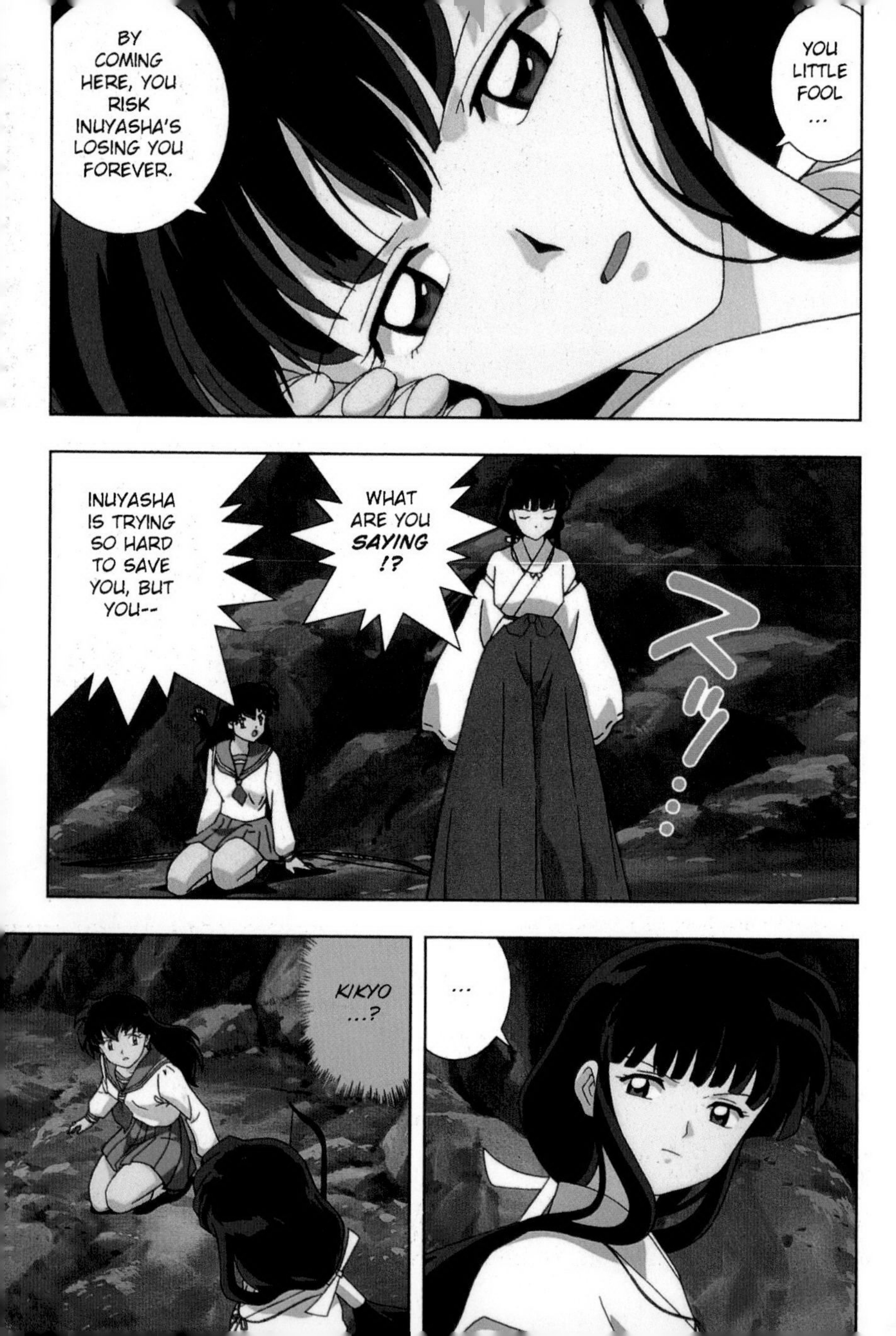
YOU LITTLE FOOL ...
BY COMING HERE, YOU RISK INUYASHA'S LOSING YOU FOREVER.
スッ…
WHAT ARE YOU *SAYING* !?
INUYASHA IS TRYING SO HARD TO SAVE YOU, BUT YOU--
...
KIKYO ...?

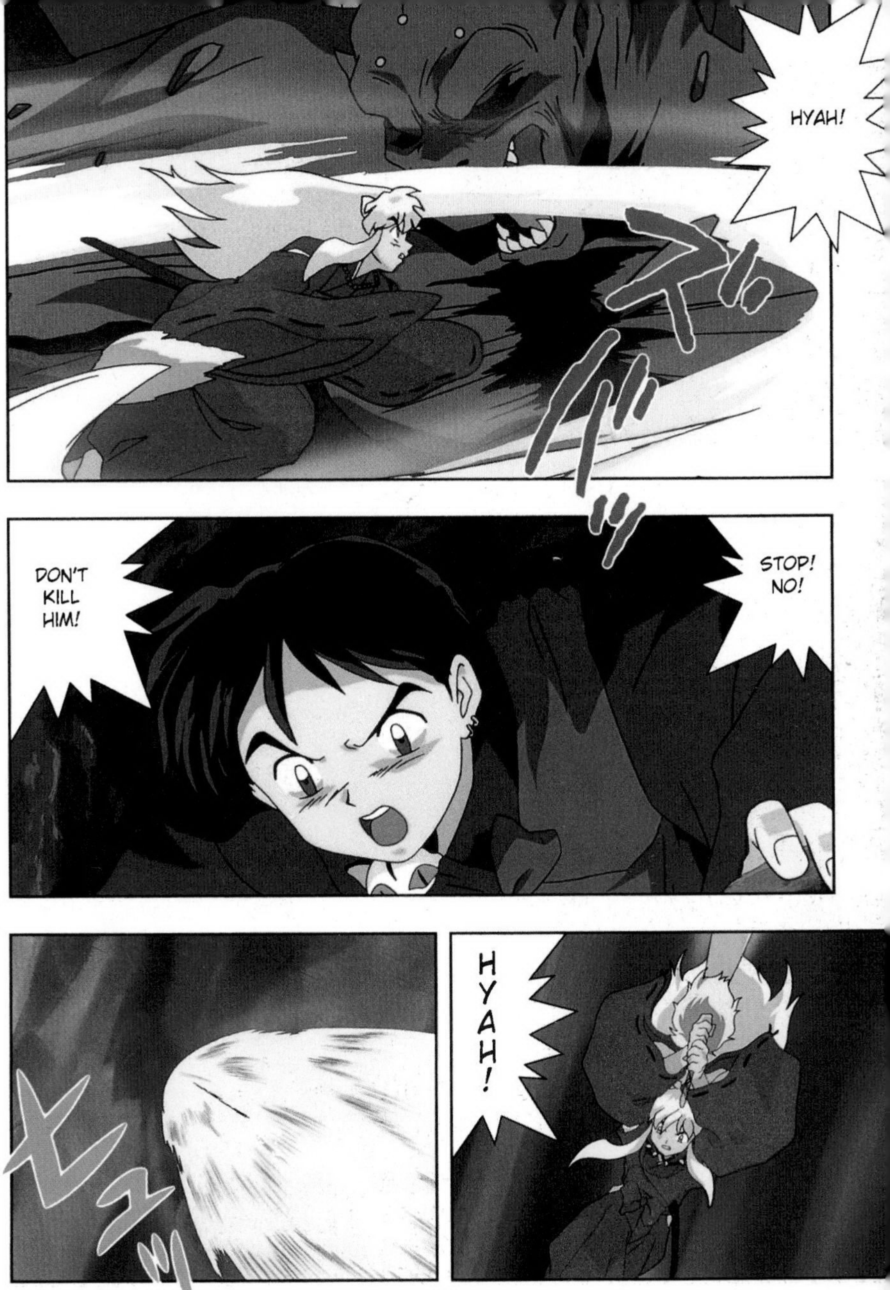
HYAH!
STOP! NO!
DON'T KILL HIM!
HYAH!

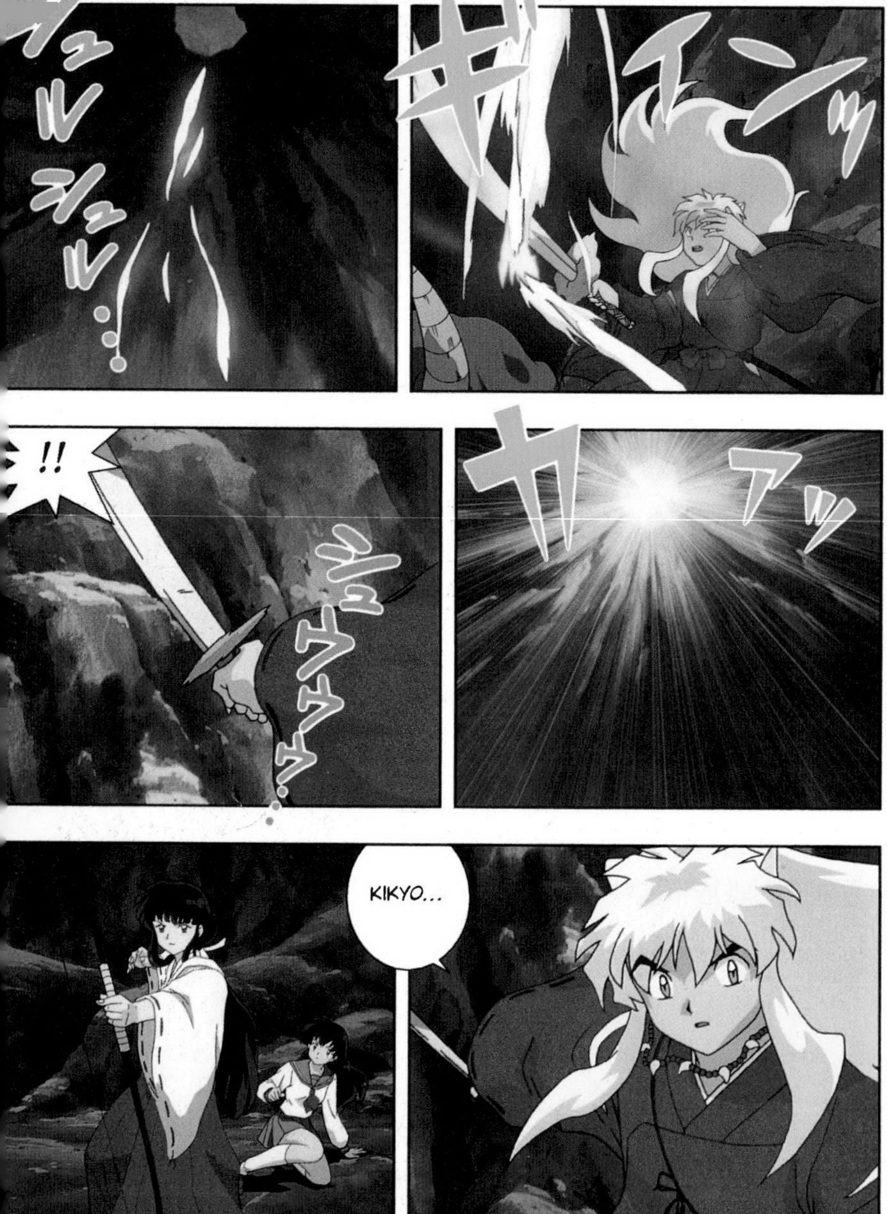
ギインッ
カァッ
!!
シュウウゥ…
KIKYO...

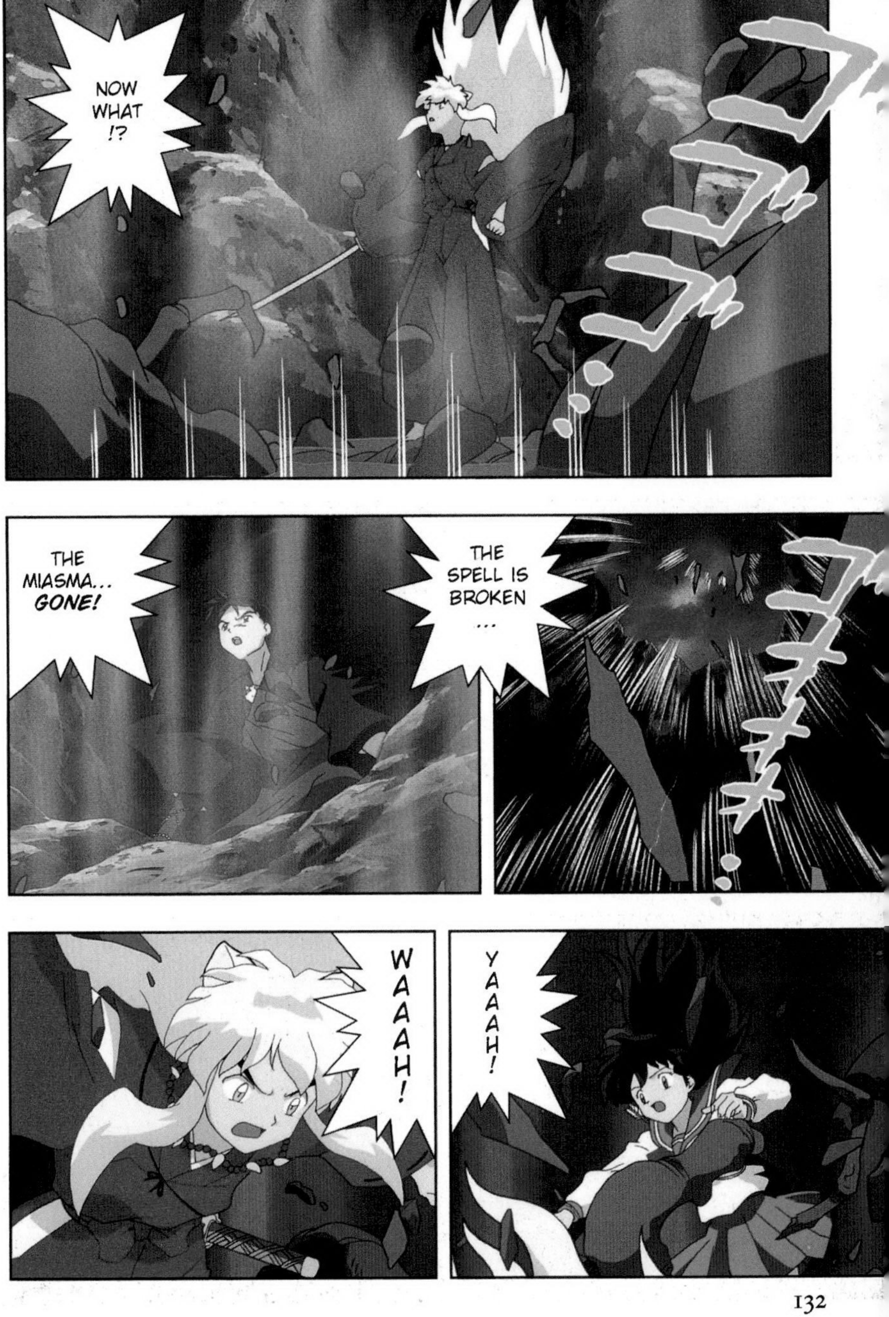
NOW WHAT!?
THE SPELL IS BROKEN...
THE MIASMA... **GONE!**
YAAAAH!
WAAAAH!

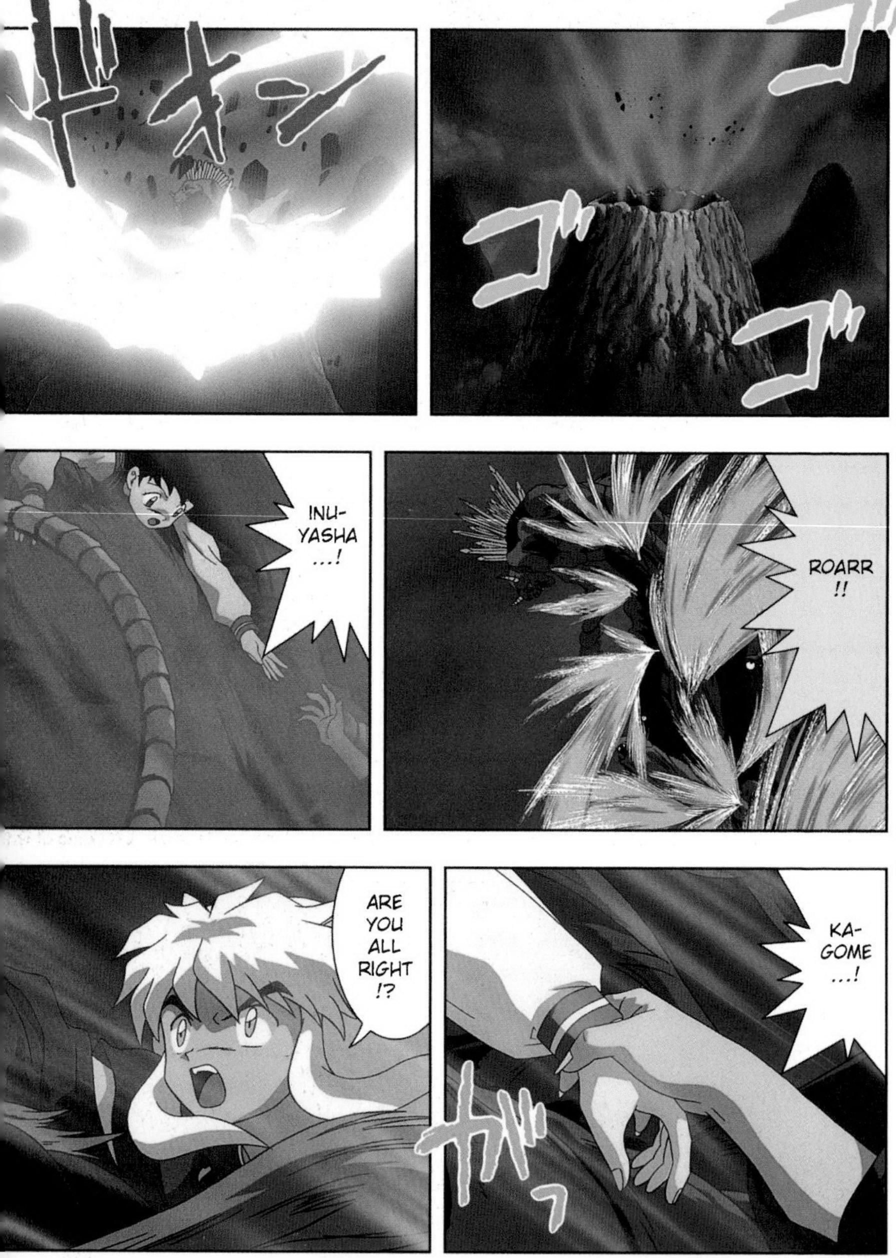
ゴゴゴ
ドオーン
ROARR !!
INU-YASHA ...!
KA-GOME ...!
ガッ
ARE YOU ALL RIGHT !?

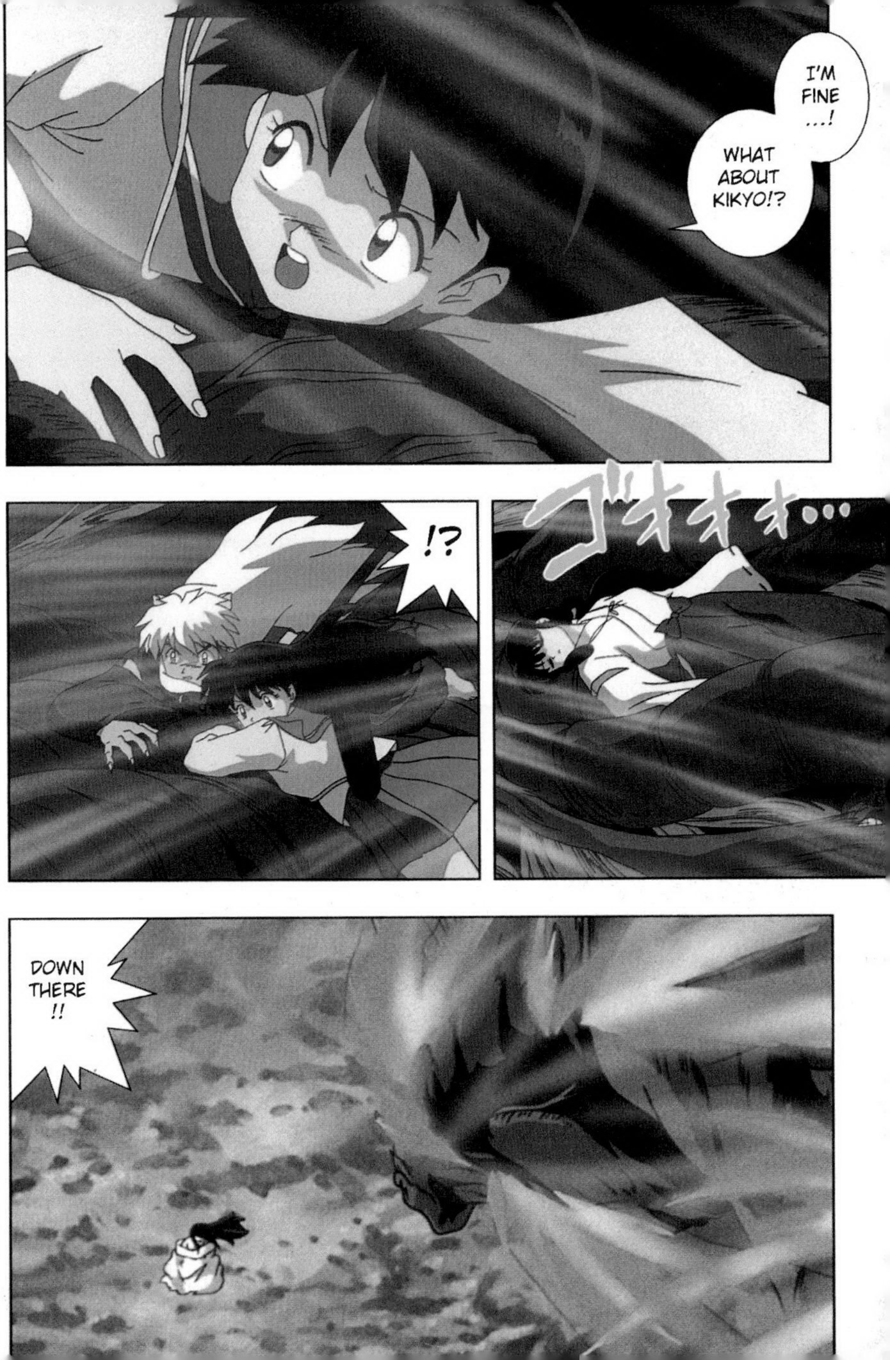
I'M FINE ...!
WHAT ABOUT KIKYO!?
ゴオオオオ…
!?
DOWN THERE !!

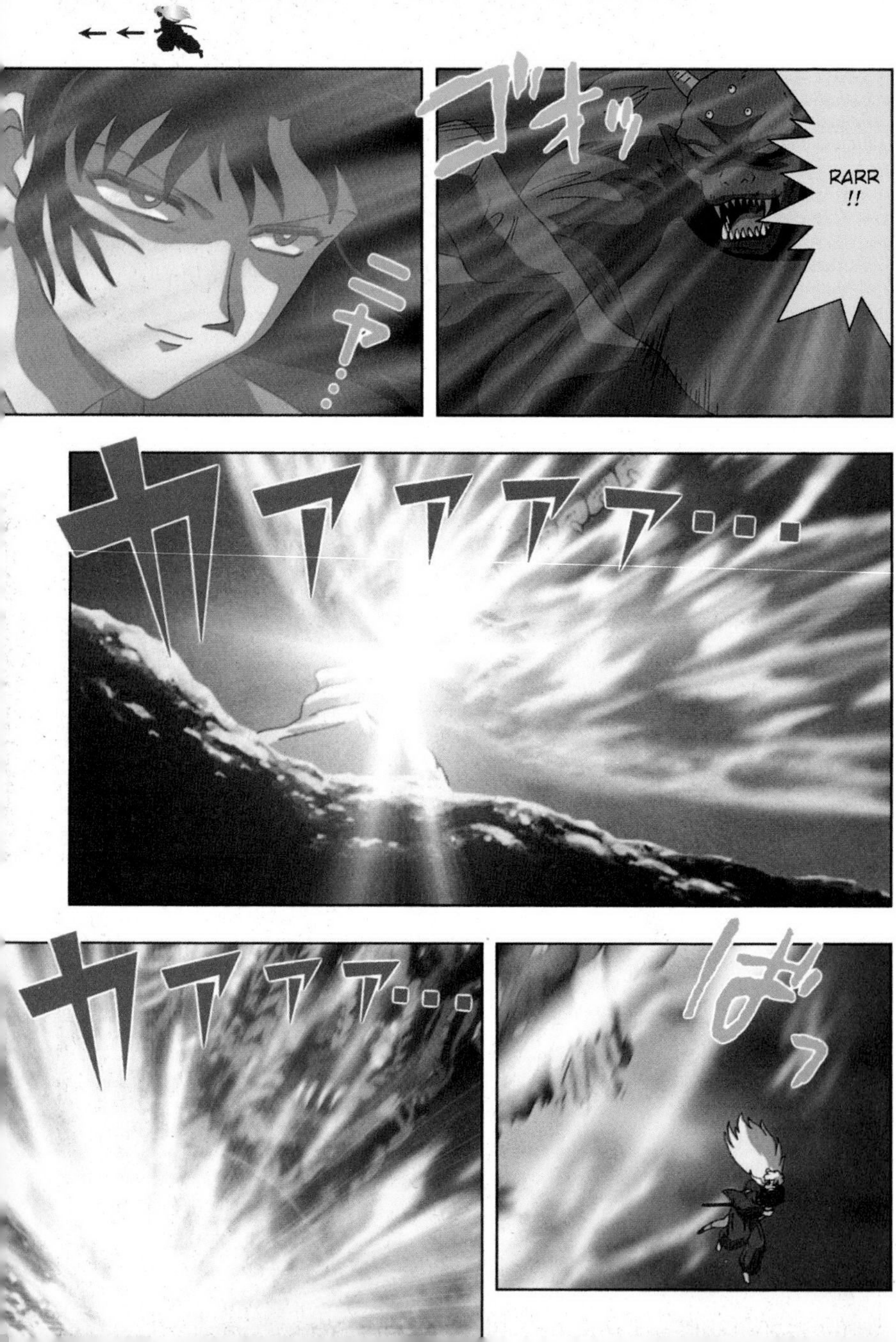
ゴキッ
RARR
!!
ニヤ…
カアアア…
ばっ
カアアア…

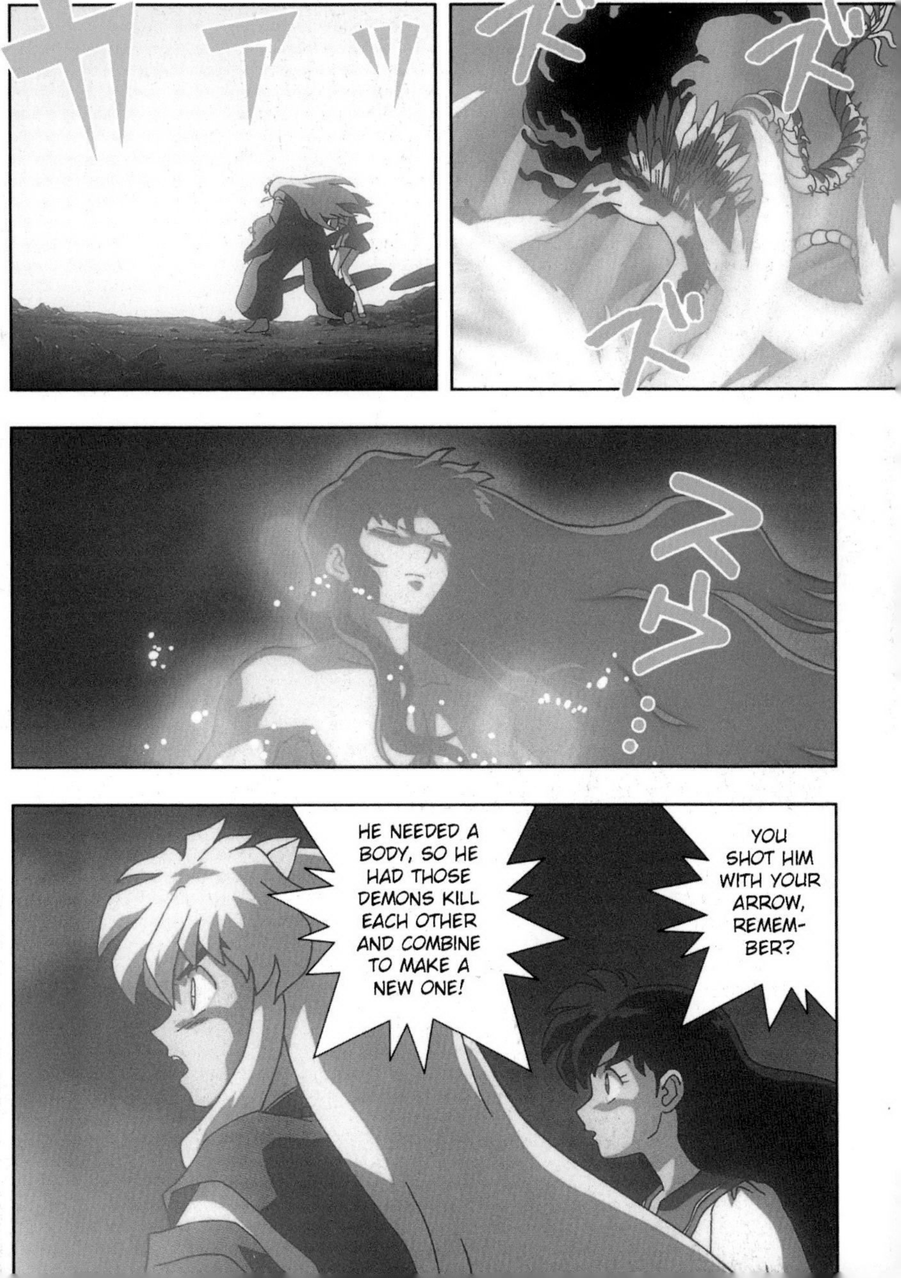

ズズズ
ヤアッ
スゥ…
YOU SHOT HIM WITH YOUR ARROW, REMEMBER?
HE NEEDED A BODY, SO HE HAD THOSE DEMONS KILL EACH OTHER AND COMBINE TO MAKE A NEW ONE!

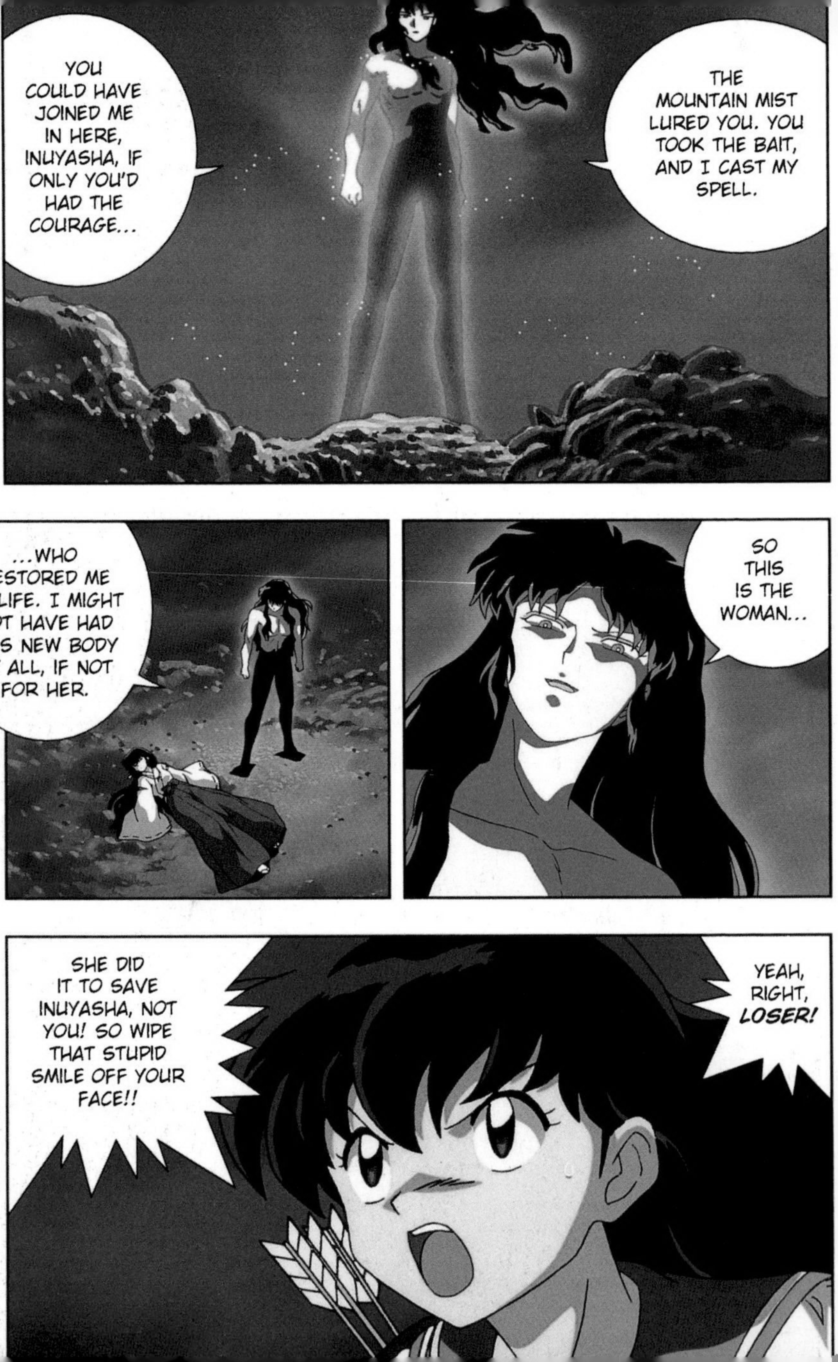
THE MOUNTAIN MIST LURED YOU. YOU TOOK THE BAIT, AND I CAST MY SPELL.
YOU COULD HAVE JOINED ME IN HERE, INUYASHA, IF ONLY YOU'D HAD THE COURAGE...
SO THIS IS THE WOMAN...
...WHO RESTORED ME TO LIFE. I MIGHT NOT HAVE HAD THIS NEW BODY AT ALL, IF NOT FOR HER.
YEAH, RIGHT, ***LOSER!***
SHE DID IT TO SAVE INUYASHA, NOT YOU! SO WIPE THAT STUPID SMILE OFF YOUR FACE!!

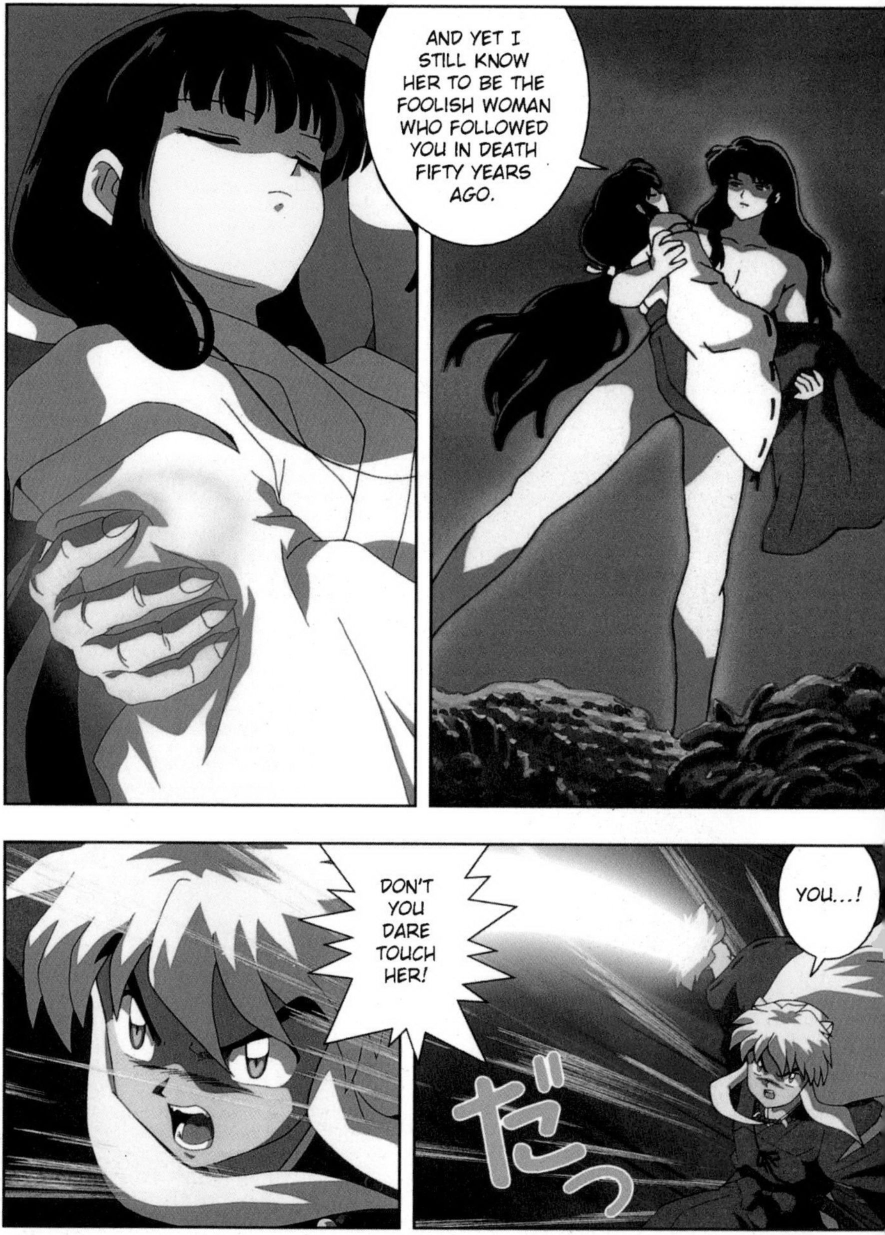
AND YET I STILL KNOW HER TO BE THE FOOLISH WOMAN WHO FOLLOWED YOU IN DEATH FIFTY YEARS AGO.
YOU...!
だっ
DON'T YOU DARE TOUCH HER!

UNH !!

INU- YASHA !

UNH ...

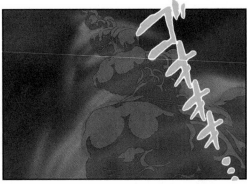

HOW DARE HE !!!

HOW DARE HE...

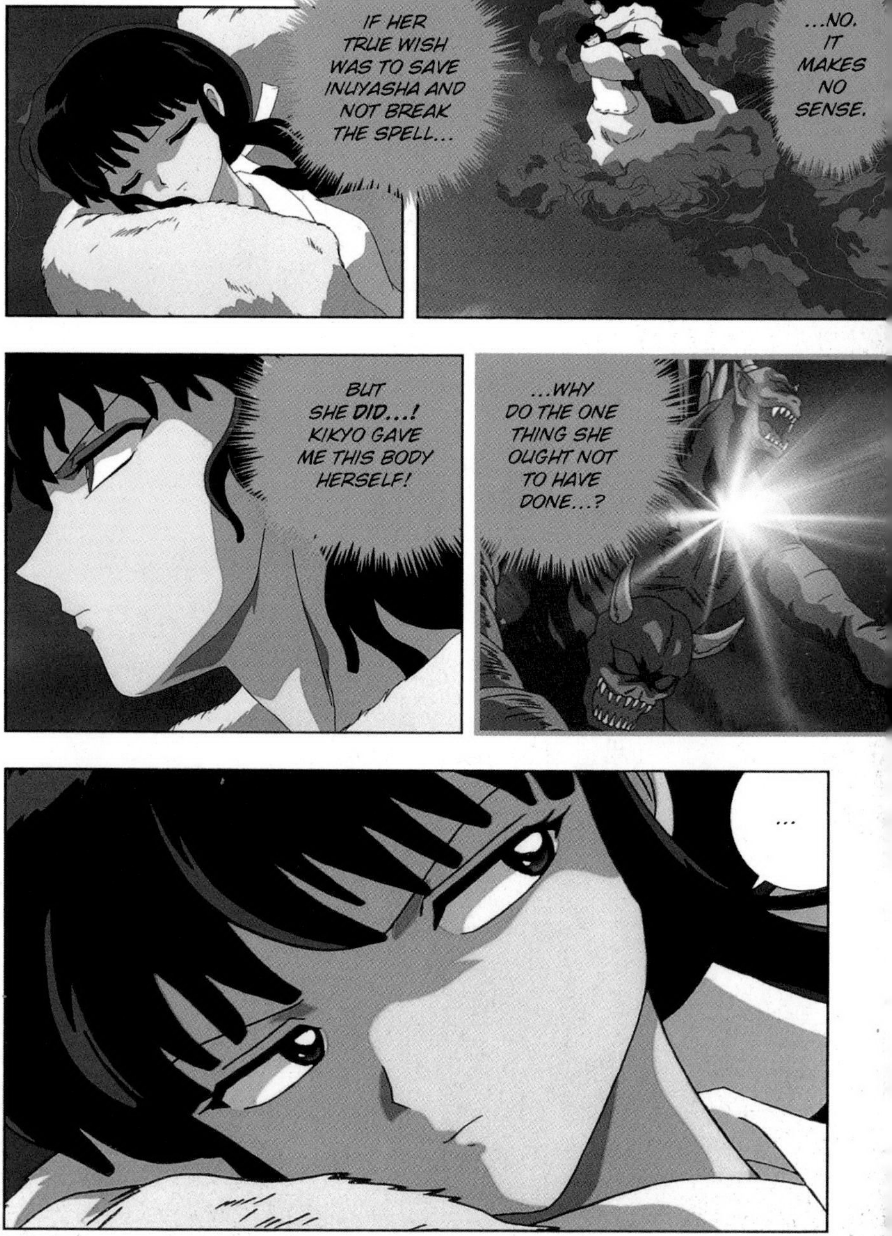
...NO. IT MAKES NO SENSE.
IF HER TRUE WISH WAS TO SAVE INUYASHA AND NOT BREAK THE SPELL...
...WHY DO THE ONE THING SHE OUGHT NOT TO HAVE DONE...?
BUT SHE DID...! KIKYO GAVE ME THIS BODY HERSELF!
...

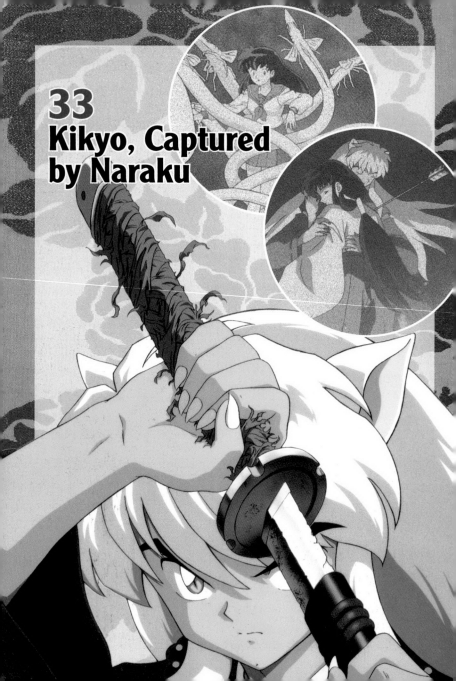

33
Kikyo, Captured by Naraku

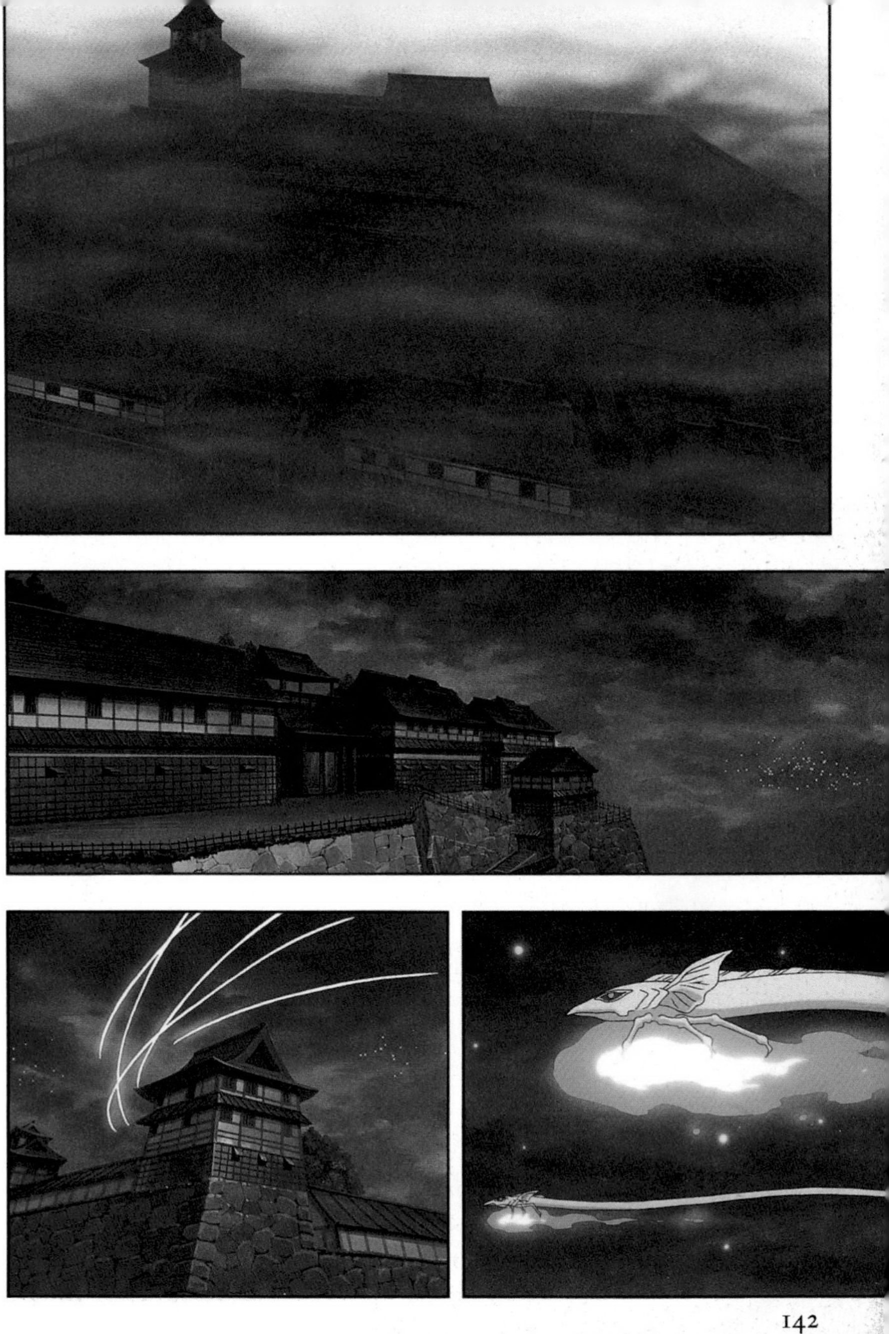

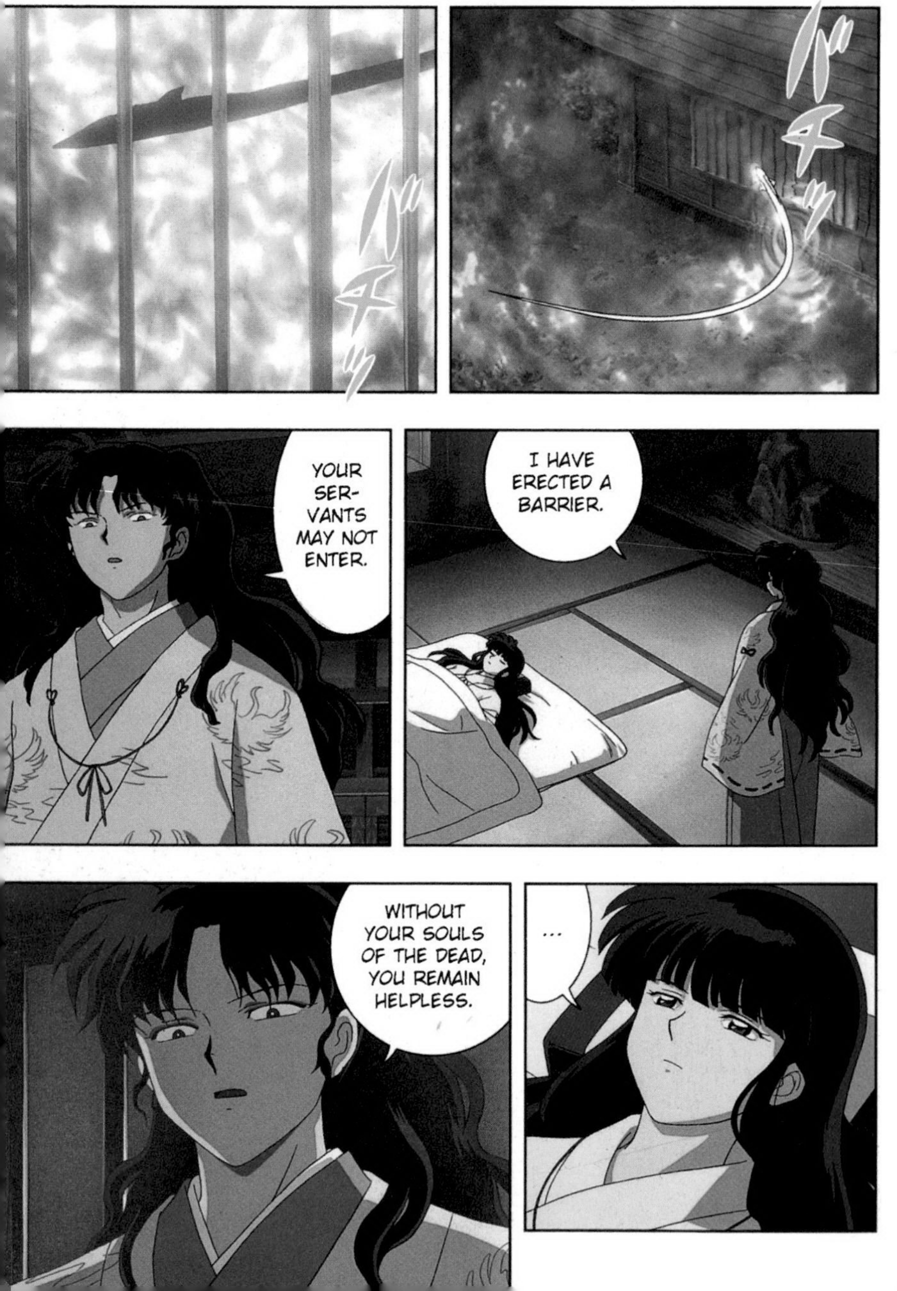
バチッ
バチッ
I HAVE ERECTED A BARRIER.
YOUR SER-VANTS MAY NOT ENTER.
...
WITHOUT YOUR SOULS OF THE DEAD, YOU REMAIN HELPLESS.

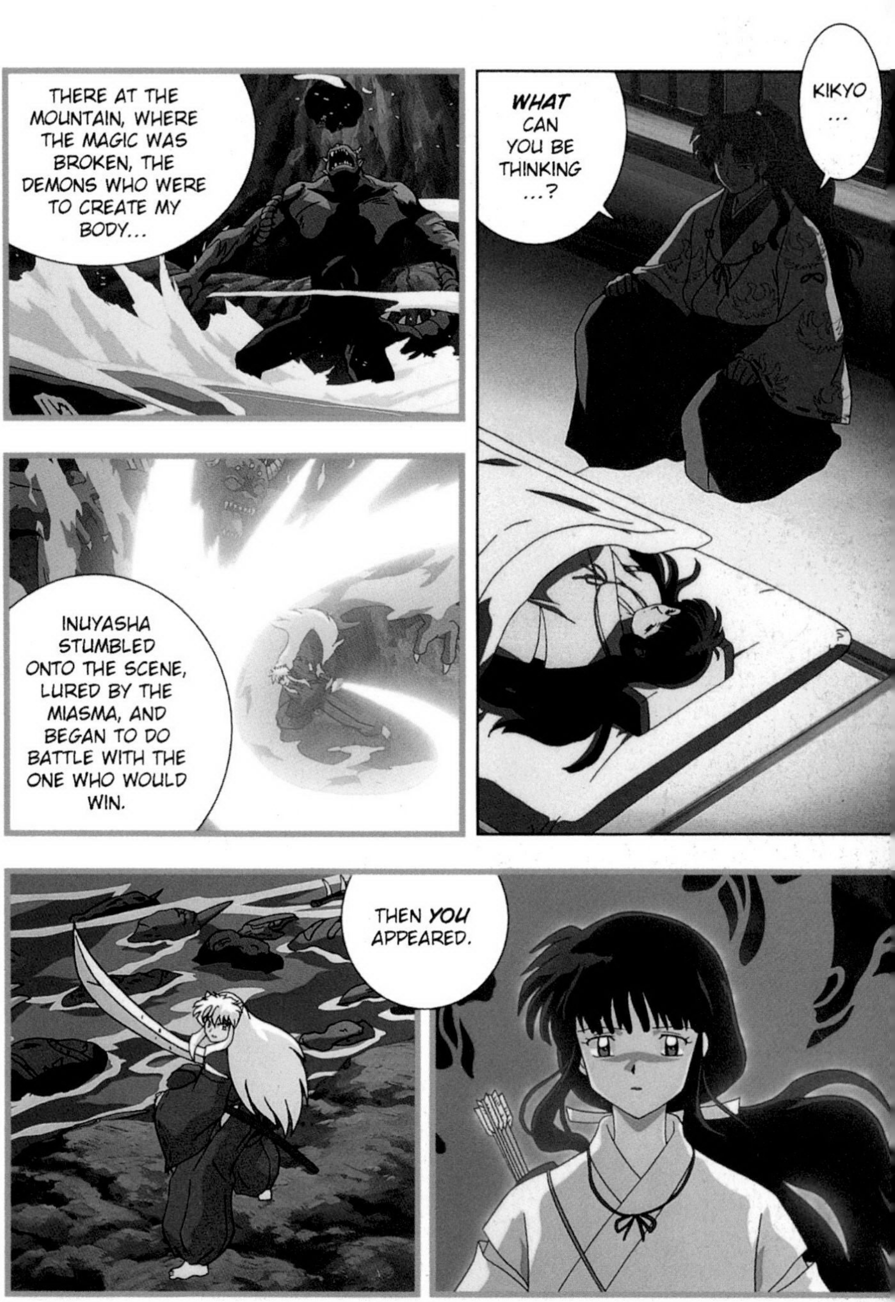
KIKYO ...
WHAT CAN YOU BE THINKING ...?
THERE AT THE MOUNTAIN, WHERE THE MAGIC WAS BROKEN, THE DEMONS WHO WERE TO CREATE MY BODY...
INUYASHA STUMBLED ONTO THE SCENE, LURED BY THE MIASMA, AND BEGAN TO DO BATTLE WITH THE ONE WHO WOULD WIN.
THEN *YOU* APPEARED.

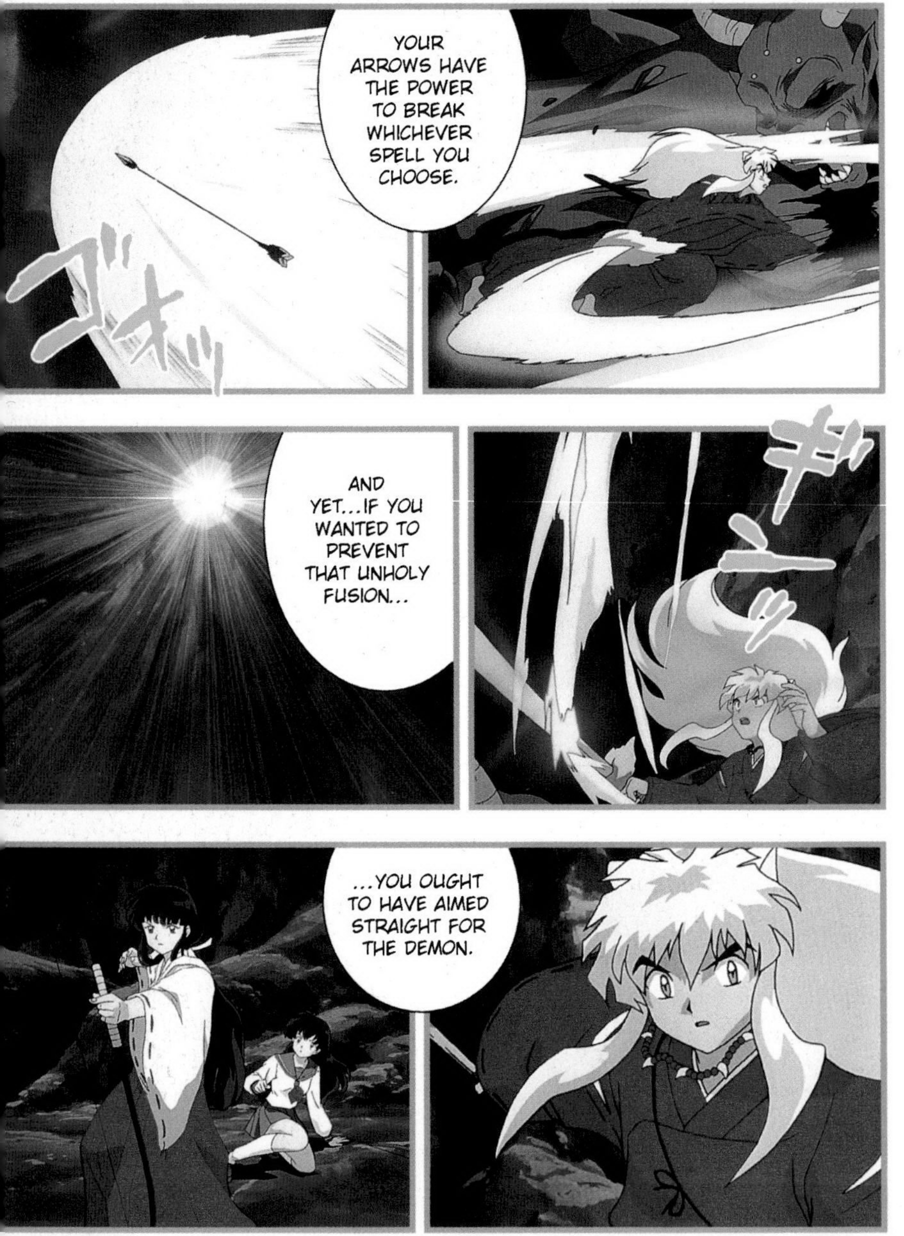
YOUR ARROWS HAVE THE POWER TO BREAK WHICHEVER SPELL YOU CHOOSE.
ゴオッ
ギュッ
AND YET...IF YOU WANTED TO PREVENT THAT UNHOLY FUSION...
...YOU OUGHT TO HAVE AIMED STRAIGHT FOR THE DEMON.

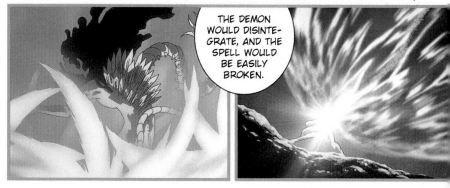

THE DEMON WOULD DISINTE-GRATE, AND THE SPELL WOULD BE EASILY BROKEN.

BUT BEFORE *THE ONE* BECAME COMPLETE, WERE YOU TRYING TO SEE WHAT LAY BEYOND...?

AND THERE YOU WERE...

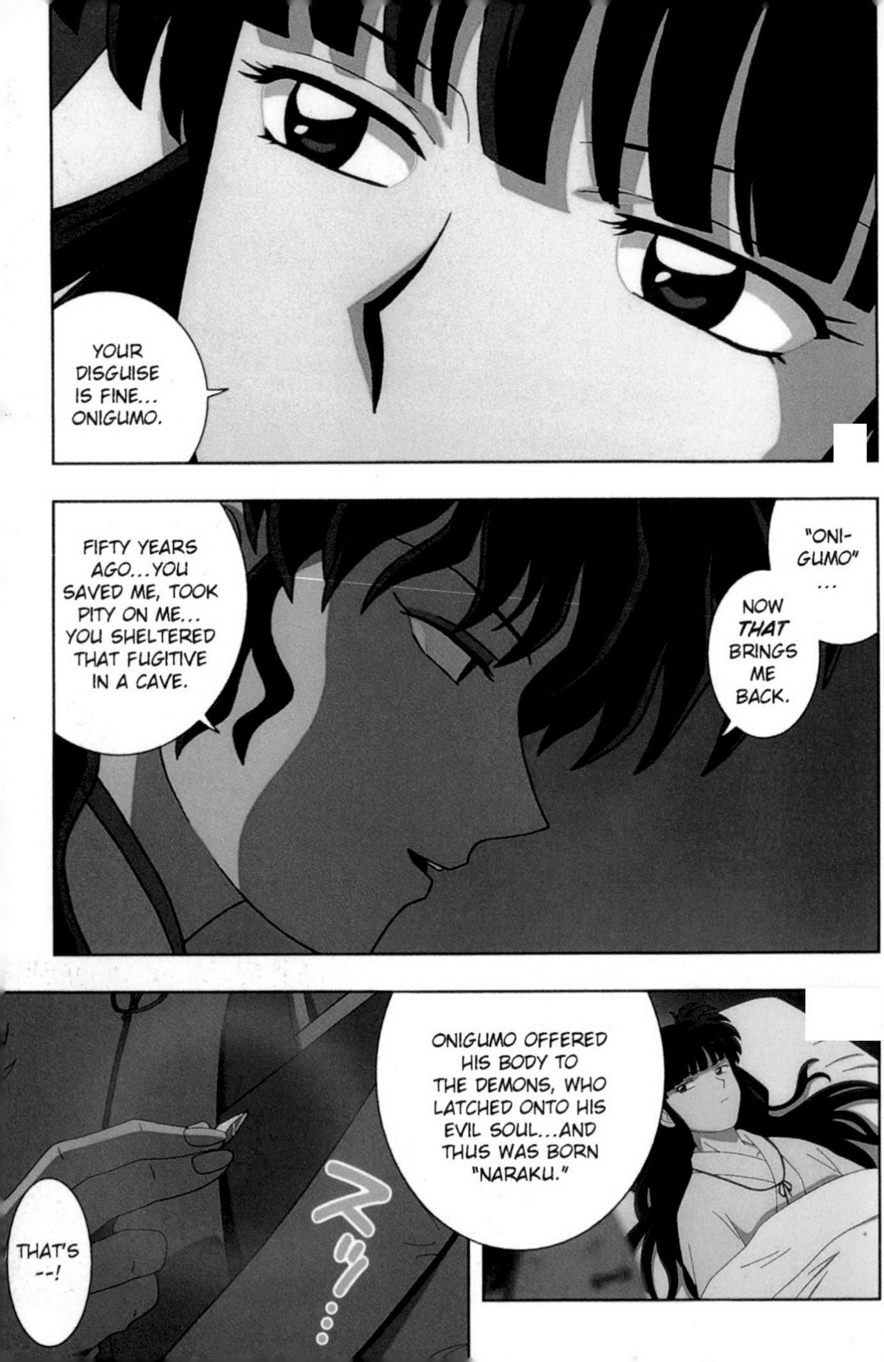
YOUR DISGUISE IS FINE... ONIGUMO.
"ONI-GUMO"...
NOW *THAT* BRINGS ME BACK.
FIFTY YEARS AGO...YOU SAVED ME, TOOK PITY ON ME... YOU SHELTERED THAT FUGITIVE IN A CAVE.
ONIGUMO OFFERED HIS BODY TO THE DEMONS, WHO LATCHED ONTO HIS EVIL SOUL...AND THUS WAS BORN "NARAKU."
スッ...
THAT'S --!

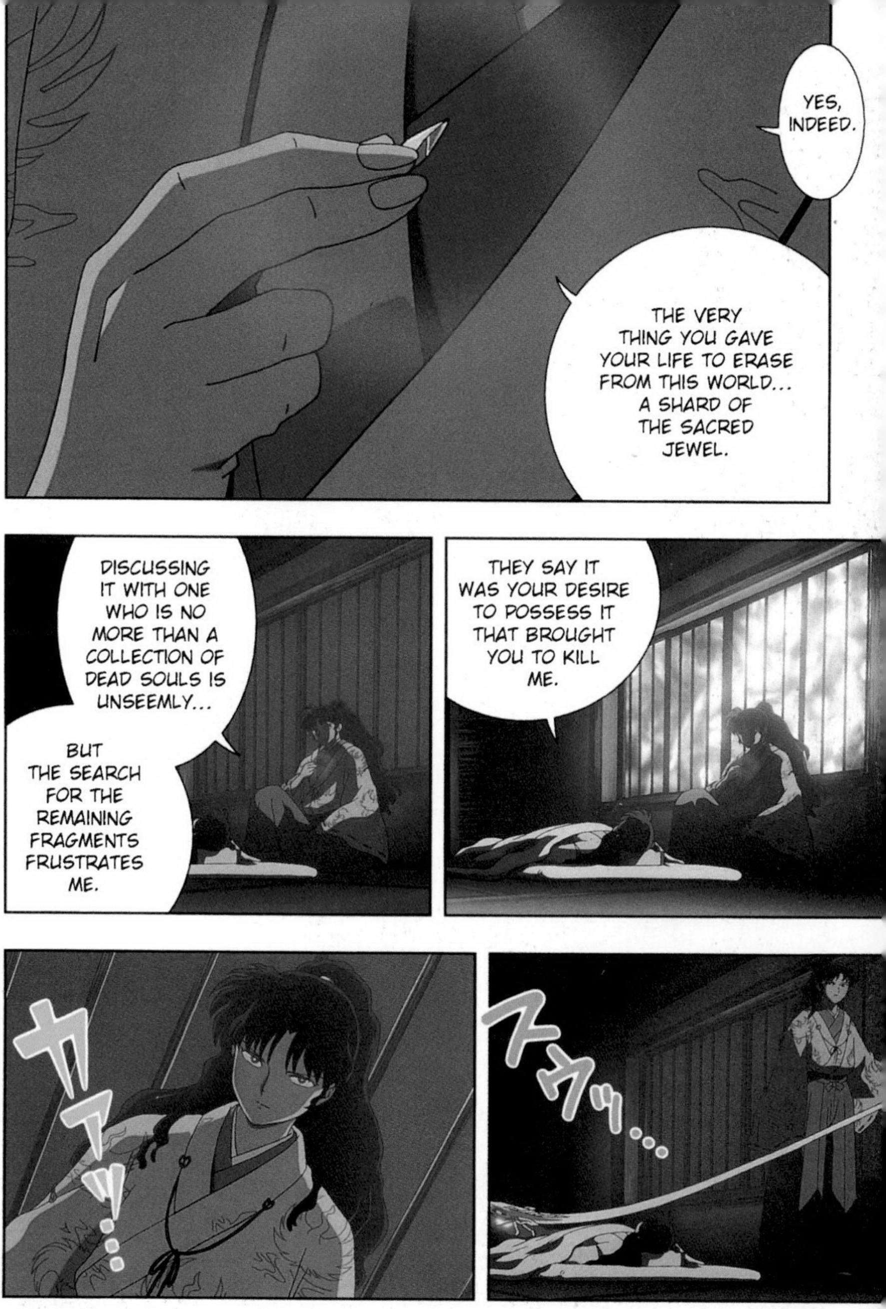
YES, INDEED.
THE VERY THING YOU GAVE YOUR LIFE TO ERASE FROM THIS WORLD... A SHARD OF THE SACRED JEWEL.
THEY SAY IT WAS YOUR DESIRE TO POSSESS IT THAT BROUGHT YOU TO KILL ME.
DISCUSSING IT WITH ONE WHO IS NO MORE THAN A COLLECTION OF DEAD SOULS IS UNSEEMLY...
BUT THE SEARCH FOR THE REMAINING FRAGMENTS FRUSTRATES ME.
スゥッ...
ヤァッ...

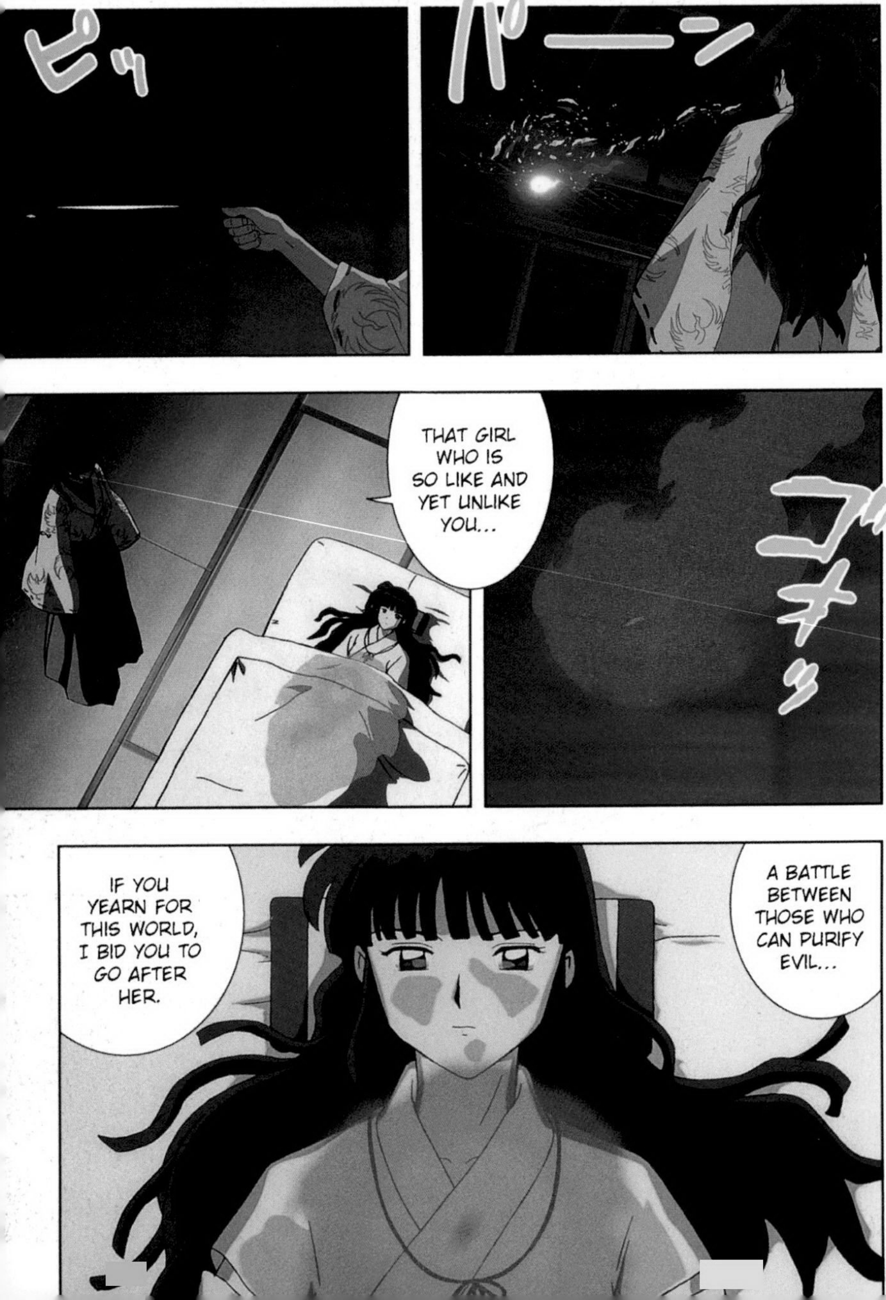
パーン
ピッ
ゴオッ
THAT GIRL WHO IS SO LIKE AND YET UNLIKE YOU...
A BATTLE BETWEEN THOSE WHO CAN PURIFY EVIL...
IF YOU YEARN FOR THIS WORLD, I BID YOU TO GO AFTER HER.

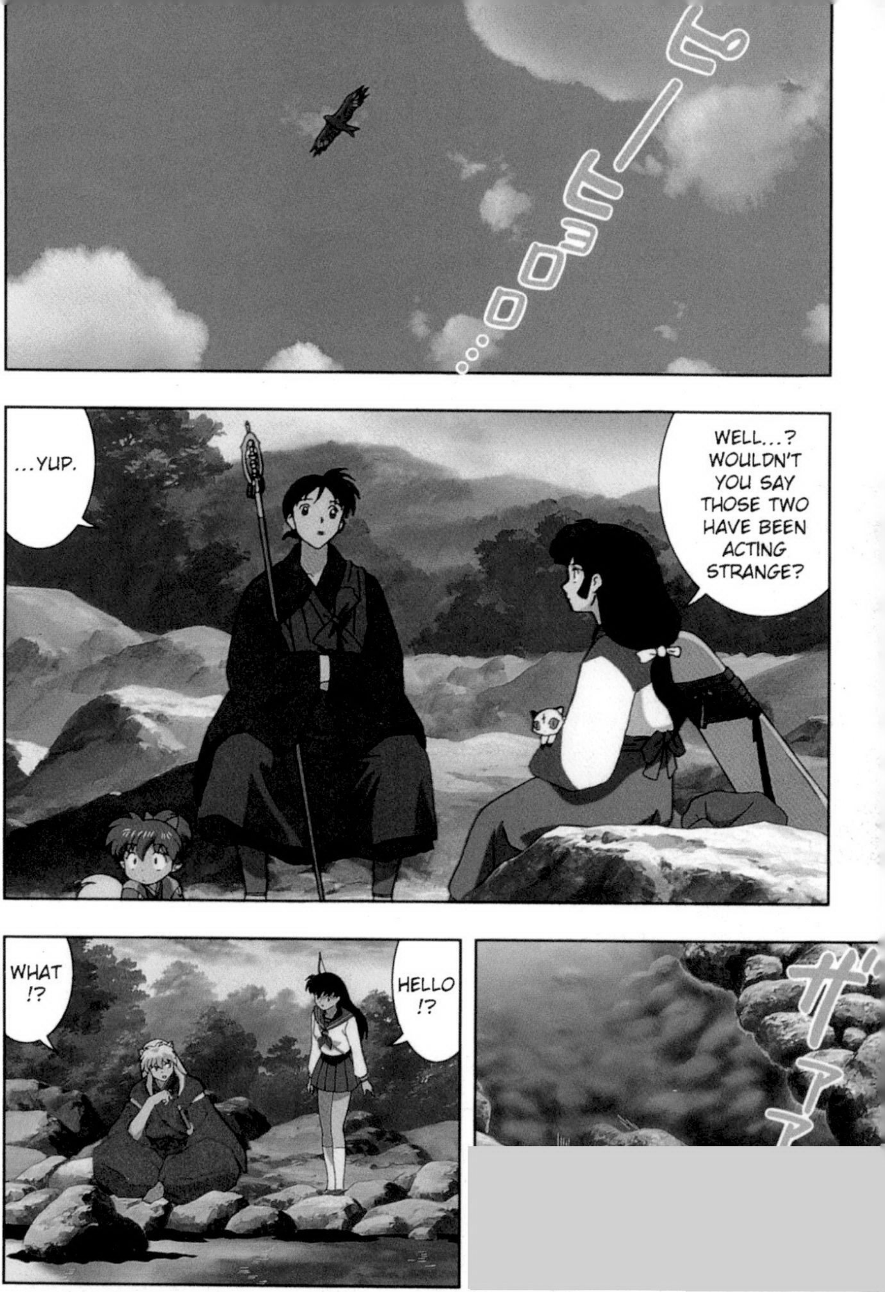
ピーヒョロロ…
WELL...? WOULDN'T YOU SAY THOSE TWO HAVE BEEN ACTING STRANGE?
...YUP.
ザァ
HELLO !?
WHAT !?

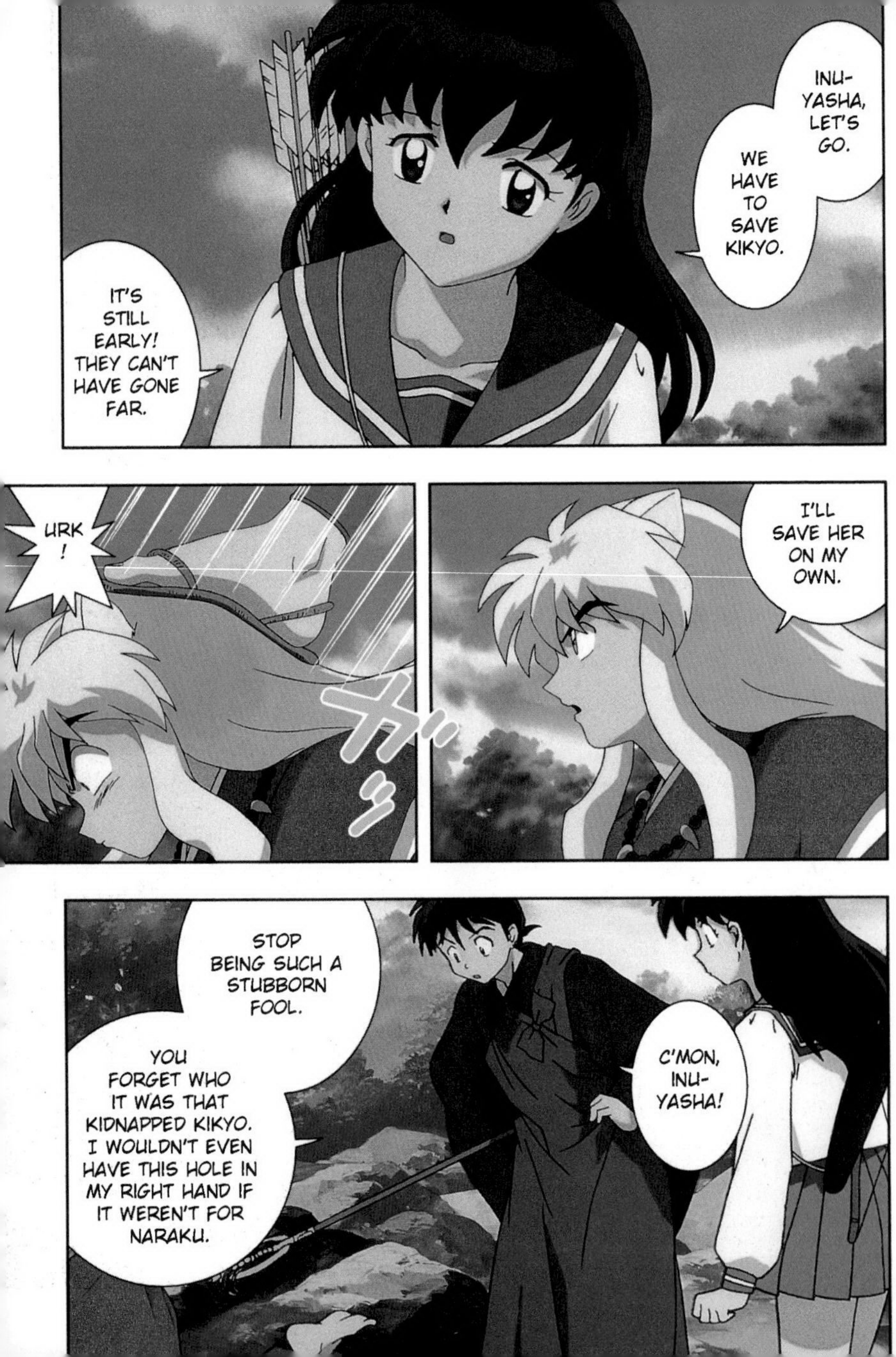
INU-YASHA, LET'S GO.
WE HAVE TO SAVE KIKYO.
IT'S STILL EARLY! THEY CAN'T HAVE GONE FAR.
I'LL SAVE HER ON MY OWN.
URK!
ガッ
C'MON, INU-YASHA!
STOP BEING SUCH A STUBBORN FOOL.
YOU FORGET WHO IT WAS THAT KIDNAPPED KIKYO. I WOULDN'T EVEN HAVE THIS HOLE IN MY RIGHT HAND IF IT WEREN'T FOR NARAKU.

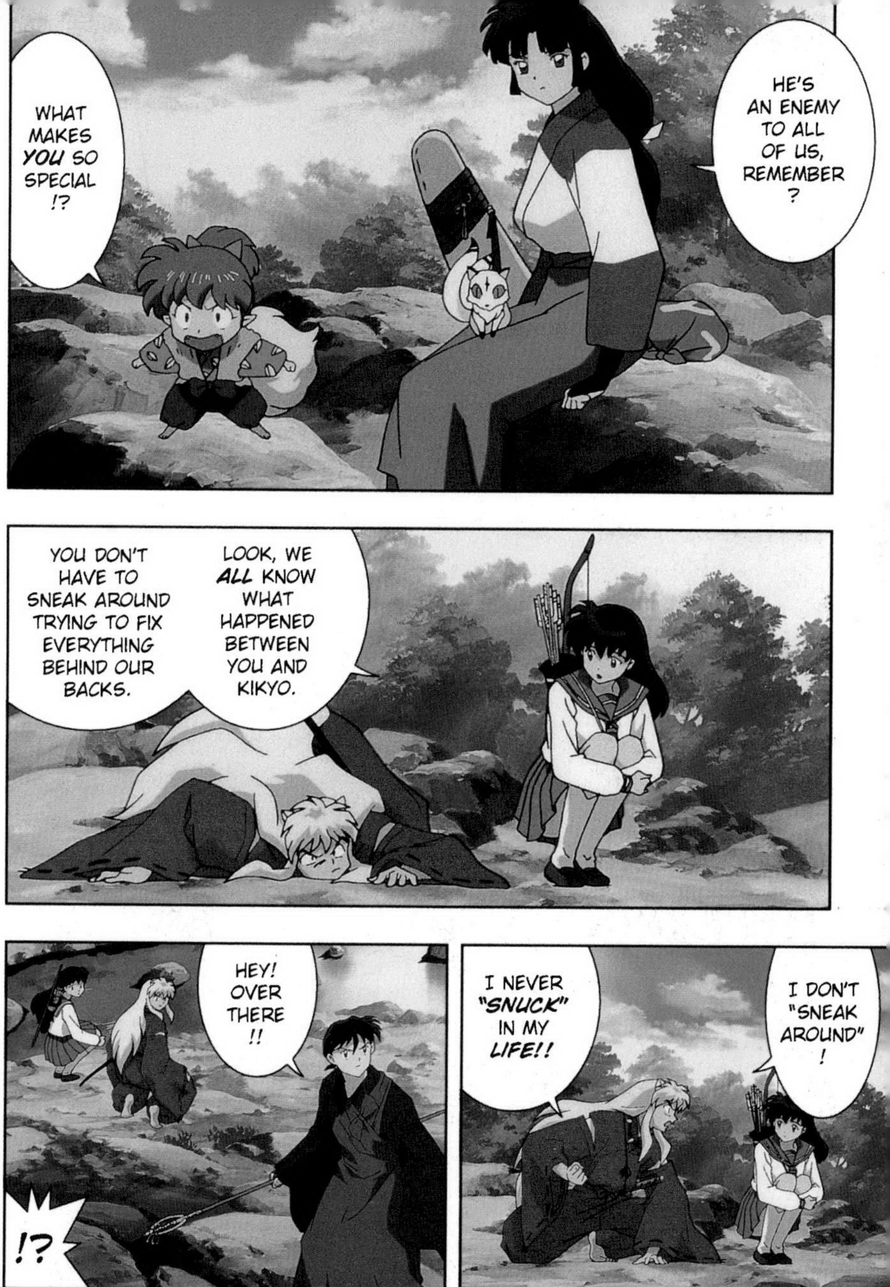
HE'S AN ENEMY TO ALL OF US, REMEMBER?
WHAT MAKES YOU SO SPECIAL!?
LOOK, WE ALL KNOW WHAT HAPPENED BETWEEN YOU AND KIKYO.
YOU DON'T HAVE TO SNEAK AROUND TRYING TO FIX EVERYTHING BEHIND OUR BACKS.
I DON'T "SNEAK AROUND"!
I NEVER "SNUCK" IN MY LIFE!!
HEY! OVER THERE!!
!?

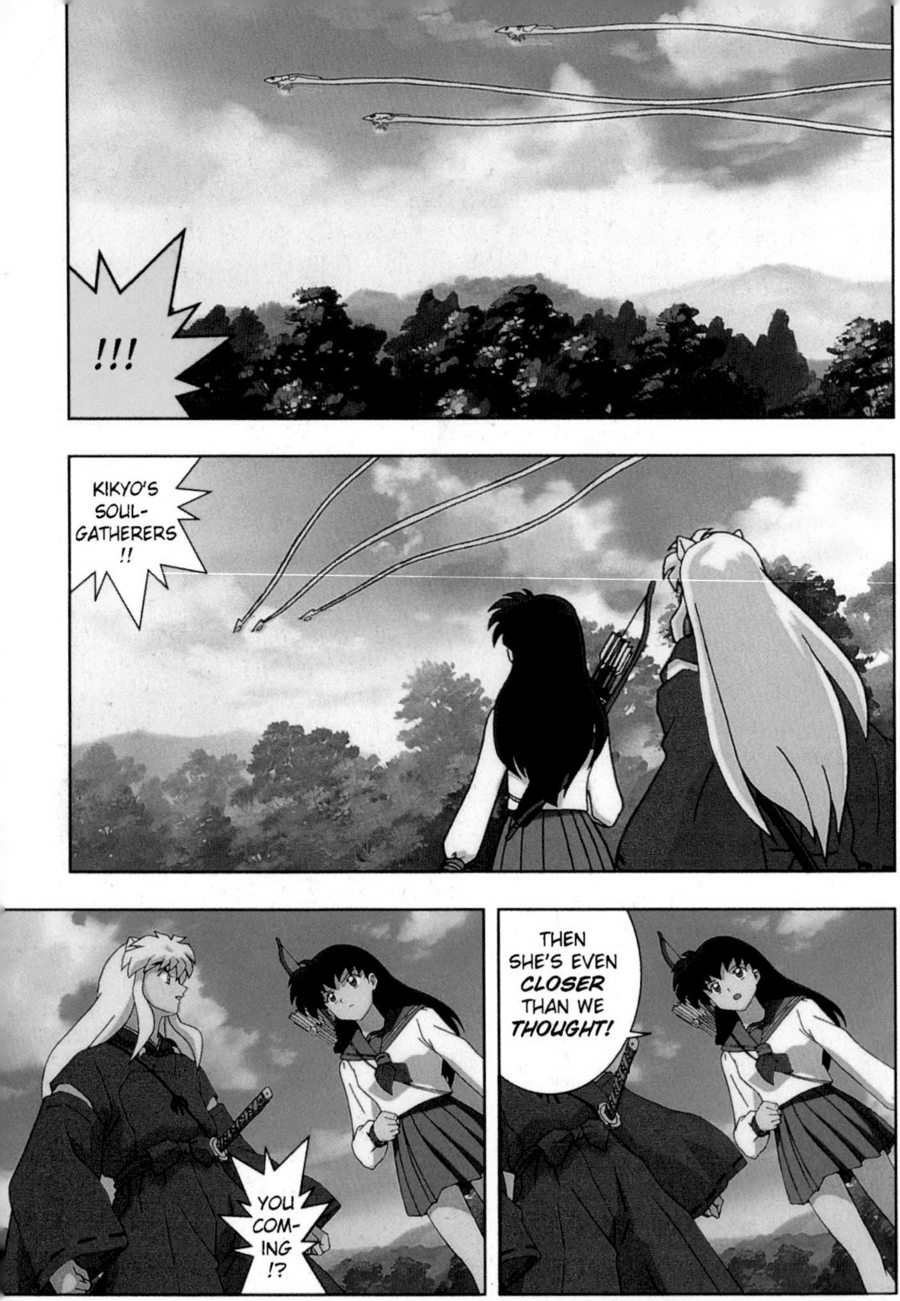
!!!
KIKYO'S SOUL-GATHERERS!!
THEN SHE'S EVEN CLOSER THAN WE THOUGHT!
YOU COMING!?

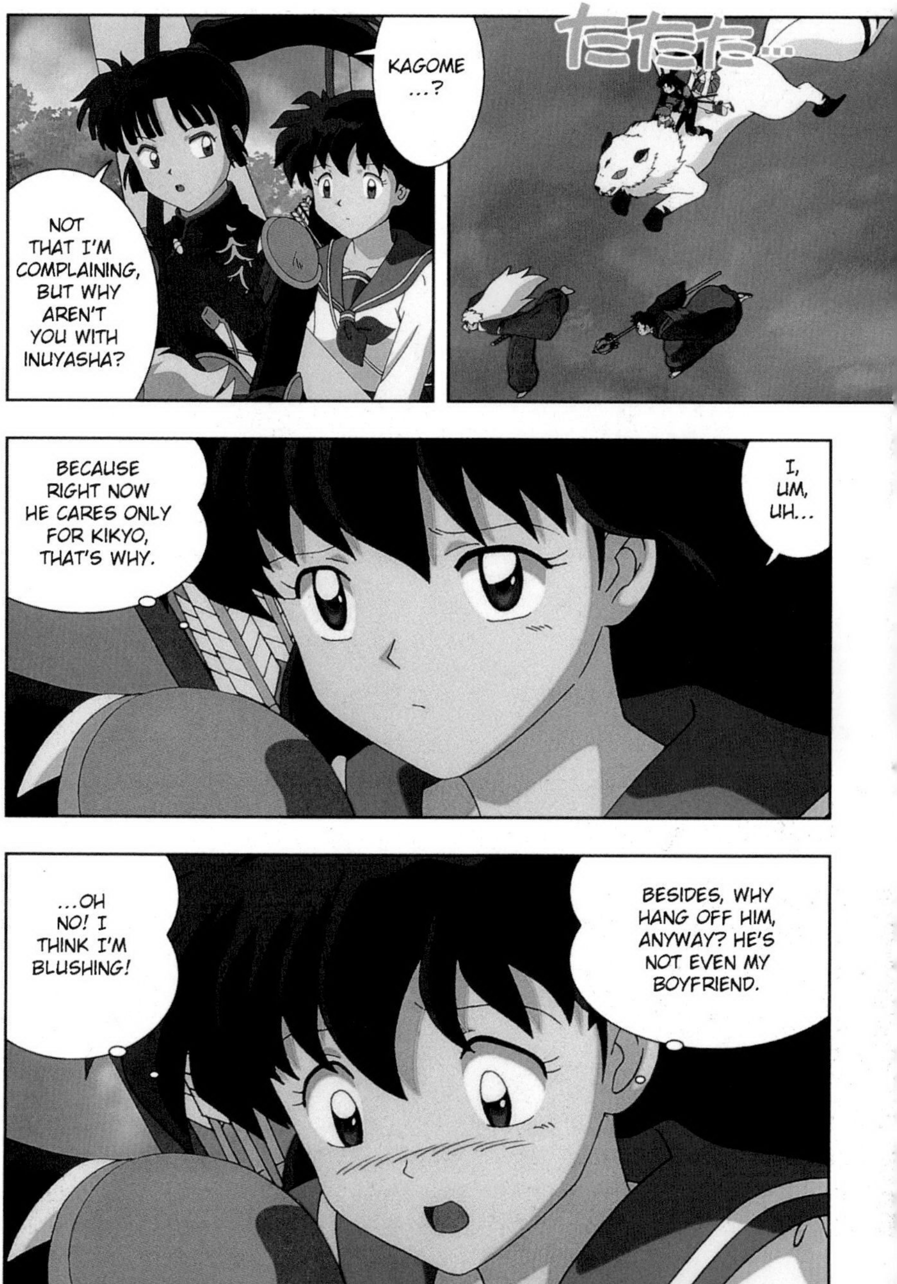
たたた…
KAGOME ...?
NOT THAT I'M COMPLAINING, BUT WHY AREN'T YOU WITH INUYASHA?
I, UM, UH...
BECAUSE RIGHT NOW HE CARES ONLY FOR KIKYO, THAT'S WHY.
BESIDES, WHY HANG OFF HIM, ANYWAY? HE'S NOT EVEN MY BOYFRIEND.
...OH NO! I THINK I'M BLUSHING!

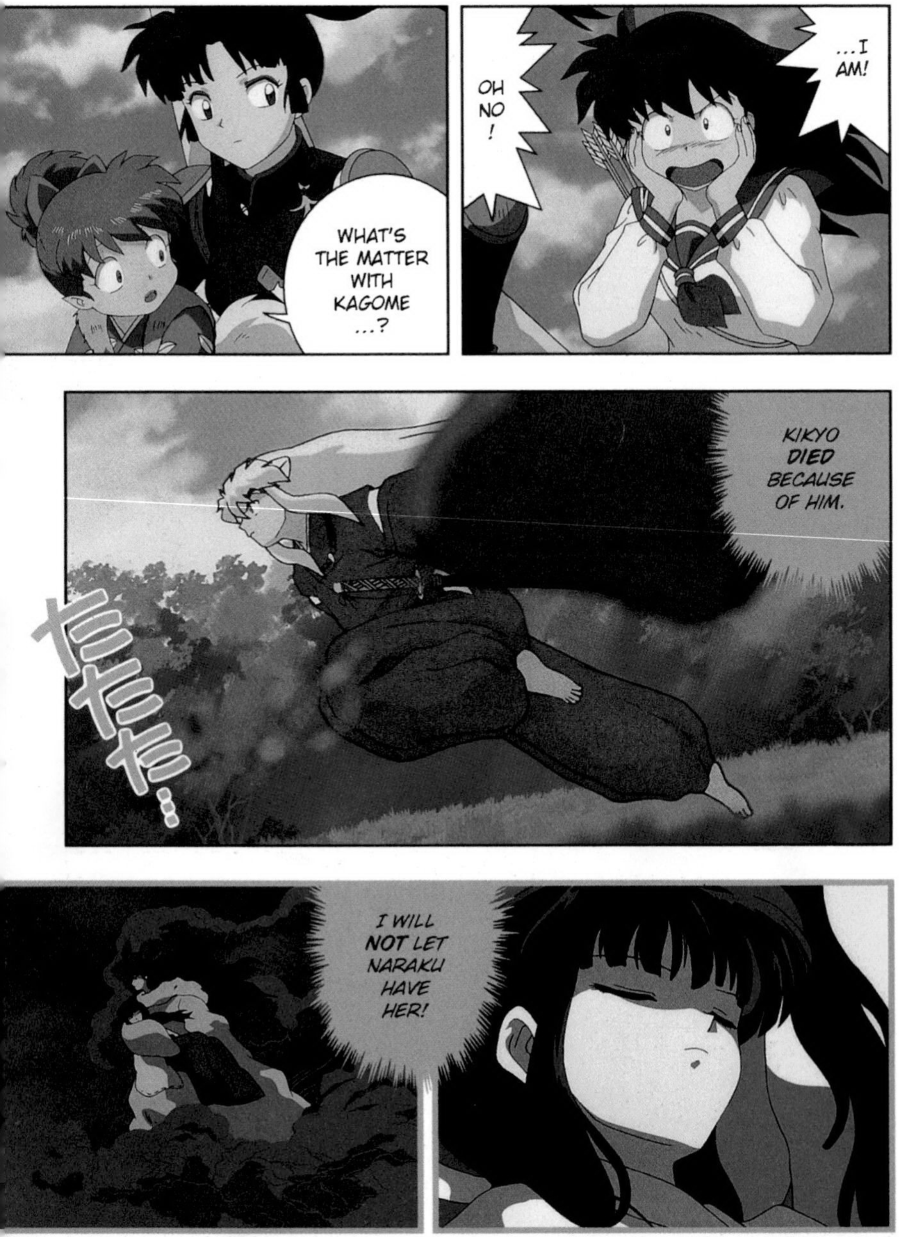
...I AM!
OH NO!
WHAT'S THE MATTER WITH KAGOME ...?
KIKYO DIED BECAUSE OF HIM.
I WILL NOT LET NARAKU HAVE HER!

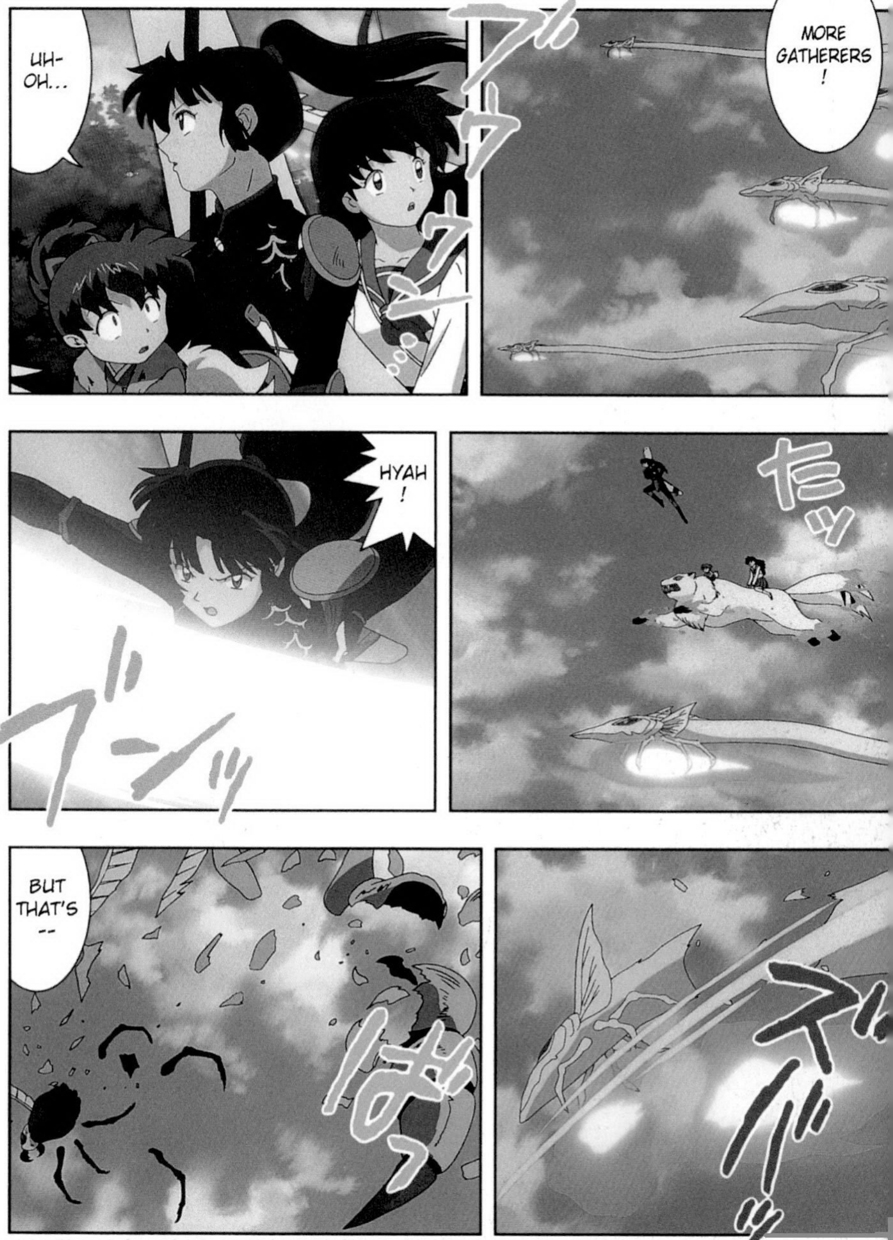
MORE GATHERERS !
UH-OH...
たッ
HYAH !
ブンッ
BUT THAT'S --
ばっ

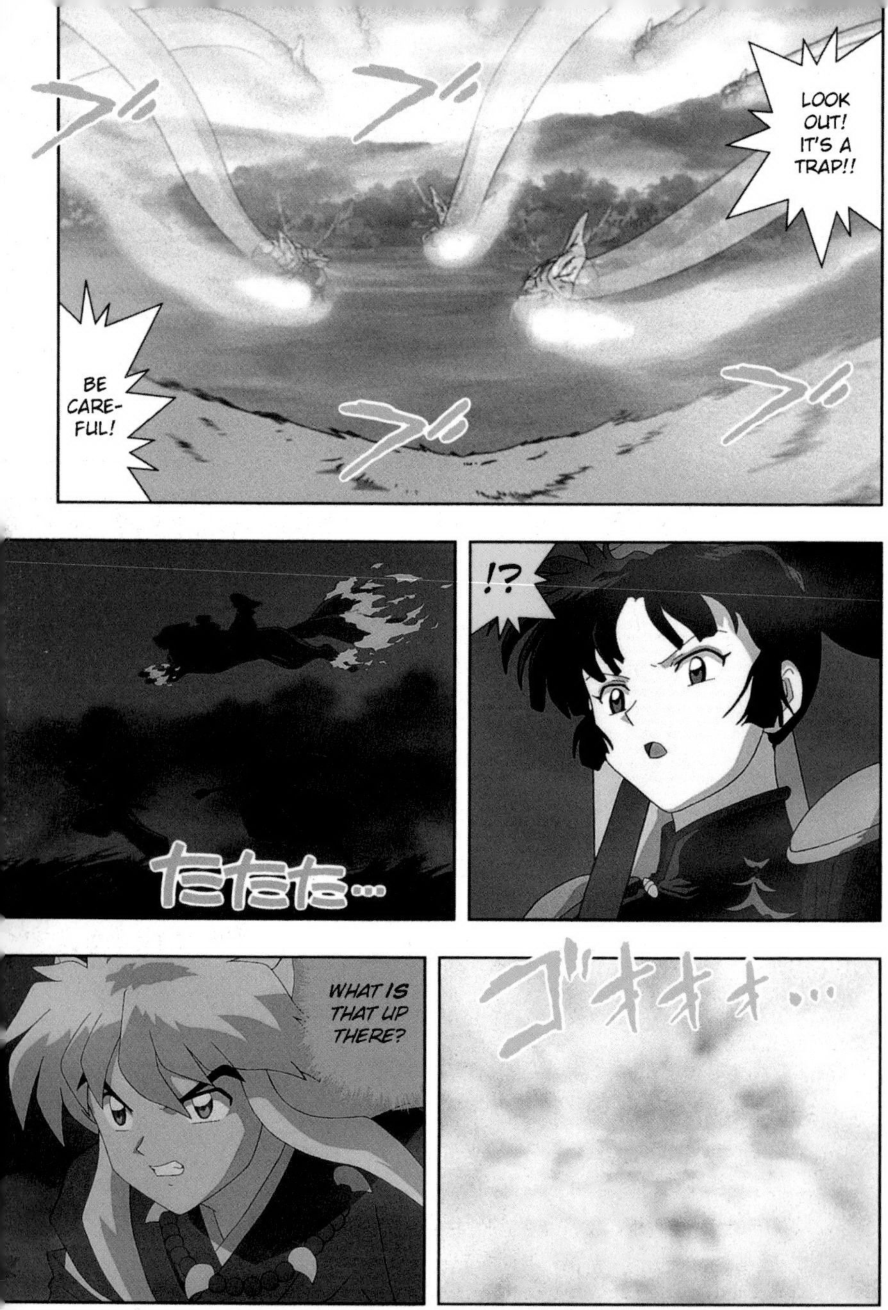
LOOK OUT! IT'S A TRAP!!
ブ
ブ
ブ
ブ
BE CAREFUL!
!?
たたた…
ゴオオオ…
WHAT IS THAT UP THERE?

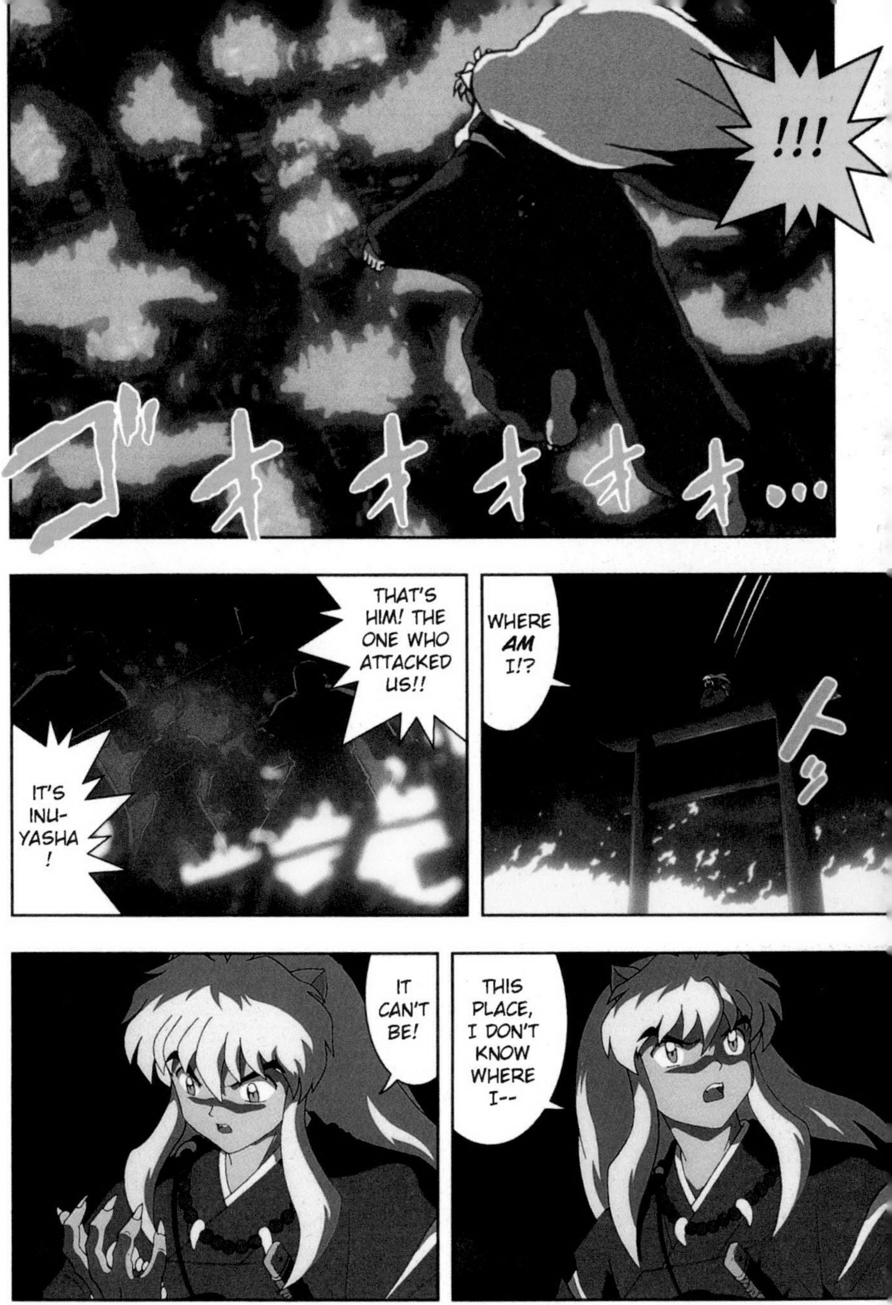
!!!
ゴオオオオオ...
WHERE AM I!?
トッ
THAT'S HIM! THE ONE WHO ATTACKED US!!
IT'S INU-YASHA!
THIS PLACE, I DON'T KNOW WHERE I--
IT CAN'T BE!

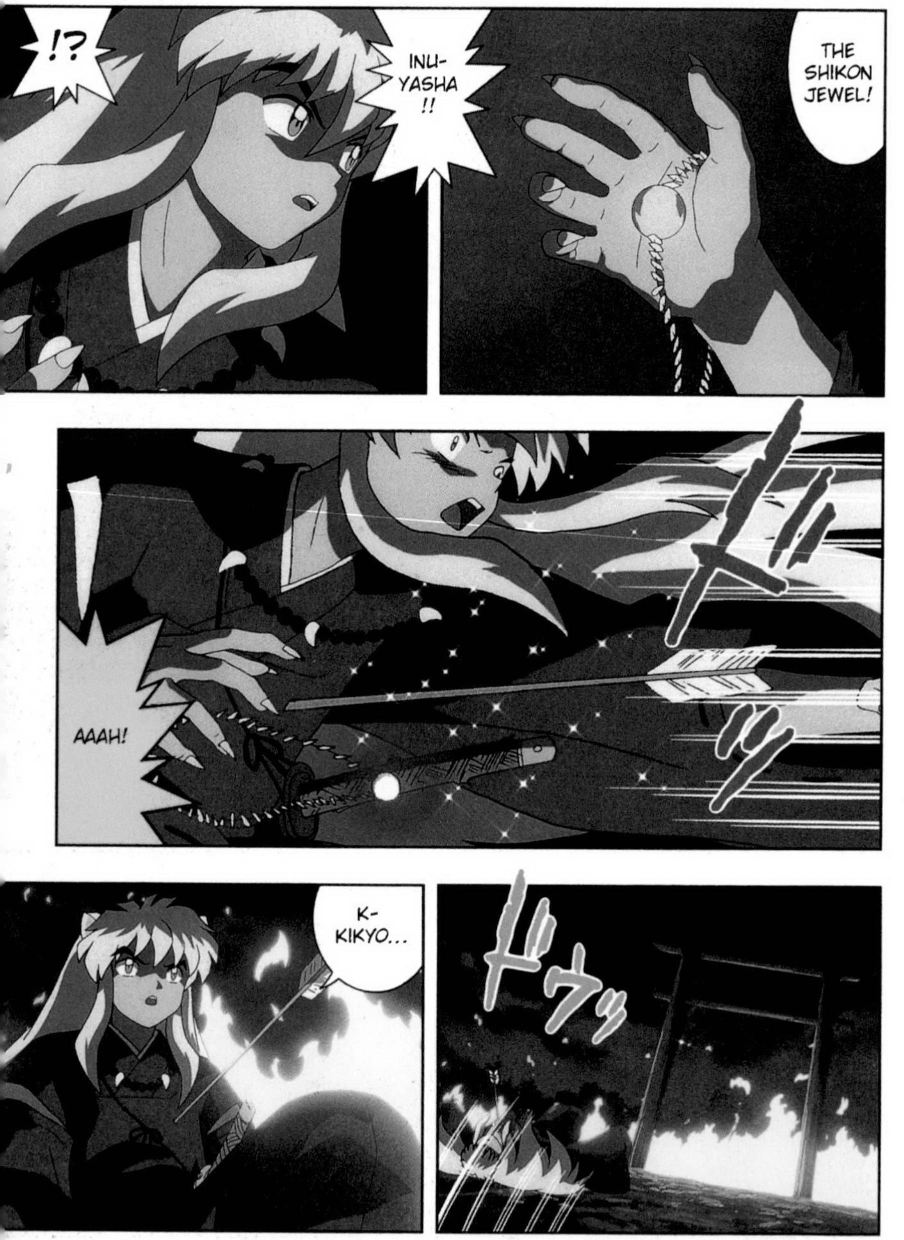
THE SHIKON JEWEL!
INU-YASHA!!
!?
AAAH!
ドウッ
K-KIKYO...

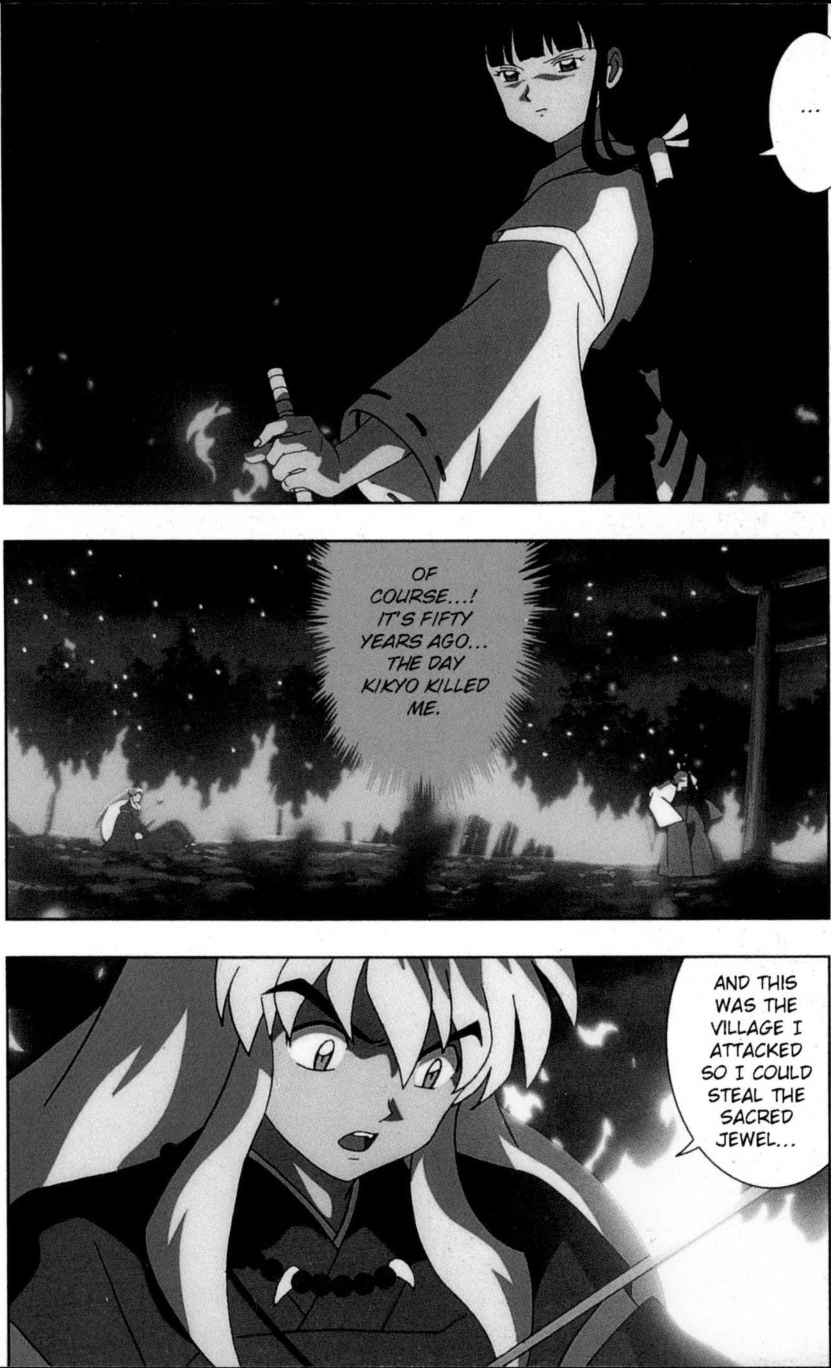
...
OF COURSE...! IT'S FIFTY YEARS AGO... THE DAY KIKYO KILLED ME.
AND THIS WAS THE VILLAGE I ATTACKED SO I COULD STEAL THE SACRED JEWEL...

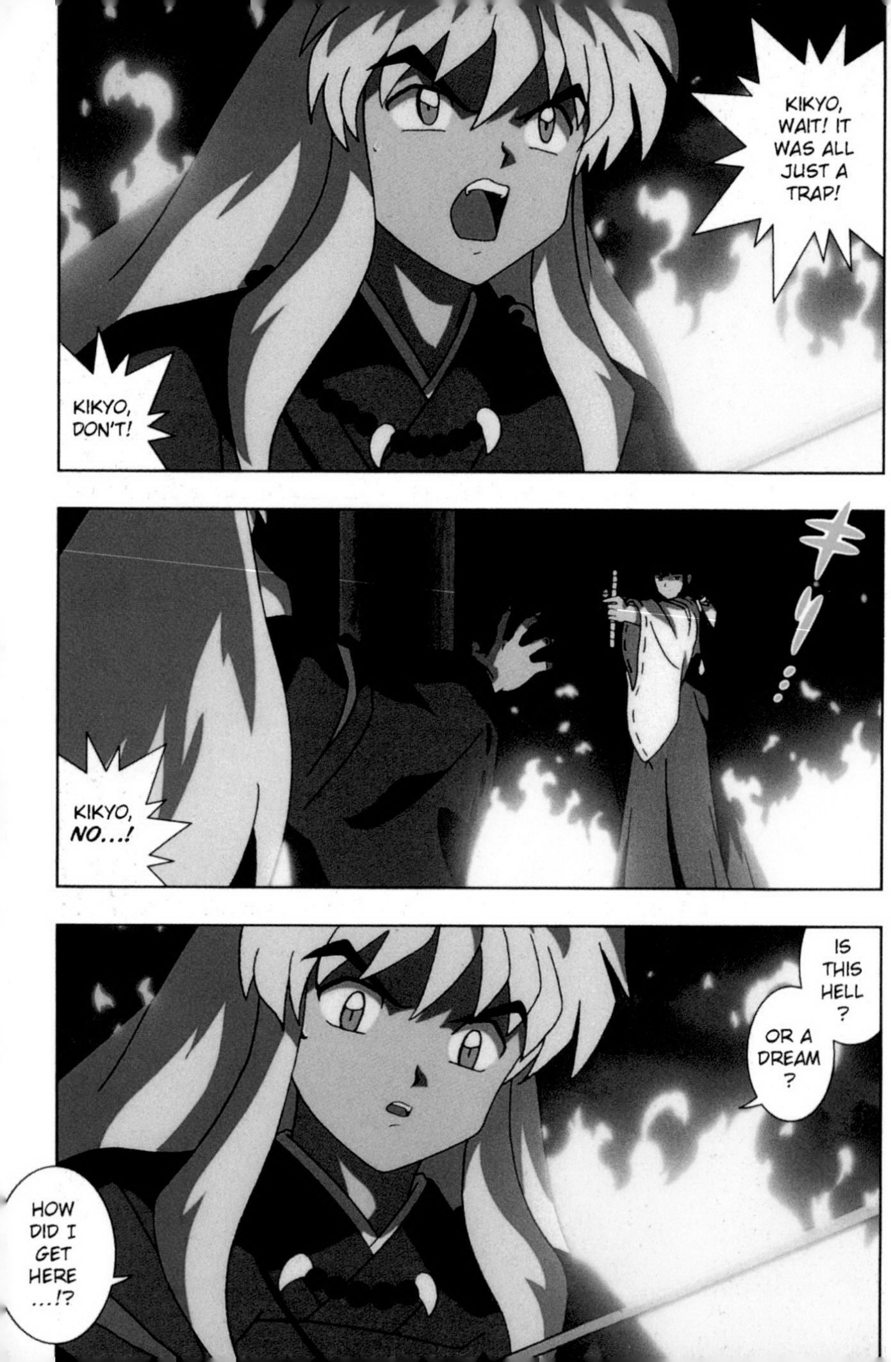
KIKYO, WAIT! IT WAS ALL JUST A TRAP!
KIKYO, DON'T!
KIKYO, *NO...!*
IS THIS HELL?
OR A DREAM?
HOW DID I GET HERE ...!?

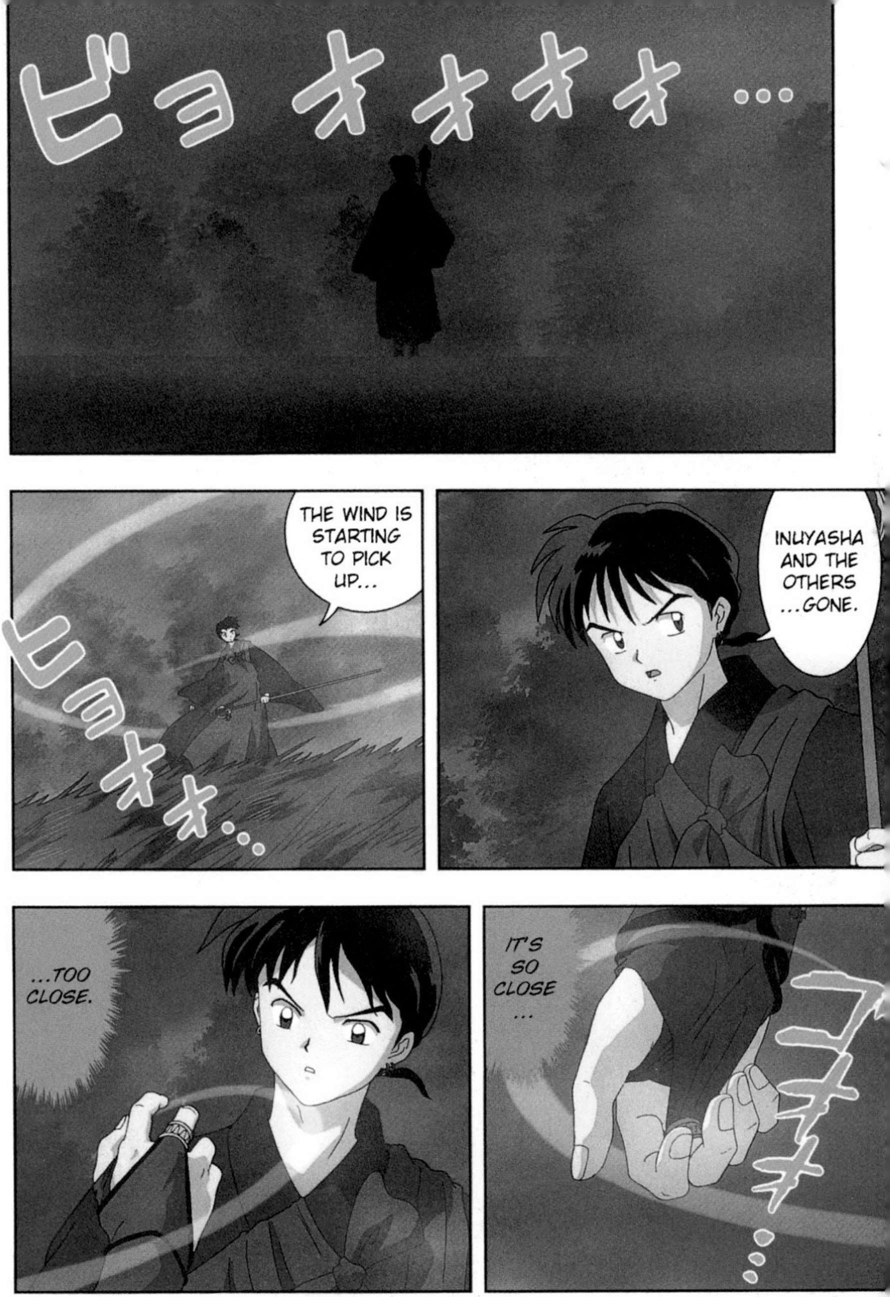
ビョオオオオ…
INUYASHA AND THE OTHERS ...GONE.
THE WIND IS STARTING TO PICK UP...
ヒョオオ…
IT'S SO CLOSE ...
コオオ…
...TOO CLOSE.

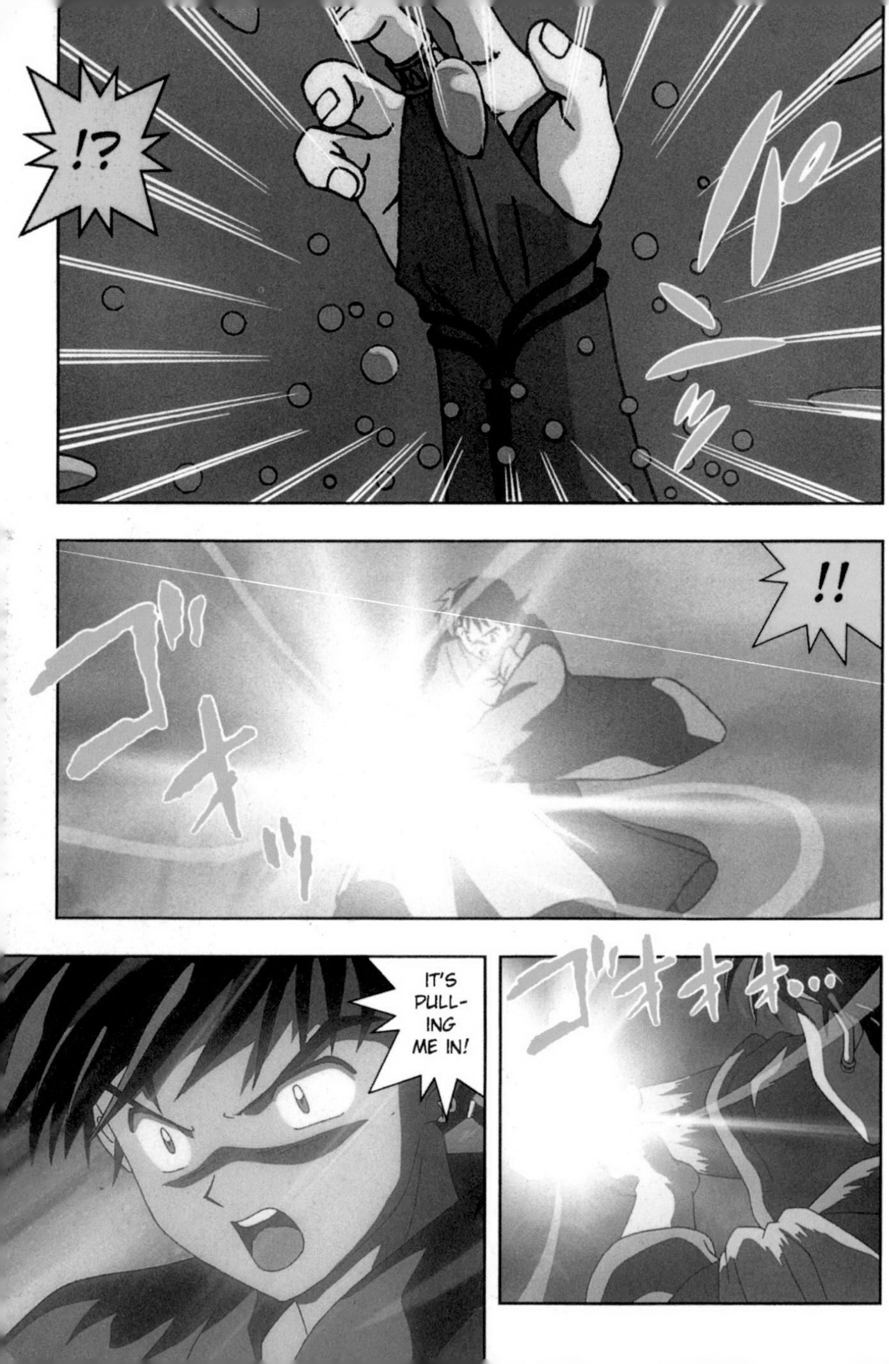
!?
!!
ゴオッ
ゴオオオ…
IT'S PULLING ME IN!

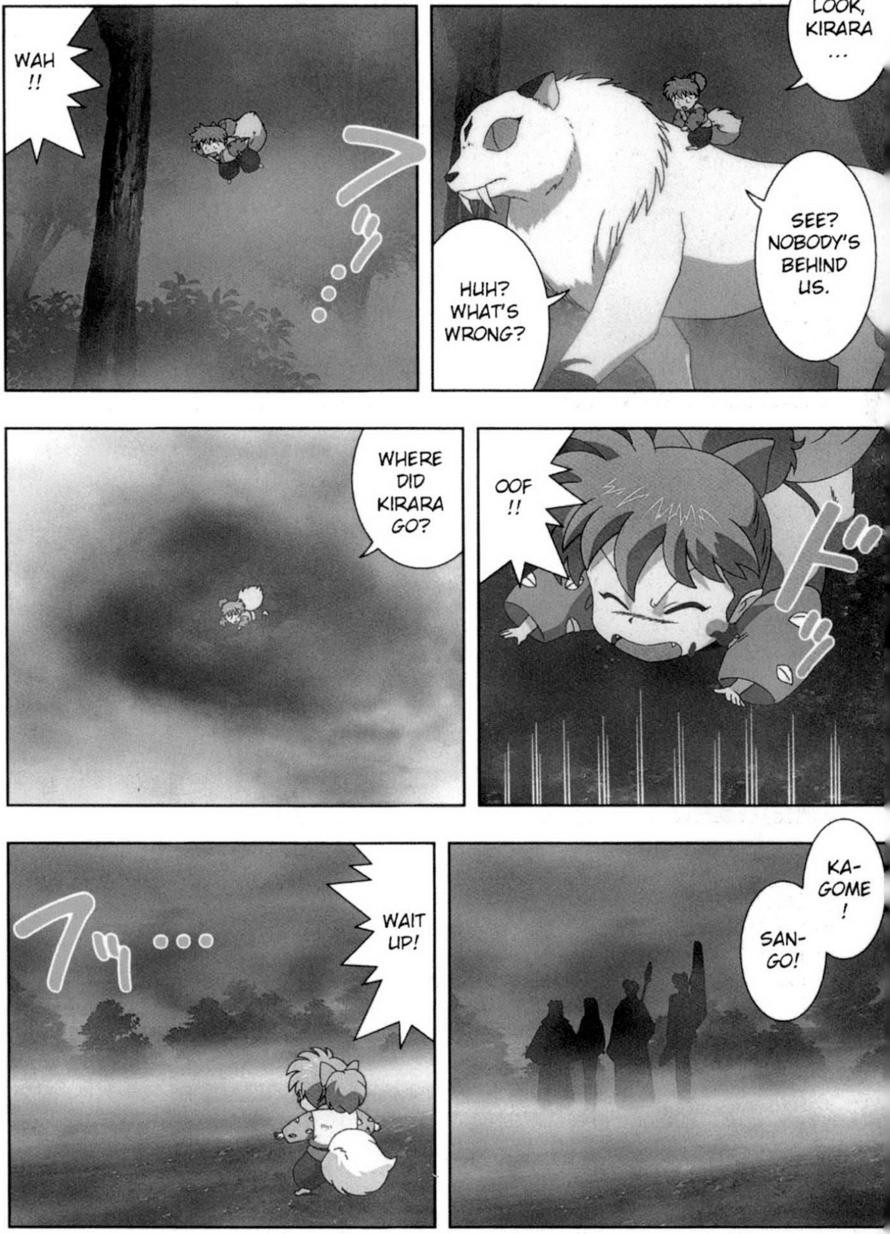
LOOK, KIRARA ...
SEE? NOBODY'S BEHIND US.
HUH? WHAT'S WRONG?
WAH !!
フッ...
OOF !!
ドッ
WHERE DID KIRARA GO?
KA-GOME !
SAN-GO!
WAIT UP!
フッ...

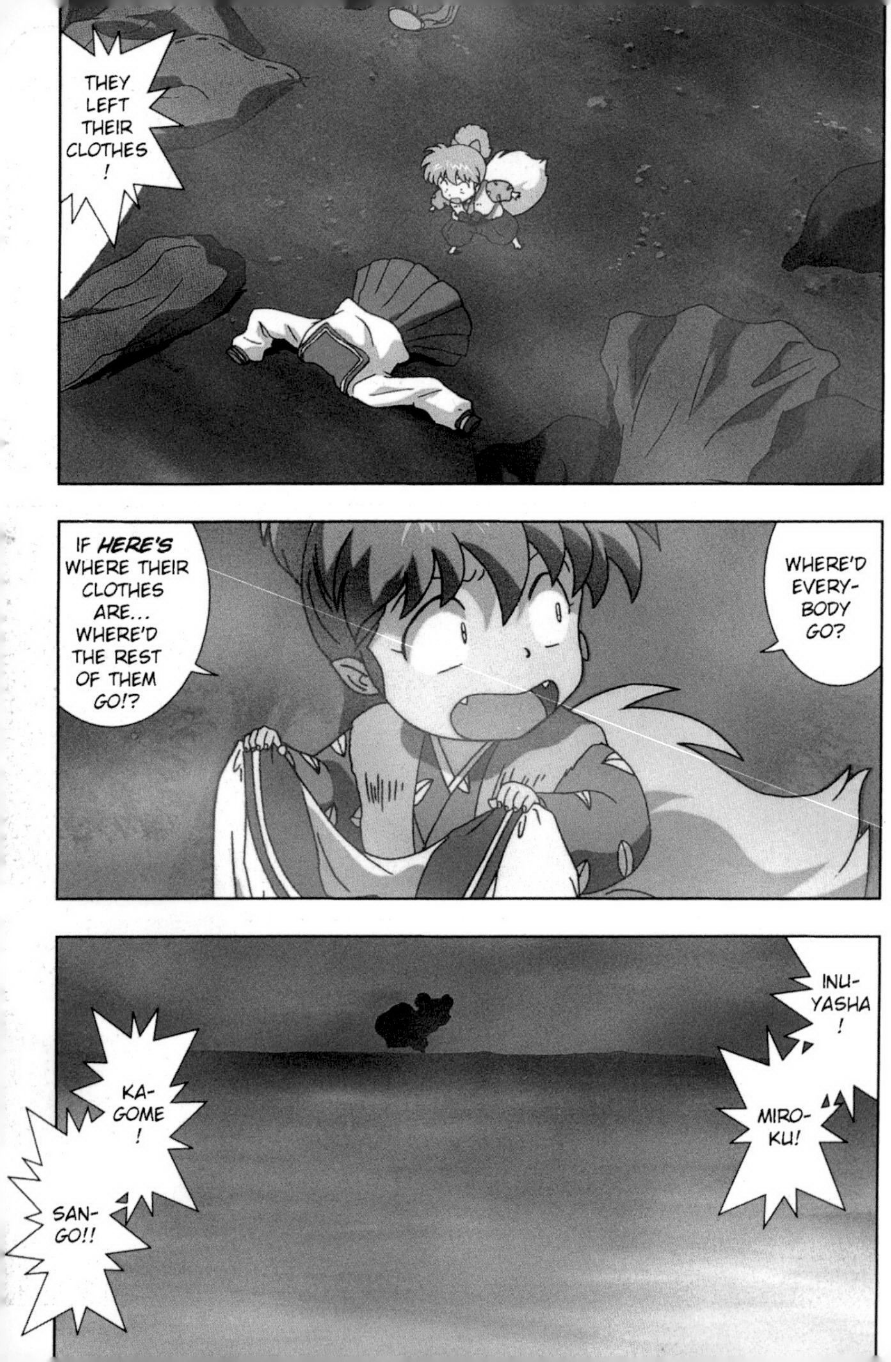
THEY LEFT THEIR CLOTHES!
WHERE'D EVERY-BODY GO?
IF ***HERE'S*** WHERE THEIR CLOTHES ARE... WHERE'D THE REST OF THEM GO!?
INU-YASHA!
MIRO-KU!
KA-GOME!
SAN-GO!!

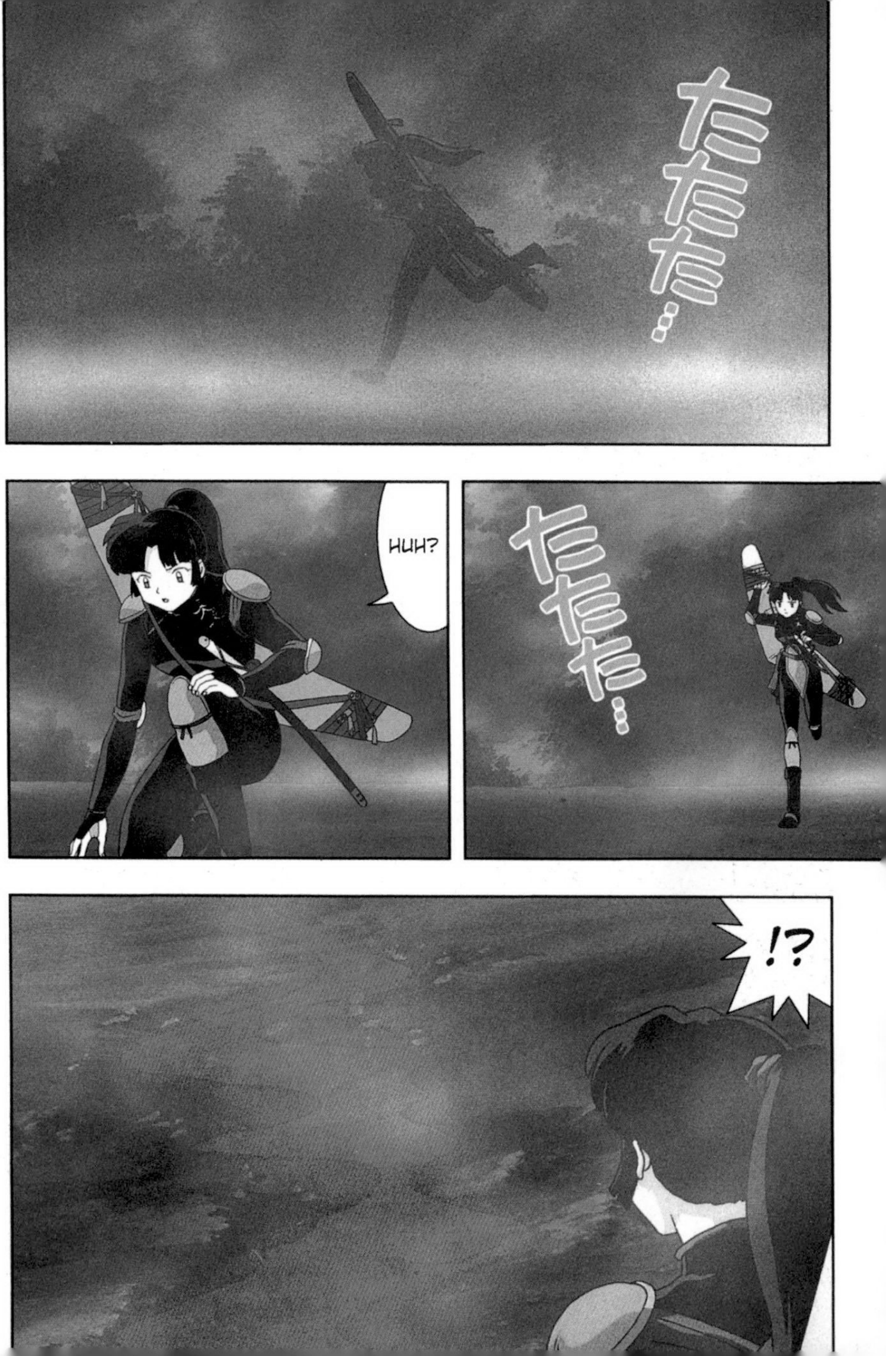
たたた…
たたた…
HUH?
!?

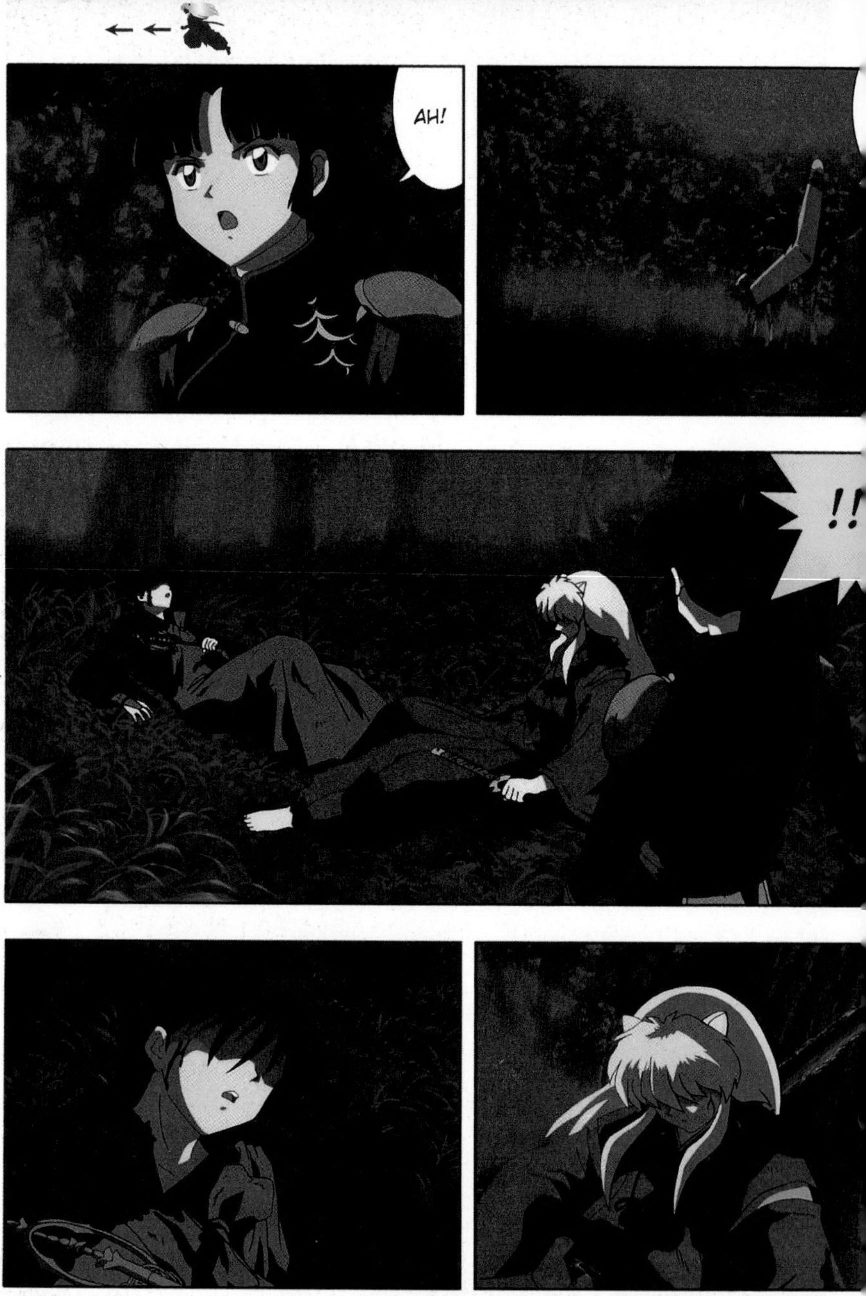
AH!
!!

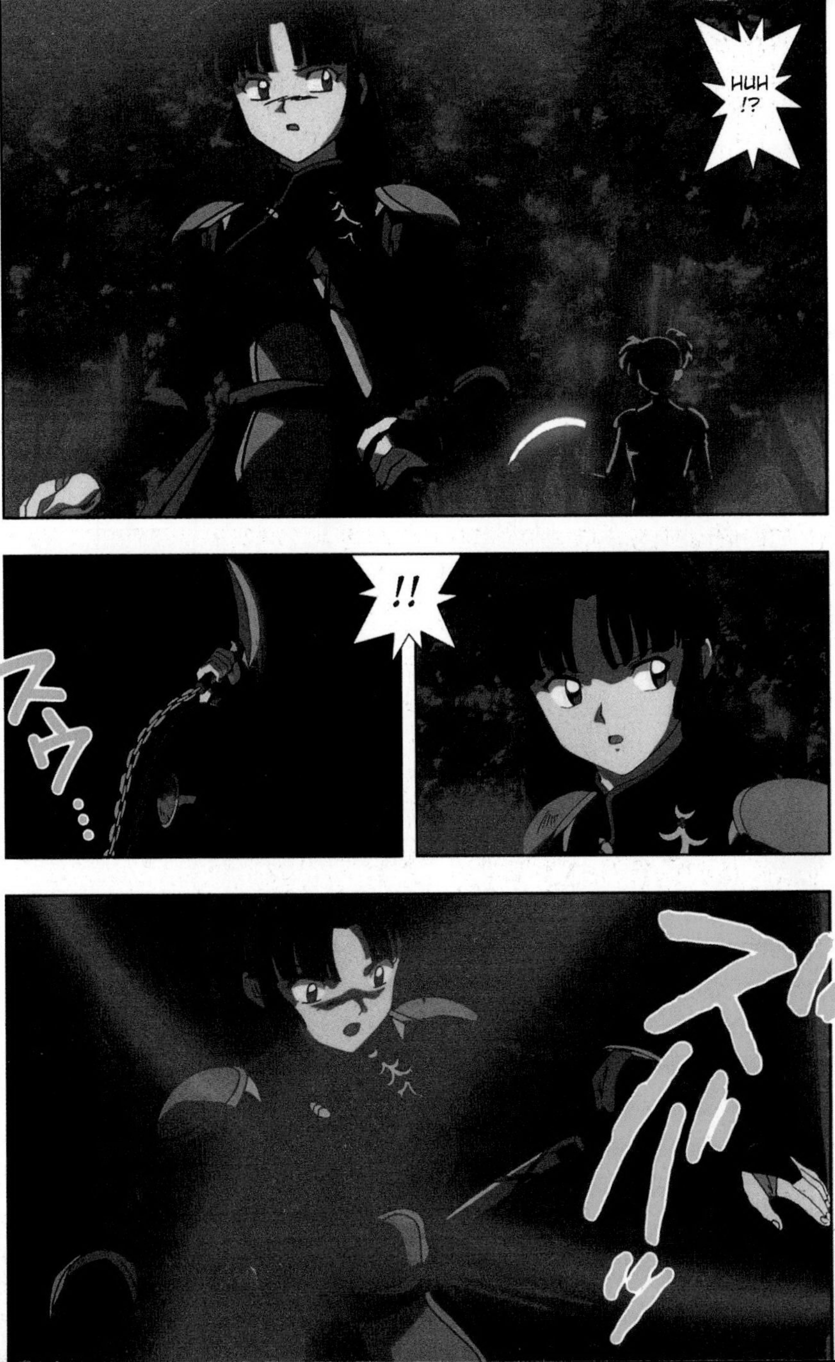
HUH !?
!!
スゥ…
ズバッ

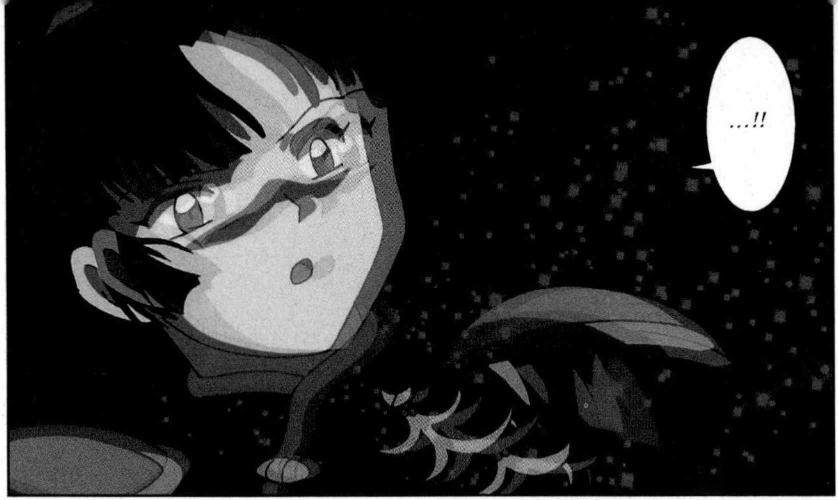
...!!
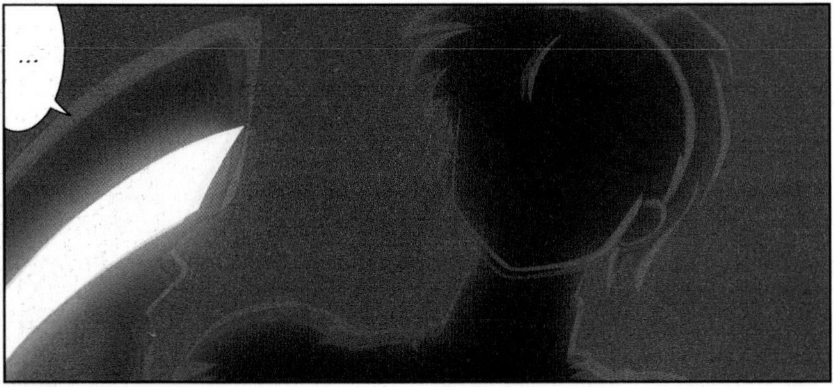
...
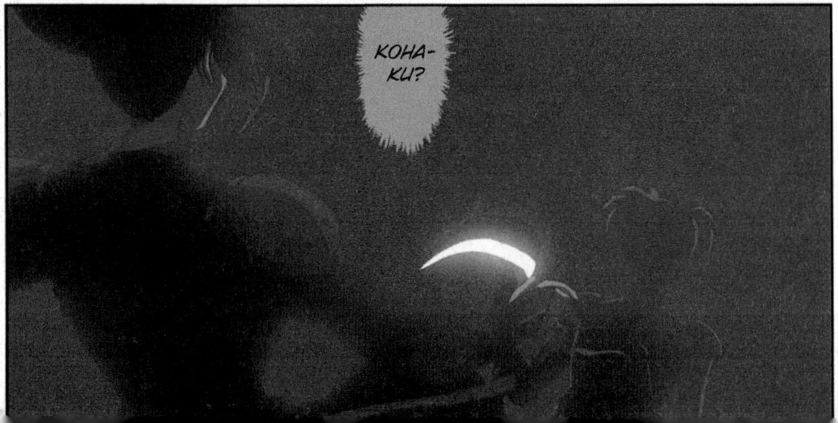
KOHA-
KU?

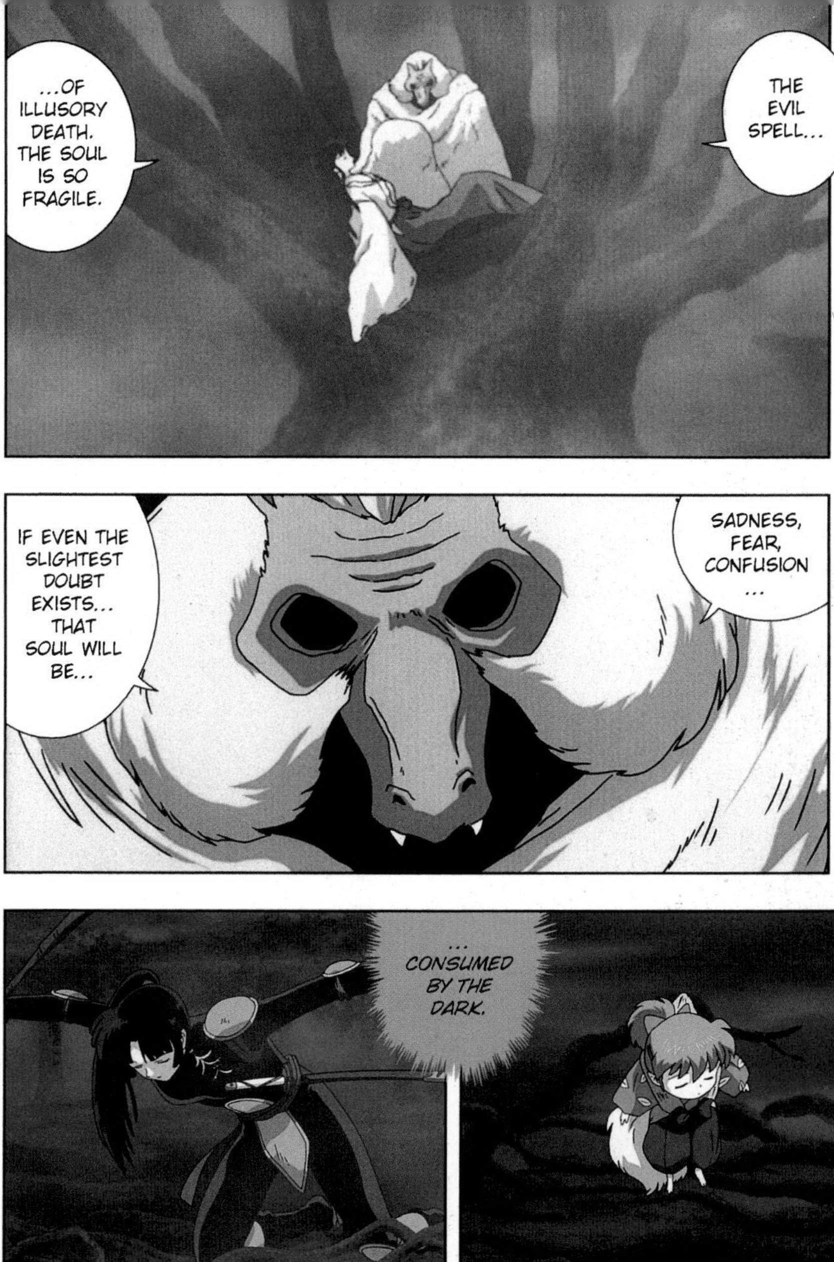
THE EVIL SPELL...
...OF ILLUSORY DEATH. THE SOUL IS SO FRAGILE.
SADNESS, FEAR, CONFUSION ...
IF EVEN THE SLIGHTEST DOUBT EXISTS... THAT SOUL WILL BE...
... CONSUMED BY THE DARK.

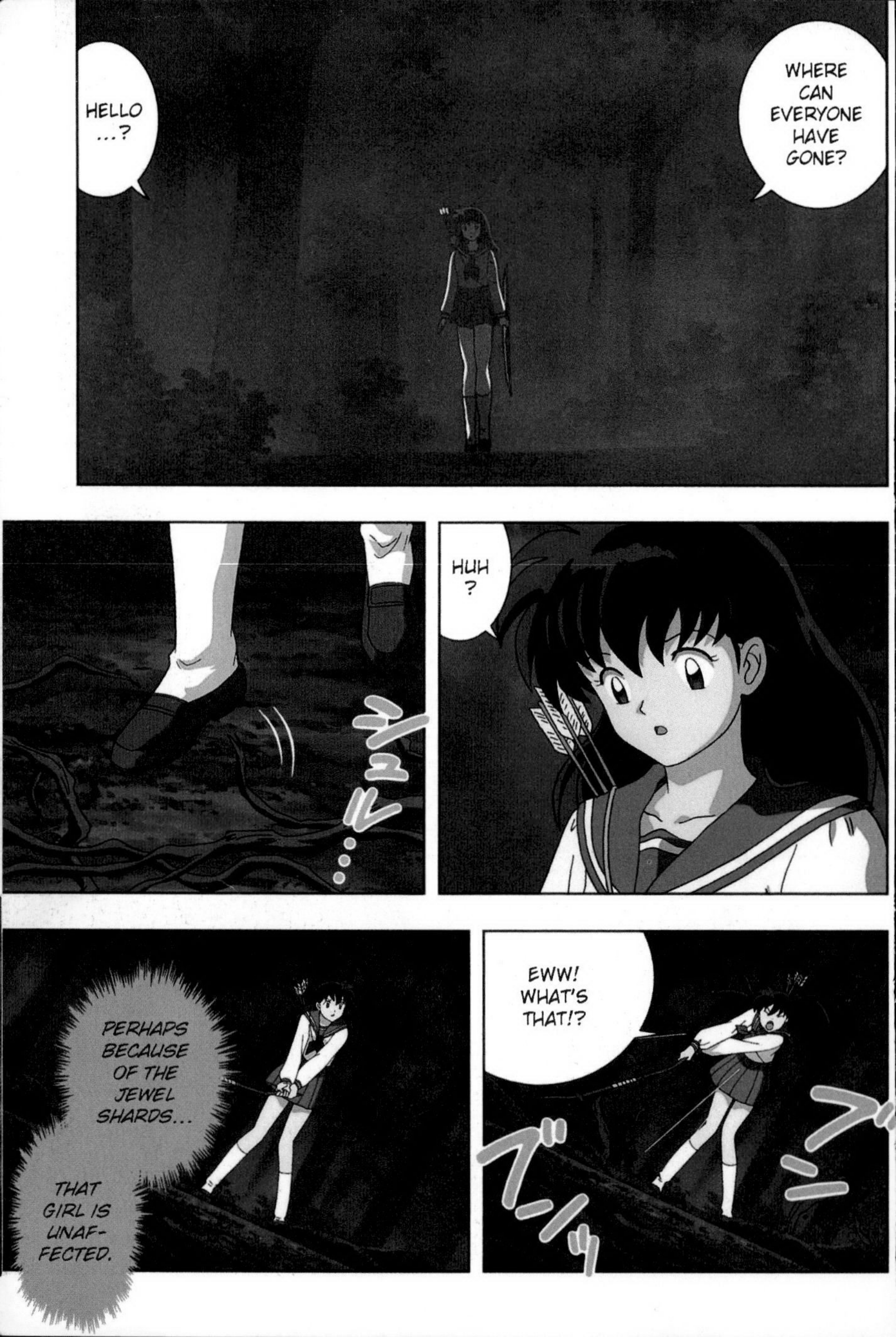
WHERE CAN EVERYONE HAVE GONE?
HELLO ...?
HUH ?
シュル...
EWW! WHAT'S THAT!?
PERHAPS BECAUSE OF THE JEWEL SHARDS...
THAT GIRL IS UNAF- FECTED.

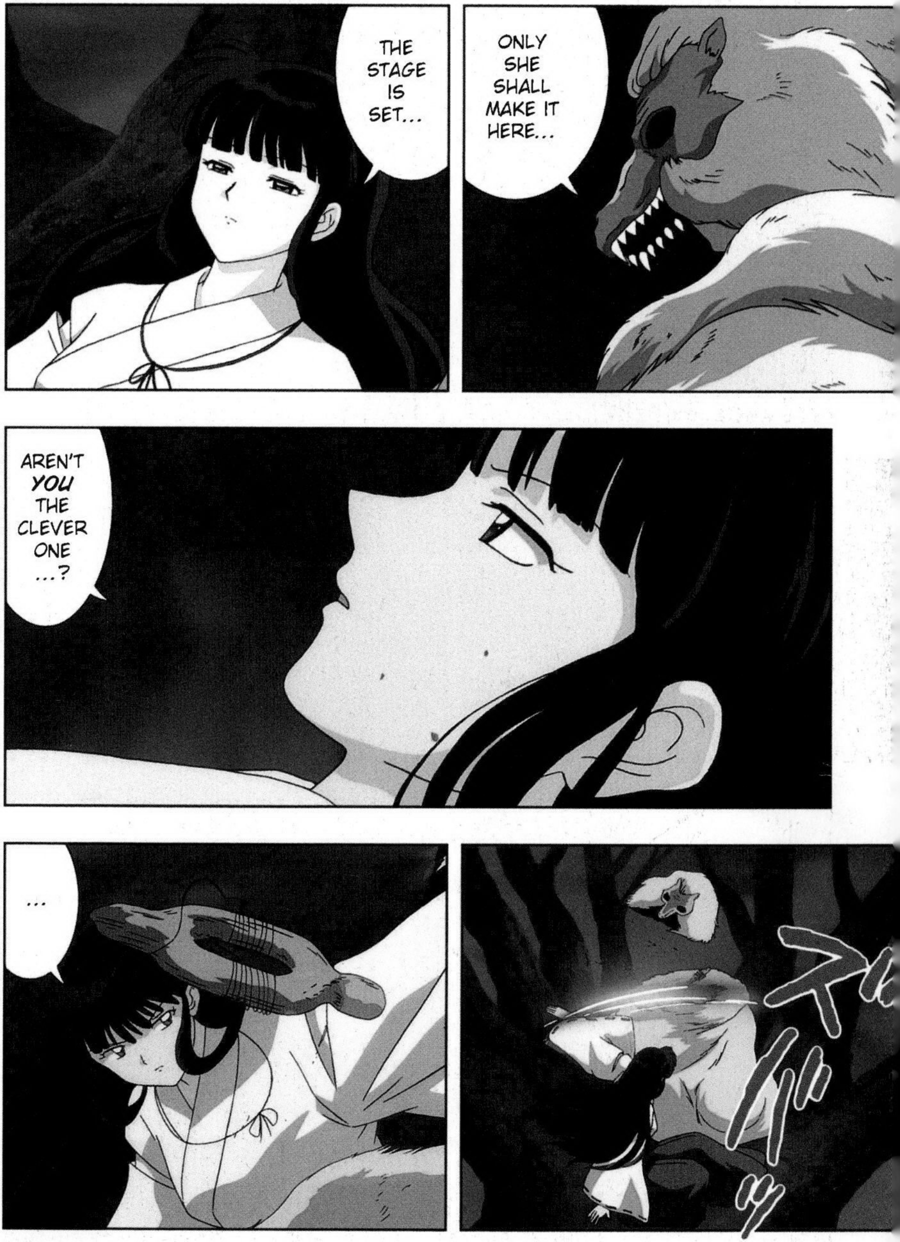
ONLY SHE SHALL MAKE IT HERE...
THE STAGE IS SET...
AREN'T *YOU* THE CLEVER ONE ...?
...

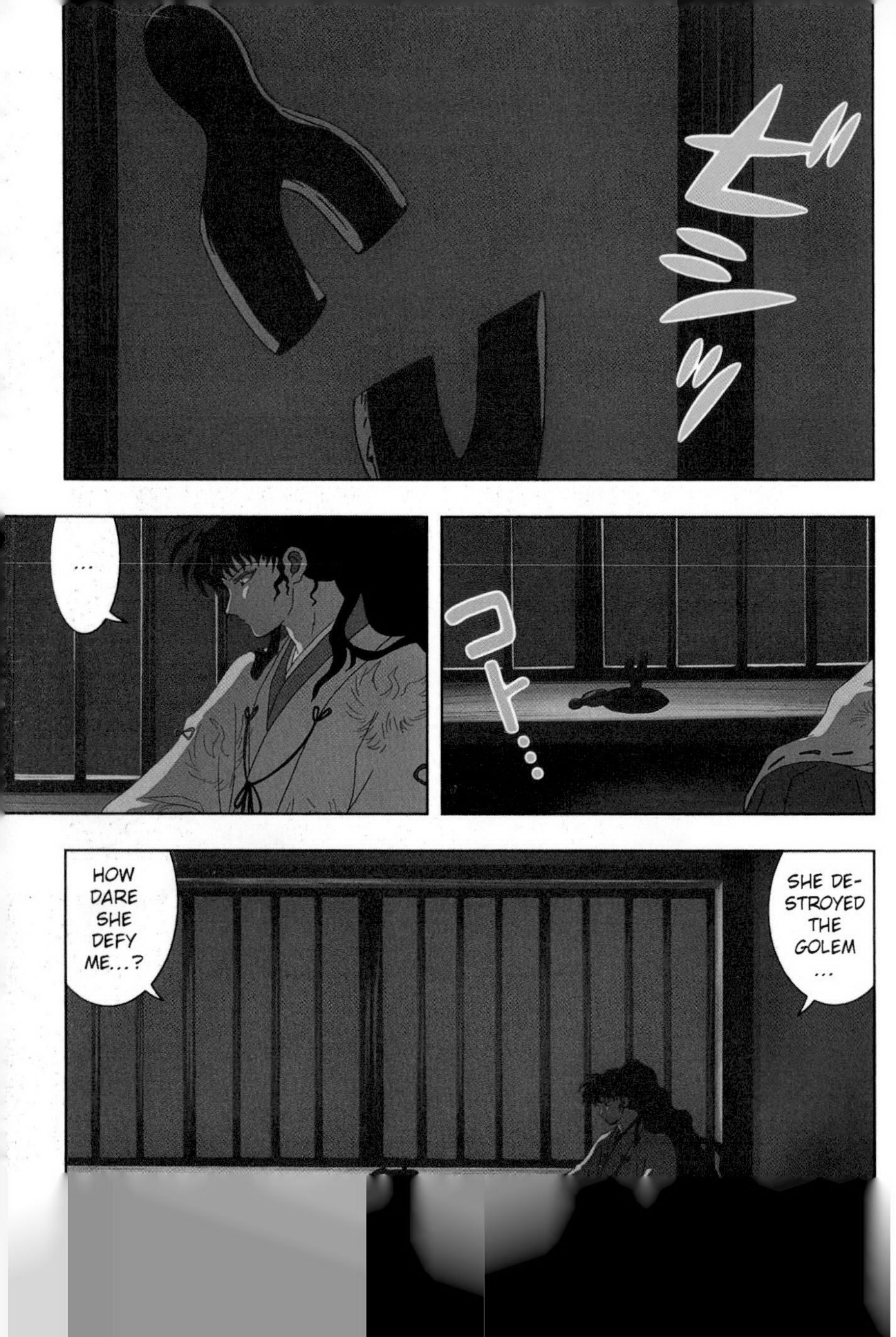
ビシッ
コト…
...
SHE DE-STROYED THE GOLEM ...
HOW DARE SHE DEFY ME...?

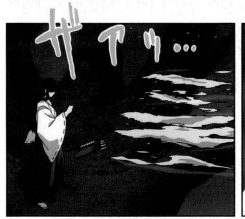

ザアッ…

シュウウウ…

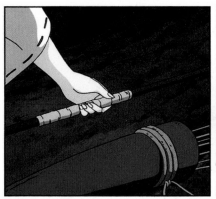

KIKYO
...

ギィ

ギィ

YOU'RE
OKAY!

KIKYO
!

たっ

174

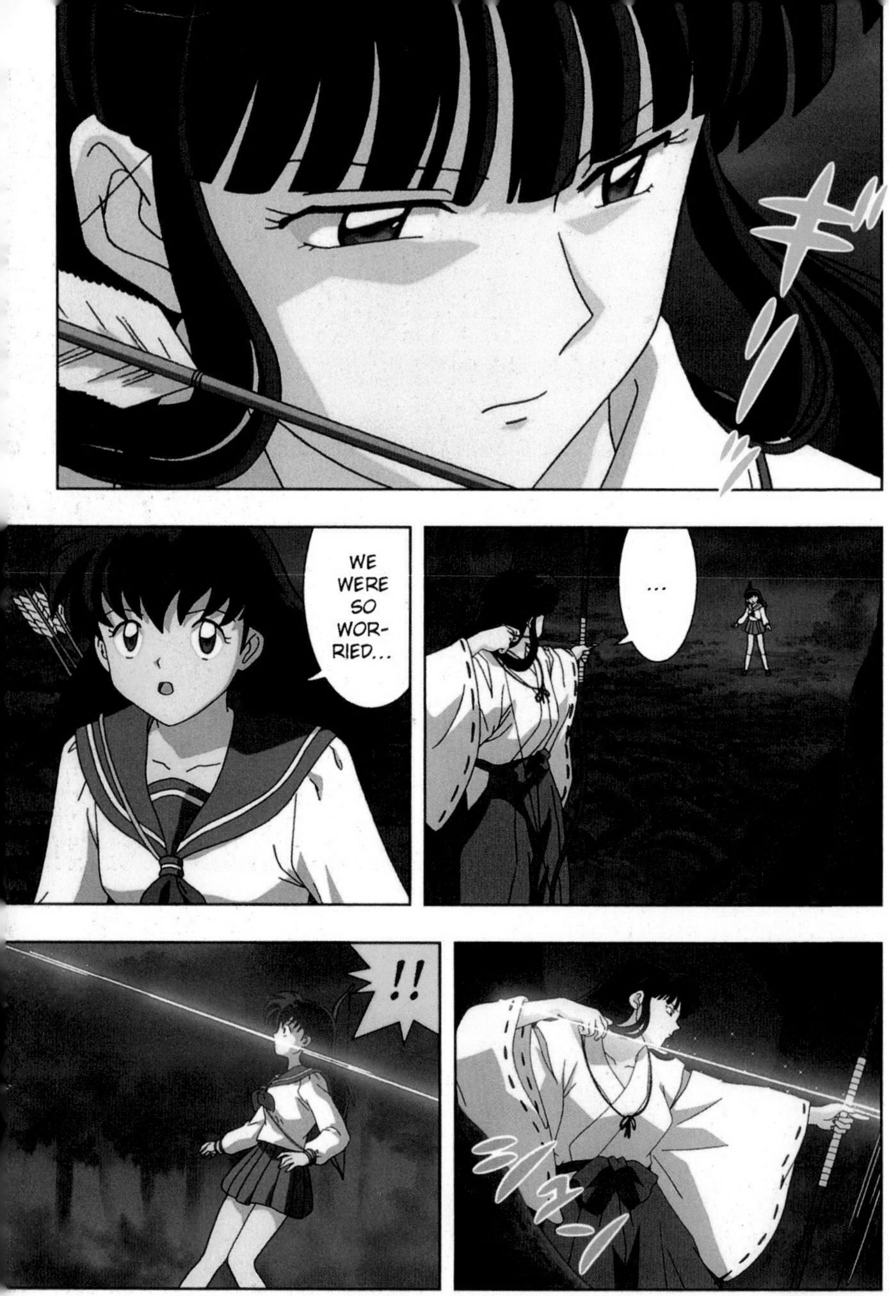
...
WE WERE SO WORRIED...
!!

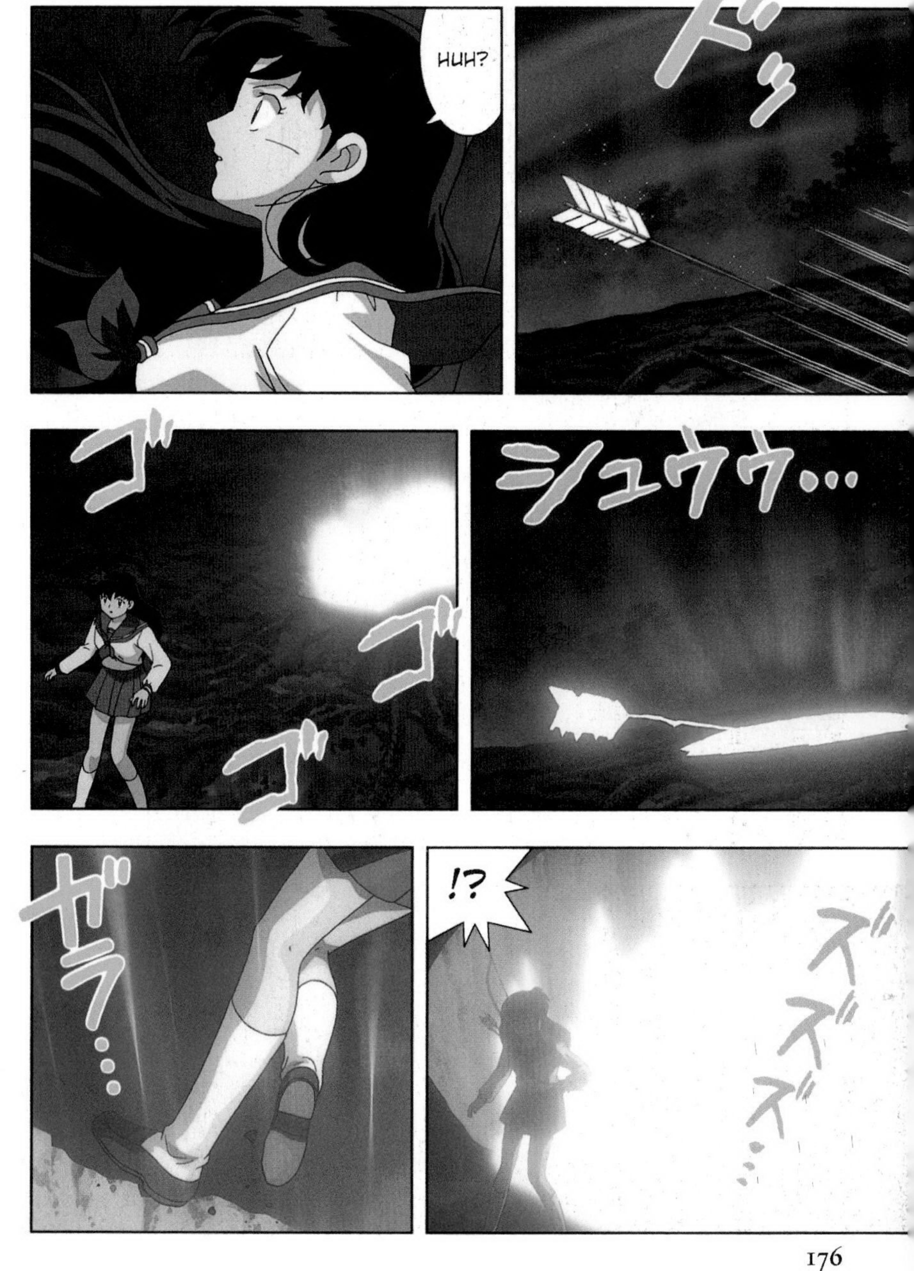
ドッ
HUH?
シュウウ…
ゴ
ゴ
ゴ
!?
ズズズ…
ザラ…

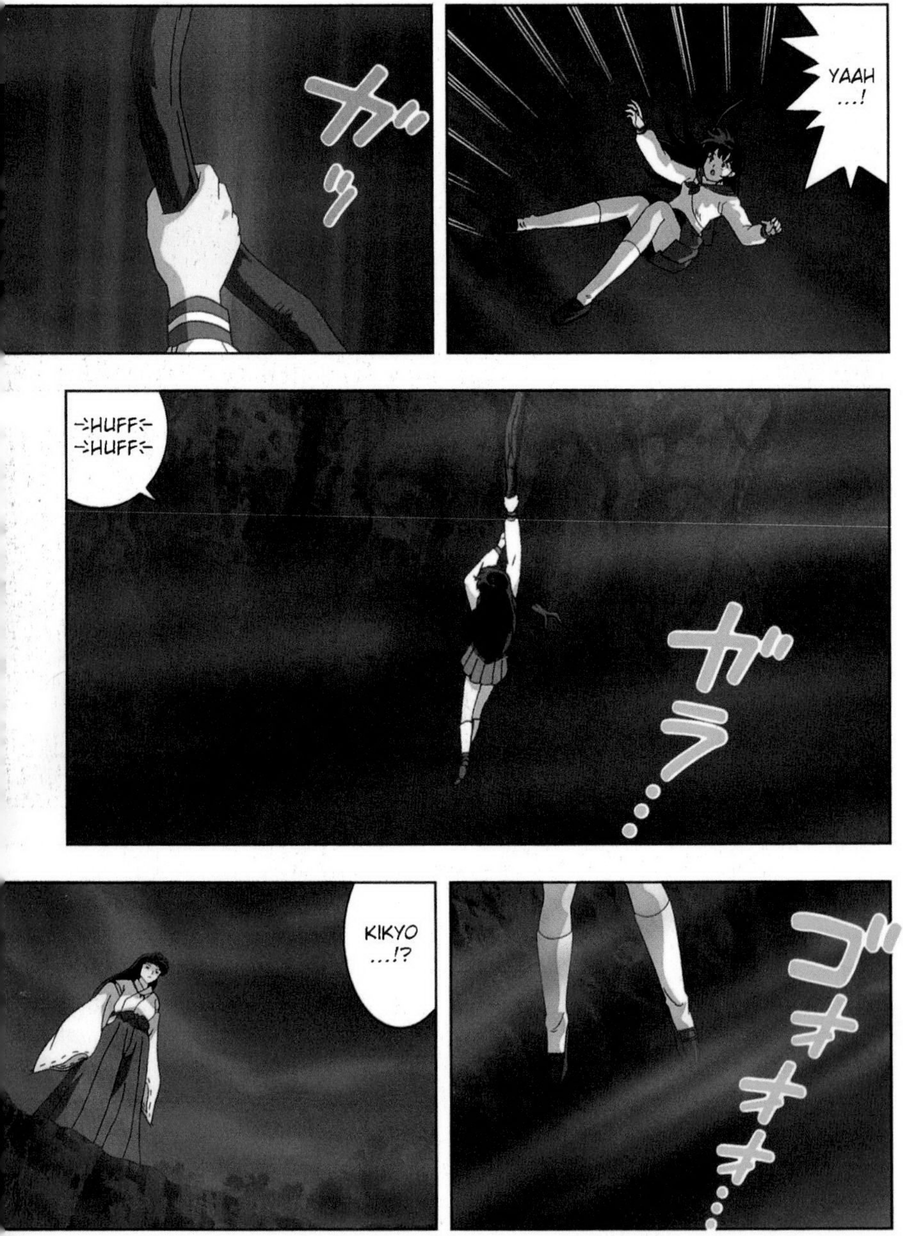
YAAH ...!
ガッ
HUFF
HUFF
ガラ…
ゴォォォ…
KIKYO ...!?

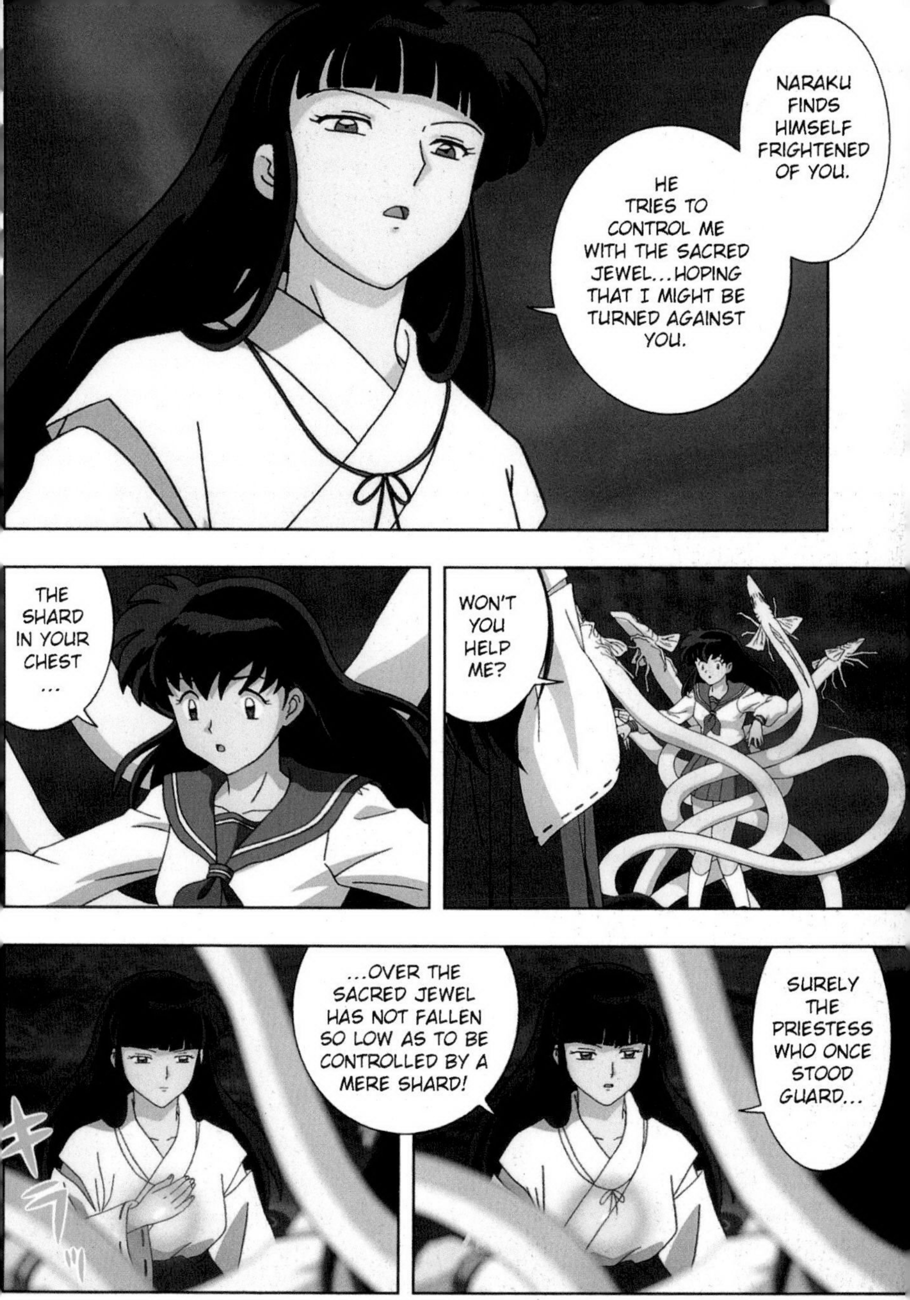
NARAKU FINDS HIMSELF FRIGHTENED OF YOU.
HE TRIES TO CONTROL ME WITH THE SACRED JEWEL...HOPING THAT I MIGHT BE TURNED AGAINST YOU.
WON'T YOU HELP ME?
THE SHARD IN YOUR CHEST...
SURELY THE PRIESTESS WHO ONCE STOOD GUARD...
...OVER THE SACRED JEWEL HAS NOT FALLEN SO LOW AS TO BE CONTROLLED BY A MERE SHARD!
キラ

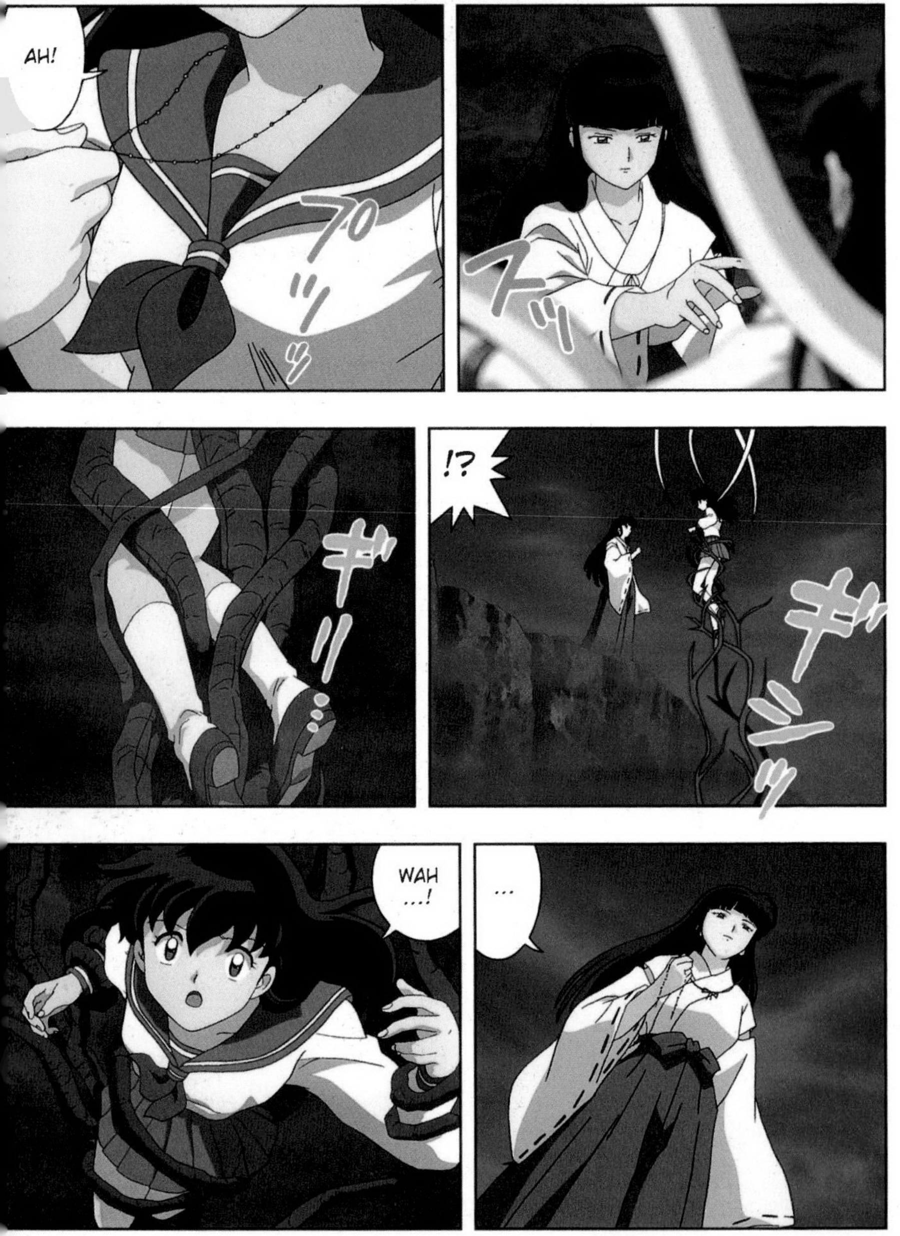
フッ
AH!
プツッ
!?
ギシッ
ギリ
...
WAH ...!

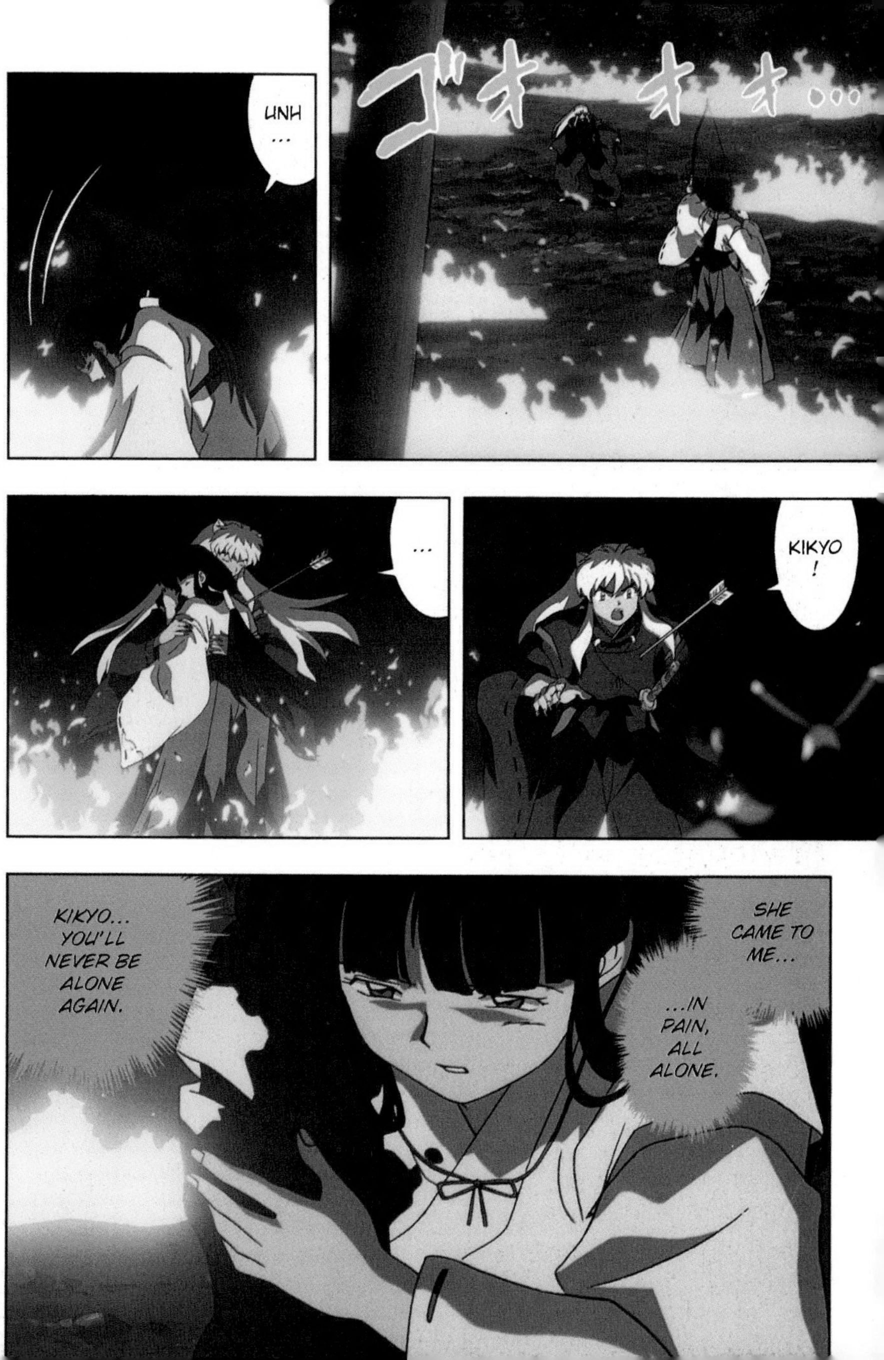
ゴオオオ…
UNH ...
KIKYO !
...
SHE CAME TO ME...
...IN PAIN, ALL ALONE.
KIKYO... YOU'LL NEVER BE ALONE AGAIN.

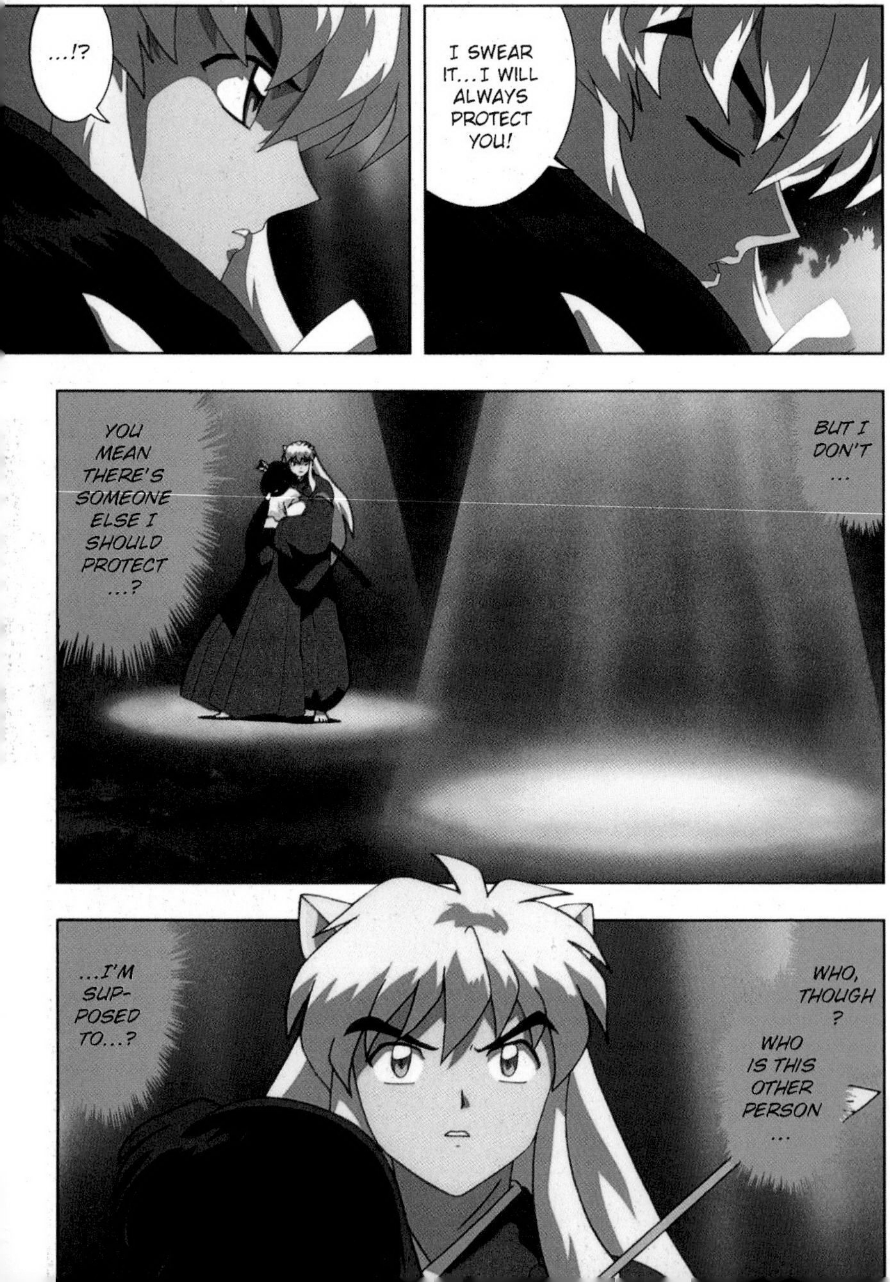
I SWEAR IT... I WILL ALWAYS PROTECT YOU!
...!?
BUT I DON'T ...
YOU MEAN THERE'S SOMEONE ELSE I SHOULD PROTECT ...?
WHO, THOUGH ?
WHO IS THIS OTHER PERSON ...
...I'M SUP-POSED TO...?

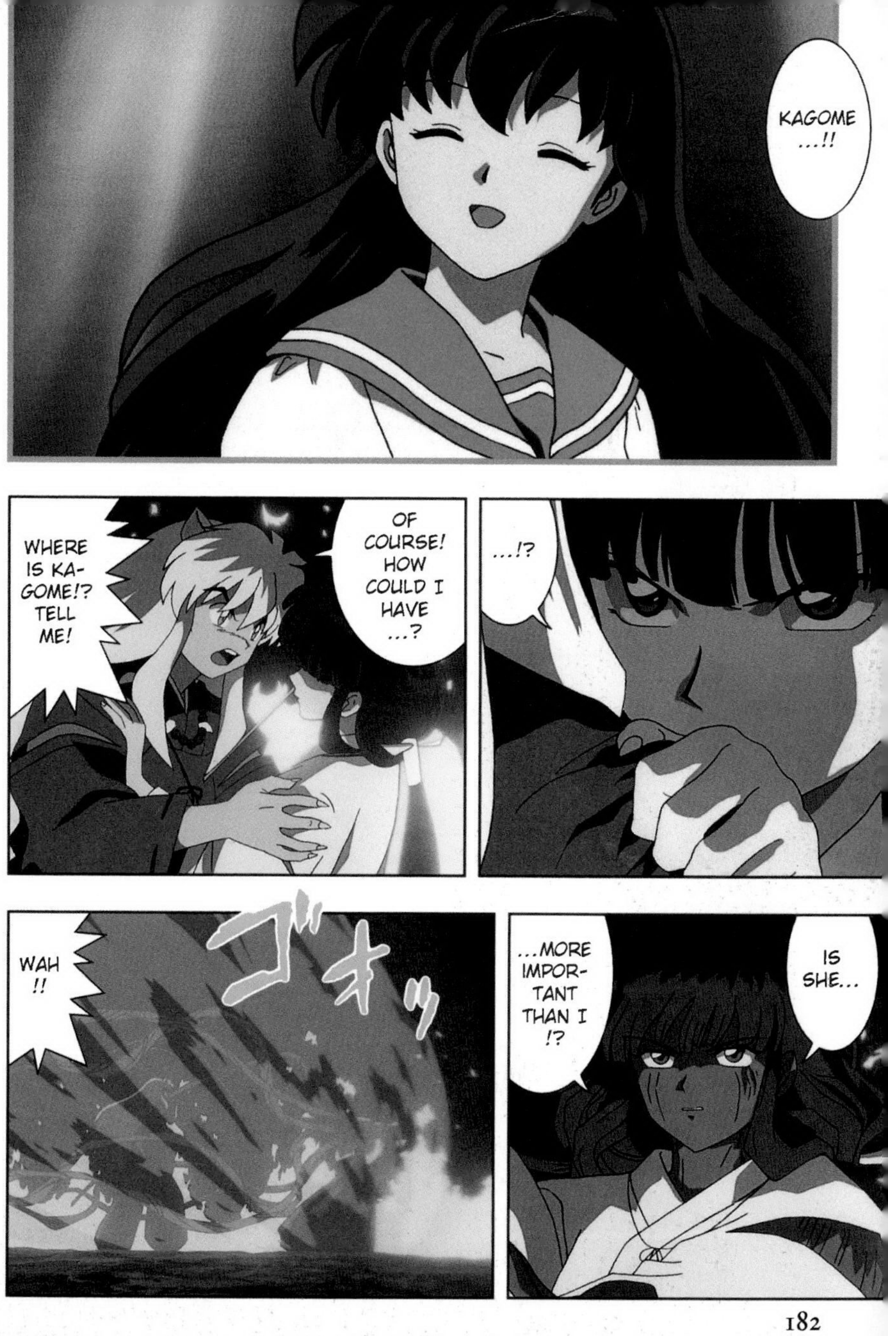
KAGOME ...!!
...!?
OF COURSE! HOW COULD I HAVE ...?
WHERE IS KA-GOME!? TELL ME!
IS SHE...
...MORE IMPOR-TANT THAN I !?
ゴォッ
WAH !!

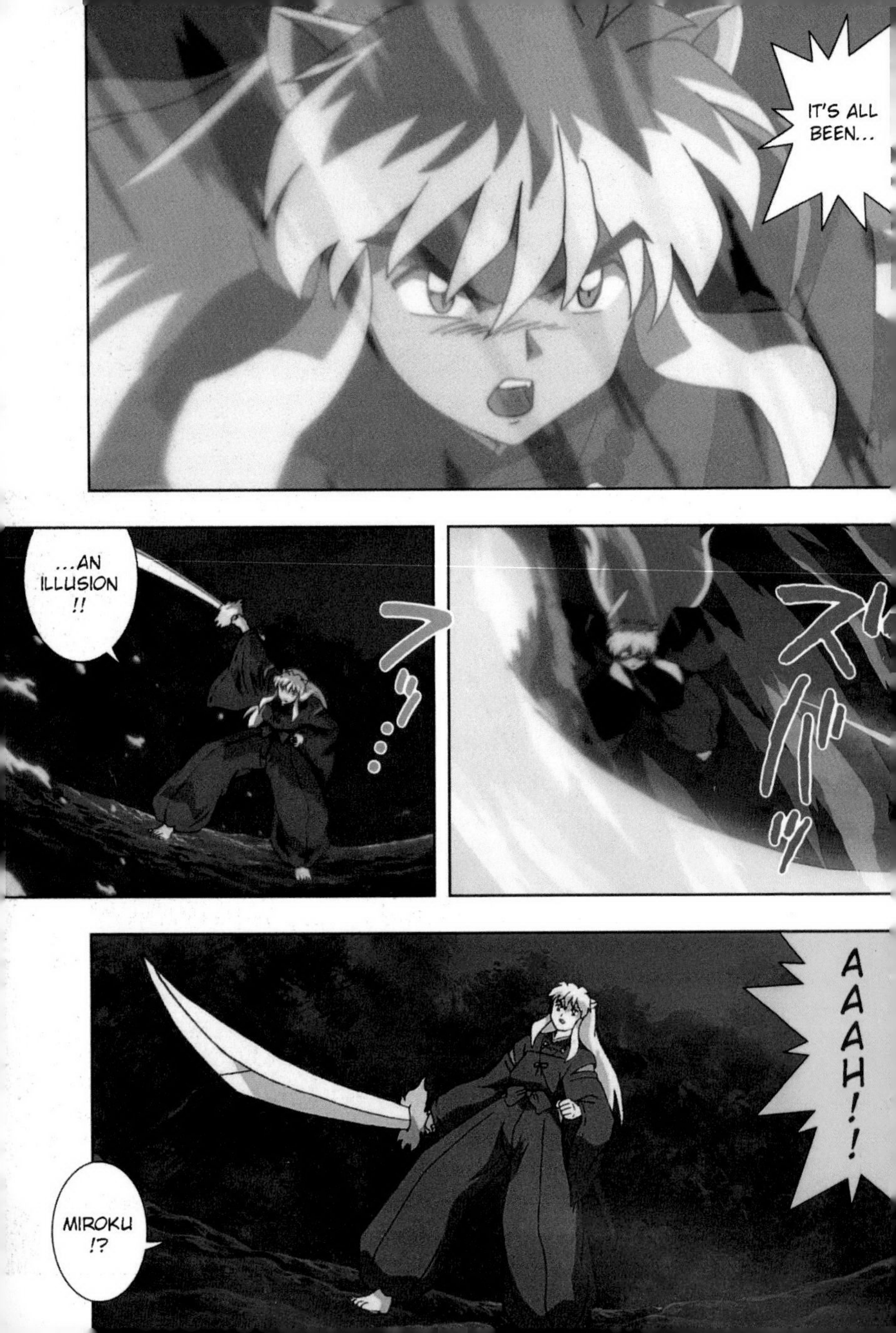
IT'S ALL BEEN...
...AN ILLUSION !!
フッ...
AAAAH!!
MIROKU !?

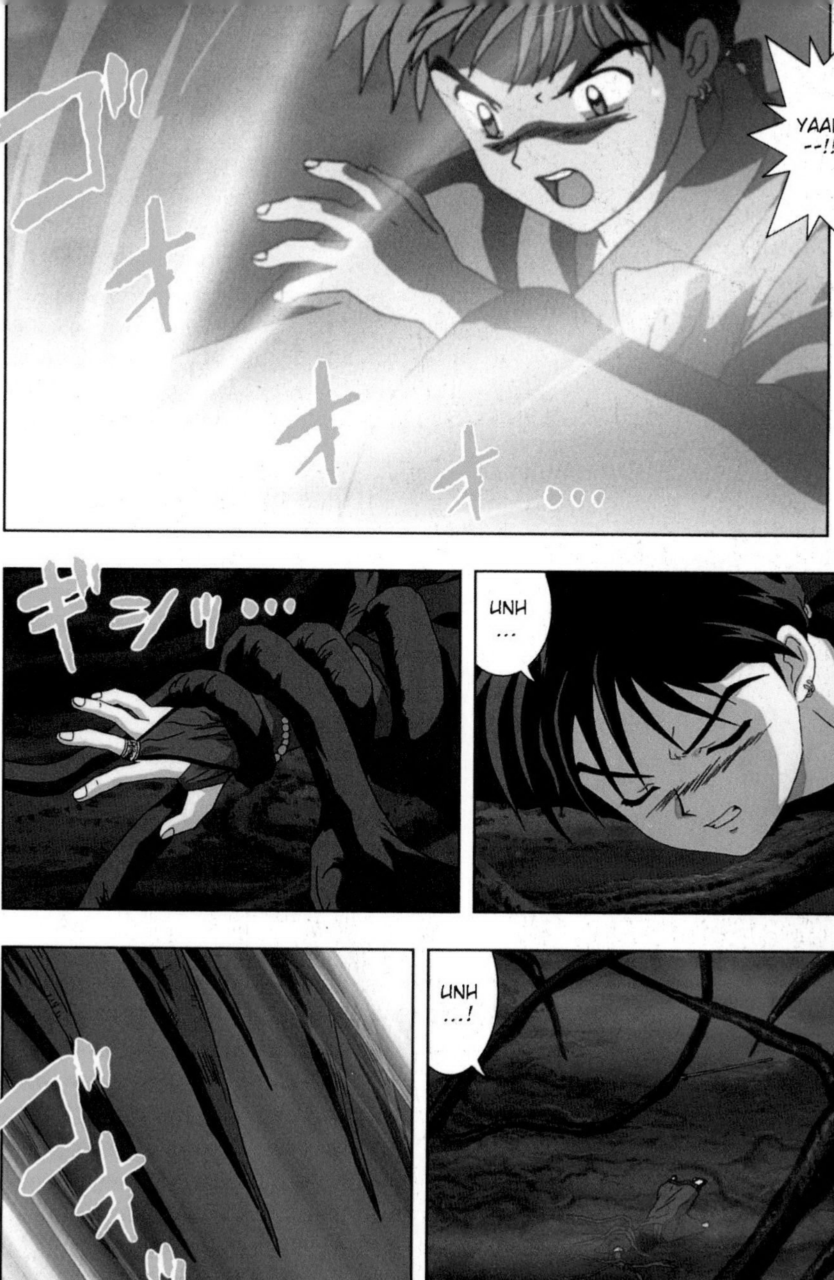
YAAH --!!
ゴオオオ…
UNH ...
ギシッ…
UNH ...!
ゴオッ

MI-
ROKU
!!

UNGH
...!

HEY
!!

YOU
OKAY?

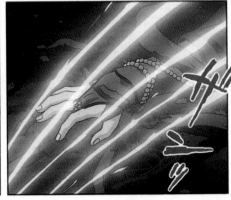

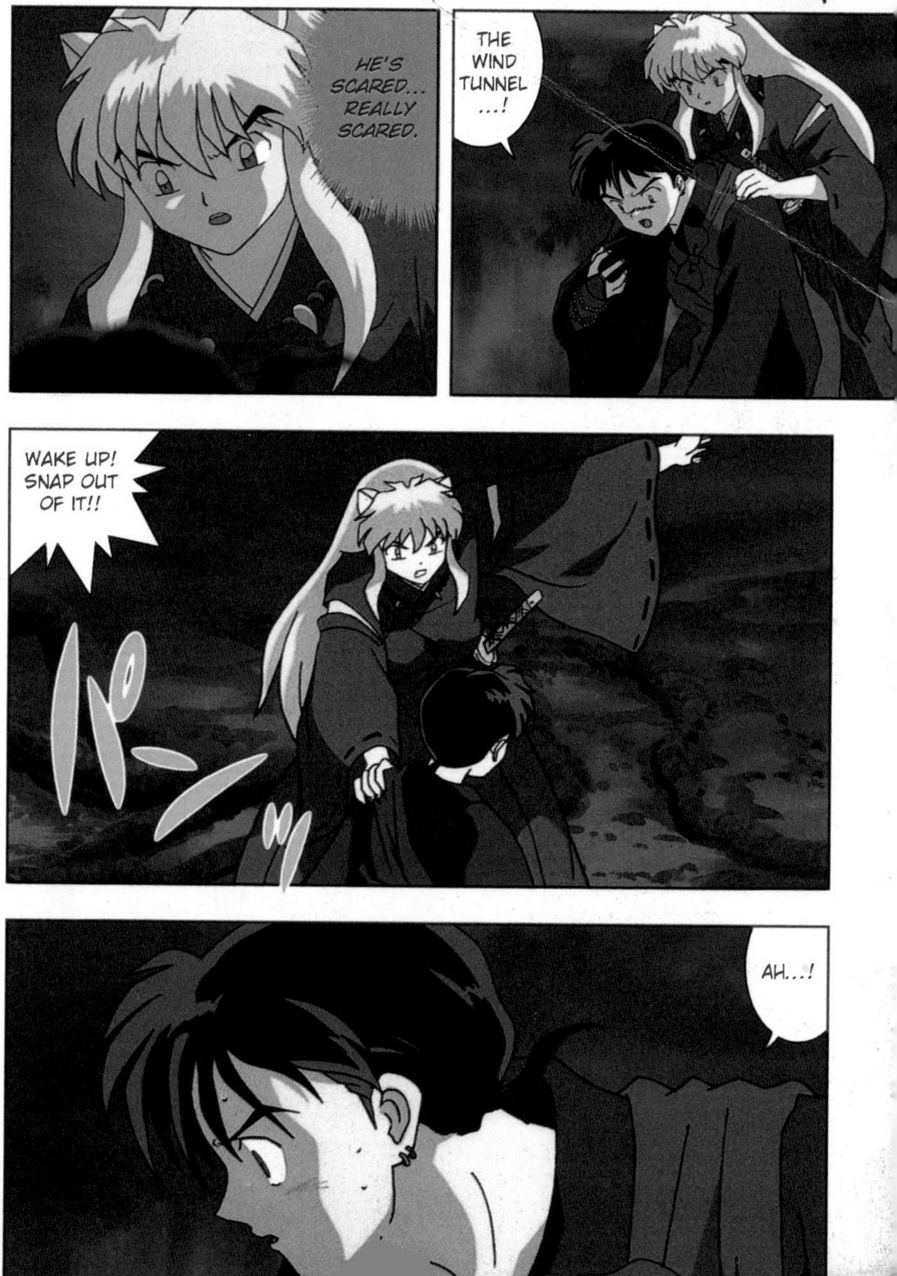
THE WIND TUNNEL ...!
HE'S SCARED... REALLY SCARED.
WAKE UP! SNAP OUT OF IT!!
AH...!

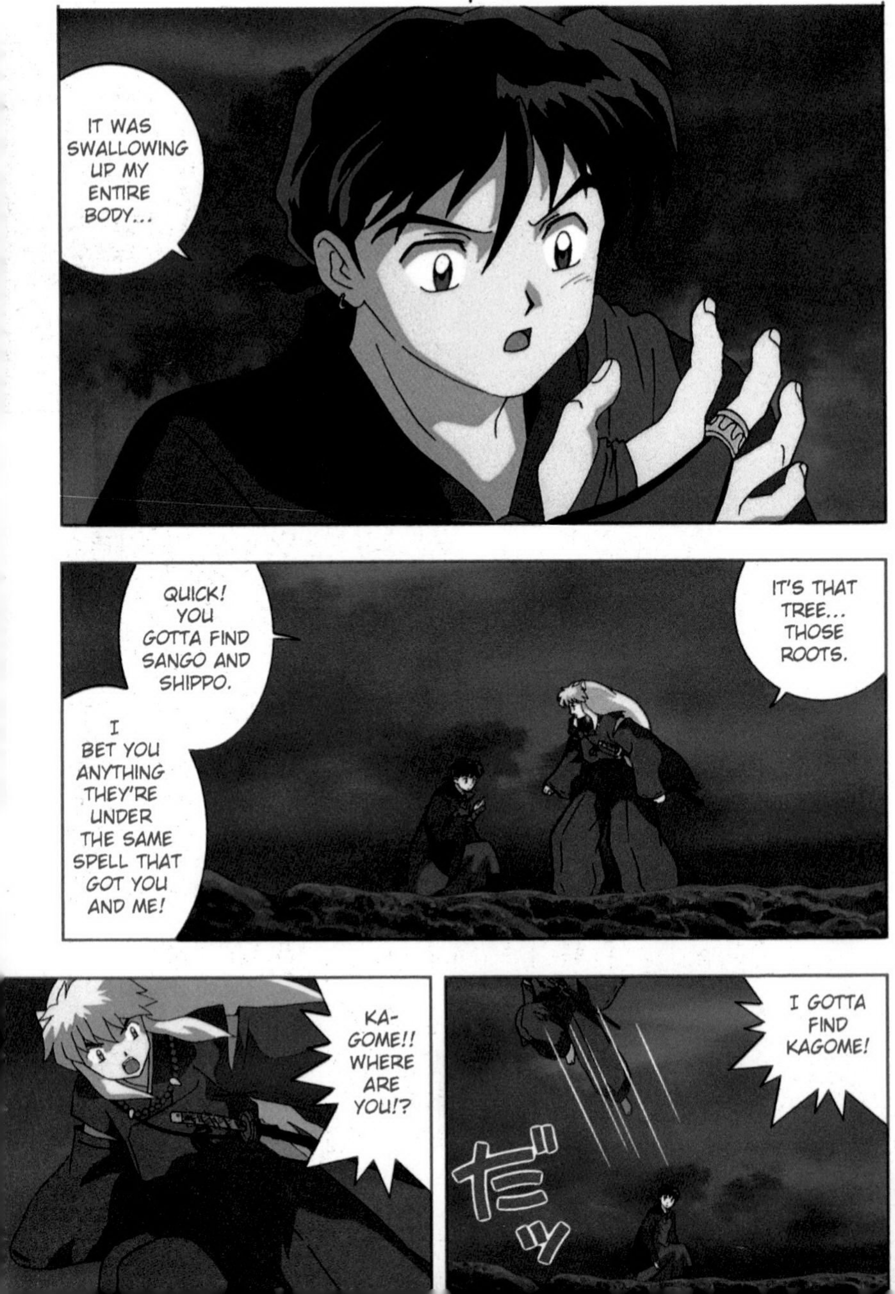
IT WAS SWALLOWING UP MY ENTIRE BODY...
IT'S THAT TREE... THOSE ROOTS.
QUICK! YOU GOTTA FIND SANGO AND SHIPPO.
I BET YOU ANYTHING THEY'RE UNDER THE SAME SPELL THAT GOT YOU AND ME!
I GOTTA FIND KAGOME!
ダッ
KA-GOME!! WHERE ARE YOU!?

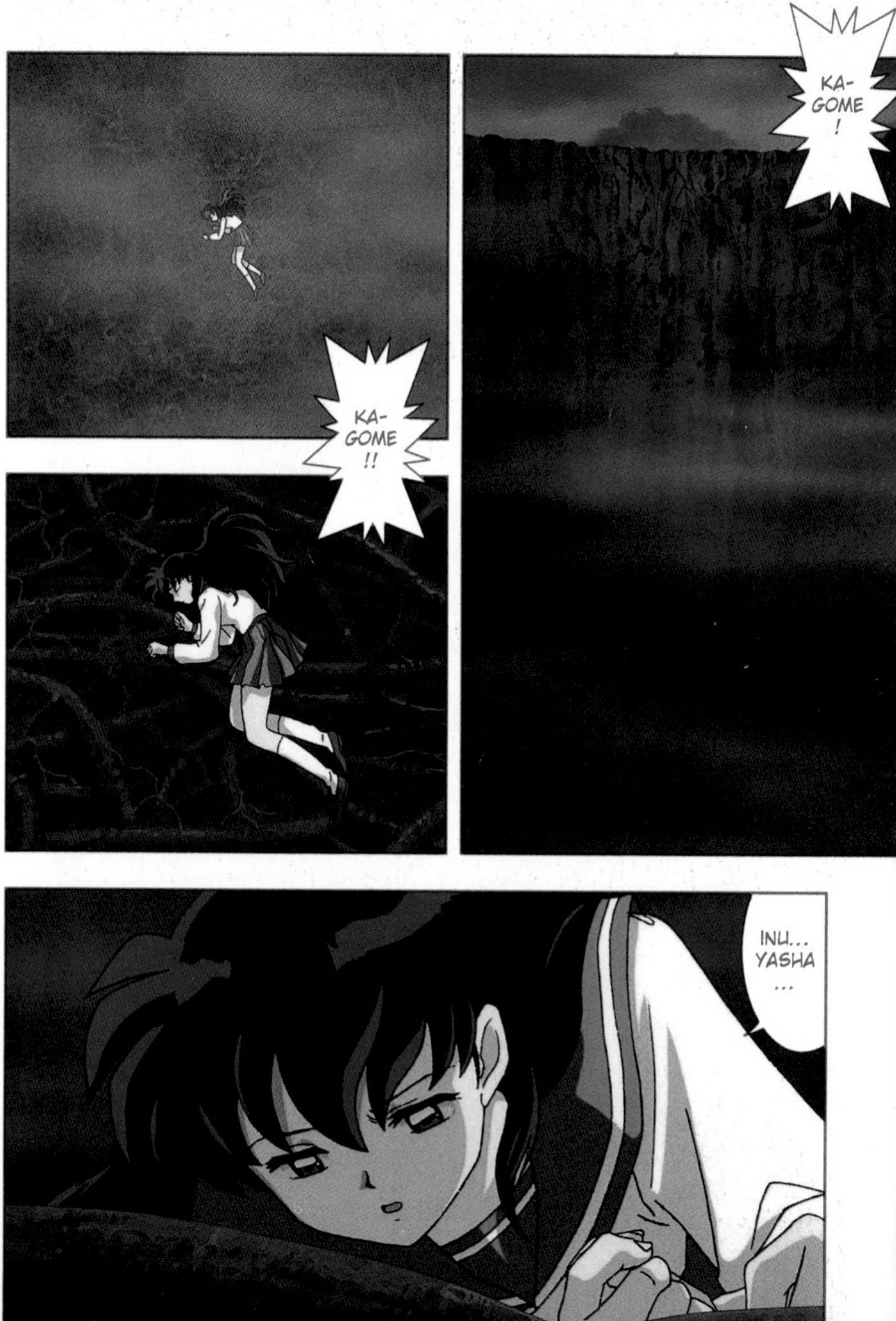
KA-GOME !
KA-GOME !!
INU... YASHA ...

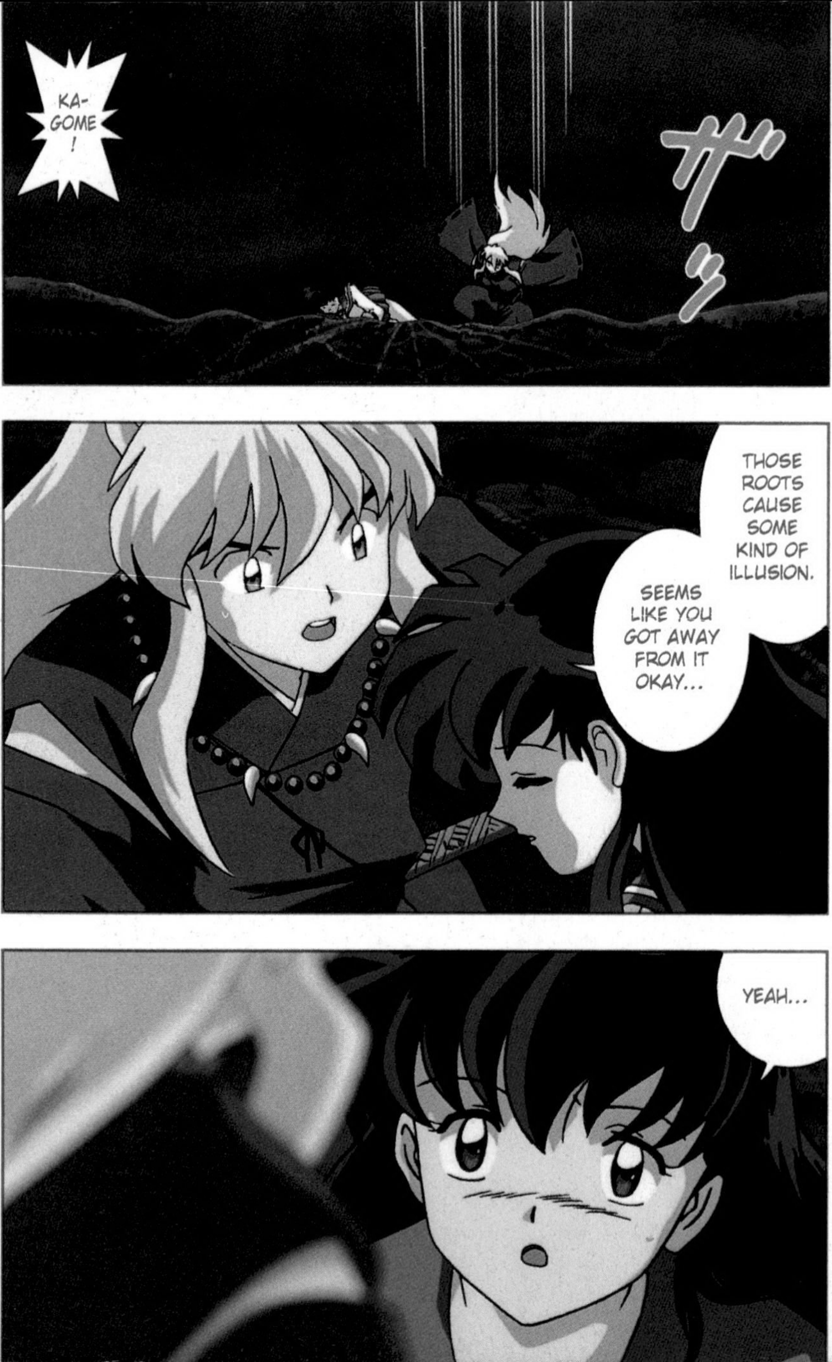
KA-GOME!
THOSE ROOTS CAUSE SOME KIND OF ILLUSION.
SEEMS LIKE YOU GOT AWAY FROM IT OKAY...
YEAH...

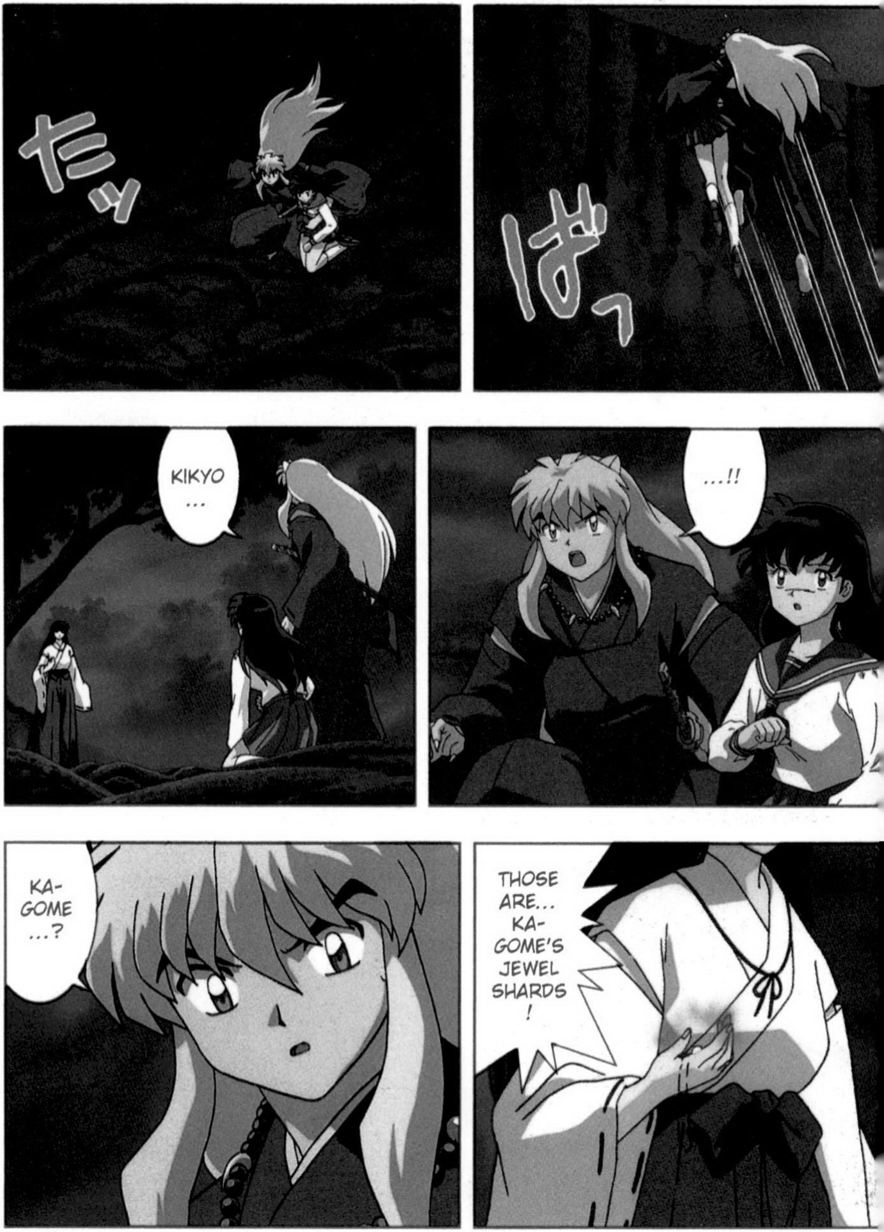
ぱっ
たッ
...!!
KIKYO ...
THOSE ARE... KA-GOME'S JEWEL SHARDS!
KA-GOME ...?

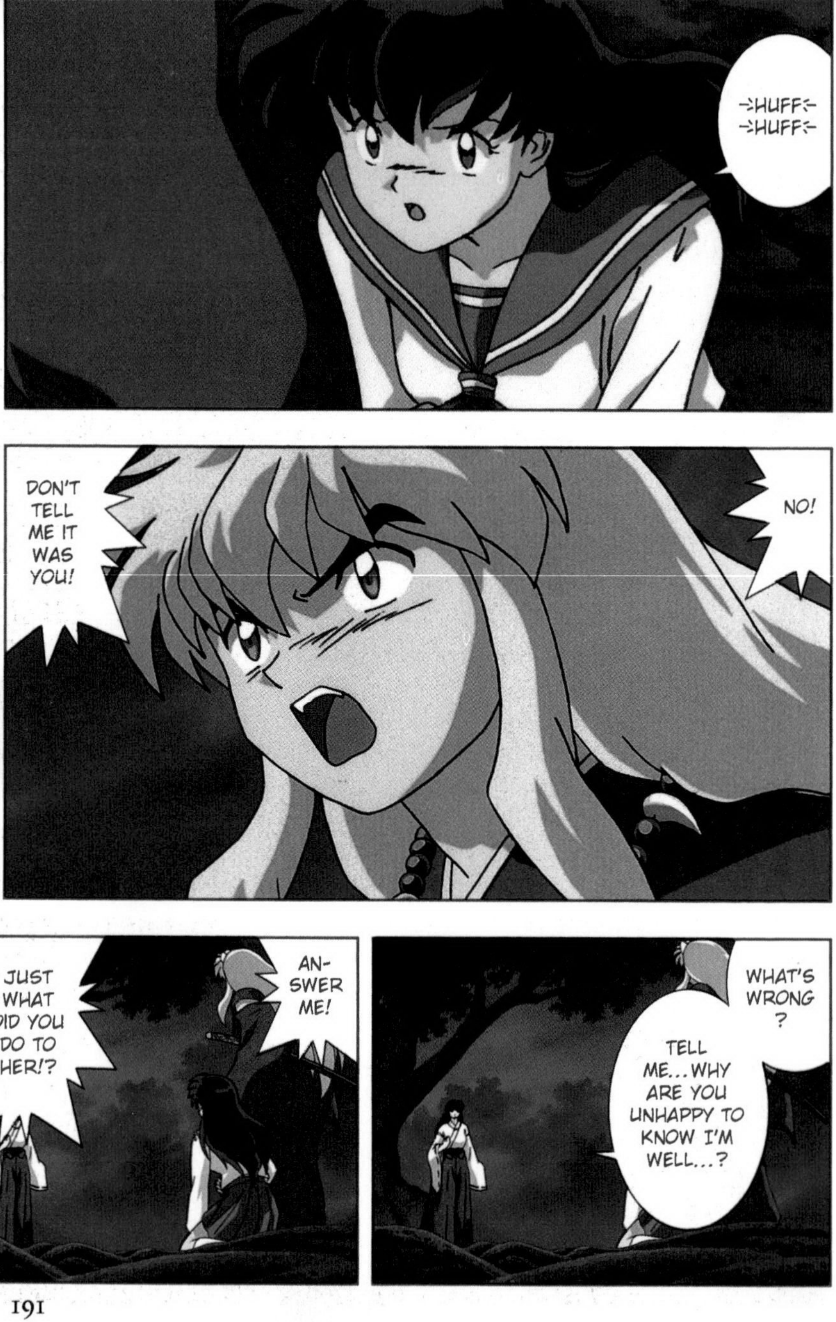
HUFF
HUFF
NO!
DON'T TELL ME IT WAS YOU!
WHAT'S WRONG?
TELL ME... WHY ARE YOU UNHAPPY TO KNOW I'M WELL...?
AN-SWER ME!
JUST WHAT DID YOU DO TO HER!?

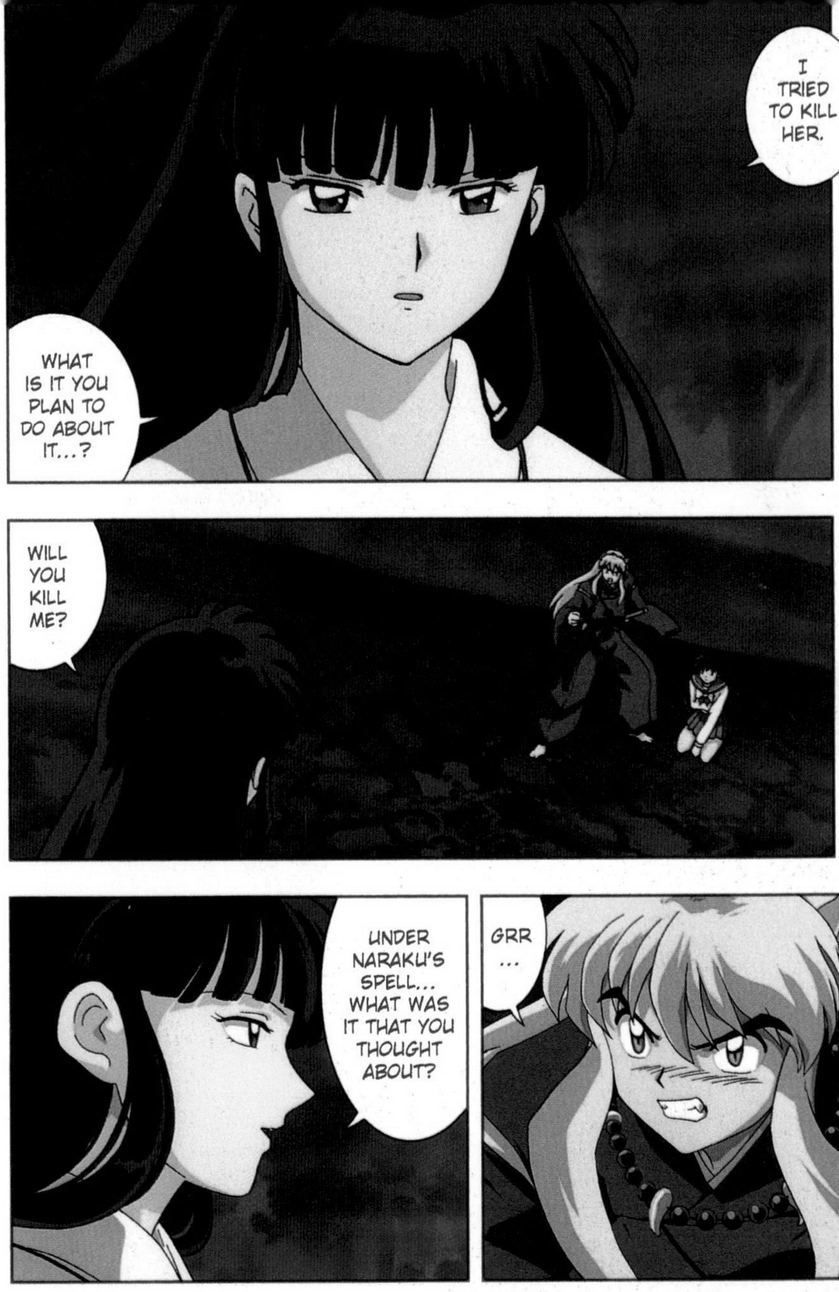
I TRIED TO KILL HER.
WHAT IS IT YOU PLAN TO DO ABOUT IT...?
WILL YOU KILL ME?
GRR ...
UNDER NARAKU'S SPELL... WHAT WAS IT THAT YOU THOUGHT ABOUT?

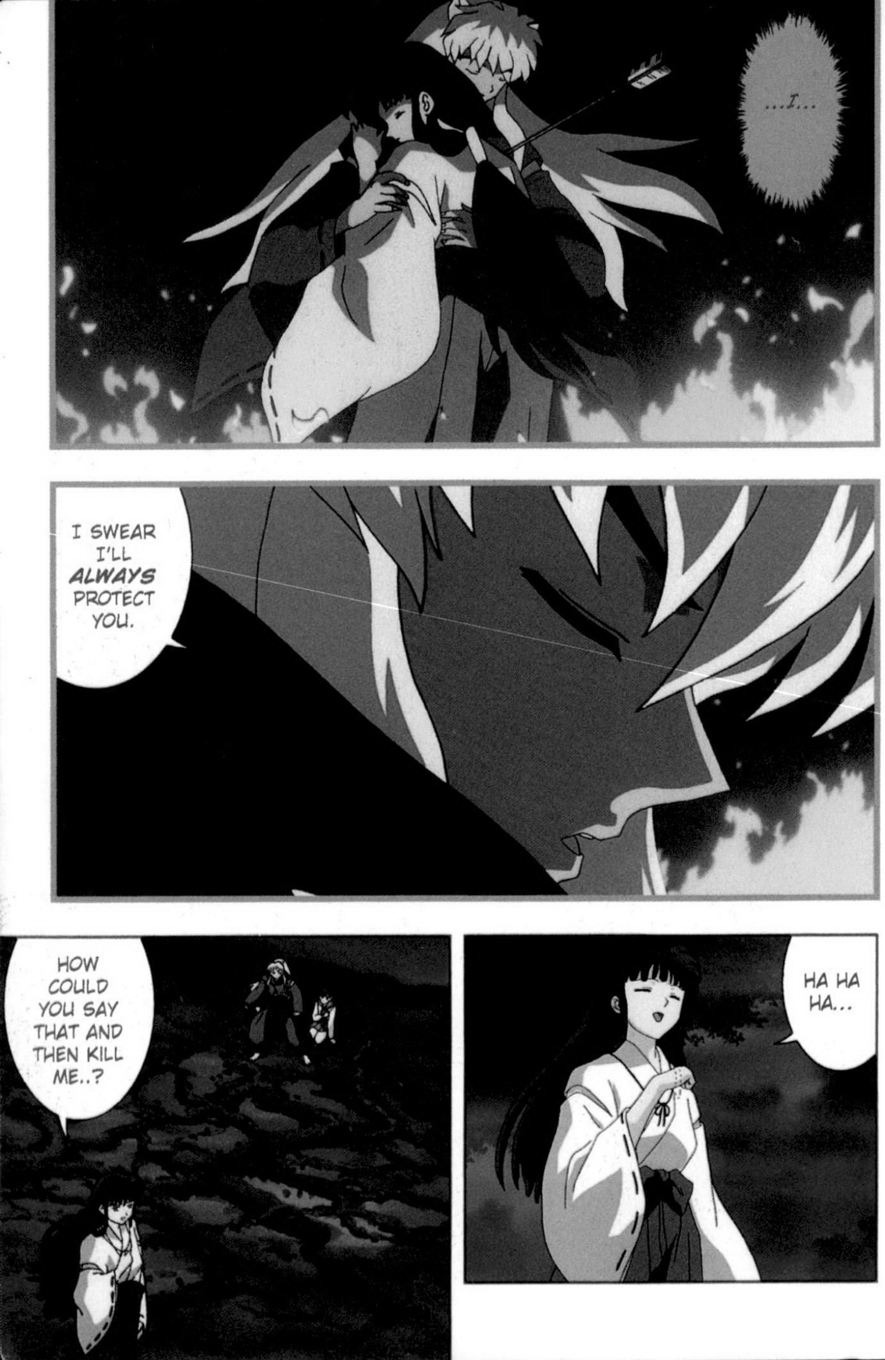
...I...
I SWEAR I'LL **ALWAYS** PROTECT YOU.
HA HA HA...
HOW COULD YOU SAY THAT AND THEN KILL ME..?

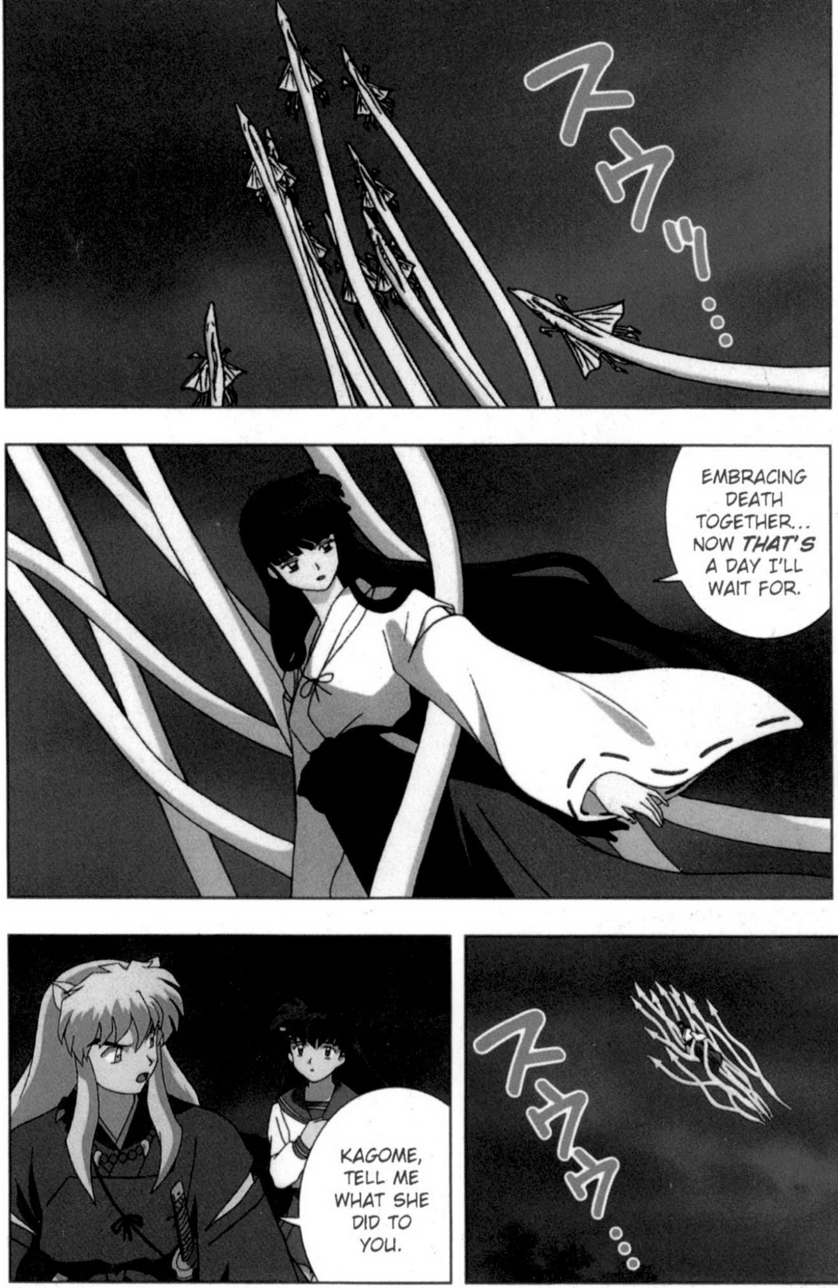
スウッ…
EMBRACING DEATH TOGETHER... NOW *THAT'S* A DAY I'LL WAIT FOR.
スゥゥ…
KAGOME, TELL ME WHAT SHE DID TO YOU.

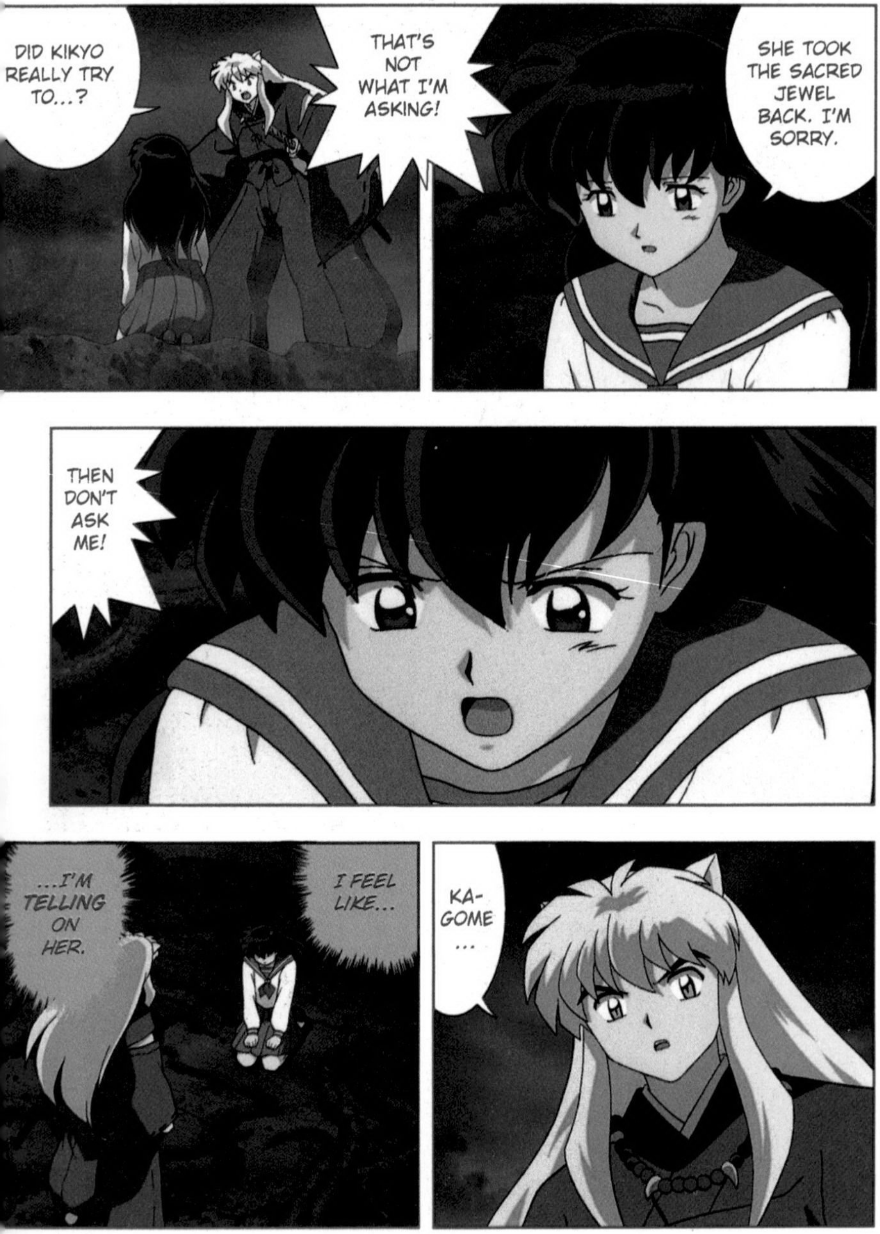
SHE TOOK THE SACRED JEWEL BACK. I'M SORRY.
THAT'S NOT WHAT I'M ASKING!
DID KIKYO REALLY TRY TO...?
THEN DON'T ASK ME!
KA-GOME...
I FEEL LIKE...
...I'M TELLING ON HER.

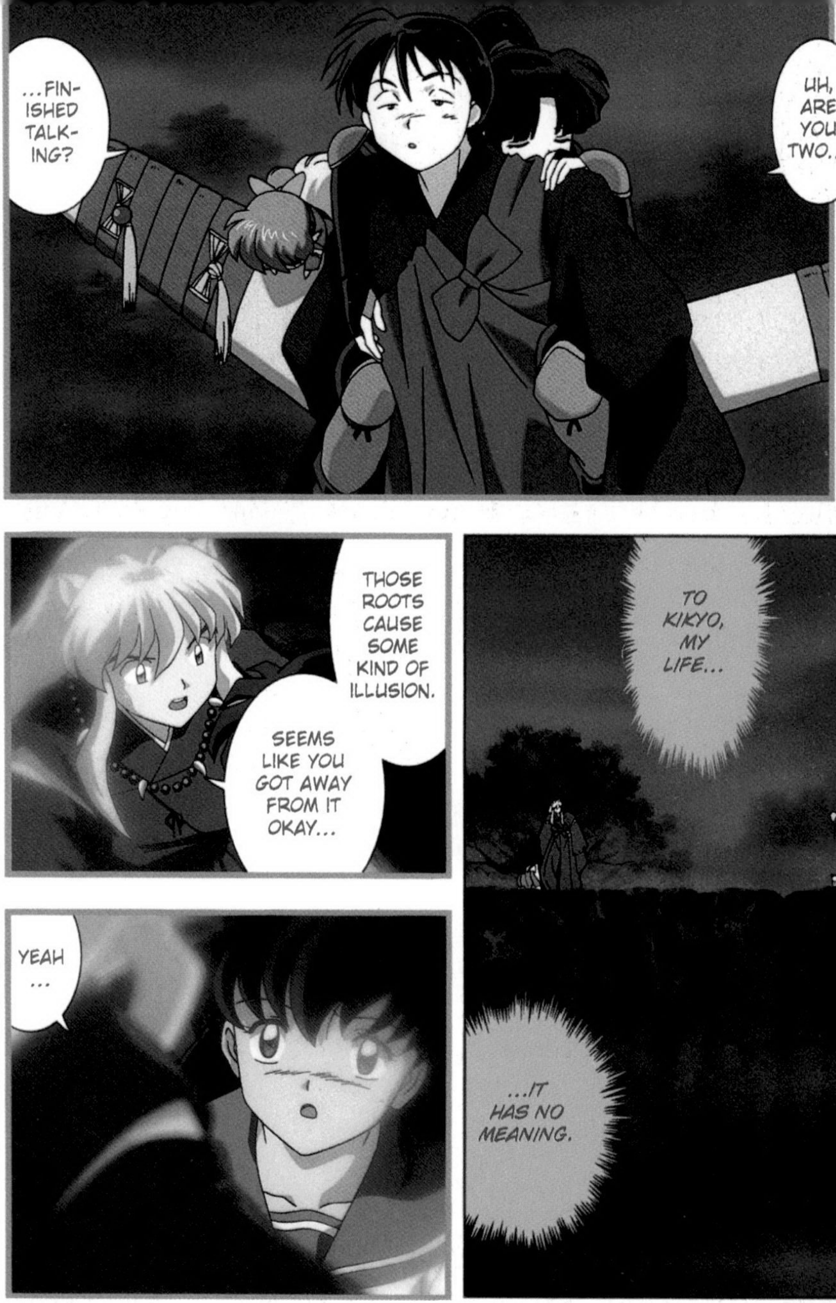
UH, ARE YOU TWO...
...FIN-ISHED TALK-ING?
TO KIKYO, MY LIFE...
...IT HAS NO MEANING.
THOSE ROOTS CAUSE SOME KIND OF ILLUSION.
SEEMS LIKE YOU GOT AWAY FROM IT OKAY...
YEAH ...

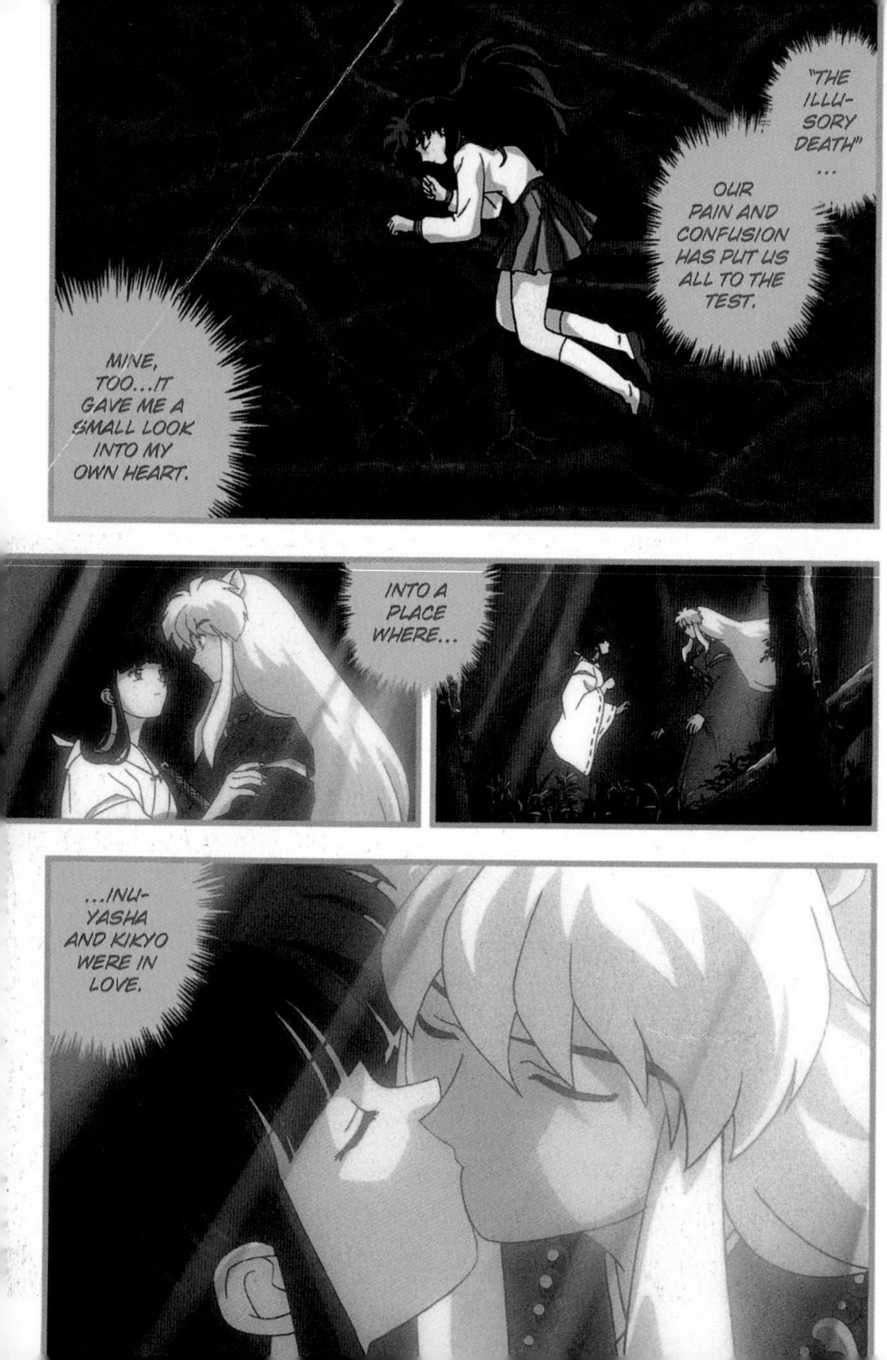
"THE ILLUSORY DEATH"...
OUR PAIN AND CONFUSION HAS PUT US ALL TO THE TEST.
MINE, TOO...IT GAVE ME A SMALL LOOK INTO MY OWN HEART.
INTO A PLACE WHERE...
...INUYASHA AND KIKYO WERE IN LOVE.

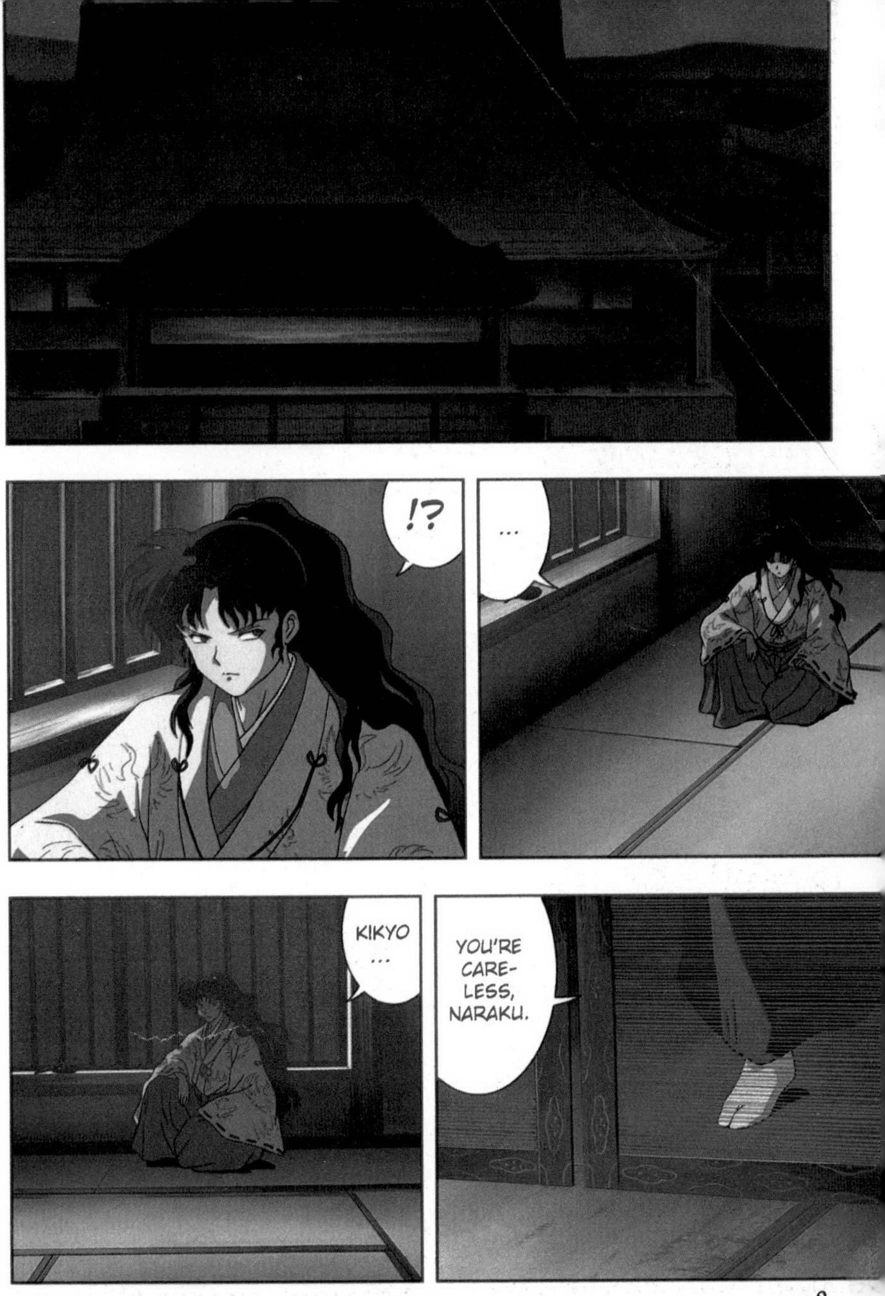
...
!?
YOU'RE CARE-LESS, NARAKU.
KIKYO ...

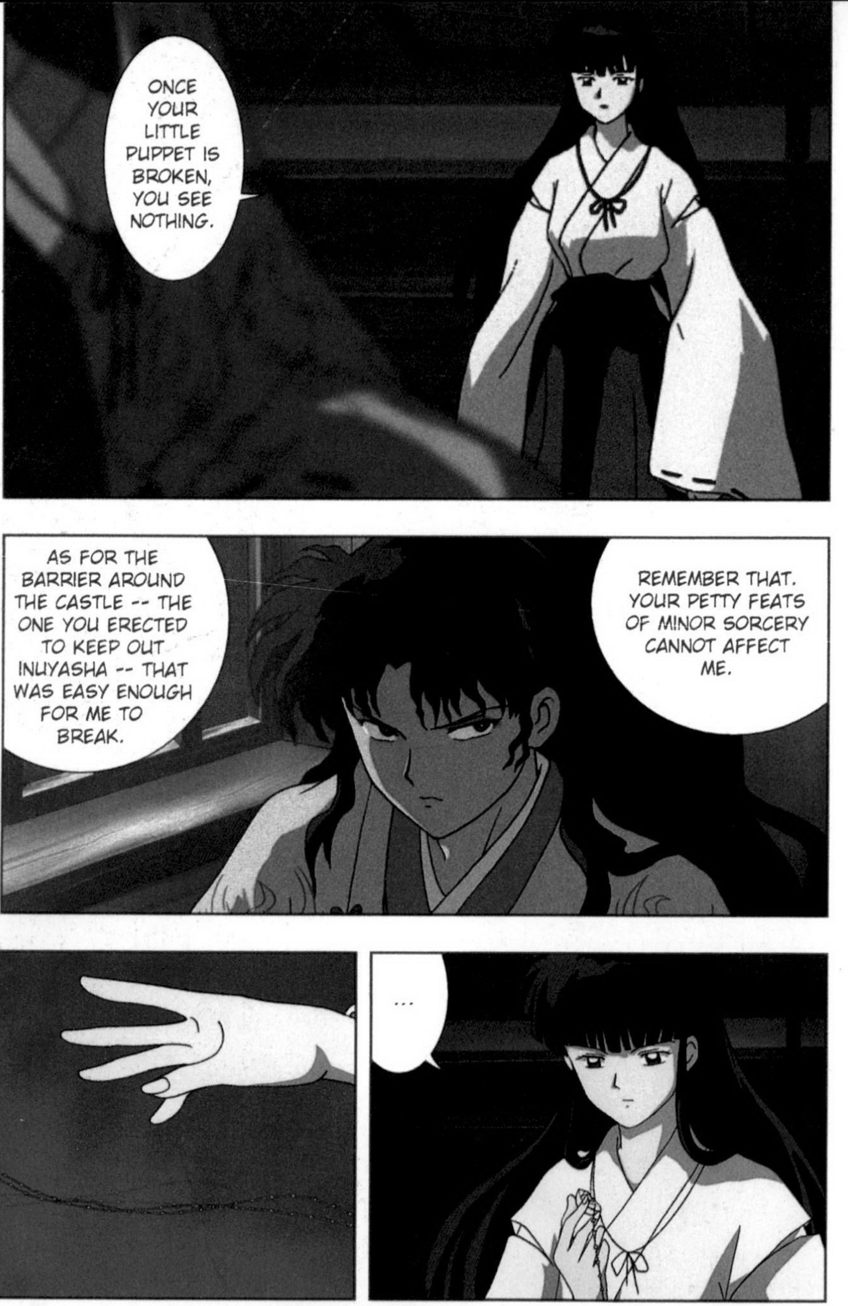
ONCE YOUR LITTLE PUPPET IS BROKEN, YOU SEE NOTHING.
REMEMBER THAT. YOUR PETTY FEATS OF MINOR SORCERY CANNOT AFFECT ME.
AS FOR THE BARRIER AROUND THE CASTLE -- THE ONE YOU ERECTED TO KEEP OUT INUYASHA -- THAT WAS EASY ENOUGH FOR ME TO BREAK.
...

...!!

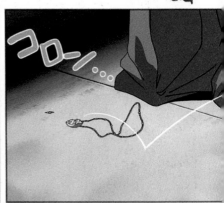

コロ─リ...

...DIDN'T YOU?

YOU WANTED IT...

I LEAVE IT TO YOU TO STAND GUARD OVER. AFTER ALL, WHO NEEDS ITS POWER MORE THAN YOU...

... DEMON NARAKU? OR IS IT...

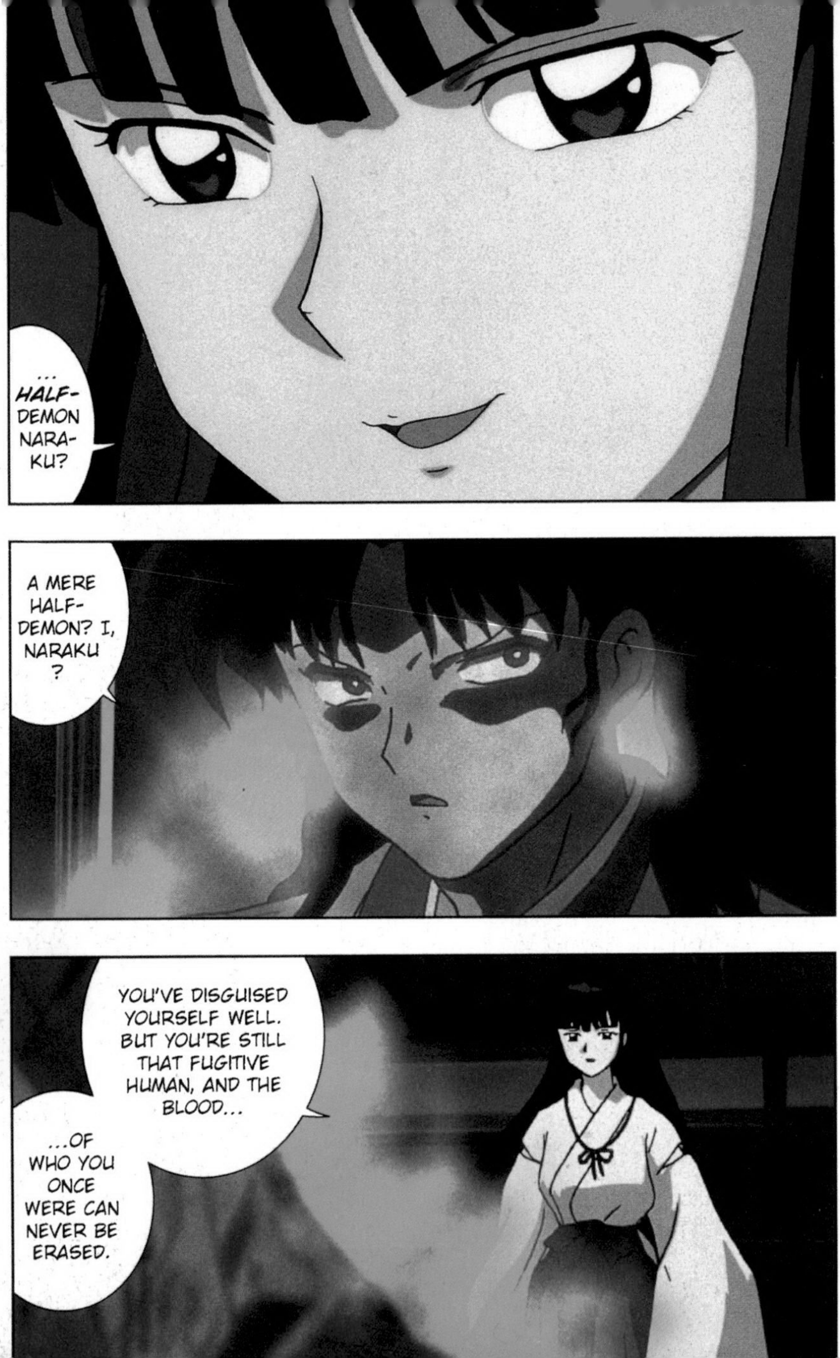
...HALF-DEMON NARAKU?
A MERE HALF-DEMON? I, NARAKU?
YOU'VE DISGUISED YOURSELF WELL. BUT YOU'RE STILL THAT FUGITIVE HUMAN, AND THE BLOOD...
...OF WHO YOU ONCE WERE CAN NEVER BE ERASED.

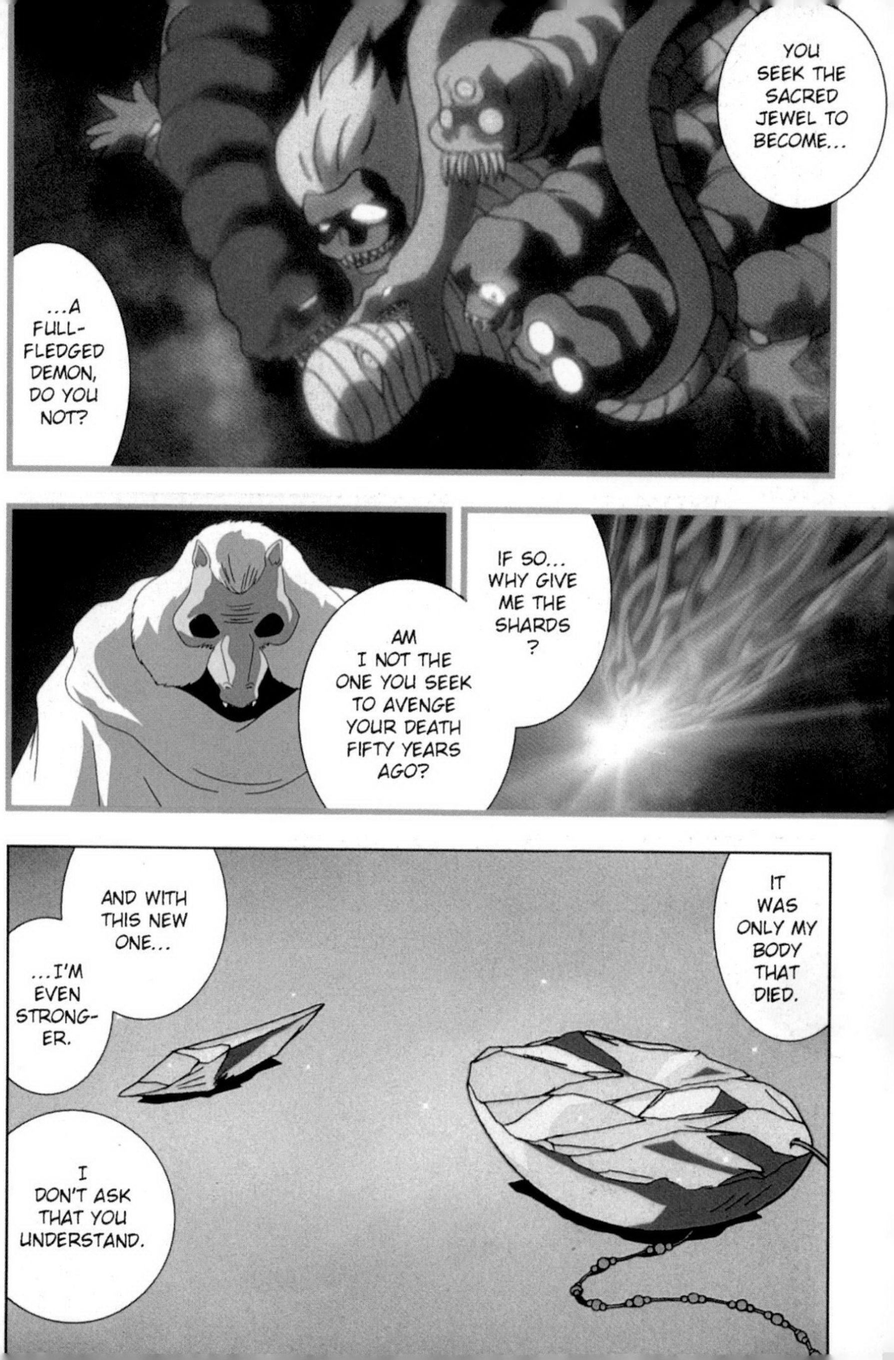
YOU SEEK THE SACRED JEWEL TO BECOME...
...A FULL-FLEDGED DEMON, DO YOU NOT?
IF SO... WHY GIVE ME THE SHARDS?
AM I NOT THE ONE YOU SEEK TO AVENGE YOUR DEATH FIFTY YEARS AGO?
IT WAS ONLY MY BODY THAT DIED.
AND WITH THIS NEW ONE...
...I'M EVEN STRONGER.
I DON'T ASK THAT YOU UNDERSTAND.

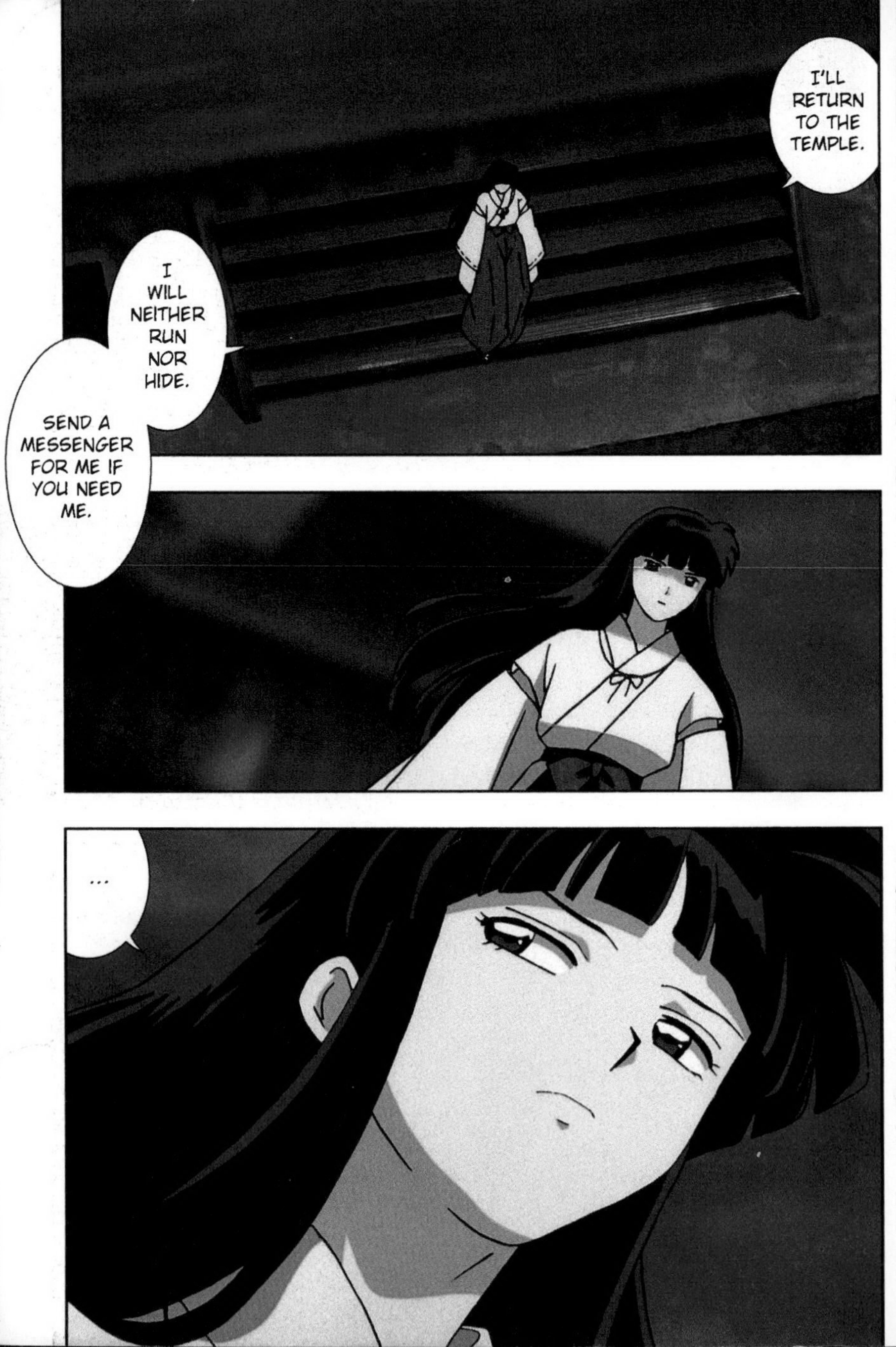
I'LL RETURN TO THE TEMPLE.
I WILL NEITHER RUN NOR HIDE.
SEND A MESSENGER FOR ME IF YOU NEED ME.
...

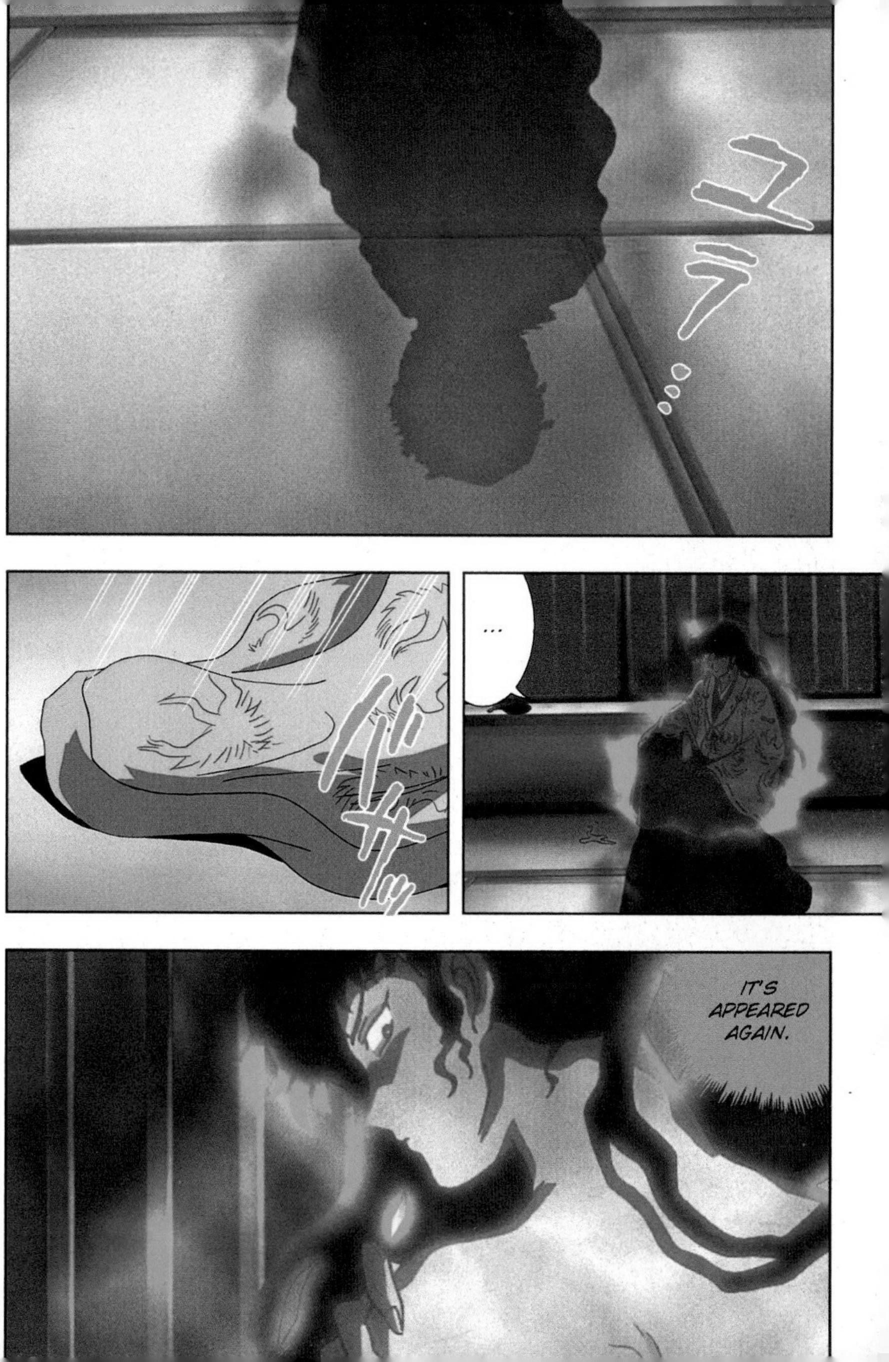
ユラ…
…
グサッ
IT'S APPEARED AGAIN.

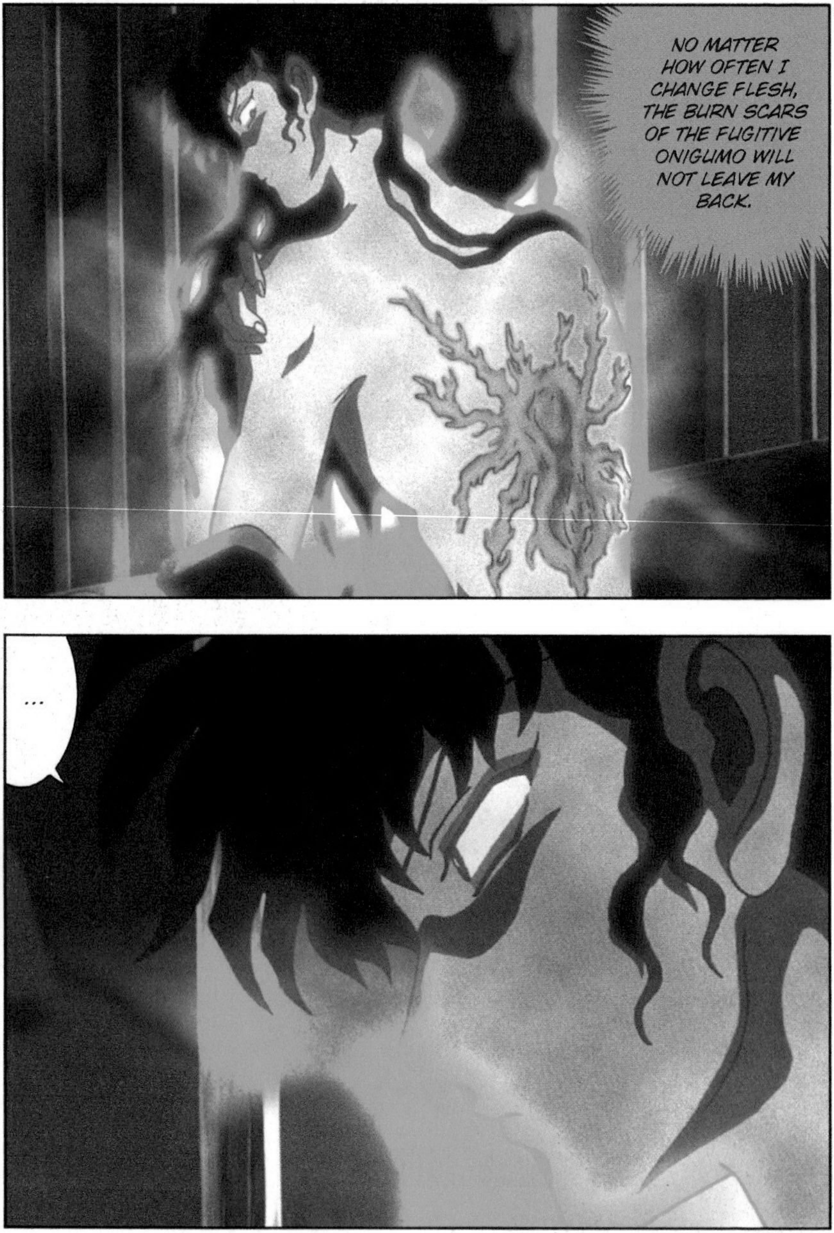
NO MATTER HOW OFTEN I CHANGE FLESH, THE BURN SCARS OF THE FUGITIVE ONIGUMO WILL NOT LEAVE MY BACK.
...

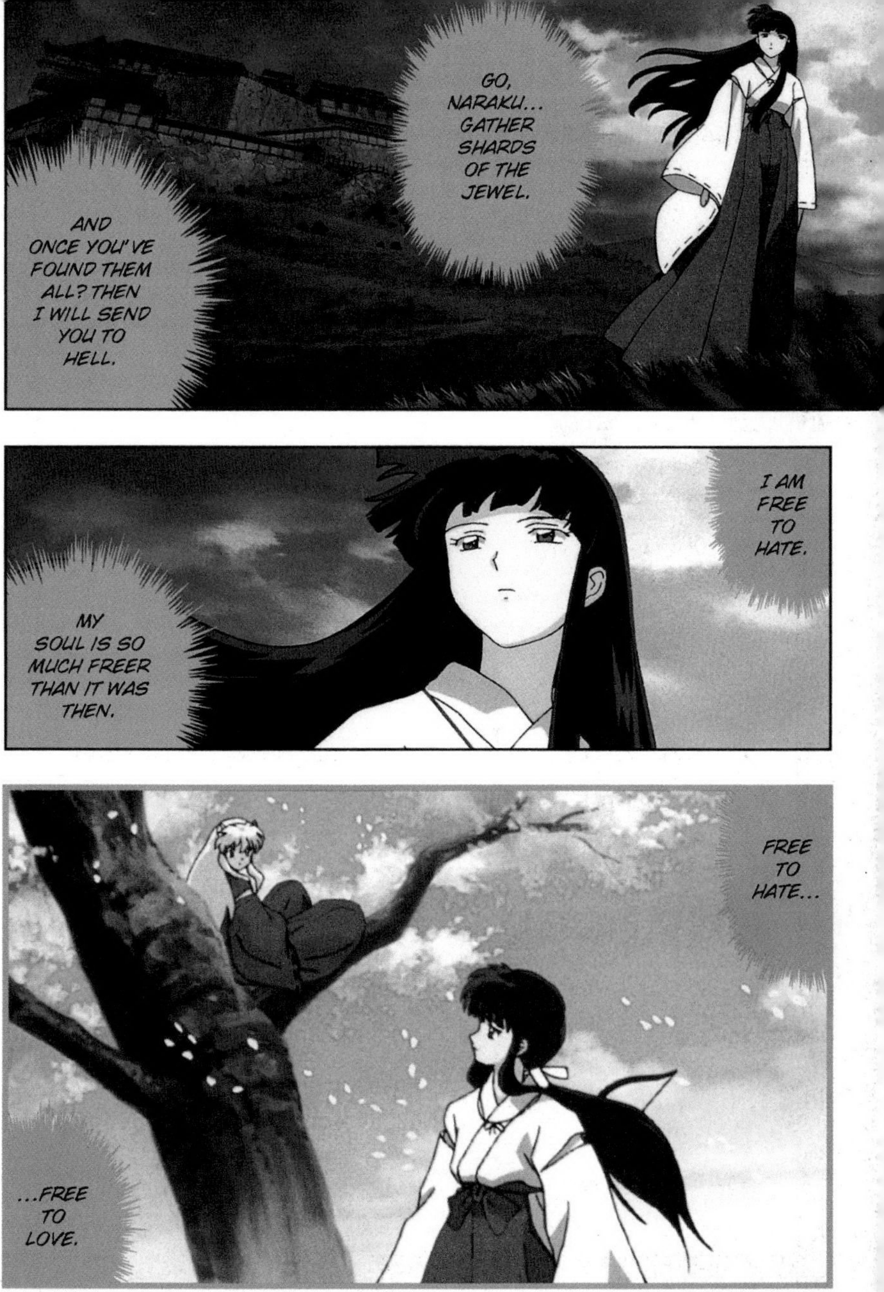
GO, NARAKU... GATHER SHARDS OF THE JEWEL.
AND ONCE YOU'VE FOUND THEM ALL? THEN I WILL SEND YOU TO HELL.
I AM FREE TO HATE.
MY SOUL IS SO MUCH FREER THAN IT WAS THEN.
FREE TO HATE...
...FREE TO LOVE.

TO BE CONTINUED...

Glossary of Sound Effects

Each entry includes: the location, indicated by page number and panel number (so 3.1 means page 3, panel number 1); the phonetic romanization of the original Japanese; and our English "translation"—we offer as close an English equivalent as we can.

36.1 FX:Za za
(Inuyasha dashes through underbrush)
36.2 FX:Ta ta ta… (running)

38.4 FX:Hyoi (Jinenji removes scary little worm)

39.1 FX:Chi chi chi… (bird sounds)
39.1 FX:Chi chi… (bird sounds)

40.1 FX:Kun kun (sniff sniff)
40.2 FX:Za (Inuyasha parts the underbrush)
40.4 FX:Doga (Inuyasha falls through dirt)
40.5 FX:Za za za…
(Inuyasha tumbles downward)

41.1 FX:Doh (Inuyasha lands in soft dirt)

42.3 FX:Neba (sound of stuff being sticky)

44.1 FX:Za za (torch flames crackling)
44.2 FX:Za za (more crackling)

45.1 FX:Pachi pachi (flames crackling)
45.4 FX:Baki
(rock breaks through wooden window)

46.4 FX:Ba (Ma appears in doorway)
46.5 FX:Ga (rock strikes hut near Ma)

47.3 FX:Ba (Kagome steps between Ma
and the mob)

48.3 FX:Bun (torches burning)

Chapter 31:
Jinenji, Kind Yet Sad

13.5 FX:Gata (Kagome's tire hits a bump)

14.3 FX:Ta ta ta… (running)

15.1 FX:Zuza (woman falls)
15.3 FX:Zuba (demon slash)
15.4 FX:Koron… (basket falls forlornly)

16.1 FX:Za (Inuyasha shoulders bicycle)
16.3 FX:Jii…
(Kagome looks pointedly at Inuyasha)

18.2 FX:Za (Inuyasha steps in front of Villagers)

22.1 FX:Hyu (rocks fly)
22.2 FX:Ga ga (rocks hit Jinenji)
22.4 FX:Kaa (Jinenji's eyes glow)
22.6 FX:Ba (Inuyasha whips out his sword)

23.2 FX:Doh doh doh doh (Jinenji thumps off)

24.2 FX:Baki (Ma breaks log over Tetsusaiga)
24.4 FX:Da (running)

26.2 FX:Gori gori (Jinenji chopping up herbs)

29.1 FX:Po (Ma puts hand to blushing cheek)
29.5 FX:Zu… (Jinenji extends bundle)

32.1 FX:Garan (spears clatter)

48.4 FX:Doh doh doh (villagers throw torches at hut)

49.1 FX:Gohh (hut bursts into flame)
49.6 FX:Zawa (buzz of crowd)

50.2 FX:Da (running)
50.3 FX:Za za za (bugs attack fallen villager)
50.5 FX:Da (Kagome and Ma move away)

51.3 FX:Gohhh... (whoosh)

52.1 FX: Kiri kiri (Kagome draws bowstring back)
52.2 FX:Shu (arrow flies)
52.3 FX:Doh (arrow strikes)
52.5 FX:Bun (monster strikes at Kagome with tail)

53.1 FX:Doga (Kagome struck)
53.2 FX:Za (Kagome falls)
53.5 FX:Shuru... (monster's tongue unfurls)
53.5 FX:Kaa (Jinenji's eyes shine)

54.1 FX:Ba (punch)
54.2 FX:Doga (Jinenji punches through monster)
54.3 FX:Shuru... (tentacle curls around Jinenji)

56.1 FX:Doka (villagers stab ineffectually at demon babies)
56.2 FX:Zuru (demon babies start to eat villager)
56.3 FX:Zan (they keep eating)
56.4 FX:Zuba (slash)

58.4 FX:Ba (Inuyasha leaping)

60.1 FX:Gu gu gu... (growling)
60.2 FX:Kaa (Jinenji's eye shining)
60.3 FX:Buchi (Jinenji breaks monster's grip)
60.4 FX:Ga (Jinenji wrestles with monster)
60.5 FX:Kaaaaa... (Jinenji's eyes shining)

61.1 FX:Bashu (Jinenji explodes centipede)

61.3 FX:Doga (Jinenji punches monster's head away)

62.1 FX:Kuru (Jinenji lumbers toward villagers)

63.2 FX:Zu—n... (Jinenji makes fist)
63.3 FX:Su... (fist comes toward prostrate villager)

65.2 FX:Koku... (Jinenji hangs his head)

68.5 FX:Ka—n ka—n (sound of field being worked)

Chapter 32:
Kikyo and Inuyasha, Into the Miasma

76.2 FX:Shuuuu... (Kikyo banishes demon)

77.1 FX:Za (footsteps in dust)

79.4 FX:Su (Kikyo walks abruptly past retainers)

80.1-2 FX:Za (Kikyo opens door)

84.3 FX:Po (droplets fall)

85.1 FX:Gohh (whoosh of demon body parts raining from sky)
85.2 FX:Da (running)
85.3 FX:Doh doh doh doh doh... (body parts hit ground)

90.5 FX:Cha (sword blades restrain Kikyo)

96.4 FX:Suu... (Kikyo's soul stealers come through window)
96.5 FX:Suuu... (soul stealers snaking around)

97.2 FX:Giri (soul stealers stealing soul)
97.3 FX:Fu... (soul leaving vassal)

116.1 FX:Gohh (whoosh)
116.3 FX:Shuuuu… (souls leaving)
116.4 FX:Fura… (Kikyo collapses)

117.1 FX:Suu… (Kikyo falls)
117.5 FX:Doh (Kikyo collapses)

120.1 FX:Da (Inuyasha running)
120.2 FX:Guo (roar)
120.2-3 FX:Doga (demon smacks Inuyasha)

121.1 FX:Za (Inuyasha lands with a smack)

122.1 FX:Pu… (chain with jewel on it breaks)
122.2 FX:Karan (jewel rolls off)
122.4 FX:Pita… (Kagome crouches down)

124.3 FX:Ta ta ta…
(Kagome running down passageway)
124.5 FX:Da (Kirara scampers off)
124.6 FX:Gui (Miroku grabs Kirara by tail)

125.4 FX:Guo (green demon reaches for Kikyo)

126.1 FX:Zuba (sword slash)
126.2 FX:Boko
(green demon knocked into cave wall)
126.3 FX:Doga (green demon strikes Inuyasha)
126.4 FX:Zuzaza…
(Inuyasha skids across the ground)

127.6 FX:Zuba (slash)

128.1 FX:Suku (Kagome stands up)

129.2 FX:Su… (Kikyo stands up)

130.1 FX:Zuba (slash)
130.4 FX:Hyu (projectile flies)

131.1 FX:Giin (projectile whooshes past Inuyasha)
131.2 FX:Shuru shuru… (projectile whooshes up
toward mouth of volcano)

98.3 FX:Goh (whooshing)

101.1 FX:Su—n… (distant thumping)
101.3 FX:Zu—n… (distant thumping)
101.5 FX:Zun… (distant thumping)

102.3 FX:Go go go (sound of bubbly whirlpool)
102.4 FX:Zan (splashing demon soup)
102.5 FX:Zaa (other demon erupts from water)

103.1 FX:Ga (dinosaur demon attacks)

104.1 FX:Doga (dinosaur demon's head falls off)
104.2 FX:Zaaa… (body parts join demon slush)
104.3 FX:Gohhhhh… (whooshing)
104.4 FX:Kaaa… (shining)

106.3 FX:Ba (Inuyasha wrests himself from
Miroku's grasp)

107.2 FX:Goh (whooshing out of demon's mouth)

108.2 FX:Yoro (Sango being unsteady on her feet)

109.1 FX:Za… (Kikyo appears from mist)
109.4 FX:Su…
(Kikyo moves past Kagome and Sango)

110.5 FX:Da (Kagome runs off)

111.1 FX:Poh… (Souls inside of Kikyo glowing)

112.1 FX:Zan (sloshing about)

113.5 FX:Goh (flames)
113.5 FX:Ta (Inuyasha runs)
113.5 FX:Dohhn (flames hit a rock)

114.1 FX:Zuba (sword slash)
114.2 FX:Doh (demon dodges)
114.3 FX:Ta (Inuyasha lands)

115.1 FX:Suu… (Kikyo appears behind Miroku)

148.4 FX:Suu… (soul catcher whooshes inside)
148.5 FX:Kaa… (Naraku's eyes glow red)

149.1 FX:Pa—n (soul catcher glows)
149.2 FX:Pi (Naraku flicks jewel shard at soul catcher)
149.3 FX:Goh (catcher hit by shard, starts to glow red)

150.1 FX:Hi—hyororo… (bird call)
150.3 FX:Zaaa… (water going over waterfall)

151.3 FX:Ga (smack)

154.1 FX:Ta ta ta… (running)

155.3 FX:Ta ta ta… (running)

156.1-2 FX:Buuuun… (soul catchers flying)
156.3 FX:Ta (Sango leaps off Kirara)
156.4 FX:Bun (slice)
156.5 FX:Zuba (slash through soul catcher)
156.6 FX:Ba (thing breaks)

157.1 FX:Bu bu bu bu (buzzing of insects)
157.4 FX:Ta ta ta… (running)
157.5 FX:Gohhh… (whooshing)

158.1 FX:Gohhhhh… (whoosh of flames)
158.2 FX:Toh (Inuyasha alights on torii)

159.3 FX:Doh (arrow imbeds itself in Inuyasha)
159.4 FX:Dohh (Inuyasha collapses)

161.2 FX:Kiri… (Kikyo draws bowstring)

162.1 FX:Byohhhh… (wind howling)
162.3 FX:Hyohh… (more wind)
162.4 FX:Gohhh… (whooshing)

163.1 FX:Pan (prayer beads explode from being wrapped around wind tunnel hole)
163.2 FX:Goh (whooshing from wind tunnel)

131.3 FX:Shuuuu… (whoosh)

132.1 FX:Go go go… (volcano starts to collapse)

133.1 FX:Go go go (rocks falling)
133.2 FX:Dohn (explosion)
133.5 FX:Ga (Inuyasha grabs Kagome's wrist)

134.2 FX:Gohhh… (Kikyo being whooshed away)

135.1 FX:Goh (whoosh)
135.2 FX:Niya… (little tricky smirk from Naraku)
135.3 FX:Kaaaaa… (shining)
135.4 FX:Ba (Inuyasha leaps clear of action)
135.5 FX:Kaaaa… (shining)

136.1 FX:Zu zu zu (Naraku starts to absorb new body)
136.2 FX:Kaa (shining)
136.3 FX:Suu… (sparkling as Naraku completes absorbing new body)

138.3-4 FX: Da (Inuyasha runs toward Naraku)

139.1 FX:Bachi (Inuyasha strikes with glowing Tetsusaiga)
139.2 FX:Dohn (blow bounces off Naraku)
139.3 FX:Gohhh… (whooshing)

Chapter 33:
Kikyo, Captured by Naraku

143.1 FX:Bachi (soul catcher hitting barrier that it can't break)
143.2 FX:Bachi (soul catcher hitting barrier)

145.2 FX:Goh (arrow flies)
145.3 FX:Gin (arrow strikes something)

147.4 FX:Su… (Naraku's jewel shard glimmers in the darkness)

163.3 FX:Gohhh… (whooshing)

164.2 FX:Fu… (Kirara disappears)
164.3 FX:Doh
(Shippo lands on ground with a whomp)
164.5 FX:Fu… (eerie wind)

166.1 FX:Ta ta ta… (Sango runs)
166.2 FX:Ta ta ta… (Sango runs more)

168.3 FX:Suu… (Kohaku's chain and sickle
thrown at Sango)
168.4 FX:Zuba (thunk)

171.3 FX:Shuru… (roots sneaking around,
trying to bind Kagome]
171.4 FX:Bun bun (Kagome shaking off roots)

172.4 FX:Zuba
(Kikyo takes off fake Naraku's head)

173.1 FX:Bishi (doll cut in half)
173.2 FX:Koto… (doll lands on ground)

174.1 FX:Shuuuu… (Kikyo grabs puppet)
174.2 FX:Zaa… (doll and phony Naraku blow
away in the breeze)
174.5 FX:Ta (Kagome steps toward Kikyo)
174.6 FX:Kiri kiri (Kikyo pulls back arrow)

175.1 FX:Kiri (Kikyo pulls bowstring tight)
175.4 FX:Shun (Kikyo lets arrow fly)

176.1 FX:Doh (thunk)
176.3 FX:Shuuu… (hissing of glowing spot)
176.4 FX:Go go go (whoosh of pit opening)
176.5 FX:Zu zu zu… (pit opens up)
176.6 FX:Gara… (Kagome slips)

177.2 FX:Ga (Kagome grabs root)
177.3 FX:Gara (Kagome dangles from root)
177.4 FX:Gohhh… (roar of wind below Kagome)

178.5 FX:Kira (jewel sparkles)

179.1 FX:Su (Kikyo reaches out)
179.2 FX:Putsu (Kikyo snatches jewel)
179.3 FX:Kishi Kishi
(soul catchers let go of Kagome)
179.4 FX:Giri… (roots squeeze tight)

180.1 FX:Gohhh… (flames burning)

182.5 FX:Goh (flames)

183.2 FX:Zuba (slash)
183.3 FX:Fu… (illusion dissipates)

184.1 FX:Gohhh… (whooshing)
184.3 FX:Gishi… (roots squeeze)
184.5 FX:Goh (roots whoosh away)

185.2 FX:Zuba (slash)
185.3 FX:Zan (nasty roots get cut away)

186.3 FX:Pan (slap)

187.3 FX:Da (Inuyasha leaps)

189.1 FX:Za (Inuyasha swoops down)

190.1 FX:Ba (Inuyasha leaps up)
190.2 FX:Ta (Inuyasha lands)

194.1 FX:Suu… (soul catchers swoop in)
194.3 FX:Suu… (soul catchers spirit Kikyo away)

200.1 FX:Koron… (Jewel shard falls to floor)

204.1 FX:Yura… (Naraku glows blue)
204.3 FX:Basa (Naraku throws off cloak)

INUYASHA ™

Rated #1 on Cartoon Network's Adult Swim!

In its original, unedited form!

maison ikkoku ™

The beloved romantic comedy of errors—a fan favorite!

Ranma ½ ™

The zany, wacky study of martial arts at its best!

$24.98

Inuyasha The Movie 3:
Swords of an Honorable Ruler

DVD In Stores Now!

The Great Dog Demon gave a sword to each of his sons—the Tetsusaiga to Inuyasha and the Tenseiga to Sesshomaru. But the Sounga, a third, more powerful sword also exists... A sword that wields a great evil that's been awakened. Can the brothers put aside their sibling rivalry to save the world from a fate worse than hell?

Includes EXCLUSIVE trading card!*

Complete your INUYASHA collections today at store.viz.com!